KT-512-858

LEEDS COLLEGE OF BUILDING LIBRARY
CLASS NO. 374 JAR
BARCODE
EDUCATION
28114

LEEDS COLLEGE OF BUILDING
WITHDRAWN FROM STOCK

Adult and continuing education

Second edition

The first edition of *Adult and Continuing Education* established itself as one of the most widely used and respected introductory texts on this important area of education. For this second edition, Peter Jarvis has made extensive revisions and has included substantial additional material to take account of the many changes which have occured in the field of adult education.

The book begins with a rationale for the provision of education for adults and analyses contemporary theory before going on to give practical advice on curriculum development and the teaching of adults.

Peter Jarvis is Professor of Continuing Education and Head of the Department of Educational Studies at the University of Surrey and has published extensively in the field of adult education, including *Adult Education and the State* (Routledge 1993) and the *International Dictionary of Adult and Continuing Education* (Routledge 1990).

LEEDS COLLEGE OF BUILDING
LIBRARY

LEEDS COLLEGE OF BUILDING
WITHDRAWN FROM STOCK

LEEDS COLLEGE OF BUILDING
LIBRARY

Adult and continuing education

Theory and practice

Second edition

Peter Jarvis

London and New York

LEEDS COLLEGE OF BUILDING
LIBRARY

First edition published 1983 by Croom Helm
Second edition published 1995
by Routledge
11 New Fetter Lane, London EC4P 4EE

Simultaneously published in the USA and Canada
by Routledge
29 West 35th Street, New York, NY 10001

Reprinted 1996, 1998, 1999, 2000, 2002, 2003 (twice)

RoutledgeFalmer is an imprint of the Taylor & Francis Group

© 1983, 1995 Peter Jarvis

Typeset in Times by Mews Photosetting,
Beckenham, Kent
Printed and bound in Great Britain by
Biddles Ltd, Guildford and King's Lynn

All rights reserved. No part of this book may be reprinted or
reproduced or utilized in any form or by any electronic,
mechanical, or other means, now known or hereafter
invented, including photocopying and recording, or in any
information storage or retrieval system, without permission in
writing from the publishers.

British Library Cataloguing in Publication Data
A catalogue record for this book is available from the British Library

Library of Congress Cataloging in Publication Data
A catalogue record for this book is available from the Library of Congress

ISBN 0–415–10242–1

In memory of
Mother, Father
and Jack
in gratitude.

LEEDS COLLEGE OF BUILDING
LIBRARY

Contents

LEEDS COLLEGE OF BUILDING
LIBRARY

Figures

Tables

Acknowledgements

Few books can be written without the encouragement, inspiration and, even, provocation of friends and colleagues. This book has all of these origins and without them it would have been the poorer. There are, however, some who deserve especial mention and to whom I am greatly indebted: Miss Sheila Gibson, Dr Alan Chadwick and Dr Colin Griffin have read all or part of the book in draft form and their comments have enriched the text considerably; the post-graduate students in the Department of Education Studies at the University of Surrey have continued to help me to clarify some of my ideas in our teaching and learning sessions; Mrs Hilarie Hall has undertaken the responsibility of transforming my handwriten draft into a typescript with expertise and efficiency.

I would like to express my gratitude to those who have given me permission to quote or reproduce from other writings: the Cambridge Book Company, New York, to quote Roby Kidd's 'Ten Commandments'; Dr Colin Griffin, to summarize most of the points he raised in his paper on continuing and recurrent education in Table 9.3; Holt, Rinehart and Winston, to reproduce Professor Dennis Child's diagram of Maslow's hierarchy of needs and Professor Robert Gagné's diagram of the relation between phases of learning and events of instruction; Jossey Bass, to reproduce two diagrams from Professor C. Houle's *The Design of Education*.

Once again, I must gratefully acknowledge the help and support of my wife, Maureen, and children, Frazer and Kierra, who have encouraged me to write, even though it has resulted in them undertaking additional family responsibilities.

Many people have helped me to produce this text but, like every writer, the final responsibility for what has been produced must rest with me.

Introduction

The study of adult education is growing in significance as the training of educators of adults is being undertaken more frequently in the United Kingdom and elsewhere. But there are few text books that seek to introduce students to a broad sweep of the field, and so this text has been prepared with this aim in view. It is hoped that students of the education of adults on ACSET I, II and III, Certificate, Diploma and Degree courses might find it a useful volume. In addition, it is hoped that other practitioners in the field of adult and continuing education will find much in this book that is relevant to their work.

With this aim in mind, the book has been very fully referenced so that readers can follow up any of the points that interest them and can also refer to the original sources. Further reading suggestions for each chapter are at the end of book, so that ideas from each chapter might be developed by interested readers. The contents of the book are wide enough to introduce students and practitioners to a variety of contemporary issues in the study of the education of adults. The aspects discussed in this book reflect the purpose for which it has been written, so that a great deal of it is devoted to the teaching and learning transaction. These have been divided into different chapters in the book for reasons of clarity but in reality such a division is frequently artificial.

The text attempts to combine the theoretical with the practical and it is hoped that those who read it will find it informative, relevant and, above all, useful.

Introduction to revised edition

This book was originally written as a text book for the first year MSc course in Adult Education which I taught at the University of Surrey, a course which has subsequently been modularized in line with many of the other changes that are discussed in this revised edition. Adult educators are only too well aware of all the changes that have happened and, no doubt, like me they are not happy with all the things that they have been forced to do, despite many of the changes having been anticipated in one form or another for a number of years. But there have been so many changes that the latter part of this book has required considerable rewriting so that much of it is new. I hope that I have captured the changes without changing the nature of the book too greatly.

Not only have there been considerable changes in the fields of study, but over the period I have changed some of my views and also have published a number of other pieces about adult and continuing education. Where I have written something since the original version of this book was published, I have tried to make reference to it, so that readers of this revised version will see how much of my own development has occurred.

In addition, the original version was written using the pronoun 'he' in the impersonal sense, and I was rightly taken to task about this soon after the publication of this book. I hope that I have rectified this throughout this present study, although I acknowledge that it has made the revision even more complex than it would have been had only the changes referred to above been incorporated.

I am most grateful to Routledge, and especially to Helen Fairlie for asking me to revise the book, and for awaiting for a slightly delayed manuscript, although the reasons for this have been due to events beyond my control. I am also most grateful to those who edited and typeset this revised version for taking the original book and all my alterations and making it into a comprehensive and comprehensible volume.

I would also like to thank those readers who made comments to the publishers about additions that they considered I should make to update this book. I hope that I have done justice to their comments, although, like every other author, I cannot blame anybody but myself for what I have written!

Over the years some people have been kind enough to tell me that they have found the original version of this book useful and I can only hope that this revised edition might also prove useful to some who use it.

Peter Jarvis

1 Towards a rationale for the provision of education for adults

Human learning is a lifelong process, one which has acquired greater significance as the speed of change in society has increased so that its members are almost compelled to keep learning in order to remain members. This is no new phenomenon; human beings have probably always had the capacity to learn throughout their lives, but in former times there was perhaps less need to do so than there is in this present age. Lifelong learning has, consequently, become a more conspicuous concept in the literature of recent years. Even so, it will be argued throughout this book that lifelong learning is not the same as lifelong education – learning and education are fundamentally different concepts. Nevertheless, it is also maintained that education should also be provided for people throughout their lives, although such provision is not, nor should be, made totally by the state.

The idea of adults returning to education is now much more taken for granted than it was even twenty years ago. However, it is still common to find the term 'education' used as if it applies only to the education of children. It is hard to change prevalent views and so the idea that education might refer to lifelong processes, or even processes that occur in adulthood, usually requires some elaboration on the term 'education'; various concepts appertaining to this are discussed in Chapter 2. The purpose of this chapter is to provide a theoretical rationale for the provision of education for adults, and this must start from the nature of both society and the individual. The chapter, therefore, commences with an examination of society and individuals within it and proceeds from there to argue that while education should be provided across the whole lifespan, the state should not be the sole provider.

THE NATURE OF CONTEMPORARY SOCIETY

Any discussion about the nature of society inevitably assumes certain theoretical perspectives, but this brief one does not seek to enter any sociological system. Rather it assumes that society is a complex social system in a state of continuous change and that change is the norm rather than the exception. It also recognizes that the educational institution is both the recipient of the pressures for change exerted by other institutions in society, especially the technological and the economic, and source of pressure on other institutions. Finally, it is recognized that individuals are moulded by the forces that are exerted upon them as they seek to discover a place for themselves in society. However, human beings are not merely the passive recipients of social pressures acting upon them, they are also able to act back upon their world and become agents who contribute to the processes of social change.

Every society produces its own culture which is carried by human beings and transmitted through interaction; but, more recently, this culture is also being stored in audio and video cassettes, in computers etc. Culture, in this context, refers to the sum totality of knowledge, values, beliefs, etc. of a society. Because of its apparent commonality among members of a society, culture seems to be a phenomenon external to the individual and objective. Actually this objectivity is more apparent than real since individuals have internalized a great deal of their own culture and shared it through social inter-action. It is the the fact that individuals do share it that provides the impression that it is actually objective and residing outside them. Consequently, culture may be regarded as 'objectified' rather than objective, and the manner by which infants acquire culture having been born into a society is illustrated in Figure 1.1.

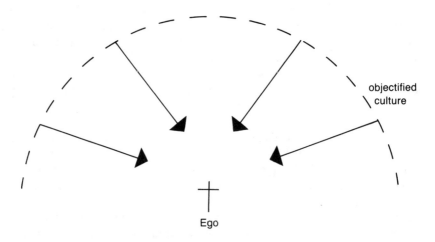

objectified
culture

Ego

Figure 1.1 The process of internalization of 'objectified' culture

All individuals have the culture of their society transmitted to them through interaction with others. The arrows in Figure 1.1 indicate the direction of the transmission in every interaction between 'ego' and 'alter'. Hence it may be seen that there is a sense in which every interaction is a process of learning and teaching. Every time an individual learns something as a result of being exposed to any of the media, the same process of learning is occurring. It is the process of socialization. There is a sense in which some facets of education may be regarded as part of the process of socialization, although the former is usually viewed as a more formal process than the latter. However, it is possible to understand precisely how Lawton (1973: 21) can regard the curriculum as a selection from culture within the context of this discussion. Obviously, the process of acquiring culture is very significant during childhood, both through socialization and education. However, sociologists regard socialization as a lifetime process having at least two aspects: primary socialization is 'the first socialization an individual undergoes . . . through which he becomes a member of society. Secondary socialization is any subsequent process that inducts an already socialized individual into new sectors of the objective world of his society' (Berger and Luckmann 1967: 150). Similarly, education may be regarded as a lifelong process and further reference will be made to the concepts of lifelong learning and lifelong education below.

It is not difficult, however, to realize that in a society where the rate of social change is very slow, such as a pre-industrial European one or a primitive tribe, it would be feasible for individuals to learn most of the cultural knowledge necessary for them to assume their place in that society in childhood. In such societies it was, and still is, only the elite – e.g. Plato's philosopher-kings, the priesthood – who continue to study esoteric knowledge during adulthood, while the remainder of the populace are regarded as having completed their education. Consequently, it is not hard to understand why a front-end model of education emerged, although it is equally obvious that such a model has little relevance to a society whose culture is changing rapidly.

From the onset of the Industrial Revolution, with the introduction of more sophisticated technology, the rate of social change increased. Indeed, change is endemic to technological societies. This means that the learning process should not cease at early adulthood. New knowledge, new ideas, new values and new practices all have to be confronted. Hence, a growth of educational provision occurred in the eighteenth and nineteenth centuries and the people were encouraged to learn more. Both children and adults were provided with additional educational opportunities and it is frequently claimed that the reason for this new emphasis on education was because a need existed to produce a competent and literate work force. Clearly this was so. Yet education, once introduced, had functions of a non-educational kind. Quoting one of Her Majesty's Inspectors for Education in London during the late nineteenth century, Kumar writes: 'If it were not for her 500 elementary schools London would be overrun by a hoarde of young savages' (1978: 248f.) Perhaps education is still being used to keep people 'off the streets', but now the subjects are a little older! Education is used for many purposes, but, clearly, it is an important agency in preparing individuals to respond to the rapid social change that is occurring. Because change is so rapid, it is necessary for individuals to keep learning, so that they should not become alienated from the culture that engulfs them.

Max Scheler (1980), as early as 1924, focused upon the effects of change on knowledge when he suggested that some forms of knowledge alter faster than others, the fastest being technological knowledge. He called this 'artificial' because it is a form of knowledge that does not persist over time, and he classified knowledge into seven types, based upon their degree of artificiality: myth and legend; knowledge implicit in the natural folk language; religious knowledge; basic types of metaphysical knowledge; philosophical-metaphysical knowledge; positive knowledge of mathematics, natural and cultural sciences; technological knowledge. Irrespective of the validity of Scheler's classification, he highlighted an important phenomenon about knowledge – that different types change at varying rates. Hence the more people's knowledge becomes outdated the more new knowledge they have to learn if they are to remain in harmony with their culture. The more technologically based the society, the more easy it is for individuals to become alienated, for all are affected by the changes in technology, as evidenced by the introduction of the pocket calculator, the digital watch and the micro-computer. Hence individuals need to learn new knowledge to prevent the onset of alienation or anomie, and lifelong learning – even lifelong education – may help them to adjust to the cultural changes prevalent in their society.

This phenomenon is even more common in the sphere of employment, with many occupations and professions being based upon knowledge that occurs at the artificiality end of Scheler's spectrum. For instance, the Advisory Council for Adult and Continuing Education's report stated:

> In recent years the obsolescence of knowledge has been most marked in the professions. Many professional bodies now encourage, and sometimes require, their members to undertake regular courses of continuing education and professional development. The need for regular updating will broaden across much more of the working population.
>
> (ACACE 1982b: 9)

Continuing education has become a reality in the professions (see Houle 1980). Additionally, some more traditional occupations have declined while others have disappeared, leaving many to seek new forms of employment and industrial training. Government retraining schemes have become a relatively common phenomenon in recent years in the United Kingdom and many forms of vocational education appear to be increasing and expanding. Indeed, Woodhall (1980: 22) estimated that in 1978–9, in the United Kingdom, a figure of £3,000 million was spent on all forms of vocational training, equivalent to one-third of the total expenditure on education and equal to about 3 per cent of all wages and salaries.

Woodhall (1988: 83f) repeated these figures whilst arguing that it is tremendously difficult to calculate the real cost of part-time education. In America, Eurich (1985: 6) cites Harold Hodgkinson, who was formerly the director of the Professional Institute of American Management Associations, who suggested that the cost of training in 1981 came close to the total cost of running the whole of America's higher education system which in that year amounted to $55 billion. The cost of providing education for the work force is, therefore, not a small addendum to the total expenditure on education each year. Technological innovation has also led to structural unemployment and this also costs countries a great deal in financial support and has to be included in any final calculations about the cost of providing vocational education.

Not only have technological innovations led to unemployment, but recent monetarist policies in Western Europe, especially the United Kingdom, and in the United States have resulted in increased unemployment and also in a gradual lowering of the age of retirement. This has resulted in more leisure time, even though it is enforced and often unwanted. In a society dominated by a work ethic, in which it has been regarded as good to work but evil to be idle, leisure has always been regarded as a mixed blessing. Consequently, it is being recognized that values about leisure will have to adapt or they will be changed, which, incidentally, illustrates a way by which values respond to social pressure. But some people have to learn how to use their leisure time and Parker (1976) has drawn a useful distinction between education for leisure and education as leisure.

That some people have to learn how to use this leisure may appear to be surprising initially but it is less surprising when it is realized that many who are now entering enforced unemployment, at an earlier stage of their lives than they originally anticipated, were brought up with the expectation that they would work until they approached the end of their lives and that not to work was regarded as malingering. Hence, the expectation of having to work for the greater part of their lives has meant that many people have not really learned how to use non-work time as constructively as they might. Yet it may actually be wrong to tell people what to do with their leisure but correct and beneficial to provide them with the opportunity to consider how they employ creatively the additional freedom that technological changes and specific economic policies have produced. One aspect of preparation for unemployment that has occurred recently has been pre-retirement education (see Coleman 1982; Jarvis 1980, 1983b; Glendenning and Percy 1990, *inter alia*) in which programme time is frequently devoted to the use of leisure.

By contrast, education as leisure has traditionally been undertaken by more educated people because many, especially those from the working classes who were unsuccessful during their initial education, have tended to shun the formal provision of leisure time education once they had completed their initial and, perhaps, their vocational education. The history of liberal adult education is a long and honourable one, being enshrined in the university extension movement and other types of provision, such as the Workers Educational Association, and the demand for it appears to be unabating (ACACE 1982b). This may be demonstrated by the many people who attend the university extension classes, local education authority classes, and courses organized by other commercial and voluntary agencies. Additionally, the creation of the Open University has demonstrated the tremendous attraction that academic study has for many people who do not possess the traditional, formal qualifications for university entry. Similar movements exist in many parts of the world

(Rumble and Harry 1982) and in America with its Free Universities movement (Draves 1980) and the provision of part-time degree education throughout the lifespan. More recently, education and the elderly has assumed increasing significance: in America, there are the elderhostels (Zimmerman 1979: 10 and 22f); *l'université du troisième age* began in France and spread throughout Europe, so that it is now to be found throughout the world and has its own international meeting. Many of these new educational movements have already shown that leisure time education does not necessarily result in any lowering of academic standards; indeed, the academic standards may be lifted in some instances. Hence leisure time education is more than hobby-type education, which is often belittled. Yet the provision of this latter form of education is also of great importance since it provides opportunity for life enrichment and reflects a positive attitude on behalf of the learner to the acquisition of new knowledge and skills. Parker (1976: 99) quotes Jary with approval when he concludes that 'the leisure centredness of liberal adult education ought not to be hidden or apologised for. It should be reocgnised and its gratifications elaborated. It should be seen as a highly distinctive form of leisure.'

If adult education can help people to relate more easily with contemporary culture, if it can help them to use their leisure time in a creative manner, if it can enrich the lives of many who undertake it, then it would appear to be quite ludicrous to relegate it to the margins of the world of education; and, clearly, its provision will become even more important since more people are living longer and hence have more actual time in their lives to learn things. 'But what is the use of learning new things when a person is old?' is a question frequently posed. Yet if learning is life enriching, as it is for many people, then the elderly have as much right as anyone else to enjoy the fruits of learning. Dewey wrote that since

> life means growth, a living creature lives as truly and positively at one stage as another, with the same intrinsic fullness and the same absolute claims. Hence education means the enterprise of supplying the conditions which insure growth, or adequacy of life, irrespective of age.
>
> (Dewey 1916: 51)

But another objection that is often raised is that 'you can't teach an old dog new tricks'. Yet is this adage true? Recent research (see Allman 1982; Glendenning and Percy 1990; Sherron and Lumsden 1978) has indicated that the elderly can and do learn effectively, even if their methods of learning may be slightly different. Old dogs can be taught new tricks!

Indeed, people of all ages are realizing that they either want, or need, to return to studying later in their lives. This has led to the growth of other important spheres of education, such as ACCESS and return to study courses. ACCESS courses began to help disadvantaged adults to gain access to professional preparation and they soon evolved to offer them the opportunity to prepare themselves to enter higher education. Some of these courses also began to offer fresh horizons for women who felt that they had been disadvantaged earlier in their lives (see Hutchinson and Hutchinson 1978). In addition, there has been a growth in courses teaching people the skills of studying, such as Richardson *et al.* (1979) and Gibbs (1981). This latter book is student centred and introduces readers to many techniques familiar to educators of adults.

Thinking people are much more able to play a part in the wider life of society, and democracies need people who are not only able to think but who are also knowledgeable about areas of social and political life. Only by having a thinking and educated populace can a democratic society be achieved; and even if the ideal of democracy is only an ideal, it is still a goal to strive towards (Jarvis 1993)! Lengrand, one of the most influential writers on lifelong education, suggested that modern democracy

> in its political, social, economic and cultural aspects can only rest on solid foundations if a country has at its disposal increasing numbers of responsible leaders at all levels, capable of giving life and concrete substance to theoretical structures of society.
>
> (Lengrand 1975: 30)

Few would want to dispute this claim and it may be through the educational process that some of these responsible leaders emerge.

As a result of major changes in society, culture is changing and adult education provision can assist people to understand the processes that are occurring and help them to adapt and take their places in a constantly renewing society. People require the provision of adult education classes to help them in their work, in their leisure and, indeed, in enriching the whole of their lives. With the provision of education for adults, one condition exists that is a necessary foundation stone for the creation of a democratic society. Yet people are not really only the passive recipients of the culture of society, as Figure 1.1 depicts, and so it is now necessary to examine the second facet of this argument: the nature of the individual.

THE NATURE OF THE INDIVIDUAL

At the start of the preceding section it was suggested that one element in the inter-relationship between individuals and their society is that they are recipients of its culture. Even so, it was stressed that there is another aspect to this process and this is exemplified in Figure 1.2. Human beings are not passive recipients of their cultural heritage, they do not have it imprinted upon a *tabula rasa* type of mind, but they receive, process and externalize it. The arrows in Figure 1.2 demonstrate that social interaction is a process of teaching and learning. During the process the recipients accept some elements of their culture, modify others and even reject some of the information with which they are presented. But they do more than merely process the knowledge and ideas, etc. that they receive, they are frequently proactive in the pursuit of the knowledge, ideas, values, beliefs enshrined in their objectified culture. (See Jarvis 1987, 1992 for a much more extensive discussion of this.)

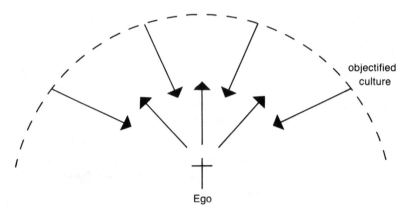

Figure 1.2 The nature of the individual in relation to 'objectified' culture

The nature of humankind has occupied the minds of philosophers and theologians for centuries and it is not the purpose of this section to encroach upon their deliberations, nor even to attempt to summarize their arguments. It is intended, however, to suggest that human beings are active participants in the learning process throughout the whole of life and that the reason for this lies both in their nature and in their relationship with the wider society (Jarvis and Walters 1993).

Figure 1.2 gives the impression that the objectified culture is static and unchanging, but this is quite untrue. Society is changing very rapidly and so the objectified culture at which the outward pointing arrows are directed has changed slightly during the period that it takes individuals to process their responses. The very fact that they themselves do not merely mirror what they receive, but process and change it is part of the process of cultural change itself. Hence, human beings are not only born into a changing culture, but they are part of the process of change. Their adaptation to this ever changing society is itself a learning process.

Initially, this section has been designed to demonstrate that human beings are lifelong learners, and in the remainder of this chapter it will be shown that they are also meaning seeking animals. It is maintained here that this endeavour of human beings to understand themselves, their society and their universe lies at the root of the learning process. Finally, it is concluded that the provision of education for people of all ages is essential because it helps to facilitate this quest to understand, which is at the heart of humanity itself.

Individuals as lifelong learners

Lifelong education, it was claimed earlier, is not a new concept but the rapidly changing social conditions of contemporary society have provided impetus for a wider acceptance of the idea. In recent years the stimulus has been strengthened by a considerable number of publications and an increasing amount of research has also been devoted to the topic. Organizations such as UNESCO have adopted it and have thereby brought it into the political arena. However, adult educators have, generally, been a major force in drawing attention to the practice of lifelong learning. One such writer on the subject has been Ronald Gross (1977) who records some of the stories of lifelong learners. Quoting from one of these, Cornelius Hirschberg, he writes:

> I am stuck in the city, that's all I have. I am stuck in business and routine and tedium. But I give up only as much as I must; for the rest I live my life at its best, with art, music, poetry, literature, science, philosophy and thought. I shall know the keener people of the world, think the keener thoughts, and taste the keener pleasures as long as I can and as much as I can.
>
> (Gross 1977: 27)

In case this sounds too idealistic to be practical, Hirschberg read on the subway to and from work each day, and during his lunchtime, for most of his business life. He estimated that he had undertaken some ten hours of serious reading each week for about 2,000 weeks – enough reading time to get at least five college degrees! His university was the world of books and the opportunity to think about the ideas he acquired from them.

Libraries, then, and museums are important adjuncts to human learning. Their existence is an indication that people seek to learn from numerous sources. Recently, adult educators have taken considerable cognizance of their significance to lifelong education and a number of studies have been published in this field, e.g. Chadwick 1980; Dadswell 1978; Dale 1980; Surridge and Bowen 1977. Additional learning facilities are provided by the media. Groombridge (1972: 27ff) regards television as a liberal educator because it makes people aware of what lies beyond their milieu, it helps them to understand each other and it provides a rich diet of imaginative experience. As long as it is recognized that what is seen and heard is actually a distillation of reality through the media process, then these claims are valid. Indeed, the British Broadcasting Corporation's charter specifically states that one of its functions is to educate. In a totally different context, Moemeka suggests that in African countries local radio can 'provide a continuous flow of educational information and messages on all aspects and endeavours that affect the lives of rural communities, and so arouse their awareness and stimulate them' (1981: 104). Travel is another medium through which individuals learn, so that many adult education institutions, schools and colleges organize visits and study tours both in the United Kingdom and abroad as part of their programme of learning activities. The arts, museums, libraries, radio and television all cater, in one way or another, for something in human beings which drives them to learn more about the universe in which they live and about other people with whom they inhabit this planet.

Hence the people about whom Gross was writing may not be exceptions, rather they may be much more common than it is generally believed. In a survey conducted by the National Institute of Adult Education (Hutchinson 1970: 52f) it was suggested that '40 per 1000 of the adult population may be enrolled in adult education classes in any one year' and that this did not include those adults attending universities, polytechnics and all colleges of further and higher education. It was also estimated that allowing 'for double counting, the number of adults engaged in some form of education or training in any one year is more likely to be about 16% of the adult population, giving a figure of about 6 million in England and Wales' (ACACE 1982a: 46).

In a much more recent survey, Sargant (1990) suggested that one-tenth of the adult population were engaged in education and that a further 16 per cent had undertaken some form of study within the previous three years. In addition, she found that a further 10 per cent were engaged in self-directed learning, which suggests that over one-third of the adult population are undertaking some form of planned learning exercises. Obtaining accurate statistics about the participation rate of adults in education is a very complicated undertaking and, therefore, in the end an estimate is all that may be obtained. The same is true in the United States. For instance, Johnstone and Rivera (1965: 33) calculated that between June 1961 and June 1962 there were at least 2,650,000 adults in full-time education, 17,160,000 in adult classes and some 8,960,000 undertaking self-education, but they recognized that these totals were no more than approximations. Nevertheless, their research highlighted the prevalence of the autodidact and they wrote that 'the incidence of self-education throughout the adult population is much greater than we anticipated' (Johnstone and Rivera 1965: 37). They had discovered millions of lifelong learners who were not using the educational services, people who wanted to learn and understand through their own direction.

Not long after Johnstone and Rivera published their monumental study another seminal research report highlighting the lifelong learner appeared. Allen Tough (1979) reported research into adults' self-directed learning projects and he suggested that self-directed education is even more common than Johnstone and Rivera indicated. He writes that it 'is common for a man or woman to spend 700 hours a year on learning projects. Some people spend less than 100 hours, but others spend more than 2000 hours in episodes in which the person's interest to learn or to change is clearly his primary motivation' (1979: 1). Tough was not concerned merely to count the odd hours of enquiry in which an individual might indulge since he considered that these could not be described as learning projects. Rather he defined a learning project as 'a series of related episodes, adding up to at least seven hours' (1979: 6). Tough, and his fellow researchers, interviewed sixty-six people in depth in their initial research and discovered that all but one of them had undertaken at least one learning project during the year prior to the interview, that the median number of projects was eight and that the mean time spent on learning projects was 816 hours. A participation rate of 98 per cent was discovered – far higher than Johnstone and Rivera would have anticipated from their research. But Tough and his colleagues employed a more intensive interview technique than Johnstone and Rivera and this method of research was one reason for the higher statistics. Additionally, Tough acknowledges that his sample was not random, so that it is not technically correct to claim that 98 per cent of the population of Canada, nor even of Ontario (where the research was conducted), undertake at least one seven-hour learning project per annum. Indeed, his statistics may be a considerable overestimation, although they might actually be correct, but they do suggest that people have a need to learn, know and understand. These various research statistics may all indicate that the human being has a basic need to learn, a need that may be as basic as any of the needs identified by Maslow in his well-known 'hierarchy' of needs.

The human being and the need to learn

Maslow's 'hierarchy' of needs is usually represented as in Figure 1.3. Child (1977: 40ff) suggested that the need to know comes at the top of the hierarchy, but in the third edition of his text he (1982: 43) has adapted this slightly and omitted the highest stratum. At the same time he has continued to highlight

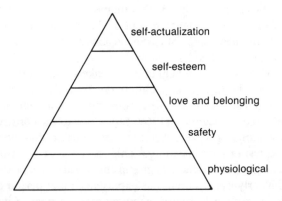

Figure 1.3 Maslow's 'hierarchy' of needs
Source: Maslow (1968)

the significance of knowledge and understanding. Maslow (1968: 60ff) certainly considered the need to know but claimed that knowledge has a certain ambiguity about it, specifying that in most individuals there is both a need to know and a fear of knowing. However, the fear of knowing may be the result of social experiences rather than being basic to the person. The need to know may be a fundamental need, even if the consequences of that knowledge may be dangerous. If this is the case, then Child's suggestion does require further consideration. Does the need to know actually occur at the apex of the hierarchy? Is there a progression through the hierarchy which occurs only when the more preponderant needs are satisfied? Is it even a hierarchy? Argyle (1974: 96f) suggests that the main supporting evidence for the hierarchy comes from the lower end but that there 'is not such clear evidence about the upper part of the hierarchy'. Houston *et al.* (1979: 297) claim that the order of needs is itself arbitrary and that the exact order is not particularly important. If the order is unimportant, then both Maslow's and Child's construction of a needs hierarchy is open to reconsideration.

Child may be correct when he suggested that the intellectual pursuit of knowledge is a higher order need but this may only be true for the academic pursuit of knowledge. But the fact that Tough (1979) has suggested that many people undertake learning projects implies that the need to learn may be quite fundamental to the human being. Indeed, it is suggested here that this need is better understood as being one to learn rather than to know and understand since individuals need to learn in order to comprehend the world in which they live and to adapt themselves to it. If this is the case, then the need to learn is quite basic and should perhaps occur lower in Maslow's hierarchy because the individual is conscious of the need to learn from very early in life, as is manifest in children from the time that they acquire the facility of language (and ask the question 'why?') and during the process of the formation of the self.

Elsewhere (Jarvis 1983c: 20–3) this theme has been expanded a little in the context of the religious development of the individual. Without seeking to rehearse that argument, some of its conclusions are summarized here because of their significance to this discussion. It is suggested that the processes of the formation of the self and of beginning to make sense of the objective world occur simultaneously during early childhood. Indeed, Luckmann maintains that a human organism becomes a self, constructing with others an 'objective and moral universe of meaning' (1969: 50). Prior to the construction of this universe of meaning, however, it must be recognized that every individual poses many questions of meaning. This process of focusing upon the 'unknowns' of human experiences begins in childhood and appears fundamental to humanity. Nearly every parent has experienced that period during which their child persistently asks questions about every aspect of its experience. Initially these questions appear to be restricted to its immediate experience but as the child's universe expands its questions of meaning change. Answers to the questions, however, demand different types of knowledge: empirical, rational, pragmatic and belief knowledge. Hence, learning initially progresses, unfettered by the boundaries of the disciplines, as a result of a process of questioning at the parameters of the child's experiences. As the questions are answered and the child acquires a body of knowledge, so the learning need is receiving some satisfaction. During early childhood these questions are overt and the learning experience explicit. When children attend school, however, teachers (and other adults) sometimes attempt to provide information that bears little or no relation to the questions being posed at that time and, therefore, the knowledge being transmitted may appear irrelevant to the recipient. Unless the teacher is able to demonstrate its relevance and create a questioning attitude there may be little internal stimulus to learn what is being transmitted. (This does not mean that the child does not want or need to learn, only that the child may not want to learn what is being transmitted.) However, by the time the child matures into an adult, answers to many of the questions may have been discovered and the adult has been socialized into the objectified culture of society. The adult appears to ask fewer questions. But during periods of rapid social change the questioning process is evoked. During traumatic experiences the accepted internalized body of knowledge may not be able to cope with the situation and the questioning process is reactivated. Schutz and Luckmann write: 'I only become aware of the deficient tone of my stock of knowledge if a novel experience does not fit into what has, up to now, been taken as a taken-for-granted valid reference scheme' (1974: 8).

In other words, when individuals' biographies and their current experience are not in harmony, a situation is produced whereby they recommence their quest for meaning and understanding. It is this disjuncture that underlies the need to learn and this has been developed much more thoroughly in later works (Jarvis 1987, 1992). While the need to learn occurs continuously throughout most of the lifespan, the religious questions are raised intermittently throughout life, so that the process is never really complete. Perhaps, as Tough has implied, questions are asked much more frequently than adult educators have generally assumed, so that the learning need is ever prevalent.

Before progressing further with this discussion it is necessary to recall Maslow's original 'hierarchy' of needs and Child's adaptation of it. Maslow suggested that there are five basic areas of need: physiological, safety, love and belonging, self-esteem and self-actualization. Child suggested that understanding and knowledge should be added to the pinnacle of the hierarchy. But it was suggested that the needs do not actually form a hierarchy and it has been argued here that the need to learn is quite fundamental to humanity and that it manifests itself during the process of the formation of the self, so that in any formulation of human needs the learning need should be specified. Hence, it is suggested that Maslow's hierarchy should be adapted and seen as a taxonomy (see Figure 1.4). This is clearly not a hierarchy but a process through which a child passes during early maturation. All the needs exist in individuals and, wherever possible, human beings seek to satisfy them. Hence the provision of education throughout the whole of the lifespan may help the learner to satisfy a basic human need, especially in a rapidly changing world in which the individual may be posing many questions of meaning. Herein may lie one theoretical base of andragogy, a point to which further reference will be made below.

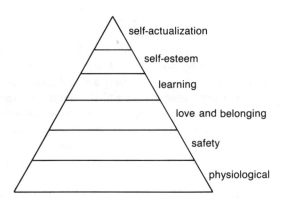

Figure 1.4 A taxonomy of human needs

Some of the ideas that occur in the above argument are similar to those adduced by Mezirow in his discussion on 'perspective transformation'. He claims that:

> to the degree our culture permits, we tend to move through adulthood along a maturity gradient which involves a sequential restructuring of one's frame of reference for making and understanding meanings. We move through successive transformations towards analysing things from a perspective increasingly removed from one's personal or local perspective.
>
> (Mezirow 1977: 157)

Mezirow has certainly raised some very significant points about the process of adult learning, to which further reference is made later, but he implies that this 'maturity gradient' is inevitable and sequential and that it relates to development and ageing rather than to the individual's response to the world, so that it is not totally similar to the position adopted here and it cannot be utilized as a rationale for the provision of education for adults.

It might be objected that if human beings have a basic need to learn, there is no need to provide education since they will seek to satisfy their learning needs in any case. However, this argument contains no substance because education, the provision of libraries, museums, etc. have all emerged as means by which individuals may learn answers to their questions of meaning. Yet it must be recognized that education *per se* is only one of a number of ways through which the learning need can be satisfied. Another answer to the objection may be posited in the form of an analogy: if safety is a need that is always going to be satisfied then there would be no reason for legislation about health and safety at work, and yet today there are probably very few people who would dispute the need for the existence of such an Act of Parliament.

SUMMARY

In this chapter it has been argued that the provision of education for adults is necessary because of the nature of contemporary society and the nature of humanity. It was suggested that there are various features in society that have to be taken into consideration, including: rapid social and cultural change; the obsolescence of technical knowledge resulting in the need for individuals working with such knowledge to keep abreast of developments; an increase in the amount of leisure time and an increasing number of people living into old age; the need to work towards a democratic society. Additionally, it has been suggested that human beings have a basic need to learn and that they are lifelong learners and that the provision of education across the lifespan is one way by which people can satisfy this basic need.

However, it was recognized at the outset that these two aspects are not discrete entities but that there is an inter-relationship between the individual and society, and that this division was made only for ease of analysis. One approach without the other is to present a false picture of reality, so a rationale for the provision of education for adults must always contain a combination of both sets of reasons proposed here.

Thus far the concepts employed have gone undefined and undiscussed, so it is now necessary to explore some of the many concepts that are discussed in the literature about the education of adults.

2 A conceptual framework for adult and continuing education

Many ideas were raised in the opening chapter without any of them being rigorously defined, and thus it is now necessary to examine some of them. It is intended to analyse the concept of education and then to apply the analysis to some of the terms in contemporary usage that relate in some way to the education of adults, during which the underlying philosophies will become more apparent. In addition, it will become clear that the same terms are employed in different ways, while, on occasions, different terms are used to convey the same meaning!

THE CHANGING CONCEPT OF EDUCATION

In the opening chapter, reference was made to the so-called 'front-end' model of education and it was claimed that while this model was appropriate for less technological societies it is no longer relevant to contemporary society. However, such a claim requires further discussion, but before this is undertaken it is appropriate that this particular model is examined. Perhaps the simplest way to illustrate the concept is diagrammatically and an adaptation of Boyle's diagram is used for this purpose (see Figure 2.1).

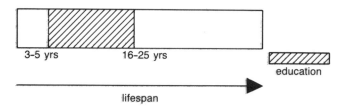

Figure 2.1 The front-end model of education
Source: Boyle (1982: 8)

This clearly demonstrates the idea that education occurs only during the formative years and that when social maturity, or adulthood, is achieved then education ceases. This idea is reflected by many writers on the subject of education. John Stuart Mill, for instance, claimed that the content of education was to be found in 'the culture which each generation purposely gives to those who are to be their successors' (cited in Lester-Smith 1966: 9). Emile Durkheim, a French sociologist and educationalist, regarded education in a similar manner: for him it was 'the influence exercised by adult generations on those who are not yet ready for social life' (1956: 71). But by the beginning of the twentieth century it was becoming more apparent that an inter-generational perspective was not adequate to describe the educational process. John Dewey (1916: 8), for instance, was forced to add a prefix to the term *education* in order to express the same sentiments as those specified by Mill and Durkheim, stating that *formal education* was necessary if society was to transmit all its achievements from one generation to the subsequent one. Today, formal education frequently refers to teaching method rather than to the structure of the educational provision, and the term most likely to be used to convey the same idea is *initial education*. This has been described as:

> going to school, including nursery school, but it could go on full or part-time into the mid-20s. After compulsory schooling, 'initial' education takes a wide variety of forms: full-time study in sixth form, university, college, poly-technic, medical school, military academy and so on; part-time day release, evening classes and correspondence courses; on the job training in the factory.
> (ACACE 1979: 9–10)

In a similar manner, Coombs and Ahmed seek to distinguish formal education from informal and non-formal education. They define it as: 'the highly institutionalized chronologically graded and hierarchically structured "education system" spanning lower primary school and upper reaches of the university' (1974: 8). Their intention is to distinguish this initial formal system from other forms of lifelong education which occur in developing countries. The idea underlying initial education is that at a given stage in the lifespan individuals have stored away sufficient knowledge and skill to serve them for the remainder of their life, so that their education is then complete.

Such a model of education is also implicit in the writings of the well-known English philosopher of education, R.S. Peters, who makes a clear distinction between education and the educated man (a term which Peters used without gender bias). Peters (1972: 9) regards being educated as a state which individuals achieve, whilst education is a family of processes that lead to this state. However, it might be advantageous to this analysis to enquire whether the educated person is an end-state. Peters' writings tend to suggest that he considers it as such, for he claims that education 'was not thought of (previously) explicitly as a family of processes which have as their outcome the development of an educated man in the way in which it is now' (1972: 7). While this seems to imply that Peters considers that the educated person is an end-state, it is possible to regard it as a social status in contrast to the uneducated person, since it is an achievement. Yet even if it is an achievement, is it possible for the educated person to undertake more education? Of course it is – but to where does the additional process lead? If it is regarded as a status, then that status remains unchanged. Peters rightly claims that to be an educated person is not to have arrived but to travel with a different view during life. Hence the educated person is being educated throughout the whole of his life. Indeed, it might be that if the state of educated man were achieved then the process must continue or else the state would be lost. Hence it is maintained here that the process is significant, perhaps more significant than the state or the end-product. Therefore, it is claimed, no initial or inter-generation aspect may be considered intrinsic to the concept of education, and since the educated person should always be in the process of being educated, the implications of having achieved a state of having been educated are misleading.

It may, therefore, be concluded that education is about a learning process and, as such, it may be seen as a response to the basic learning need in humankind that was discussed in the previous chapter. However, not all learning is educational. Few people would deny, for instance, that indoctrination is a learning process but they would almost certainly wish to deny that it is an educational one, so that specific criteria need to be adduced in order to ascertain whether any learning process is educational. Elsewhere (Jarvis 1983a), this has been worked out in some detail, so that it would be repetitive to do more than summarize that discussion here.

Peters (1966: 23ff), following Wittgenstein, claims that education like many other phenomena is too complex to define but he suggests that there is a family of similar phenomena that may be regarded as education. He puts forward three sets of criteria for consideration as a basis for education, but they were not regarded as totally satisfactory, so that other criteria were suggested: education must involve a learning process; the learning process should not be a single event; the process should be planned rather than haphazard; education is essentially a humanistic process because knowledge is humanistic and because the process involves human beings as learners and, also, maybe as teachers; learning has to involve understanding, which is essentially a quality of critical awareness. Before a definition is offered it is necessary to examine the term 'humanistic' within this discussion. Dewey claims that knowledge is essentially 'humanistic in quality not because it is about human products in the past, but because of what it *does* in liberating human intelligence and human sympathy' (1916: 230). He goes on to suggest that any specific matter that does this is essentially humane, so that in this context humanistic has two facets: it is concerned about the welfare and humanity of the participants and it is humane. Hence this makes claims that the educational process is normative and idealistic. Education may now be defined as 'any planned series of incidents, having a humanistic basis, directed towards the participants learning and understanding' (Jarvis 1983a: 5). This definition is very broad since it is the common factor in the multitudinous branches of education, and it is possible to modify and adapt it, so that the definition may reflect the meaning added to the basic idea when a prefix is placed before the term education, e.g. lifelong education requires only that 'and which may occur at any stage in the lifespan' be added to the end of the definition. Hence it may be seen that this basic definition of education does not restrict education: to any specific learning process; to any time in life; to any specific location; to any specific purpose. It is, therefore, maintained that the front-end model of education, depicted in Figure 2.1, is only one branch of education rather than being the total educational process. It is recognized, however, that it is difficult to change people's attitudes towards education and that this front-end model of initial education is equated with education *per se* in many people's minds, and thus the education of adults is still often viewed as an optional extra added after initial education has actually been completed, so that it remains marginal to the institution of education in society.

This definition will be considered in relation to the various branches of education that are relevant to the education of adults; but, prior to embarking upon this, it is necessary to clarify the relationship between teaching, learning and education.

TEACHING, LEARNING AND EDUCATION

Tough (1979) demonstrated that many of the adults' learning projects were completely self-directed and that neither a teacher nor an educational institution was necessary to their successful implementation. Yet it would be difficult to claim that many of these projects were not educational. It might be more true to claim that the more self-directed the project the greater the likelihood that learners can respond to their own learning needs and also self-actualize in the process, thus demonstrating the humanistic nature of education itself. Consequently, it may be seen that while the learner is an essential element in the educational process, the teacher is not. Learning may, and often does, occur without teaching but the extent to which teaching can occur without learners and learning is much more debatable. A teacher may claim to have taught a subject and say that nobody learned anything – but would the claim actually be correct? If nobody had learned, had the teacher actually taught or only tried to teach but not succeeded? Teaching, it is claimed here, is dependent upon learning, but the converse is not true.

Teaching may be regarded as the intention to bring about learning (Hirst and Peters 1970: 78), but if it is unsuccessful it may be viewed as an unsuccessful attempt to teach rather than unsuccessful teaching. Unsuccessful teaching may occur when some learning has resulted from the teaching but when all the intentions have not been achieved. Learning is often defined in behavioural terms and Hilgard and Atkinson, for instance, define it as 'any more or less permanent change in behaviour which is the result of experience' (1967: 270). However, the acquisition of new knowledge need not result in behavioural change, but learning has occurred. Hence this definition is not accepted here. It will be recalled from the last chapter that learning was put into the context of the acquisition of culture and it is, therefore, proposed to regard learning as any process of receiving and assessing any aspect, or aspects, of culture. It has been defined elsewhere as the process of transforming experience into knowledge, skills, attitudes, values, emotions, etc. (Jarvis 1987, 1992). This will be discussed further in the next chapter.

Many different learning processes occur during the human lifespan, but not all of them may be considered educational, since it must be borne in mind that any definition necessarily excludes those phenomena that are not in accord with it. Hence the definition adopted above includes many aspects of learning but it does not incorporate them all. Self-directed learning, for instance, may always be considered to be educational but others may never be so regarded, e.g. indoctrination. However, there are other learning processes, i.e. learning through being instructed, that might be considered educational in some instances but not in others. Learning may occur in some instructional situations which may not be considered educational because the quality of interaction between instructor and learner was such that the latter failed to self-actualize or no longer felt esteemed or accepted by the instructor. Clearly there are some teaching techniques that rarely allow for the learner's own humanity and experience to surface, and when these techniques are employed some questions must be raised about the extent to which the learning process is educational (see Jarvis 1983a: 80–93 for further analysis).

From this brief discussion it may be seen that because education is regarded here as a humanistic process, it is seen as one in which the value of the human being and the quality of interaction between teachers and learner, when it occurs, are paramount to it. Where these high ideals are not manifest in the learning process then the extent to which it is educational is open to doubt. Nevertheless, it must be borne in mind that this humanistic analysis is only of value if the process is one in which planned learning and understanding occur.

ADULT EDUCATION AND THE EDUCATION OF ADULTS

At first sight the terms adult education and the education of adults appear to mean precisely the same thing, and Hostler (1977: 58) seems to employ them synonymously; but, because of the history of the former term, there is a considerable difference between the two which will become apparent in the following discussion.

The term 'adult education' carries specific connotations in the United Kingdom which imply that it is specifically liberal education, and this also has a stereotype of being a middle-class, leisure time pursuit. Underlying this implication is the idea that the adult's education has been completed and, during leisure time, the adult self-indulgently improves or broadens existing knowledge, skills or hobbies. Hence, these implications reflect a conception of a front-end model of education and, perhaps because of the prevalence of this perception of education, it is hardly surprising that adult education is regarded as marginal. Obviously much adult education, especially that provided by Local Education Authorities, University Extension, etc., will occur during leisure time, but leisure need not be equated with the pursuit of only the creative arts or physical or domestic skills. Leisure time activities do not preclude any form of learning, whether aesthetic, athletic or academic, but they may have been undertaken for the sheer enjoyment of learning rather than for a vocational purpose. Hostler rightly states that 'one quite common error is to imagine that because liberal education is not undertaken for the sake of results, it does not *have* any results' (1978: 134; emphasis in original). Clearly it often does have results. The existence of the Open University in the United Kingdom, and similar institutions in other parts of the world, bears witness to the fact that leisure time education for adults can and does produce results – in the learner, in the academic work produced (even research projects for higher degrees) and in the award of academic degrees. In the first instance, then, it must be recognized that the term 'adult education' has a social definition as being a form of liberal education undertaken by those people who are regarded as adults. Even so, it should be noted that this is a social rather than a conceptual definition and that this is why it is important to distinguish between adult education and the education of adults. However, the definition of adult still complicates this discussion.

A number of major differences occur in the analysis of the term adult and it is necessary to summarize them here. Wiltshire (1976) suggested that adult education might also be understood as an educational process conducted in an adult manner. Taken to its logical extreme this interpretation would allow for children in schools to be regarded as participating in adult education if the process in which they were engaged was conducted in an adult fashion. However, Wiltshire was aware of this possible interpretation and suggested that an adult also has to be mature, experienced and over twenty years of age, a figure that appears to be somewhat arbitrary. Even though it is possible to agree with Wiltshire that adulthood also implies maturity and experience, it is harder to accept that these are either absolute or discrete, or that they occur at a specific biological age. Hence, it is necessary to pursue this discussion about adulthood a little further and to return to the matter of an adult learning environemnt in a subsequent chapter.

Paterson (1979) discusses the concepts of adult, education and adult education, but since he regards education as the process of developing learners as persons, he is a little restricted in his analysis of adult education. Nevertheless, he views adulthood as a status, involving certain responsibilities, entered into at a specific age. He (1979: 1) claims that people are deemed to be adults because of their age but, although they are not necessarily mature, they are expected to behave in an adult manner. Adult education is, therefore, different from other forms of education because of the nature of its students and this may be an answer to Legge's (1982: 3) question about whether there is a need to have a sharp dividing line between child and adult. That the term is employed may be an even more significant reason why it requires analysis. By contrast to Paterson, Knowles (1980: 24) suggests that the basis for treating people as adults is that they behave as adults and that they perceive themselves to be adults. Like Legge, he does not regard the distinction between adulthood and childhood to be absolute, recognizing that during the individual's lifespan the process of transition is both gradual and continuing. However, it might be objected that Knowles' subjective approach is rather circular, and to some extent it is since he defines 'adult' by 'adult', so that the conception of social maturity might be employed here. When an individual is regarded as having reached a level of social maturity in which he can assume a responsible position in society he may be regarded as an adult. Knowles goes on to state that clarification of the term 'adult education' is more difficult because it is used with at least three different meanings: the process of adults learning; a set of organized activities carried out by a variety of institutions to achieve specific educational objectives; a field of social practice. Knowles describes the last of these three, a combination of the other two, as bringing 'together in a discrete social system all the individuals, institutions and associations concerned with the education of adults' (1980: 25).

It is clear from this brief discussion that in any analysis of the terms 'adult education' and 'education of adults' the definition of the term 'adult' is deceptively difficult. In a sense, it might be easier to employ the term 'post-compulsory education' to overcome this problem, but this term does not convey the same wealth of meanings as does the word adult. Hence, it is suggested here that, following Knowles, adulthood refers to the fact that both individuals' own awareness of themselves and other people's perceptions of them accord them with the status of adulthood within their own society. The education of adults, therefore, refers to those learning processes undertaken by people who have achieved the status of adult. At the same time it has to be recognized that there is also an institutionalized adult education service and that, on occasions, the words are used to refer to it.

At this stage it is possible to draw some conclusions about the two terms under discussion in this section. In the United Kingdom 'adult education' is used within a liberal education framework, sometimes carrying with it implications of a front-end model of education. For these reasons, it is more desirable to employ the term 'education of adults' because this may refer to any educational process undertaken by adults, whether liberal, general or vocational, and located in the spheres of adult, further or higher education or outside the institutional framework entirely. This terminology also implies that education is not completed at any stage in the lifespan and, indeed, that the education of adults may begin in the period of initial education and, for some people, it continues into post-compulsory sectors. Additionally, it will be recognized that the term has some overlap with the idea of continuing education, which will be referred to later in this chapter. However, the term 'education of adults' is a broad term and one that encourages the development of a separate sphere of study within education, a point to which further reference will be made. Clearly this latter usage is very similar to the American use of the term 'adult education', so that the different implications in the terminology should be borne in mind when reading the literature from either nation. While these differences are unfortunate, they do reflect the differing historical traditions of the two nations.

LIFELONG EDUCATION

Once the front-end model of education is rejected the way is open to formulate other approaches to the subject, one being that the process of education begins in childhood and continues throughout the lifespan. While lifelong education as an ideal has recently been adopted by the United Nations Educational, Scientific and Cultural Organization (UNESCO) it is not really a new concept:

> It is common place to say that education should not cease when one leaves school. The point of this common place is that the purpose of school organization is to insure the continuance of education by organizing the powers that insure growth. The inclination to learn from life itself and to make the condition of life such that all will learn in the process of living is the finest product of schooling.
>
> (Dewey 1916: 51)

While not everyone would agree with Dewey's understanding of the purpose of the school organization, they may well agree with the sentiments expressed in the remainder of the quotation. Later in the same passage, Dewey continues:

> Since life means growth, a living creature lives as truly and positively at one stage as at another, with the same intrinsic fullness and the same absolute claims. Hence education means the enterprise of supplying the conditions which insure growth, or adequacy of life, irrespective of age.
>
> (Dewey 1916: 51)

For Dewey, education is one of the major foundations of a rich life but it is a foundation that need not be laid at the beginnings of life or in childhood, it is one that may be laid at any stage of life and then built upon. While Dewey has not been particularly relevant to a great deal of thinking about adult education in the United Kingdom, his influence has been far greater in the United States. Among his disciples was Lindeman – author of *The Meaning of Adult Education* (1961, first published 1926) – whose own influence continues to be extended through existing practitioners in the field.

Soon after Dewey's influential book, from which these quotations have been drawn, appeared in America, an important document about adult education was published in Britain. A.L. Smith, chairman of the committee that produced the famous 1919 Report, wrote:

> That the necessary condition is that adult education must not be regarded as a luxury for the few exceptional persons here and there, nor as a thing which concerns only a short span of early manhood, but that adult education is a permanent national necessity, an inseparable aspect of

citizenship, and therefore should be both universal and lifelong.

(Smith 1919: Introductory letter para xi: 5)

This far-sighted statement, like many others in the Report, was loudly acclaimed but never implemented, so that the idea of lifelong education remained an ideal. Yeaxlee returned to the subject and claimed that

the case for lifelong education rests ultimately upon the nature and needs of the human personality in such a way that no individual can rightly be regarded as outside its scope, the social reasons for fostering it are as powerful as the personal.

(Yeaxlee 1929: 31)

Here, then, lies an argument for lifelong education, very similar in substance to that produced earlier in this study; yet this case was made in the United Kingdom over a half a century ago, since which the concept has remained dormant for many years.

It was not until after the Second World War that the term gained prominence again and this was because organizations such as UNESCO adopted it, influenced by such writers as Lengrand (1976). Thereafter many publications, emanating from UNESCO, have developed and expounded the concept. The Faure Report (1972) advocated that education should be both universal and lifelong, claiming that education precedes economic development and prepares each person for a society that does not exist but which may do so within his lifetime. The Report claims that education is essential for human beings and their development and that, therefore, the whole concept of education needs to be reconsidered.

In 1976, lifelong education appeared to have 'come of age' when the Lifelong Learning Act was passed into law in the United States. This law authorized the expenditure of $40 million annually between 1977 and 1982 on lifelong education (Peterson *et al.* 1979: 295). However, Peterson and his associates were forced to conclude that while 'lifelong education and learning policies are gaining favour in numerous foreign countries, notably Scandinavia, there are at the moment signs of slackening progress [in America]' (1979: 423). Despite this rather gloomy assessment there are signs of innovation in lifelong education in America, in such institutions as elderhostels (e.g. Zimmerman 1979).

Higher education is also gradually changing its direction and beginning to practise policies of lifelong education, although this process is extremely slow. Kulich (1982b) documents how Canadian universities are moving in this direction and Knapper and Cropley (1985) trace the implications of the idea of lifelong learning for higher education. Williams (1977) actually claims that lifelong education is the new role for institutions of higher education. While this assertion is supported here, it is recognized that some universities have found it very difficult to adapt to these demands and some of them have actively resisted such changes. Nevertheless, with the gradual growth in part-time higher education and the introduction of schemes of credit transfer changes are occurring which might result in higher education providing opportunities for education throughout the lifespan.

Having briefly reviewed some of the main developments in lifelong education, it is now necessary to formulate its definition. Dave regards lifelong education as 'a process of accomplishing personal, social and professional development throughout the lifespan of individuals in order to enhance the quality of life of both individuals and their collectivities' (1976: 34). Lawson has tried to show that such a wide conception of education 'fails to distinguish between the general mass of formative influence that shapes us or between the general learning which an intelligent being undergoes in adapting to circumstances' (1982: 103). He pleads for a more careful analysis of the claims that are made on behalf of lifelong education. While Lawson is clearly right to criticize Dave's approach, since it offers no real definition of education, Lawson himself does not offer an alternative. Even so, in his discussion Lawson does seem to be in danger of including the content of what is taught and learned in the educational process, rather than regarding the actual content as incidental to the process. It seems, therefore, that a *via media* between the too limiting approach of Lawson, on the one hand, and the too broad approach of Dave, on the other, is required and it is suggested that a modification of the definition of education offered earlier fits into this category. Lifelong education is, therefore, any planned series of incidents, having a humanistic basis, directed towards the participant's learning and understanding that may occur at any stage in the lifespan.

Lifelong education is, therefore, a concept and an ideal which remains rather meaningless unless it is actually implemented. This has occurred in different ways and in various places and each different approach contains within it its own philosophy. Three major perspectives have occurred: continuing education, recurrent education and community education. Each is examined in turn and, finally, the concept of the learning society is discussed.

CONTINUING EDUCATION

As the education of adults began to develop, there was considerable confusion and overlap between the different terms; indeed, there still is. For instance, a symposium, organized by Jessup in 1969 was published as 'Lifelong Learning – a symposium in Continuing Education' and the discussion paper published by the Advisory Council for Adult and Continuing Education states: 'Continuing education has long been a popular idea among some people concerned with the education of adults. It has gone under a variety of names in different countries: education permanente, lifelong education, recurrent education' (ACACE 1979a: 7). This report is clear that continuing education should not be regarded as further education in the manner in which this currently exists in the United Kingdom. However, the above quotation actually raises at least three major questions: To what extent is continuing education conceptually different from lifelong education? Is continuing education actually synonymous with further education? What is the relationship between continuing and recurrent education? The last of these three questions is discussed in the following section, but the first two are explored here.

Venables defines continuing education as 'all learning opportunities which can be taken up after full-time compulsory schooling has ceased. They can be full-time or part-time and will include both vocational and non-vocational study' (1976: 19). But McIntosh (1979: 3) disagrees with the definition, suggesting rather that continuing education refers to post-initial rather than post-compulsory education. The logic of this suggestion is quite clear from the previous discussion on the education of adults: initial education may continue for longer than compulsory education, so if continuing education followed compulsory education it would actually commence during initial education for many people. Hence, it may be concluded here that continuing education is post-initial education, but that it is not synonymous with lifelong education. Lifelong education makes no distinction between initial and post-initial education whereas continuing education refers only to the latter part of lifelong education and is, therefore, only one branch of education.

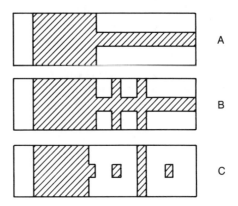

Figure 2.2 Models of continuing education

Figure 2.2 indicates that continuing education may take a number of forms: A suggests some form of continuous part-time education and is less frequent than other forms; B suggests that continuous education can be both full-time and part-time, this is even rarer than A; C is the most realistic as it implies that continuing education is intermittent rather than continuous. There are similarities between this concept and that of recurrent education, which will be discussed later in this chapter.

Continuing education, however, is not the same as further education for a number of reasons: further education is post-compulsory but not necessarily post-initial; further education tends to imply a specific level of study whereas continuing education does not; further education is usually pre-vocational, vocational or academic while, conceptually, continuing education need not be directed towards any course assessment or award.

From this discussion it is clear that continuing education differs slightly in its conceptualization from any of the previous terms that have been thus far elaborated upon. Yet the name of the Advisory Council linked together adult and continuing education and this same coupling occurs in a number of national organizations, such as the American Association of Adult and Continuing Education; so how does it differ from adult education? It was pointed out earlier that adult education has connotations of hobbies and skills in part-time leisure education and that this is much narrower and more specific than the education of adults. Continuing education embraces aspects of personal, social, economic, vocational and social education (Venables 1976: 23–4) and may actually equate to the concept of the education of adults rather than to adult education. Indeed, the Advisory Council issued two reports, one on adult education (1981) and another on continuing education (1982a), so that it is clear that in the Council's thinking the specific connotations of adult education, as already discussed, were seen separately from those of continuing education. Nevertheless, when the National Institute of Adult Education changed its name, it was to National Institute of Adult Continuing Education, which linked the two terms firmly together. Indeed, the term continuing education has tended to incorporate adult education in a variety of ways, so that university extra-mural classes are regarded as continuing education, etc.

Having accepted the implications of McIntosh's definition it is now necessary to explore these in further detail. The first significant point is that the concept appears to be a politically neutral one neither making reference or criticism of the initial education system nor implying any form of evaluation of the total contemporary education system. Perhaps its apparent neutrality may be taken to incorporate a conservative bias, thereby making it a politically acceptable term. But because the term appears neutral it is acceptable to people of all political persuasions, which may be a reason why Sockett was able to claim that in 'the last five years Continuing Education has gradually worked itself up the national education agenda only to be stopped in its tracks by economic factors' (1981: 5). The past ten years have demonstrated something of the truth of this analysis.

While it is certainly true that some forms of continuing education have been harshly treated as a result of the recent economic depression, the British government has certainly financed a considerable amount of continuing vocational education and pre-vocation education under the auspices of the Manpower Services Commission before it was replaced, PICKUP, the local TECS (Training and Enterprise Councils), etc. Indeed, government policy towards the education might be summarized by a claim made initially in the 1960s by Clark Kerr and his colleagues:

Industrialization requires an educational system functionally related to the skills and professions imperative to its technology. Such an educational system is not primarily concerned with conserving traditional values or perpetuating the classics; it does not adopt a static view of society, and it does not place great emphasis on training in the traditional law. The higher educational system of the industrial society stresses the natural sciences, engineering, medicine, management training – whether private or public – and administrative law. It must readily adapt to new disciplines and fields of specialization. There is a relatively smaller place for the humanities and the arts, while the social sciences are strongly related to the training of managerial groups and technicians for the enterprise and the government. The increased leisure time of industrialism, however, can afford a broader public appreciation of the humanities and the arts.

(Kerr *et al.* 1973: 47)

While the philosophy underlying this claim might be questioned by many adult educators, it is clear that a great deal of government policy in the United Kingdom and elsewhere has been towards supporting continuing education that has a vocational bias whilst expecting liberal adult education to be more self-financing.

Continuing education is, therefore, a term which refers specifically to post-initial education, and it has assumed a dominant place within the current terminology because it refers to both vocational and non-vocational education. Indeed, the professions have introduced the term *continuing professional education* (CPE) and this has become widely accepted for all forms of in-service training, although Houle (1980) refers to this as continuing learning. Cervero (1988), however, regards continuing professional education as a significant area of educational activity, introducing educators to the continuing education occurring within a number of different professions. In a similar manner, Jarvis (1988) endeavoured to explore the continuing education developments in the United Kingdom for an American audience.

While the conceptual definition of profession is debatable, professions are occupations based upon a circumscribed area of knowledge, and since that knowledge base is likely to be artificial, in the sense used in the opening chapter, it is necessary for each profession to ensure that its practitioners keep abreast with the latest developments in the field. Hence, Apps cites the definition of continuing education provided by the Accrediting Commission of the Continuing Education Council of the United States as:

the further development of human abilities after entrance into employment or voluntary activities. It includes in-service, upgrading and updating education. It may be occupational education or training which furthers careers or personal development. Continuing education includes that study made necessary by advances in knowledge. It *excludes* most general education and training for job entry. Continuing education is concerned primarily with broad personal and professional development. It includes leadership training and the improvement of the ability to manage personal, financial, material and human resources. Most of the subject matter is at the professional, technical and leadership training levels or the equivalent.

(1979; 68f.: emphasis added)

Professionals clearly provide their members with many updating programmes in continuing education but this has led to considerable debate about the extent to which the professions should make it mandatory for their members to attend such courses. Additionally, universities, polytechnics, colleges of further and higher education, business schools and the professions themselves are all offering continuing education provision for the professions, so that unless a national policy is actually drawn up and implemented problems and disputes might occur. Alford (1980) highlights how some of these problems – of competition between educational providers; of finance; of the political nature of accreditations – are occurring in America. These are all issues that have to be confronted in the United Kingdom, unless the 'law of the jungle' is to become manifest in continuing education (see Stephens 1981: 138). The policy of the Conservative government in the United Kingdom throughout the 1980s has been to treat education as a commodity to be marketed, so that Stephens' 'law of the jungle' could have been written more aptly as the 'law of the market'. This approach to education and the whole of culture in late modern society has been nicely summarized by Bauman:

Literature, visual arts, music – indeed the whole of the humanities – was ... set inside market-led consumption as entertainment. More and more the culture of consumer society was subordinated to the function of producing and reproducing skilful and eager consumers ... ; in its new role, it had to conform to the needs and rules as defined, in practice if not in theory, by the consumer market.

(Bauman 1992: 17)

Yet there is a danger that a national policy might restrict innovations, so that too tight a control might be as damaging as no control at all to the development of continuing education.

Continuing education may, therefore, be seen to be a continuation of the educational provision beyond initial education, especially in the vocational sphere, and it is also a concept that implies no criticism of the present system. Indeed, its major concerns seem to focus upon the provision of vocational continuing education, access to it and extension of it. However, its presence by virtue of offering no criticism of the current structure of education actually serves to reinforce the status quo, so that it is inherently conservative. No such claims may be legitimately made about the next form of education strategy to be discussed in this chapter, for recurrent education has certainly had some radical claims made on its behalf.

RECURRENT EDUCATION

If UNESCO adopted the term '*lifelong education*' then '*recurrent education*' was the concept espoused most frequently by the Organization for Economic Cooperation and Development (OCED) until the 1980s, when the term appeared to fall into disfavour. Brought to the attention of a wider audience in the late 1960s by Olaf Palme, it gained currency through the publications of OECD and, in the United Kingdom from the mid-1970s, through the discussion papers and other documents produced by the Association of Recurrent Education. There is some agreement about the definition of the term, which is perhaps summarized by the following, rather tautologous, suggestion that recurrent education is 'the distribution of education over the lifespan of the individual in a recurring way' (OECD 1973: 7). This is a little broader than an earlier definition proposed by OECD that recurrent education 'is formal, and preferably full-time education for adults who want to resume their education, interrupted earlier for a variety of reasons' (OECD 1971, cited by Kallen 1974). These two definitions have been selected because they indicate two conceptions of recurrent education, which may be illustrated in the manner shown in Figure 2.3.

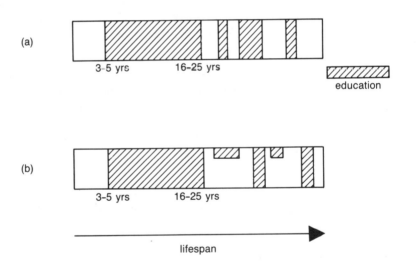

Figure 2.3 Alternative models of recurrent education
Source: Boyle (1982: 8)

In (a) it may be seen that the education is full-time but in (b) it is either full-time or part-time, and it may be recalled that continuing education might also assume a full-time or a part-time form, so that it would be legitimate to ask whether these two terms are synonymous.

One of the most significant features of recurrent education was the belief that individuals should have a right to a specified amount of full-time formal education during their lifetime, and that this need not have been taken during their formative years. Indeed, Gould (1979) not only regarded this as a moral argument about the equality of educational opportunity but he also related it to a wider perspective of equality of occupational opportunity. It was, therefore, regarded by some exponents as a radical, moral strategy for lifelong education. Unlike continuing education, which appears to occur in a piecemeal manner in response to expressed or perceived needs, etc., recurrent educationalists regarded their approach to be a 'comprehensive alternative strategy for what are at present three unrelated sectors: a) the conventional post-compulsory educational system . . . b) on-the-job training of all kinds . . . c) adult education' (OECD 1973: 25).

Houghton has claimed that recurrent education

> was the first new idea in education this century . . . . It represents one of those very rare shifts in the framework of thinking which Kuhn has described. Its emergence marks the beginning of the end of the dominant apprenticeship paradigm in education.
>
> (Houghton 1974: 6)

Clearly this is a massive claim but, at the same time, recurrent education does offer a radical alternative system, one that its exponents claim to be realistic in the light of contemporary society (e.g. Flude and Parrott 1979). Others may have viewed recurrent education as a reaction to the technological innovations in society rather than a radical alternative idea. However, not all exponents of recurrent education actually expected the whole education system to be radically changed, as Cantor indicated when he described its emergence in the United Kingdom.

> It is hardly surprising therefore to discover that recurrent education is not at all systematically organized in the United Kingdom; indeed many of its critics would argue that there is as yet little official recognition of the need to make systematic provision for it. However, education in the United Kingdom does contain elements of recurrent education upon which to erect a more systematic provision.
>
> (Cantor 1974: 6–7)

Obviously Cantor thought that a system would emerge, perhaps with a few policy decisions to aid it on its way. Indeed, this type of presentation reflects a less radical approach to recurrent education and seems to coincide with a continuing education perspective; this approach is also reflected in some of the later OECD publications (e.g. OECD 1977).

Since some exponents of recurrent education tend to present a more radical approach to education and others have embraced the more moderate continuing education perspective, it is not surprising that some theorists have extended this distinction to other respects of the curriculum. Griffin (1978), for instance, has focused upon the main aspects of teaching and learning in the curriculum: aims, content and method. He suggested that recurrent educationalists tend to be more student centred, have a more integrated approach to content and generally have a more romantic curriculum perspective, while those who had adopted a continuing education approach will have a more classical perspective on curriculum issues. While he has tended to polarize continuing and recurrent education, he admitted that he has undertaken a tentative exercise. However, he raised many valuable points about these two forms of education, and this might have been even more insightful had he also sought to incorporate some of the other philosophical issues espoused by many adult educators.

One of the main practical features in recurrent education is the idea that full-time education may be embarked upon later in life by some people. Having a right to full-time education later in life is both inconvenient and expensive to employers and governments and so it is hardly surprising that with the economic stringency of the 1980s and the advent of 'new right' politics that the idea of recurrent education disappeared from the political and educational agendas. Indeed, it even fell into disfavour with OECD, and the Association of Recurrent Education in the United Kingdom also adopted a new name – the Association of Lifelong Learning. One aspect of recurrent education which has survived, however, is paid educational leave. This was recognized in some of the early OECD literature (OECD 1973: 70–2), where discussion occurred about the extent to which paid educational leave should be a statutory right or whether it should be the result of negotiations between employers and employees. By the time that the OECD had actually published this document, France had already introduced legislation which allowed for up to 2 per cent of a firm's labour force to take leave of absence at any one time and for 1 per cent of the wage bill, rising to 2 per cent by 1976, to be spent on employee education (OECD 1975: 35).

Other European countries were also introducing similar legislation and the International Labour Organization called for each member state to formulate and apply a policy of paid educational leave (Convention 140: 1974). Killeen and Bird (1981) investigated the extent to which paid educational leave existed in England and Wales and concluded that between 15 per and 20 per cent of the total work force received some paid, or assisted, educational leave in the year of the study, 1976–7, which approximated to six days per person for courses organized by the employing organization and twelve days per person attending courses mounted by other organizations. They noted that this educational leave is not evenly distributed, younger workers being more likely to be released than older ones, and that the courses tended to vocationally based and had a qualification as one of its end products. Bryant (1983) reported a similar research project in Scotland in which he recorded the same type of picture as that discovered in England and Wales. Mace and Yarnit (1987) also record a number of examples of paid educational leave, including developments in London (Workbase), Sheffield (Take Ten – a day off to study each week for ten weeks) and Liverpool (Second Chance to Learn): this book of readings is an important one since it seeks to address the issue of why low paid and disadvantaged groups get fewer opportunities for educational development than do the more advantaged groups. In addition, the book reports on the 150-hour programme in Italy, which is an exemplar of what can be done with careful planning.

One writer who has continued to use the term recurrent education is Tuijnman (1989), whose use of the data from the 50-year longitudinal study of men in Malmo, Sweden, has shown how significantly adult education and occupation are related. He demonstrated, for instance, that adult education has significant positive effects on occupation and career development. Tuijnman suggests that 'men who participate in adult education tended to view their lives as more "full,", "worthwhile," "rich," and "interesting" than those who did not take part in such activities' (1989: 228). Tuijnman's research was only with men so that, while it might be postulated that the same would be true for women, he does not produce data to demonstrate it.

Killeen and Bird (1983: 38ff) demonstrated clearly the conceptual confusion surrounding the education of adults since they referred to paid educational leave as part of the system of continuing education. Their emphasis reflects the fact that the term continuing education has greater currency in the United Kingdom than does recurrent education, even though it might not be quite so refined conceptually. Since continuing education is a much more nebulous concept, having no undertones of radicalism, it is hardly surprising that it has gained so much support and that it is incorporating elements of recurrent education within it. It is perhaps also significant to note that the term recurrent education has appeared less prominently in some of the later OECD publications (OECD 1977).

Recurrent education, then, has two major stands: a more radical one that regards it as a strategy for the reform of the whole education system and perhaps also the wider society, while the more conservative stand is less ambitious in its claims, preferring rather to regard it as a reformist approach to implementing lifelong education. There is, therefore, a marked difference in the philosophy of the two stands and yet they both recognize that while education may not be continuous after initial education it should be lifelong, a right that all people should receive and that sufficient provision should be made for them to do so.

COMMUNITY EDUCATION

Occasionally a word appears in the English language that becomes ideologically acceptable for a period of time. 'Community' is such a word and it was widely accepted in the United Kingdom in the 1960s and 1970s as representing something intrinsically good and right. Perhaps this was because a certain nostalgia was present in society at that time for a world that was past. Hence the idea of community education appeared to be accepted with almost the same uncritical appraisal as the term community was received. This process was aided and abetted by the fact that it is a confused and multifarious concept. In order to begin to appreciate some of these facets it is necessary to understand the use of the word community.

In sociology the main meaning of the word stems from the work of the German sociologist Toennies (1957), who wrote in the last century about social change. He recognized that a change in the type of human relationships was occcurring from one which may be seen as personal and long lasting (community) to one that was formed by association. Hence, the term 'community' assumed a distinctive meaning in sociology referring both to personal relationships and to the fact that they should be established within a specific locality. Toennies actually considered that these personal, long lasting relationships were disappearing as society became more urban and its members more mobile. Thus it is not surprising that the term assumed an ideological significance in an increasingly impersonal and individual society, especially in the period that it did, when stress was being placed upon human values and the value of humanity in general.

A second, but quite similar, use of the term refers to those groups of people who live together in a specific place, e.g. a monastery, and where the value of the community life is extolled. Here people interact in a personal manner in a specific locality but the boundaries of the community are even more tightly drawn. Thirdly, the word is sometimes used without reference to the personal relationships, when it refers only to the locality, e.g. the people of such-and-such a community. This is perhaps the most common use of the word, although there is one other that is employed very frequently; in this instance it refers to 'extra-mural' in its widest sense, so that a community nurse, for instance, is one who cares for her patients outside the walls of the hospital, etc.

Consequently, it is easy to comprehend how difficult the term 'community education' is to understand, since all of these meanings of community are inter-related and confused in the diverse educational processes that are often classified as being a part of community education. It is, therefore, not surprising that an analytical philosopher, such as Lawson (1977), should point out this conceptual confusion and raise doubts about the phenomenon. However, other adult educators, e.g. Kirkwood (1978), considered that Lawson's approach, while valuable, was rather conservative and not entirely correct. Perhaps it would be true to say that new forms of adult education generally arise in response to expressed needs or demands and that in their initial stages they are not classified in any manner, so that Lawson's analytical approach is a necessary reflection upon the innovations that are occurring within the education of adults.

From the above discussion it is possible to distinguish at least three different types of education which might be labelled community education: education for action and/or development education in the community; extra-mural forms of education. Lovett *et al.* (1983: 36ff.) also sought to distinguish between different forms of community education and they suggested four types: community organization/education; community development/education/; community action/education; social action/education. However, for the purposes of this analysis the three types of community education distinguished here will now be more fully discussed.

Education for community action and/or development

Perhaps the most well-known exponent of this position is Paulo Freire, who maintains that education can never be neutral. He formulated his ideas in Latin America, against a background of illiteracy and poverty, and his thinking reveals the synthesis of Christian theology, existentialism and Marxism that has been quite dominant amongst certain groups of intellectuals in Latin America over the past two or three decades. While his ideas developed in a Third World situation, they are relevant to the United Kingdom and America, as London (1973) shows. Even though much of Freire's work has been written in Portuguese, it is widely available in English (see bibliography). He emphasized that education should make the learners critically aware of their false consciousness and of their social condition. In becoming aware, they should reject many of the myths erected by the ruling elite that prevent them (the learners) having a clear perception of their own social reality. Having undergone a process of demythologization, learners should act upon the world to endeavour to create a better society. Clearly Freire's radical, but moral, approach is one that many will criticize, especially those who for varying reasons wish to see education as a neutral process.

Freire is not alone with this perception of education, although few other writers have formulated it in such a sophisticated manner. Among those in the United Kingdom whose approach to education is similar to Freire's is Lovett (1975, 1978, 1979, 1980, etc.) who has worked both in inner-city Liverpool and, more recently, in Belfast in Northern Ireland. Lovett suggests that some adult educators see 'the role of adult education in community action ... as ... providing the working class with an effective educational service so that they can take full advantage of the educational service *and* make the best use of their individual talents and abilities.' (1975: 155; emphasis in original). In his work in Northern Ireland, Lovett (Lovett *et al.* 1983) has continued to work out these ideas and subsequently offered a model of different types of community education. More recently, Kirkwood and Kirkwood (1989) have endeavoured to apply Freire's ideas in a community education project in inner-city Edinburgh. They record how they adapted his educational techniques to their own situation, although the project is certainly less radical than some of Freire's own ideas.

In America, perhaps the most well-known institution organizing radical adult education of this type is Highlander. Highlander was founded by Myles Horton in Tennessee and worked with labour unions and citizenship groups. It played a significant role in the civil rights movement in the United States and its work is becoming increasing well documented (Horton 1990).

But should adult educators be involved in the action in the community? Newman suggests that there are conditions under which the adult educator 'should not try to stop short of involvement in community action' (1973: 26) but by contrast, other adult educators consider that while they should be prepared to teach activists what to do, they should not actually be involved in the action (Flude 1978: 163). Flude's position shows that one who adopts a more radical position in the continuing education/recurrent education debate may be a little less radical in the community action/community development discussion. Clearly, however, there are legitimate differences in approach on this issue and it would be quite unwise to attempt to draw conclusions about the extent to which educators of adults should, as part of their teaching, be involved in community action.

At the same time, it is clear that education is an essential tool in the process of community development. Fordham *et al.* (1979) document a project, undertaken by the University of Southampton, in which they were involved in seeking to establish and strengthen adult education provision in an informal educational setting in a working-class housing estate in Havant. Here the educators were concerned to develop adult education for the sake of the whole area rather than as a response to the demands of potential students. In this instance, the educator is taking the initiative rather than merely publishing a prospectus and awaiting enrolments. It would be quite possible to record a multitude of community development projects in which adult education has played a major role but perhaps it is wiser to note here that the journal of the International Council of Adult Education, *Convergence*, usually carries reports of a number of these enterprises from developing countries and, recently, *The International Journal of Lifelong Education* has also published similar studies.

Education in the community

Perhaps the earliest formal education of this type stemmed from the work of Henry Morris, who was responsible for the establishment of community colleges in Cambridgeshire before the Second World War (see Jennings n.d.), and whose ideas were influential in their introduction in Leicestershire shortly afterwards (Fairbairn 1978). From these beginnings have grown the larger urban educational and social complexes, such as the Abraham Moss Centre in Manchester and the Sutton Centre in Nottinghamshire. One of the central ideas of these schemes is that the school should be the focal point of the community, in a similar manner to that of the parish church in medieval times, and that adults should be able to attend classes in these centres. As a result of his work in Liverpool, Midwinter concludes that:

> Education must no longer be open to caricature as a few hours at school for a few years in . . . pre-adult life. It must be viewed as a total, lifelong

experience, with the home and the neighbourhood playing important parts, and everybody contributing to and drawing on this educative dimension of the community.

(Midwinter 1975: 99)

However, he does not specify all the advantages of comprehensive schools including adults among their learners, but Mary Hughes (1977: 226–32) sees many advantages in allowing adults to attend community schools at the same time as children, not the least being that it is education on the cheap. In America, the community college concept has also been implemented and comprehensive programmes are offered for younger and older students who wish to study (Yarrington 1979: 86–94).

Fletcher (1982), who conducted a five-year research project at the Sutton Centre, shows how a multi-purpose centre can be beneficial to all the participating organizations, how the school children are able to participate in adult classes and how adults are enabled to join with children in learning during the day. He shows how this approach can be beneficial to all concerned provided that there is some adaptation in the way that the initial education is organized. These large urban educational complexes have also been introduced in other parts of the United Kingdom, and a similar community school complex established in the suburbs of Grenoble, in France, was also influenced by these developments. Clearly educational innovation is occurring throughout the world and much of it could be discussed under this sub-heading. Poster and Krüger (1990) have brought together a number of examples from different countries in the Western world, highlighting some of the ways in which educationalists are reaching out into the community.

Adult education beyond the walls

Extra-mural adult education is a term usually restricted to university adult education extension classes where staff form the universities teach in the community, or the university employs part-time staff to teach liberal adult education classes under its auspices in the wider community. Recently, the term has assumed some significance with other educational institutions organizing educational classes in their local communities. However, these forms of educational outreach are rarely regarded as community education, even though they are examples of education 'beyond the walls' of the educational institution. By contrast, Head (1977) records how he, with the aid of a social work student on placement, was able to work in an informal manner with older, single men in a day centre teaching them how to write letters and how this exercise developed into a wider educational exercise. Head was involved in an endeavour that some adult educators might classify as community education while others might regard it as adult basic education since the learners were the end product of the educational exercise.

This point might be further demonstrated since it will be recalled that Tough's research suggested that many individuals undertake learning projects during the course of a year and that these are frequently undertaken outside the normal educational institution. In addition, Brookfield (1979) records how he discovered a leaderless discussion group which met to learn more about specific subjects and how he was able to provide material for the group although he never attended it. Other adult educators will also be aware of the existence of similar gorups and even, perhaps, have been involved in helping establish such groups without necessarily attending them. Certainly, since the advent of the Open University an increase in the number of such groups will almost inevitably have occurred as students meet together informally to discuss their studies. Perhaps the most well-known recent development in this approach to adult education has been the University of the Third Age, a movement founded in Toulouse in 1973 and which has grown rapidly since that time. It was established in the United Kingdom in 1981. This is not a university in the traditional sense, although it is more closely associated with the university system in some parts of the world than others, but it is an organization formed for older adults to enable them to meet together in interest groups to teach and learn from each other. Universities of the third age exist in many parts of the world, organizing extensive non-formal educational programmes and, more recently, forming their own international network. Perhaps the development of educational technology has also resulted in an increase in the number of autonomous learning groups, but it is to be doubted whether this form of education beyond the walls would be regarded as community education.

Having reviewed a number of different types of adult education that might be classified under the heading of community education, taking into account the various usages of the term community, at least two questions remain to be answered: is there any theory of community education and is there anything distinctive about it?

Fletcher (1979: 67) suggests that there are three premises in community education:

– the community has its needs and common causes and is the maker of its own culture
– educational resources are to be dedicated to the articulation of needs and common causes
– education is an activity in which there is an alternative between the roles of student, teacher and person

He goes on to argue that certain implications follow from this in terms of centre or periphery activities, formality and informality and democratic control. This, in turn, results in active and reactive processes. However, perhaps Fletcher is guilty of reification of the concept of community in the first of these premises and he might have argued that there are groups and categories of persons in the locality who have common causes who may be helped by the allocation of educational resources, e.g. the underprivileged. Then the philosophy underlying the theory would be one of responding to certain forms of social inequality in order to produce a less unequal society in which more people interact on an inter-personal basis, so that the locality begins to generate its own community ethos. It would, therefore, be a matter of social policy and educational commitment to divert educational resources to the under-privileged and, as such, it would reflect the philosophy that led to the creation of educational priority areas in initial education. However, this argument still fails to differentiate between community education and other forms of education of adults, such as adult basic education or educational programmes for immigrants etc. How does community education differ from these? This is one of the more difficult questions, and community education is not distinct unless it is seen to be an educational response to social inequality. But if it is only a response of this nature, adult basic education could be equated with it. Hence the intended outcome of the response might be important, so that community education might be regarded as a response to social inequality, the aim of which is development in the location or action in order to improve the standard of living, the quality of the environment, etc. in the vicinity. If this argument is accepted then the sociological concept of community which involves both the quality of human relations and a specific locality is that which forms the basis of community education. Indeed, this position is reflected in Fletcher's own definition of community education as 'a process of commitment to the education and leisure of all ages through local participation in setting priorities, sharing resources and the study of resources' (1979: 7). Another approach would be by extending the definition of education offered earlier in this chapter to include the sociological concept of community, so that community education is any planned series of incidents, having a humanistic basis, directed towards the people in a specific locality learning and understanding how to enrich the quality of human relationships and social living in that area. Such a definition allows for both community development and community action.

This argument leads to the logical conclusion that the second and third types of education described in this section, i.e. education in the community and adult education 'beyond the walls', are merely innovations in lifelong education and should not really be classified as community education, since its distinctive feature is the community in which the learners will be involved rather than the development of the learners for their own ends. The alternative position would be for any form of education that relates to any of the definitions of community with which this section commenced being regarded as community education. If this were to be accepted, then the parameters of community education would be broadened to include many forms of adult and lifelong education that have been discussed here, resulting in the concept becoming so broad as to be almost meaningless. Nevertheless, it has to be recognized that the concept is used in this broad way in the educational vocabulary, for a variety of reasons, and that its use in a non-radical manner tends to neutralize the force of the more radical connotations.

THE LEARNING SOCIETY

Community education refers to specific types of non-formal education occurring outside the formal educational organization, but the final concept discussed in this chapter sets its boundaries much more widely. The learning society is a futuristic concept, an ideal, that draws together many of the ideas and ideals raised in this chapter. Although it is futuristic, it may be possible to detect its emergence as rapidly changing levels of technology provide people with the social conditions necessary for, and make people aware of, the opportunities to extend their learning throughout the whole of their lives. However, unless the provision of educational facilities occurs it is doubtful if it could be claimed that the conditions were in place for such a society; and there is a danger of equating the provision of educational facilities with the idea of the learning society. In the Royal Society for the Encouragement of Arts, Manufactures and Commerce's (RSA) investigation into lifelong learning, for instance, the learning society was defined as 'one in which everyone participates in education and training throughout their life. It would support them as citizens, in their employment and leisure' (cited in Molyneux 1922: 7). Clearly this definition runs the risk of confusing 'education' with 'learning', something which Hutchins' definition did not do. He wrote that it

is a society in which everyone has begun a liberal education in educational institutions and is continuing liberal learning either in such institutions or outside them, a society in which there are true universities, centres of independent thought and criticism is one in which values may be transformed.

(Hutchins 1970: 134)

Indeed, he offers a vision of the ideal: 'A world community learning to be civilized, learning to be human . . . . Education may come into its own' (ibid.).

Thus it may be seen that at the foundations of the learning society are values accorded to learning as being 'normal and commonplace' and education is regarded as an 'inherent human right of all its citizens' (Boshier 1980: 1). The learning society, it must be recognized, is learner based, has no barriers of access and provides a flexible but lifelong system of education. It is society organized in such a manner as to make all kinds of learning available to everyone on a full-time or a part-time basis. Hence Boshier (1980: 1–2) claims that a learning society cannot emerge through additional learning programmes being grafted on to existing provision, rather it requires a deliberate policy and definite changes in curriculum aims especially in initial education.

While a learning society might be emerging, a number of major constraints exist to inhibit its progress, including: the idea that education should have an aim other than learning for its own sake; the prevalence of the idea that education is only initial education; the understanding of leisure as being something which is uncreative and of little value, so that it is only malingerers who have it. It is perhaps interesting that leisure should no longer be related to education since the word school is derived from a Greek word *skhole* which means 'leisure spent in the pursuit of knowledge' (Collins English Dictionary 1979). Perhaps a rediscovery of the original meaning of the word school is necessary in a learning society. But Tough, Brookfield, Sargant and other researchers have all shown how people do use their leisure in learning, so that it may be necessary to understand the fact that people do use their leisure in this way and emphasize this more frequently than educators do at present. However, the front-end model of education remains a constraint to the emergence of a learning society which means that the concept of education learned by trainee teachers should include a lifelong rather than a learning process provided for children, and that they should see a major function of the school in society as being an institution which helps children discover the joy and skills of learning so that they can spend much of the remainder of their lives so doing. Indeed, Husen (1974), among others who have written on this subject, suggests that schooling has to change considerably to accommodate the learning society.

Clearly there is considerable evidence that more educational facilities are being made available to adults, so that some of the basic provisions are being put into place for the creation of a learning society. Indeed, the British Broadcasting Corporation recently held a conference on the contribution that broadcasting can make to a learning society, and from a survey of 1,030 people it found that many wanted 'practical' programmes and ones that could be tied to accreditation in some way. Nature programmes and documentaries were the ones from which viewers felt that they learned the most (Straw 1992). Many forms of education for adults are becoming regarded as mainstream education rather than an optional extra, as attitudes towards education and training alter. There are a variety of reasons for these innovations, although the main ones probably relate to the speed of social and technological change. Without opportunities to learn, people would be unable to keep abreast with developments in society. Perhaps Hutchins' ideal is still a long way off, but since a changing society must be a learning one, more opportunities now exist than ever before for people to learn throughout their lifetime.

SUMMARY

This chapter has sought to illustrate some of the philosophies and concepts apparent in the current discussions about the education of adults. Initially, the front-end model of education was discussed and it was suggested that such an approach is not particularly relevant for education in contemporary society, so that a humanistic definition of education was offered, i.e. that education is any planned series of incidents, having a humanistic basis, directed towards the participants' learning and understanding. Education is seen, therefore, as an idealistic process in which the humanity of the participants is paramount.

The education of adults was regarded as any process directed towards the participants' learning and understanding, where the participants regard themselves and are regarded by others as socially mature. The reasons for the use of the term education of adults revolve around the fact that adult education carries liberal education connotations while a great deal of educational provision is vocational in nature. However, liberal adult education provision must lie at the heart of the learning society which has, above all, one conception of education as its basis: that education is a lifelong process of learning and developing – which is an ideal at which to aim.

Three strategies for implementing lifelong education were discussed: continuing education tends to be gaining wide acceptance but it is a conservative concept that casts no aspersions on the present system; recurrent education seems to be being incorporated into the continuing education system but it is a more radical conceptualization, especially among some of its exponents, which implies that the current system needs radical reform so that everybody may receive an equal entitlement of education at some stage during their life; community education was also shown to be a rather confused concept and it was suggested that the concept should be restricted to those educational processes in which the learners intended to use their learning to improve the quality of life in a specific locality, while other forms of education generally classified under this heading might be better regarded as other innovations in lifelong education.

This chapter has, therefore, endeavoured to clarify some of the contemporary concepts and to show in the process some of the underlying philosophies and trends in current society. However, it has become apparent throughout this chapter that the provision of education for adults is a political phenomenon; its provision is a matter of governmental policy and, on occasions, some of its forms assume a radical political orientation. No educational provision can actually be regarded as an apolitical phenomenon. Having examined these concepts it is now necessary to examine the adult learner and adult learning, a subject that forms the basis for the next two chapters.

3 The adult learner and adult learning

Earlier in this book it has been argued that learning is a basic human need, so that the process of learning occurs in most people throughout much of their life. Hence, it is maintained that lifelong education should be regarded both as a human right and as a fundamental necessity in any civilized society in order that all people can respond to their learning needs, fulfil their potential aned discover a place in the wider society. For too long education has been regarded as 'something done to children' and at some stage in adolescence, or soon after, it is completed – except for the minority who continue to attend educational institutions. Even though the many may never darken the doors of an educational institution again in their lifetime, it does not mean that they have ceased to learn and, therefore, some continue in the process of self-education, even if the learning that they provide for themselves might not always be quite so enriching as they may have received had they availed themselves of the wider educational provision. Much of this learning may have been covert and, despite the work of Candy and similar research projects (see Candy 1991 for a recent bibliography and analysis), the actual amount of learning per adult remains unknown and, perhaps, unknowable. However, in these past two decades an increasing emphasis has been placed upon adult learners and their learning, and many studies about these have appeared, to which some reference has already been made. Consequently, this chapter focuses upon these aspects and contains two main sections: the adult learner and adult learning. In the following chapter some of the writers about adult learning are examined.

THE ADULT LEARNER

Previous discussion highlighted the problem of defining the term adult and concluded that adulthood is reached when individuals are treated by others as if they are socially mature and when they consider themselves to have achieved this status. However, such an approach does not really appear to enrich the debate about the adult learner a great deal, nor does it contribute much to the theory of adult learning, so that it is necessary to pursue this discussion a little further at this point.

The self

It was noted in the first chapter that the self-concept is central to learning theory. Jarvis (1987, 1992), following George Herbert Mead, has argued that the mind and the self are learned phenomena, since the brain stores memories of experiences, probably from the time that the baby is still in the womb and certainly from the time of birth. Hence, the brain is the storehouse of memories from which emerge the mind and the self. Luckmann (1967: 48–9) argues that during the early years the individual self becomes detached from its immediate experience in the interaction with other persons. This detachment leads to an individuation of consciousness and permits the construction of schemes of meaning, since these respond to the learning needs that the evolving self develops. This, in turn, results in the self integrating the meanings that have evolved in response to the learning questions which have arisen from previous experience. Hence, ultimately, a self is formed that integrates the 'past, present and future in a socially defined, morally relevant biography'. There is, therefore, a sense in which the self transcends its biological body, reaching out to the socio-cultural environment and responding to pressures from it in a dialectical relationshp in order to create a sense of meaning, as was illustrated in the opening chapter.

This chapter raises philosophical questions about the nature of human beings that cannot be avoided in any consideration about the adult learner. It will not be pursued much further here, however, since it is beyond the scope of this study, although this particular problem is explored in Jarvis (1992). Suffice to note that, if this argument is accepted, the person has two major components: the self and the physical body in which the former is contained. This is an important conclusion since the ravages of time clearly have their effect on the physical body, but what of their effect on the self? Following Luckmann's argument, it may be seen that every new experience is interpreted by the self and has a meaning given to it which is then integrated into the meanings of past experiences stored in the mind. This ultimately results in a system of meaning or a body of knowledge that helps the person interpret 'reality'. But what if the physical body and even the brain itself begin to deteriorate during adulthood? Does it not affect the ability of the self to process these experiences in a meaningful way? Luckmann might respond in the negative to this, at least until such time as the brain ceases to function efficiently or at all. In recent years, psychologists have tended to support this conclusion.

Until fairly recently it was thought that when human beings achieved biological maturity they reached a plateau and, after a few years, they began to deteriorate. Thorndike (1928), for instance, concluded that the ability to learn 'rises until about twenty, and then, perhaps after a stationary period of some years, slowly declines' (cited in Yeaxlee 1929: 41). However, this argument has come under some criticism in recent years and Allman (1982) summarizes some of these later research findings. She records how Horn suggested that there are two forms of intelligence: fluid, which stems from the biological base, and crystallized, which is capable of growth through the major part of life since it is influenced by the social processes that the individual experiences. In the same paper she points to Birran's 'discontinuity hypothesis' which states that

> the biological base ceases to be the primary influence on behaviour after physical maturation is complete and as long as the biological base does not enter into a hypothesized critical range of pathology, it will not regain supremacy of influence.

(Allman 1982: 47)

From these and other studies, she concludes that since adulthood is not the end-product of childhood and adolescence, lifelong education becomes a means of facilitating future adult development. In a similar fashion, one of the foremost investigators of education and ageing, Gisela Labouvie-Vief concludes that 'much of what we now know about the educability of adults is in need of revision' (1978; 249) as a result of recent research on the topic. Therefore, the old adage that 'you can't teach an old dog new tricks' is not only misleading but it is also inappropriate since older people can and do learn new things.

The physical capabilities of the adult, however, do decline after they have reached a peak in late adolescence or in early childhood. Verner summarized these as including: 'sensory decline; loss in strength; lengthening of reaction time; decline in sexual capacity; changes in skin texture, muscle tone and hair colour; and a gradual decline in overall energy' (1964: 18). He suggests that there are a few physiological losses that are very significant in the process of adult learning: loss in visual acuity, loss in audio acuity, loss of energy and the problems of homeostatic adjustment. Since these all affect adult learning and, therefore, adult teaching, they need to be taken into consideration. However, these physiological changes may induce adults to underestimate their powers to learn and so reinforce the perception that education is something that occurs early in life.

Nevertheless, irrespective of the conditions of the physical body, the individual self continues to interact with others within the same socio-cultural milieu enabling the person to continue to construct a universe of meaning. If other people are withdrawn then that dynamic tension between the self and the wider society, which is at the heart of learning, disappears and people may begin to doubt themselves, suffer senility, anomie, etc. But do adults always learn when they are interacting with other people? Clearly many situations are familiar so that individuals do not have a traumatic experience in every interaction and the amount of new knowledge gained may be minimal and it may merely reinforce that which is already known. But on other occasions the discrepancy between what individuals know and the meaning that they give to their experiences is greater and then the learning experience becomes more explicit. Schutz and Luckmann state:

In the natural attitude, I only become aware of the deficient tone of my stock of knowledge if a novel experience does not fit into what has up until now been taken as a taken-for-granted valid reference scheme.

(Schutz and Luckmann 1974: 8)

Thus it may be argued that given specific social situations every adult is a learner, whereas in familiar experiences the knowledge gained merely reinforces that which the individual already has. Yet there is a sense in which this argument suggests that the motivating force for learning is a discordant experience between the self and the socio-cultural environment, but it would be unwise to suggest that this is the only reason for undertaking such an activity. Tough (1979: 44–62) shows how complex these reasons are and it would not do the sophistication of his argument justice to attempt to reproduce it here; suffice to note that Tough discusses many reasons, among which are: pleasure, esteem, desire to employ what is learned, satisfying curiosity, enjoyment gained from the content of what is learned, completing unfinished learning, and social benefits.

Characteristics of the adult learner

It may thus be asked, who is the adult learner? Clearly Tough's finding of 98 per cent of his sample, discussed earlier, appeared to be rather high and that might be accounted for by his methodology. Yet Peters and Gorden (1974), in a similar piece of research, discovered that 91 per cent of their sample of 466 had also conducted learning projects. Other research has supported these findings, so that it does appear that the majority of adults actually undertake learning projects and that, from the above argument, every adult is a learner.

However, adults who learn through enrolling on a course at an educational institution may be of specific types. It is much more difficult to discover the statistics for, and the characteristics of, the latter types of person than it might appear on the surface. Chanley *et al.* (1980: 7) suggest that about 16 per cent of the adult population of England and Wales attend post-secondary education in any one year. However, their statistics for vocational education appear to be incomplete, so that this figure is probably an underestimate. Sargant 1991: 69) suggests that 17 per cent of the population are trying to teach themselves informally, while 10 per cent actually enrol on a course. In all, she suggests that 36 per cent of the population have enrolled on a course or have studied informally over the three years prior to her research. In a piece of research conducted in 1980, but not published until 1987, Woodley *et al.* (1987: 169) conclude that mature students do not represent a cross-section of the population: mature students tend to be from the service classes and the younger students tend to enrol in courses that lead to a qualification, although mature students tend to have some educational qualifications already. This certainly supports other research that has shown that those who have some education want more of it, for a variety of reasons.

By contrast, Johnstone and Rivera (1965) report that over 20 per cent of the American population attended education in the year commencing June 1961, but this figure included full-time students and those whom they classified as self-directed learners. Cross (1981: 51), reporting the statistics from the National Center for Educational Statistics in America, suggests that some 12 per cent of the American population over the age of 17 years were engaged in some formal, organized adult education, but this excluded those studying for an academic qualification. ACACE (1982b: 15) discovered that 47 per cent of the sample interviewed claim either to have taken part at some time or to be currently engaged in some form of post-full-time education or training, 12 per cent were engaged in a study at the time of the research and another 10 per cent had been during the three-year period prior to it, and that 'large numbers of the population are interested in using their (leisure) time actively rather than passively in a wide variety of ways' (ACACE 1982b: 27). Killeen and Bird (1981: 20) calculated that between 3 and 4 million people received some sort of educational leave during 1976–7 but this was not always on a full-time basis. However, from these varying figures it is clear that accurate statistics are difficult to obtain and that, since the social provision of education is changing rapidly, any statistics discovered in one year may have little relevance a few years later.

Research into who joins tutorless discussion groups and who attends voluntary organizations in order to learn is still in its infancy and it might be unwise to estimate numbers, although Verner (1964) suggests that the same type of people participate in formal community life as those who participate in adult education. However, it will be interesting in the coming years, as research into the University of the Third Age begins to be published, to see if Verner's assumptions are true.

It is, therefore, necessary to try to summarize some of the findings about the type of person who actually participates in adult classes. Charnley *et al.* conclude that:

> the adult education service has attracted a variety of students, but the student body is not distributed in a way which reflects the class structure of the population as a whole. The exceptional case of extensive working class participation is adult literacy where special funds were made available. The tendency [is] for the higher socio-economic groups ... to take fuller advantage of the provision.
>
> (Charnley *et al.* 1980: 37)

None of the more recent research tends to question this conclusion, even though it reflects the position at the end of the 1970s. Two reported studies demonstrate the validity of this conclusion. Sidwell (1980: 309–17) conducted a survey of sixty-three evening and nine day classes in modern languages for adults in Leicestershire between November 1978 and May 1979. In all 1,139 students were sent a questionnaire and a response rate of 41.7 per cent was achieved. Women outnumbered men, over 75 per cent of the respondents could be classified as coming from the non-manual socio-economic classes, and 71.5 per cent had already studied a language during their initial education. The modal age group was between 30 and 34 years. Jarvis (1982b) studied a small adult education centre in a Surrey village during the academic year 1979–80 in which 477 students registered. Of the 368 respondents to a questionnaire, 87.8 per cent were women and many classified themselves as housewives. Of the remainder, the great majority were from non-manual backgrounds, 62 per cent were in the age group 22–45 years and only 5.7 per cent of the respondents were over 65 years. The Advisory Council survey also discovered that women students outnumbered men, but only slightly, and that the adult student body is predominantly under the age of 45, and that its social class is concentrated heavily in the C1 grouping, which is lower middle class. Statistics from American research also point to similar findings: higher participation rates among women, among the 17–34 years age group, among the more wealthy and the better educated (Cross 1981: 54). Cross concludes that the amount of formal schooling is the one variable most significantly correlated to educational interest and participation in adulthood. This conclusion is in accord with the phenomenological argument of Schutz and Luckmann (1974) who write that individuals are likely to repeat their past successful acts because it enables them to act upon the world in a confident manner. Bourdieu (1973) called this cultural capital. Support for such a position would also come from behavioural psychology since repetition of past successful acts may be interpreted as a reinforcing action.

It would be difficult to specify the type of person in professional occupations who attends in-service continuing education. However, some evidence may be found in the work of Rogers (1962) who discovered that those professional practitioners most likely to introduce innovations to their practice were those who were better educated and who kept up with recent developments by reading the professoinal journals and who attended professional association meetings and conferences. Hence the place of the professional journal and the regular conference assumes a significance that the educator of adults has to take into consideration. For other occupations, Killeen and Bird (1981) suggest that young male workers are more likely to receive paid educational leave than any other category of the work force, which provides additional evidence for the current feminist argument.

Few mature people enter the field of higher education as full-time students although many more study part-time, especially with the Open University. Hopper and Osborn (1975) investigated mature students in three universities and one polytechnic and discovered that there were more men than women and that they had, on the whole, received more than the basic minimum education required by law but that many of these students had been socially downwardly mobile since leaving school, so that they re-entered the educational system from socio-economic class III (non-manual). By contrast, those who had been upwardly socially mobile tended to enter it from socio-economic class II. They also noted that many of the students had a low sense of personal self-esteem and that they tended to experience a sense of marginality. More recently, Roderick *et al.* (1981) have conducted a similar study in Sheffield and they also discovered that more men than women were mature students and that the median age of male students was lower than that of the female students. However, they also noted that a surprising number of the mature students were either separated or divorced. They suggest that 'in cases where marriages run into difficulties, some women become alarmed at their lack of qualifications and consequent inability to earn enough to support themselves and their children' (1981: 53) and so they return to full-time education. However, it would be a feasible interpretation to suggest that the marriage breakdown also frees some people to return to full-time education. They also record data from 520 mature students who applied to one of the universities of Birmingham, Leeds, Liverpool, Manchester and Sheffield for the years 1977 and 1978: 69 per cent were men, 49 per cent were under 30 years of age and only 11 per cent were over 40 years; 48 per cent were married but only 6 per cent were separated or divorced; 25 per cent were already in the professions and a further 20 per cent were in clerical employment.

More recently, Tight (1991) has undertaken research into part-time higher education and he points out, quite correctly, that there is little government policy on this subject. He characterizes the part-time student in higher education thus:

> Part-time students are different from full-time students, and they form a more diverse group. They tend to be older ... with the majority in their twenties and thirties. The older part-time students naturally tend to be married, and to have children. Most part-time students are male, although this pattern is rapidly changing ... they are overwhelmingly middle class – but part-time students show great evidence of social mobility.
>
> (Tight 1991: 106)

He points out that many of them did not do well at school and that they gained entry qualifications through part-time study. He also records that there is a disproportionate number in London and the south-east, and that many of them travel considerable distances in order to continue their studies. As universities and colleges are being forced into the market for more students, they are beginning to innovate and more part-time courses are beginning to emerge. Hence any picture of the part-time student in higher education may change considerably over the next decade.

Since its foundation in 1969, the Open University has enabled many mature students to study part-time for a degree whilst remaining at home and continuing in their employment. Throughout the period of its establishment it has maintained and published full statistical reports about its students. McIntosh (1974) noted that in the early years of its establishment there was a downward shift in the age of those who registered, that school teachers predominated amongst the first students although there was an increasing number of students without any formal educational qualifications in the first few years.

However, she (1974: 59) pointed out that only 8 per cent were objectively working class, although 15 per cent classified themselves as such, and she considered that many Open University students are socially upwardly mobile. Rumble (1982) recorded how the proportion of school teachers studying in the Open University has declined as teaching in the United Kingdom has moved towards an all-graduate entry. He showed how each year between 1970 and 1980 more men than women have applied to study with the Open University but that the overall trend has been for an increasing number of women to apply. However, the male applicants classified as either in a skilled trade or other manual occupations have never exceeded 10 per cent of the toal number of applications nor has the number having no formal education qualifications ever exceeded 12 per cent. The majority of those applying for the Open University are under 40 years of age, with less than 1 per cent of the total number being over the age of 65 years.

Thus it may be concluded that the majority of adult students tend to come from non-manual occupations, to have been relatively successful in terms of examinations in their initial education and to be under 45 years of age. Men predominate in vocational courses and in full-time higher education but women are more likely to attend classes that do not lead to a qualification. However, the proportion of women entering the Open University does appear to be approaching that of men.

Motivation to study

The question remains, however, about the reasons why mature people wish to attend educational institutions, and many pieces of work have investigated this topic, indeed research into participation is among the most established areas of investigation in adult education. Courtney (1981) claims, quite correctly, that research in this area has been rather sporadic in Britain although there were two very early pieces, i.e. Hoy (1933) and Williams and Heath (1936). The National Institute of Adult Education's report *Adequacy of Provision* records that 'the two main reasons for going to classes were "work" and "know more about the subject/learn the correct way"' (Hutchinson 1970: 59). The Advisory Council research discovered that:

> Men attach more importance to the idea that education is a means to getting on in the world: women give rather less emphasis to it. Such a difference is not large – a matter of 7 per cent less agreement in the case of women – but it confirms what has been said elsewhere in this report about the contrast between the male and female view of continuing education.
>
> (ACACE 1982b: 41–2)

Both Woodley *et al.* (1987) and Sargant (1990) confirm this conclusion and it is clear from this research that men tend to have a slightly more instrumental attitude towards education than do women. In contrast to this work, the research in the United States has been much more consistent and elaborate (see Houle 1979; Courtney 1981; Cross 1981). Cross (1981) indicates that four main methods have been employed to investigate this phenomenon: in-depth interviews, motivation scales, questionnaires and, what she calls, hypothesis testing. Space forbids a full account of all the work published but a brief résumé of some of the findings are included here. Houle (1979: 31–2) draws the general conclusion that participation in any type of educational activity is usually undertaken for a variety of motives rather than a single one, and that these usually reinforce each other. Houle (1961) himself formulated an early and useful typology within which to classify these motives: goal-orientated learners, activity-orientated learners and those whose main orientation is learning for its own sake. Within each of these classifications a number of different motives can be specified. This typology has formed the basis of a number of analyses but Johnstone and Rivera (1965: 46) classified the motives of their sample in the following manner: prepare for a new job; help with the present job; become better informed; spare-time enjoyment; home-centred tasks; other everyday tasks; meet new people; escape from daily routine; other or none – a miscellany of unclassifiable responses. They go on to show how motives to participate vary with different subjects studied and with the age, sex and socio-economic position of each respondent. They conclude that:

> there are very pronounced ways in which the uses of adult education differ across the range of social classes. At lower socio-economic levels adult education is used primarily to learn skills necessary for coping with everyday life.
>
> As one moves up the social class ... they shift ... to getting ahead .... In general, there is an overall shift away from learning for the purpose of basic life adjustment ... [to] enrichment of spare time.
>
> (Johnstone and Rivera 1965: 159–60)

Other research projects have subsequently employed different typologies to these and yet the overall findings do not differ greatly. Burgess (1974), for instance, identified seven basic orientations to adult education, which were a desire: to know; to reach a personal, social or religious goal; to take part in a social activity; to escape; to comply with formal requirements. Morstain and Smart (1974) highlighted six clusters of reasons: social relationships; external expectations; social welfare; professional advancement; escape/stimulation; and cognitive interest. In a later piece of research, Aslanian and Brickell (1980) interviewed 744 adult learners by telephone and discovered that 83 per cent of them specified a life transition as the motivating factor that caused them to start learning, e.g. a change in employment. While their research method might have biased their response, it does point to the significance of analysing the life-world of learners in order to understand both their motivation and their approach to learning.

Wlodkowski (1985) suggests that there are six major factors that affect motivation, a concept which he concedes is most difficult to define but which relates to the reasons why people behave in the manner that they do; these factors are: attitudes, needs, stimulation, emotion, competence and reinforcement. He suggests 68 different techniques which are designed to increase achievement in learning. This study, however, is much more specifically on the motivation to learn than it is on the motivation to enrol on a course of student, i.e. on participation.

It is quite clear from all of these research findings that most of the main reasons for participating in adult education classes lie in a cluster of orientations that are quite similar, despite the fact that different researchers employ their own terminology. The reason for participation does not always lie within learners but in the dynamic tension that exists between learners and the sociocultural world. Yet if there is a need to learn and if most people actually embark upon learning projects there must be reasons why so few people appear to attend formal educational provision. Carp, Peterson and Roelfs (1974) suggest three sets of factors which inhibit participation: situational barriers, institutional barriers and dispositional barriers. They suggest that cost and time are the major hurdles, and this is in accord with Charnley *et al.* (1980: 37) who also focus upon fees as a major issue in leisure time education, but they also suggest other factors, such as a lack of flexibility in the adult education service which prevents some people from attending. The Advisory Council's research (1982b) noted that some 15 per cent of their respondents had not participated in any form of post-initial education nor did they wish to do so in the future but that there were others who had not participated in the past but wish that they had or who wish to do so in the future. In addition, there were some 15 per cent of the sample who wished that they had participated in the past, hoped to do so in the future, but who had never actually been involved in any form of post-initial education. Hence this research, while not specifying why non-participants had not actually been involved in post-initial education suggests that it would be unwise to assume that non-participants are all opposed to any participation in education.

Since the first edition of this book, liberal adult education in the United Kingdom has had to become even more market orientated and, as a result, there have been more studies about participation and non-participation. McGivney's (1990: 66–118) research isolated five groups who are under-represented in liberal adult education: unskilled/semi-skilled manual workers; unemployed people; women with dependent children; older adults; ethnic minority groups. She (1990: 79) records the most frequently mentioned deterrents to participation, which are:

1 lack of time – cited most frequently by unskilled workers and young mothers
2 negative effect of school experience – from both the unemployed and the unskilled
3 lack of money – cited by unemployed and by women and older people
4 lack of confidence – cited by the black groups

5 distance from classes – elderly, women with dependent children and ethnic minority groups all mentioned this
6 lack of childcare – mentioned by mothers with dependent children
7 lack of day-time opportunities – mentioned by women and older adults
8 education is regarded as irrelevant by unskilled people
9 lack of transport – cited by mothers with dependent children, older adults and ethnic minority groups
10 reluctance to go out at night – mentioned by women and elderly adults.

These ten deterrents provide a wide variety of reasons why these groups of adults do not participate and if adult education is to attract them it needs to address some of the problems. Without financial support from the Government, it is clear that the adult education service cannot reduce fees a great deal. Perhaps this is one of the attractions of the University of the Third Age which, because of its non-formal approach to education, has fewer overheads. However, the fact that it has relatively low membership fees means that its existence is regarded by some adult educators as a threat to the liberal adult education service.

In addition to these five groups, McGivney also notes the fact that those adults with basic education needs are another category which are inhibited from participating because of their insecurity, distrust, low aspirations, limited time, dependence, negative attitudes towards education and shame at the low level of their achievement. Each of these reasons reinforces the theory of cultural capital which was discussed above.

Sargant (190: 114) points out that non-participants have similar leisure time interests as the remainder of the population but with a slightly lower level of activity. McGivney discusses how adult educators need to target the non-participant groups, and this reflects clearly the philosophy of adult education being a commodity to be marketed. However, Sargant (1990: 111) raises a significant moral question about the extent to which adult educators should actively intervene and seek to persuade non-participants to learn. In a market-oriented service, this question might not often be raised, but the extent to which adult educators have the right to create felt learning needs in people is a question which might be addressed.

This section has attempted to draw together a wide range of material to describe the adult learner: it claimed that every adult is a learner but that there are definite characteristics of and types of person who attend the variety of educational provision that exists. Clearly adult learners who join educational institutions are younger and tend to be middle class but this does not mean that the remainder of the population do not learn or that they may not want to join in formal educational provision. Having looked at the adult learner it is now necessary to examine adult learning.

ADULT LEARNING

A theory of adult learning has been implicit in much of the previous discussion but it is now necessary to make this explicit. It will be recalled from the opening chapter that learners were located within their socio-cultural framework and that it was suggested that both the learners and their socio-cultural milieu have to be taken into consideration when endeavouring to construct a theory of adult learning. The socio-cultural milieu may itself be divided into two distinct elements: the objectified culture of a society and the means by which it is transmitted to individuals. But the individual may also be regarded as a duality of the self and the physical body in which it is located. Hence, there are at least four factors that need to be taken into consideration when framing any theory of learning.

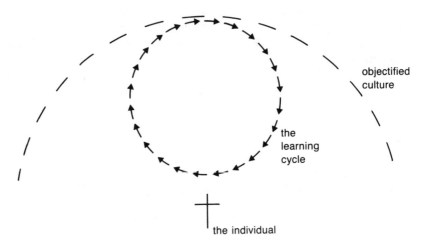

Figure 3.1 A learning cycle implicit in the individual in his socio-cultural milieu

Implicit in Figure 1.2 (Chapter 1) is a learning cycle and this may be demonstrated in more detail, as shown in Figure 3.1, from where it may be seen that the dialectical relationship between individuals and their culture (Figure 1.2) may be regarded as the learning cycle in Figure 3.1. A potential learning situation occurs when there is a dynamic tension between individuals' experiences and the agencies of transmission of the culture of the society. But before this is discussed in greater detail it is necessary to clarify each of the elements in the process.

Culture

In sociological literature this term refers to the sum total of knowledge, beliefs, ideas, values, practices, etc. prevalent in a specific society. Yet culture is neither static nor objective but it is a dynamic phenomenon affected by the pressures of changing technology, the forces of economics, political ideology, etc. As was shown earlier Scheler (1980) as early as 1926 demonstrated quite clearly that the elements of culture change at varying paces, so that while it is depicted here as a rather static homogeneity it is actually more like a patchwork quilt with each little element altering at a different rate to every other. This means that there is always new knowledge, values, beliefs, skills, etc. for learners to acquire and, at the same time, it may also result in them having to 'unlearn' older knowledge or skill, etc. in order to maintain a harmonious relationship with their cultural milieu. (The term 'unlearn' was deliberately placed in quotation marks since it is frequently used in this way, but the process is not one of unlearning – that is going back to where they were before they had learned whatever they are now unlearning – they have actually learned that their current state of knowledge is insufficient for their present situation and that they have to continue to learn and build upon what they have previously learned, since it is impossible to go back in time.) Many people, especially among the elderly, find it difficult to keep abreast with all the changes and the anomie that they experience is sometimes manifest in such phrases as, 'I don't know what the world is coming to these days'. Yet only a selection of culture (a curriculum) is ever transmitted to or acquired by individuals because of its extensiveness and complexity, so there are always new things to learn.

Culture is, therefore, a dynamic phenomenon open to the influences of a multitude of pressures, including that of individuals, as Figure 3.1 illustrates. Comprehension of the dynamic nature of culture is, however, quite essential to understanding the nature of human learning.

Agencies of cultural transmission

Culture is not a thing but a phenomenon, it exists nowhere objectively but it is internalized in the human mind, and the raw data of culture are contained in the printed word, or the cassette tape, etc. Hence the agencies of cultural transmission are themselves varied and operate in different ways, since some of these are technological, e.g. radio and television, whilst others are through personal interaction. Basically, it is through language that culture is transmitted, although not exclusively so since artists communicate through their own chosen media. However, learners are the recipients of cultural transmission and there are times when they are able to choose for themselves what they learn and how they learn it: they are self-directed learners. On other occasions learners receive cultural transmissions through different media, such as the printed word, which has become the basis of distance learning.

Whenever a person interacts with another there is usually a two-way process of transmitting and receiving individual interpretations and analyses of some aspects of culture (see Figure 3.2). Thus in almost every interaction ego and alter are both teachers and both learners and their interaction may be interpreted as a negotiation of their differing understandings of the aspect of culture which impinge upon their meeting. This is a significant feature in the education of adults since both teacher and student bring to the human interaction their own experience and their own analyses of the culture within which they interact. A number of writers in the education of adults highlight this point although it is perhaps most explicitly discussed by Freire (1972b: 53). However, it is rare for any human interaction to be on perfectly equal terms, so that the direction of the flow is more likely to be in one direction than the other. Hence, if ego is a pupil and alter a school teacher, it might be claimed that the lower arrow, in Figure 3.2, would be the more prevalent because the child has more to learn from the teacher than the teacher has from the child. While this claim is perfectly valid it is, perhaps, much more debatable than it appears! However, the interaction in some forms of teaching and learning may be depicted, as in Figure 3.3. This form of interaction occurs when ego is unable to communicate with alter, e.g. when alter's status is much higher than ego's, in some forms of instruction, in the formal lecture, or when the mode of cultural transmission is via technological media. Even in these situations, ego processes the information that is received rather than having

Ego   Alter

Figure 3.2 The two-way transmission of individual interpretation of selections from culture

alter

ego

Figure 3.3 A unidirectional transmission of culture

it merely imprinted on the mind, although it might be argued that in many instances there is insufficient critical awareness, so that a form of imprinting actually occurs.

The self

The self is that detached individuation of consciousness that expands as its experiences increase in number, so that it evolves into a sophisticated, complicated, but often fragile phenomenon. Hilgard and Atkinson (1967: 481–3) suggest that there are four aspects of the self that should be noted: it may be an agent; it is continuous; self-perception is largely dependent upon the extent to which others accept, or reject, the individual; it is the embodiment of values and goals. Kidd (1973: 126), by contrast, specifies four other aspects of the self: what is actually said and done; feelings about behaviour; how others perceive the actor; the ideal self – constant but changing throughout the lifespan. In contrast, Lovell (1980: 115) has suggested that the self includes three main elements: self-image, ideal self and self-esteem. More recently, Jarvis (1987, 1992), building upon the work of George Herbert Mead (Strauss 1964), has argued that both the self and the mind are learned phenomena that emerge through the same process of transforming experiences into knowledge, skills, attitudes, values, feelings, etc. which are stored in the brain and from which emerge both the mind and the self. It is from this body of knowledge etc. that individuals are able to impose meaning on their own situations and experiences.

The concept of self is rather complex but ill-defined and yet the self is most significant in playing both the role of teacher of adults and that of an adult learner. To be a teacher is an adult role but it is much less clearly defined in relation to other adults. Additionally, since the learner's role is designated by modern society to be one performed by young people, adult learners' self-perceptions may be in opposition to the way in which they understand that their role should be performed (see Harries-Jenkins 1982: 19–39). Hence comprehension of the concept of self is quite crucial to both the theory and the practice of teaching adults.

The physical body

Children are born into the world, they have existence in time and space, and they have life. Fundamentally, they are living human bodies with the potential for human being. Through existence these bodies may develop and become fully-fledged human beings and it is through the process of learning which has been discussed above that the social human being actually emerges and then continues to develop throughout life.

The human being may be perceived as both body and self, although these two are not separate entities; the former reaches its peak during adolescence, or in the early twenties, and then after a period it begins to decline.

By contrast, with the majority of people the mind and the self continue to develop throughout the lifespan. Certain physical abilities, such as sight and hearing, become less efficient during later life and this affects adults' efficiency in receiving the elements of culture that are being transmitted to them, so that it is most essential that awareness of this should be taken into consideration when designing any premises for adult education or any teaching and learning programme for adults.

Having discussed these four elements in the process of learning it is now necessary to turn to the process of learning itself; so the next section of this chapter expands upon the learning cycle illustrated in Figure 3.1.

The learning cycle

The significance of each of these factors to the process of adult education is apparent from the above discussion and each of these elements will be referred to frequently in this and subsequent chapters. However, it must be recognized that everybody's experience is unique and as individuals grow older so their uniqueness is even more apparent. This is not to deny each child is unique but merely to state that since adults have had more experience of life the more likely they are to manifest their differences. Hence generalizations only seek to convey a sense of the norm rather than specific situations.

It will be recalled from Figure 3.1 that in the process of learning there appears to be a cyclic relationship between individuals and their objectified culture as they both process and internalize the objectified culture and thereafter, externalize it through social interaction. Hence, it is now possible to develop a learning cycle, taking into consideration the foregoing discussion (see Figure 3.4).

Thus learning may be regarded as a process of receiving and assessing any element of culture, by whatever means it is transmitted. Such a definition is much wider than those frequently cited by learning theorists: learning is 'a relatively permanent change in behaviour that occurs as a result of practice' (Hilgard and Atkinson 1967: 270) or learning is 'any more or less permanent change in behaviour which is the result of experience' (Borger and Seaborne 1966: 14). Both of these definitions emphasize a change in behaviour as being an element of learning but this is too restrictive because it would necessitate the exclusion of the acquisition of new cognitive knowledge unless it resulted in behavioural change. The definition offered by Brundage and Mackeracher is much closer to that suggested here: they state that adult learning 'refers both to the process which individuals go through as they attempt to change or enrich their knowledge, values, skills or strategies and to the resulting knowledge, values, skill, strategies and behaviour possessed by each individual' (1980: 5). However, this is a rather cumbersome definition, which while it conveys many of the main ideas suggested in this section it does not actually capture the totality of the argument. Consequently, learning is defined

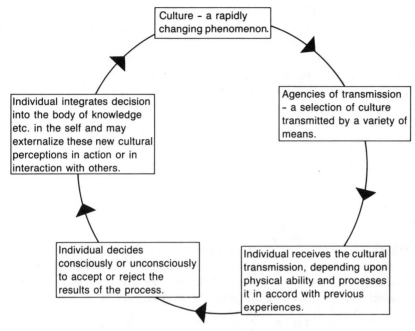

Figure 3.4 A learning cycle

here as the process of transforming experience into knowledge, skills, attitudes, values, feelings, etc.

This learning cycle represents a process and it is clear that there are two major facets to the process and these represent the teaching and learning processes: there is a selection of culture transmitted to the learner that may be regarded as an approach to teaching (this will be discussed subsequently) and there is also the learner's selection of culture which may be perceived as student-centred learning and which is quite significant in the education of adults. However, before these approaches are discussed it must be recognized that not all that is transmitted to the learner is automatically received and processed and that there are different theories of learning.

Basic theories of learning

Merriam and Caffarella (1991) have typified the variety of learning theories into four types: behaviourist, cognitive, humanist and social. In many ways this is a useful framework within which to examine the variety of learning theories that have been produced over the years, although it has to be recognized that these are not discrete types and that considerable overlap exists between them and, indeed, the latter two coincide in many of the ideas presented in this book. At the same time, it may be seen that there are ideological under-pinnings to the different theories and, most certainly, there are implicit statements of the human condition to be discovered in each theory. The significance of this is that no theory is value free so that the theories of learn-ing cannot be divorced from the wider world of ideology and belief. In this section, behaviourist and cognitive theories will first be discussed and then experientialist theories will be examined, which are both social and humanistic.

Behaviourist theories

Two forms of behaviourist theory are discussed here: connectionism and conditioning.

Connectionist or 'trial and error' learning

Perhaps the first theory to gain recognition was 'trial and error' learning, which is sometimes referred to as connectionism. This was propounded by Thorndike (1928) towards the end of the last century, and as a result of his research with animals he expounded three laws, that of:

- readiness, which relates to the circumstances under which the learner is satisfied, annoyed, etc.
- exercise, which refers to the process of strengthening the connection discovered between stimulus and response by practice
- effect, which relates to the process of strengthening, or breaking, any connection as a result of the consequences of any action.

Basically, this theory propounds a quite fundamental way of behaving: that if the learner discovers some act or explanation to be effective or valid it will be repeated until such time as the consequences of the action no longer produce the desired or expected results. By virtue of starting with the learner it is hardly surprising that Thorndike was able to pursue his work into adult learning.

Conditioning

In contrast to Thorndike, the following two theories commence with the teacher. Perhaps the most well-known of all psychological research into learning is that of Pavlov (1927), who proposed the theory of classical conditioning. Briefly stated, this theory asserts that the learner learns (is con-ditioned) to associate the presentation of a reward with a stimulus that occurs fractionally prior to it. Thus Pavlov's dogs salivated at the sound of a bell since they had been fed when this had been rung on previous occasions. Operant conditioning, however, occurs when the response is shaped by the reward, so that after every action that approaches, approximates or achieves the desired behaviour the learner receives a reward. This form of conditioning is expounded by Skinner (1951) who has more recently argued that 'man is a machine in the sense that he is a complex system behaving in lawful ways, but the complexity is extraordinary' (Skinner 1971: 197). Throughout this latter book, Skinner suggests that conditioning can explain all learning and that the exciting possibilities for the future lie in what human beings will create of humankind. Skinner has grappled with the philosophical problems of behaviourism but he may not be able to convince everyone that his perspective is quite so all-embracing as he suggests. Even so, there is a great deal of research evidence to support many of the claims of the behaviourists.

There are a number of problems with the behaviourist approach, two of which are briefly discussed here. Firstly, the definition is conceptually confusing: Hilgard, Atkinson and Atkinson suggest that learning 'is a relatively permanent change in behaviour that occurs as the result of prior experience' (1979: 217). However, the change of behaviour is a product whilst learning is a process which occurs before the change of behaviour, so they cannot be the same thing. Secondly, much of the behaviourist research into learning has been conducted on animals, so it has not been possible to research the thought processes that occur during learning, and thus the research methodology is suspect for the claims that are made about the findings. This does not deny that there are behavioural changes as a result of learning, only that learning is the change in behaviour.

Not all conditioning may be intentional, nor is it all conscious, but it certainly occurs during the process of the education of adults. Lovell (1980: 35), for instance, suggests that classical conditioning has occurred when students choose an evening class or a subject because the tutor had created a warm, friendly atmosphere. By contrast, the process of grading within assignments or praising a reticent student for contributing to a group discussion are both aspects of operant conditioning.

Cognitive theories

Perhaps the most influential learning theorist has been Piaget (1929, *inter alia*), who postulated a number of stages in the process of cognitive development which he related to the process of biological development during childhood:

Stage 1 Sensori-motor when infants learn to differentiate between themselves and objects in the external world, and this occurs during the first two years of life.

Stage 2 Pre-operational thought, children classify external objects by single salient features, and this spans the period from about two to four years.

Stage 3   Intuitive, when children think in classificatory terms without necessarily being conscious of them, a stage that stretches from pre-operational thought to about seven years of age.

Stage 4   Concrete operations, between seven and eleven, children begin to think using logical operations.

Stage 5   Formal operational thinking which occurs after the above stage when children take early steps in abstract conceptual thought.

Piaget's work has been very influential in education and it has also provided a basis for two other well-known thinkers in this area, Kohlberg (1981), who has written about moral development, and Fowler (1981), who has concentrated on faith development.

However, Piaget's final stage was reached before adulthood, so his theories have not been influential amongst adult educators. Allman (1984), however, points to a number of pieces of psychological research that suggest that adult thought processes do still change and develop during the lifespan, and she concentrates especially on Riegel's (1979) idea of dialectic logic which demands the ability to tolerate contradictions and which enables the tensions within them to generate new ideas.

Kohlberg's (1981) work on moral judgement is amongst the most well-known developments of the Piagetian approach; he demonstrates how moral theorizing develops in stages with age and his work becomes increasingly significant both as it gains recognition and also as people are beginning to ask the ethical questions once again, including those surrounding adult and continuing education. The basic premise is that learning is constructivist and that the knowledge gained through the process can be analysed thereafter, but that it is only at different stages in human development that the meaning of the moral concepts can be grasped and operationalized. Hence, younger children have a simpler conceptual understanding of moral knowledge than do those who have developed through a number of previous stages. But, like Piaget, most of Kohlberg's work has thus far been applied to children although its significance of the education of adults must be noted here.

However, cognitive theories also have another basis, and this is to be found in the work of the Gestalt theorists.

Gestalt theory

Another theory of learning that has been based upon research with animals has emerged with Gestalt psychology. The word Gestalt actually means shape or form, and as early as 1912 Max Wertheimer postulated that the individual did not perceive the constituent elements of a phenomenon but that he perceived them as a totality. He formulated the 'Law of Prägnanz' in which there are four aspects of perception: similarity, proximity, continuity and closure. Similarity refers to the fact that people group phenomena by their similar salient features rather than by their differences; proximity refers to the fact that individuals group phenomena by their closeness to each other rather than by their distance from one another; continuity refers to the fact that objects are often perceived in relation to the pattern or shape that they constitute in their totality; closure refers to the fact that there is a tendency to complete an incomplete representation so that the whole is perceived rather than the incomplete parts (see Child 1981: 73–4). From the holistic perspective Köhler (1947) suggested that solutions to problems appear to come abruptly, as by a flash of insight, and that they are achieved because the insight emerges from the perception of the relationship between the different factors rather than in response to separate stimuli. Whilst this theory has a number of attractive features, especially since it is recognized that some people are holistic learners, the idea of insight or intuition almost demands that it should be rooted in an earlier process, either socialization or an earlier learning experience, so that it would be unwise to regard all learning in such an inspirational manner.

Other cognitive perspectives

There have been a variety of other researchers who could be discussed under this heading, including Gagné, Ausubel and Bruner. Gagné (1977) proposed an eight phase model of learning, which may be summarized as follows:

- Motivation – expectancy;
- Apprehending – attention: selective perception;
- Acquisition – coding: storage entry;
- Retention – memory storage;
- Recall – retrieval;
- Generalization – transfer;
- Performance – responding;
- Feedback – reinforcement.

This model has certain attractions in terms of its logical progression. However, it is that logic which seems to oversimplify the process slightly, as will be seen later in this chapter. Other aspects of Gagné's work are discussed more fully in the next chapter.

Gagné clearly focuses upon memory in this model and Child (1981: 112–34) depicts the information-processing model of memory quite clearly when he suggests that learning begins with a stimulus which is partially picked up by a sensory register and processed through selective perception to the short-term memory. The short-term memory has a limited capacity, so some of the information is retained but some other is lost at this stage. He then suggests that what is retained is coded and stored in the long-term memory from where it can be recalled or rehearsed. Child's emphasis on memory loss here points to the fact that there is a sharp decline in what is remembered immediately after the event: with only 58 per cent being retained after 20 minutes, according to Ebbinghaus, 44 per cent being retained after an hour and only 33 per cent after a day (Child 1981: 119). The loss of memory in this manner indicates that rehearsing that which is stored soon after a learning event will almost certainly add to the amount of material that is remembered and that systematic repetition thereafter continues to aid recall.

As will be pointed out in the following chapter, Gagné also postulated that there are different types of learning, so he was not just concerned with recall of facts, etc. Another theorist who emphasized the distinction between rote learning and meaningful learning is Ausubel *et al.* (1978). For him, learning is a process of constructing new meaning. This is a feature that Mezirow (1991) has also focused upon in his work on perspective transformation in adult learning, to which further reference is made below. Dahlgren actually defines learning this way: 'To learn is to strive for meaning, and to have learned something is to have grasped its meaning' (1984: 23–4).

Marton and Säljö (Marton *et al.* 1984: 39–40) in a piece of research into the way that students learned from reading discovered that those who focused on the text and tried to remember it never really learned what it was trying to convey, but those students who adopted a deep approach to learning tried to understand its meaning.

The final theorist to be examined here is Bruner (1979), whose work is almost exclusively about the education of children. However, his work on discovery echoes that discussed above. He suggests that

> the degree that one is able to approach learning as a task of discovering something rather than 'learning about' it, to that degree there will be a tendency for the child to work with the autonomy of self-reward or, more properly, be rewarded by discovery itself.
>
> (Bruner 1979: 88)

Naturally, this points self-directed learning theorists in the direction of a cognitive strategy that underlies the motivation of some self-directed learners. Bruner also suggests that the main problem that individuals have is in memorizing what they have learned and he, echoing the early Gestalt theorists, suggests that the way that the material is organized is related to the amount that can be recalled.

It would be possible to review other theorists who have written about learning from within a cognitive framework, but this introduction points to the fact that learning is viewed as a complex set of processes having different outcomes. Other theorists have adopted different approaches although, naturally, their analyses overlap in some ways.

Experience and learning

Experiential learning theory has become quite central in recent years to a great deal of thinking about learning in the education of adults. This is not surprising in the light of the fact that adult education itself has become quite learner-centred and that a great deal of vocational education has emphasized the work experience, and even learning in the workplace (Marsick 1987). But it is quite significant that the concept of experience itself remains largely unexplored by those learning theorists who write about it. Weil and McGill (1990), for instance, do not have a single entry in their index for experience, even though the whole book is about experiential learning. At the same time it is important to recall that philosophers have examined this concept and that a variety of major works exist on the subject, e.g. Dewey (1985), Husserl (1973), Oakeshott (1933). Oakeshott does make the point, however, that experience 'of all the words in the philosophic vocabulary, is the most difficult to manage' (1933: 9). Consequently, the concept of experience needs discussion here, so that it becomes more possible to understand experiential learning. It is suggested below that there are two distinct forms of experience, and that learning is different in both of them and that these learning processes relate to both the classroom and practical learning.

The concept of experience

Life might be described as a passage through time, so time must be the starting point of any discussion of experience. Human existence is situated within time and emerges through it, and it has been argued elsewhere that learning is the process through which the human, as opposed to the biological, being grows and develops (Jarvis 1992). In a simplistic sense time is experienced as a matter of past, present and future. But the present is always problematic because immediately people try to conceptualize their present it becomes a past event, so that more realistically people think about time as a matter of past and future, although the act of experiencing is itself something that occurs at their intersection. Indeed, it is possible to argue that for the most part people live their lives almost unconscious of the passing of time: they act in a taken-for-granted manner. Bergson (Lacey 1989) called this 'duration', which is the almost unconscious passing of time. However, he is clear that there is still a consciousness of the passing of time even when people act in an almost taken-for-granted manner, but it is a low level of consciousness. This taken-for-grantedness lies in the fact that people are in harmony with their socio-cultural environment, they do not have to think too deeply before they act because, almost instinctively, they seem to know how to act in those particular circumstances. It is not, however, intuitive but the result of previous learning experiences. They are bringing their past learning to bear upon a present situation and they experience it in a meaningful manner, appearing to act instinctively.

However, another significant point about this is when people cannot act in such a manner. Elsewhere (Jarvis 1987), this is called disjuncture. Disjuncture occurs where there is not taken-for-grantedness between people's past learning experiences and their present situation. In other words, they have to stop and think. Time appears to stop, indeed time appears to be frozen at this point. Herein lies experience with a heightened consciousness. No longer can previous learning cope with the present situation, people are consciously aware that they do not kow how to act. They have to think, to plan or to learn something new. Learning then always begins with experiencing, there can be no learning that does not begin with experience although the level of consciousness of the learner plays a significant part in both the experience and the ensuing learning.

Experiencing, then, may be conceptualized, on one level, as the subjective awareness of a present situation. However, that awareness occurs only in the light of previous experiences, and consequently the subjectivity is determined by individuals' past biographies and the socio-cultural milieu in which they experience situations. People bring to every new situation their own past, although the extent to which they are themselves aware of this is a point that Freud's researches have illustrated.

In experiencing, there is a combination of the biographical past with a sensation, or perception, of the present 'external' situation although, on occasions, that 'external' situation can actually be a memory of a previous experience which occurs during contemplation. Adults bring to potential learning situations their memories of the interpretations which they have placed upon past experiences, and this has both advantages and disadvantages for learning. Memory certainly affects the experience in a variety of different ways.

'I can't remember like I used to' is a common expression among adults and one that many educators of adults hear frequently from their students in the teaching and learning situation. The expression tends to give credence to the front-end model of education, but is it correct? Obviously it reflects an experience or else the person would not utter the exclamation, and yet Rogers points out that

> a young man and a man in his late fifites would both be able to remember and repeat an average of eight randon numbers recited to him. But what does change is that if the older man is asked to remember something else between the time he was first given the numbers and the time he was asked to repeat them, he is less likely to remember the original numbers than the young man.
>
> (Rogers 1977: 59)

Yet older people do have many more commitments than younger people and often study part-time, so additional information, etc. might be given to them from a variety of sources which will make it harder to recall the information to be learned. Hence, this means that teachers of adults should provide opportunities during their teaching and learning sessions, so that adults have time to begin the process of storing the information that they have gained. Additionally, it might not be wise to discourage last minute revision when adult learners are required to sit a traditional examination. Knox (1977: 435) also points out that adults are only more likely to retain information that they receive if it is meaningful to them and they are able to integrate it into the store of knowledge that they already have. All of these findings refer to what is now called the short-term memory, but once the material is stored in the long-term memory it can be recalled, and most people are familiar with the very elderly being able to recall, from their long-term memory, information that they learned decades before.

The experience of time is another factor in the adult's learning process and one that is often forgotten in discussions about learning. Bundage and Mackeracher note a significant point when they state that children and young adults 'tend to measure time as "time from birth"; adults past 40 tend to measure time as "until death"' (1980: 35–6). Hence, as time becomes shorter, so the learning needs focus more acutely upon the problems of the immediate present and previous experience becomes increasingly important to the older person. It may be, therefore, that certain subjects are more appropriate to the psychological orientations of different age groups: history, for instance, may be a more popular study for those whose orientation is already towards their past experiences than would be mathematics. However, more research is required to investigate the extent to which there is any correlation between preferred 'learning' topics, age and orientation towards time.

Throughout their lives adults accumulate a wide range of experiences which they store up in their memories and which they bring with them to every learning situation. Memories, then, influence the interpretations placed upon experience, since they are individual and personal. Perception of the situation is largely determined by individual biography and it is, therefore, subjective and individual. Learning, it has been argued elsewhere (Jarvis 1987), is the process of transforming that present experience into knowledge, skills, attitudes, values, emotions, etc.; it is a matter, therefore, of modifying the individual biography, which in its turn will affect the manner by which future situations are experienced.

The discussion thus far focuses upon the idea of sensing or perceiving a situation, and this is 'primary experience', but Husserl makes the point that experience is frequently not direct in this sense, but indirect. He points out that once a person describes an object or an event, the description becomes an indirect experience for anyone listening to it. Indirect experience occurs through linguistic communication and this is 'secondary experience'. Secondary experience usually occurs in combination with primary experience because what is experienced directly, through the senses, is both the situation/interaction and the words or meanings that are communicated are only indirectly experienced through the language, picture, music, and so on. In a sense, Kolb's (1984) learning cycle incorporates the possibility of two modes of experience, because it allows for the learning process to start either with the concrete experience, or anywhere else on the cycle, including that of generalizing and conceptualizing, although the cycle is normally assumed to begin with the concrete experience.

It is suggested that experience is a subjective awareness of a present situation, the meaning of which is partially determined by past individual learning. Consequently, the experience is not merely of something external, but of the fusing of the external with the individual biography. There are two modes of experience – either directly through the senses, or indirectly through linguistic communication – and individuals can and do learn through both modes of experience.

Kolb and Fry claim that the learning cycle may begin at any stage and that it should be a continuous spiral (see Figure 3.5). It will be noted that there are elements of previous theories in this cycle, which is quite understandable since no one theory of learning is able to explain the complexity of the many forms of learning that occur. Additionally, it may be questioned as to whether there is an implicit behavioural definition of learning contained within this cycle. Nevertheless, it does raise significant issues about learning from experience. In addition, Kolb and Fry suggest that the movement in the vertical axis represents a process of conceptualization while that on the horizontal axis represents the variation between active and passive manipulation. They claim also that each quadrant represents a learning style.

The emphasis on this learning cycle is rightly upon concrete experience but it must be recognized that individual learners perceive phenomena

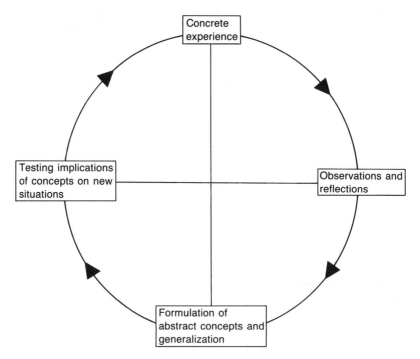

Figure 3.5 An experiential learning cycle
Source: Kolb and Fry (1975: 33–7)

differently and that some of those variations in perception are related to differences in the learner.

Understanding learning

Kolb's learning cycle does appear rather simplistic for such a complex process, so Jarvis (1987) tested it with a variety of groups of adult learners. They demonstrated that it is an oversimple description of the learning processes. Over a period of about fifteen months in 1985 and 1986 groups of adults participated in this project.

All the participants were first invited to write down a learning incident in their lives. They were asked to state what started the incident, how it progressed and, finally, when and why they concluded that it was completed. Having undertaken this exercise they were then paired in order to discuss their different learning experiences and it was suggested to them that they might like to examine the similarities and the differences in their experiences. Thereafter, two pairs were put together and they then discussed their four different learning experiences. At this time, they were asked if they would draw a simple model of their joint learning experiences, and some of them actually constructed some quite sophisticated models of learning.

The first time this exercise was conducted the groups were asked to feed-back their ideas at this point for a general discussion. Thereafter, they were given a copy of Kolb's learning cycle and it was suggested to them that they might like to adapt it to relate to their own experiences (Figure 3.5). Participants were informed that the cycle was not necessarily correct and that they were free to adapt it in any way that they wished, so that it would relate to their experiences. From the feedback from the first set of groups a more complex model of learning was constructed by modifying the above learning cycle but also which related to the findings of each of the groups of four people. Whenever this exercise was repeated thereafter, the last stage each time was to introduce some of the adaptations of Kolb's cycle that had emerged from the previous time that this had been undertaken.

This exercise was conducted on nine separate occasions both in the UK and in the USA, with teachers of adults and teachers of children, with university lecturers and adult university students who were teachers of adults in their full-time occupation, with younger people and with some not so young participants, with men and women. In all about 200 people participated in the exercise, although the sample was middle class and not tightly controlled. A complex model of learning was constructed as a result of the research. This model was subsequently tested in seminars etc. over another nine-month period, again both in the UK and the USA, with some 200 or 300 people participating in these. The final model appeared, with a full description of this methodology in a book (Jarvis 1987), and is shown in Figure 3.6.

The complexity of the learning process can now be seen, and while it is not proposed to examine the model here in great detail, it is proposed to look

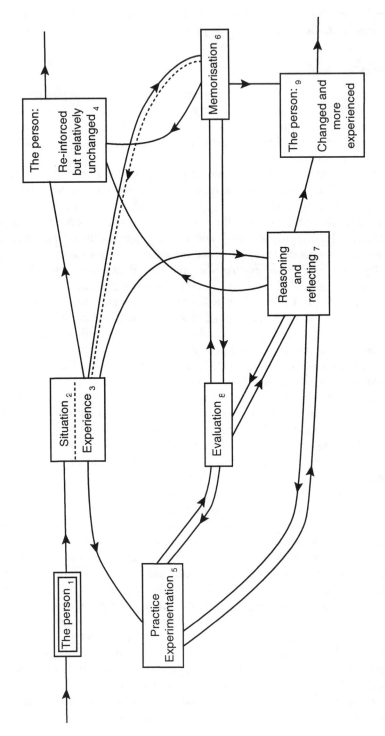

Figure 3.6 A model of the learning processes

at the variety of learning routes that can be traced through it. Basically, it is suggested that there are nine types of response to an experience and that they may be classified into three fundamentally different categories: non-learning, non-reflective learning and reflective learning. Each of these three categories contains three types and in the reflective learning stratum there are two forms of each of the three types. Now the purpose of this analysis is to relate each of these types to a wider social context, and this is undertaken in the next three sections.

Non-learning

It is very clear that people do not always learn from their experiences and so the first group of responses are non-learning ones: presumption, non-consideration and rejection. Each of these three sub-types is now described briefly.

Presumption

This is the rather typical response to everyday experience. Schutz and Luckmann describe it thus:

> I trust the world as it is known by me up until now will continue further and that consequently the stock of knowledge obtained from my fellow-men and formed from my own experiences will continue to preserve its fundamental validity . . . . From this assumption follows the further and fundamental one; that I can repeat my past successful acts. So long as the structure of the world can be taken as constant; so long as my previous experience is valid, my ability to operate upon the world in this and that manner remains in principle preserved.
>
> (Schutz and Luckmann 1974: 7)

While this appears almost thoughtless and mechanical, it is suggested here that this is the basis of all social living because it indicated that they are in harmony with their environment. It would be quite intolerable for people to have to consider every word and every act in every social situation before they undertook it. Hence, a great deal of life is lived on the basis of previous learned experiences, and presumption is a typical response to a familiar situation.

Non-consideration

For a variety of reasons people do not respond to a potential learning experience: perhaps because they are too busy to think about it or perhaps because they are fearful of its outcome, etc. Thus it may be that non-consideration is another response that occurs quite commonly in everyday life to potential learning experiences.

Rejection

Some people have an experience, think about it but reject the possibility of learning that could have accompanied the experience. For instance, think of an elderly person experiencing the complexity of modernity and exclaiming, 'I don't know what this world is coming to these days!' Here is a possible learning experience, an experience of the complex modern world, but instead of probing it and seeking to understand it, the person rejects the possibility. While the illustration here is with the elderly, it could have been with the not so elderly, with bigots, who look at the world and say that they will not have any opinion/attitude changed by it, etc.

Non-reflective learning

These forms of learning are those which are most frequently socially defined as learning. For the sake of convenience the three that have been isolated in this research project are: pre-conscious, skills learning and memorization. The factor above all else that enables them to be placed within one stratum together is that they do not involve reflectivity.

Pre-conscious learning

This is one on which there is little research. It occurs to everybody as a result of their having experiences in the course of their daily life about which they do not really think or about which they are even particularly conscious. They occur at the periphery of the vision, at the edge of consciousness, etc. Ruth Beard (1976: 93–5) calls this incidental learning and she suggests that people develop such phenomena as schemas of perception as a result of these experiences. Other scholars who have been interested in this approach include Mannings (1986), who researched incidental learning in an adult education institution, and Reischmann (1986), who presented a paper at ACACE in which he talked about learning *en passant*. Now this research project was not itself aimed at analysing this type of learning, although a number of the respondents mentioned this possibility during the research itself. It is similar in approach to the next two forms of learning.

Skills learning

This is traditionally restricted to such forms of learning as training for a manual occupation or the acquisition of a high level of physical fitness through training. However, some learning in preparation for a manual occupation is certainly not non-reflective, so this has to be restricted to the learning of simple, short procedures that somebody on an assembly line might be taught. These skills are often acquired through imitation and role modelling.

Memorization

This is perhaps the most commonly known form of learning. Children learn their mathematical tables, their language vocabularies, etc. Adults, when they return to higher education, sometimes feel that this is the type of learning that is expected of them and so they try to memorize what such and such a scholar has written, etc. so that they can reproduce it in an examination. Hence, the authority speaks and every word of wisdom has to be learned, memorized.

Reflective learning

Thus far it has been shown that learning tends to be reproductive, simply because that is the way in which it is frequently defined socially. It was suggested that non-reflective learning could not do other than to reproduce the social structures of society, but this is not true of reflective learning. These forms of learning involve the process of reflection, and thinkers such as Freire (1972a, 1972b, *inter alia*), Mezirow (1977, 1981), Argyris (1982, *inter alia*), Schon (1983, *inter alia*), Kolb (1984) and Boud *et al.* (1985) have all examined the process of reflection. Because of Freire's work it might be assumed that all reflective learning has to be revolutionary, but this must not be assumed to be the case. Reflective learning is not automatically innovative. But before this is discussed it is necessary to examine the three types of reflective learning that were discovered in this research: contemplation, reflective skills learning and experimental learning.

Contemplation

This is a form of learning that behaviourist definitions of the phenomenon make no allowance for, and yet in many ways this might be viewed as a very intellectual approach to learning because it involves pure thought. This is the process of thinking about an experience and reaching a conclusion about it without reference to the wider social reality. The religious type of terminology was carefully chosen since it allows for meditation, as well as the thought processes of the philosopher and the activities of the pure mathematician.

Reflective skills learning

This is called reflective practice in the book *Adult Learning in the Social Context*. This is one of the forms of learning that Schon (1983) concentrates upon, when he points out that professionals in practice think on their feet. In the process they often produce new skills as they respond to the uniqueness of their situation. Indeed, it was pointed out earlier that there are not many forms of skill that are learned in a totally unthinking manner, and so this may be regarded as a more sophisticated approach to learning practical subjects.

It is not only learning a skill but learning about the knowledge undergirding the practice and, therefore, why the skill should be performed in a specific manner.

Experimental learning

This is that form of learning in which theory is tried out in practice and the end-product of the experimentation is a form of knowledge that relates fully to social reality. This approach to learning relates very closely to Kelly's (1963) understanding of human beings as scientists, seeking always to experiment on their environment.

It was pointed out above that these three forms of learning do not always have to be innovative, or change orientated. It may be recalled that Argyris has two types of learning, and in discussing these he made this point:

> First is the misunderstanding that the goal of Model II implies that Model I is somehow bad or ineffective and should be suppressed. On the contrary, Model I is the most appropriate theory in use for routine, programmed activities or emergency situations (such as rescuing survivors) that require prompt, unilateral action. We must not forget that the strategy of all organizations is to decompose double loop problems into single loop ones. The major part of everyday life learning in an organization is related to single loop learning. Double loop learning is crucial, because it allows us to examine and correct the way we are dealng with any issue and our underlying assumptions about it.
>
> (Argyris 1982: 159–60)

For Argyris, then, the more innovative forms of learning are crucial but the other approaches are just as significant. While he employs the terms single and double loop, it is proposed to utilize the terms conformist and innovative relective learning here. Both of these terms now need to be discussed. Botkin *et al.* (1979) employ the terms maintenance and innovative learning and these reflect the ideas contained here. It will be recalled that Freire (1972a, 1972b, *inter alia*) recognized that there were two types of response in his forms of education: the one he called the 'banking concept of education' in which the learning was non-reflective, and the other he called 'problem posing education' in which he thought the learning would be innovative. However, Freire has not really constructed a full typology of learning and he has omitted some of the intermediate forms and, consequently, his problem posing education relates only in part to innovative reflective learning. In contrast, Habermas (1971, 1972) has three forms of learning: the technical, the practical and the emancipatory. His emancipatory form is similar to Freire's problem posing form of education and not precisely the same as the innovatory reflective learning that is discussed here. The word innovatory is preferred to emancipatory because the connotations of this word are revolutionary and while innovation might be revolutionary, it does not have to be. Hence the word seeks to convey change, rather than only revolutionary change.

Having examined the different types of learning, it is now necessary to return to the discussion about learning from experience. It will be recalled that there are two forms of experience – primary and secondary. Learning occurs whenever experience is transformed, whether it be primary or secondary, and so experiential learning is a much more complex concept than it often appears to be.

Learning from primary experience

Most of the literature on experiential learning is actually about learning from primary experience, that is learning through sense experiences, and, unfortunately, it has tended to exclude the idea of secondary experience entirely. At the same time there has been no agreement about the idea of experiential learning among those who have embraced the term. Weil and McGill, for instance, highlight this point by suggesting that experiential learning may be categorized into four villages (their term):

Village One is concerned particularly with assessing and accrediting learning from life and work experience . . .
Village Two focuses on experiential learning as a basis for bringing about change in the structures . . . of post-school education.
Village Three emphasizes experiential learning as a basis for group consciousness raising . . .
Village Four is concerned about personal growth and self-awareness
(Weil and McGill 1990: 3)

In a sense these are all subsections of learning from primary experience and in this sense the division is useful since it enables a variety of forms of learning from primary experience to be categorized. Unfortunately, the idea of practical experience, internship, is missing from this categorization, but in professional education it is a most important form of learning. Significantly, there may be a reason why it might be missing, or even why it might be included within the second village, and that is because the practical experience is not regarded so much as learning but as the application, or transfer, of previous classroom learning into practice.

However, the practice situation is actually one in which potential learning experiences do occur. Indeed, transfer is a misleading idea, since when students enter the practical situation for the first time, they are entering a new learning situation and this is true irrespective of how much learning has occurred in the classroom before that new experience happened – they are now having for the first time a primary, rather than a secondary, experience about practice and they experience it differently. However, they are bringing to the new learning situation their biographies, so that the more that they have learned form previous experiences, the more likely they are to have some knowledge which they can use in the present situation.

In order to understand the process of learning from primary experience it is necessary to have a theory of action. Elsewhere (Jarvis 1992) it has been suggested that there are three forms of non-action and five of action. Now the significant thing about these five latter forms is that these constitute a process of habitualization:

- creative/experimental;
- repetitive;
- presumptive;
- ritualistic;
- alienating.

In certain training situations this process is part of the objective – that is to get individuals to perform a skill unthinkingly but which then becomes a taken-for-granted situation, from which no learning can occur. Learning occurs when people act creatively/experimentally or repetitively, that is in the first two stages of the process, and additionally in some non-action situations, that is when individuals do not know how to behave in a specific situation. Therefore, it is important in internship to provide situations where people have the opportunity to learn from their own primary experiences.

Obviously when a student enters the practical situation there are many primary experiences that the students have for the very first time; some of these are ones where action is possible, albeit of a creative/experimental form because they have learned what to do previously. At the same time, others are potentially non-action situations, because the students have not learned about it in the classroom and they have no biographical knowledge to bring to the situation. It is a potential learning situation because the students do not know how to act and they learn from trial-and-error, observation of others' performances, or from questioning other skilled performers (or mentors) and then acting – but this action is always experimental/creative in the first instance. In none of these situations do students have the knowledge or the skill to cope with the situation and their subsequent experience of it in an unthinking, or intuitive manner, and so there is disjuncture between the students' biography and experience and, consequently, a potential learning experience has occurred. If the students have already had some instruction in the classroom about this type of situation, then they bring an informed biography to the situation and this affects their experience. At the same time they have to stop, plan their actions and so on before they can act. Any experience in which they have to stop, think, plan, and so on, is a potential learning experience. At the same time, if they have had no previous instruction in the classroom then they may not be in a position of being able to act at all, and non-action occurs.

In primary experience, people enter a situation, experience it subjectively and they can either act or else they can reflect upon the situation. If they act, it is usually with a high level of consciousness, monitoring all aspects of the action, thinking about it and evaluating its relevance etc. to the situation. They have done this as a result of recalling to mind their previous learning experiences and then they have weighed up the possible alternatives and acted on the best possible evidence. Now this is using previous learning in new situations and testing it to see if it works. If it does, then it was valid knowledge, but if it does not then it may be regarded as invalid and rejected.

It is here in practice that skills are actually learned from practical experience. Individuals use their classroom learning, but they still have to plan their actions, monitor them, and maybe reflect upon them, and then learn from their new experiences. The point here is that in planning the action, skill, etc. the students have used their biographical knowledge and acted upon that knowledge. They have not acted mindlessly or thoughtlessly: they have acted in the probability that their intended outcomes will be achieved, and they learn from the outcome. Herein lies the relationship between theory and practice – it is a pragmatic relationship in which the two coincide only if the theory works out precisely in practice. However, there are always many contingencies in practice that prevent intended outcomes from occurring. No generalized theory can take into account all the possible contingencies that might prevent the outcome occurring – the relationship between theory and practice must always be one of probability. The better the theory, the greater the chance of it resulting in the successful outcome of a practice; the greater the knowledge of that theory the greater the chance that the intended outcomes will be achieved. But no theory can be perfect and contingencies always occur and so no theory is or should be a perfect fit. Indeed, primary experience is a learning experience, it is here that the practitioner learns whether the theory has validity; it is here that the practitioner learns which rules to remember and which to forget; it is here that practitioners try out the good practices they have observed in their peers and occasionally experiment with the bad ones in order to be certain that they were poor; it is here that the practitioner experiments and learns new knowledge from primary experience. Here, in the primary situation, the practitioner learns from primary experience and tests the validity of the learning from the secondary experience.

Learning from secondary experience

Secondary experience is one which occurs most frequently in education and it is through secondary experience that a great deal of theory is taught and learned. This also facilitates the argument of the following section. Secondary experience is mediated, and usually linguistic: it occurs through normal conversation, listening to lectures and debates, and any form of monologue, dialogue, and so on, including listening to the media. In a sense, it is always interactive. In addition, reading books and other forms of linguistic and pictorial communication may be classified under this head. Simply, it is a matter of meaning being communicated through words and pictures but, simultaneously, there is direct sense experience with the other persons in the interaction, with the book or with the media, etc. rather than with the phenomenon, event or meaning being discussed, described, etc. in the communication. This is the form of interaction which Habermas (1984, 1987) calls a theory of communicative action, and which Mezirow (1991) has developed into his theory of transformative learning.

Perhaps the most common image of education is that of the teacher lecturing to a class of students, an image that many educators of adults have wanted to play down. Yet to do this is to deny the significance of speech and conversation to the learning process. A great deal of everyday life consists of interaction and dialogue. Provided teaching is dialogue and not prolonged monologue, then it remains a valid exercise and relates to everyday experiences. In everyday life people converse about a variety of things, such as an overseas vacation, and so on. Often only the speaker has a direct experience of the situation being discussed and the other participants in the conversation have an indirect experience through the speech. In other situations, none of the participants may actually have had a direct experience of the subject contained in the communication, and yet it can still be meaningful. Consequently secondary experience is a common everyday occurrence.

Learning occurs in secondary experience through the communication of meaning: words are given meanings, pictures are interpreted in meaningful ways, and so on. Communication is meaningful. The process of communication of meaning is threefold: the speaker encodes the meaning in words, the words are spoken, or transmitted through some other medium, and the receivers decode the meaning, or they interpret the communication for themselves. The fact that they decode the experience, or that they interpret the communication for themselves, is important to understanding the process of having a meaningful experience; it is not an experience of an objective phenomenon by the listeners or the readers – the experience of meaning is one in which the listeners have played their part by giving meaning to the words and by bringing their own biographical past to the surface. The experience is a total whole in which the words are heard and interpreted, and the experience they have is made subjectively their own. In this sense of interpretation, all secondary experience is hermeneutical.

Precise communication can only occur if these three stages are carried out exactly and the speaker's objective in communicating specific meaning is fully achieved. If what the speaker is saying is already known, or assumed, by the hearers then they simply take for granted what they hear. If the meaning being communicated is new but unproblematic, then they may merely seek to memorize it and the disjuncture between what they already know and what they received is not great. However, there is another level of communication – that of communicating truth propositions. If the hearers doubt the validity of what they hear, or even if they merely wish to test it out, then they stop and reflect upon the meaning of the communication. Suddenly the communication is bounded by time and the hearers turn time back upon itself, as it were, as they seek to analyse the truth, or validity, or even the practicality of the communication. At this point there may be a considerable awareness of disjuncture as the hearers question the meaning being communicated, and one aspect of testing out the validity of the communication may be the extent to which it works in practice.

Here, then, is the process of learning from secondary experience. Meaning, validity, truth, but also description and so on, are communicated by the originator of the communication and that communication may itself produce different reactions in the learners, and different forms of learning may occur. This depends on what the learners bring to the meaning experience, it depends upon their biography and their interpretation of the words and phrases employed in the transmission. Descriptive communication and telling people something may merely produce non-reflective learning, but questions about validity or truth may produce both non-reflective or reflective forms of learning. A number of factors will determine what type of response the learners make, among them the reputation of the speaker, the topic under discussion and the extent to which the hearers think that meaning and truth are objective and unchanging. If people are aware that any encoding of meaning or truth is a subjective and social process, then they might adopt something of a healthy scepticism to what they hear or read; but, unfortunately, this is not always the case.

When new information, whether it be meaning or truth, is learned then it is incorporated into the learners' biography and can be utilized in future experiences. Having examined the process of learning from secondary experience, it may now be seen that theory can be and usually is taught through this method. However, the theory being taught must be generalized and it is difficult to relate it to specific situations or contexts. But learners can learn both reflectively and non-reflectively through secondary experience and what they learn is incorporated in their biography and brought to future experiences, including primary ones.

This section has examined four major elements in a theory of experiential learning, and it will be recognized that this is a complex theory because the learners are also experiencing within a socio-cultural context, which cannot be omitted from any theoretical analysis of learning. While experiential theorists are right to emphasize the individual, it must always be the person-in-social-context that is the subject of discussion. This conclusion is quite significant when learning is related to teaching, since the way that the teacher creates the learning environment etc. will influence greatly the way that the situation is experienced and, subsequently, the ensuing processes of learning.

Adults who are under a great deal of stress, are overstimulated or anxious do not learn as well as those who are stimulated to respond to their learning situation in a normal manner (Brundage and Mackerarcher 1980: 26–32). They are much more likely to learn efficiently when they are in a location in which they feel free to express themselves without inhibition. It is for these reasons that adults, returning to study, need to be treated with the greatest consideration and also why the first class of every adult session requires careful organization by the tutor. Belbin and Belbin (1972: 168) record instances of individuals undergoing in-service training who are so anxious about passing the examination at the end of their course, that they resign from their jobs rather than risk failure, since they consider that they would lose face with their colleagues if the latter occurred. Hence, teachers of adults need to be sensitive about the emotional state of their learners, a facility that may be more significant in the educator of adults than many of the others generally assumed essential to the teacher's role.

Thought and reflection clearly play a significant role in the learning processes and people obviously have a propensity to utilize their thought processes in different ways. For instance, one person might seek to jump to conclusions about the nature of a potential learning situation and act accordingly whilst another may seek to weigh up every aspect of the situation and think about it. In a similar manner one person might be more affected by the situation within which the experience occurs whilst another be less affected, etc. Obviously, these different personality traits reflect different cognitive styles and a whole literature has emerged in learning theory about these (see Knox 1977: 443–9; Kolb 1984: 61–96). Table 3.1 summarizes some of these findings.

It must be recognized that there is a tendency in Table 3.1 to overlap but it is produced in this way to show the extent to which learning styles differ. This is a significant element in teaching adults that needs to be considered carefully by the educator. Few of the pieces of research demonstrate any relationship between learning style and learning effectiveness in adults since most of the research has been conducted with children.

The physical body

That the physical body declines once it has reached its peak is a self-evident phenomenon and, to some extent, the learner's ability to assimilate information and process it is related to the level of physical health. Knox states:

> Physiological conditions and physical health can affect learning and cognition in various ways. Sensory impairment, such as poor vision or hearing loss, can restrict sensory input. Inadequate cerebral circulation or stress can impair memory. Ill health can restrict attention given to external events.
>
> (Knox 1977: 410)

From the above it is clear that the educator of adults must be aware of these findings and ensure that the teaching and learning environment is such that any ill-effects of the physical condition are minimized. Additionally, it is known that as human reactions slow down it is more difficult for adults to sustain a high rate of learning and if they are expected to undertake learning at too fast a pace they experience stress and anxiety which leads to unsatisfactory situations in which learning is either inhibited or prevented. But once adults are enabled to learn at their own pace, when they feel free and unpressurized,

Table 3.1 Learning styles

Learning style	Comment
Active versus passive	It will be seen from the learning cycle that some learners may actively seek out information and these are self-directed learners, while others may be more passive in the receipt of information provided for them.
Assimilator versus accommodator	Kolb (1984: 78) describes the assimilator as one whose dominant learning abilities are abstract conceptualization and reflective observation, and the accommodator as one whose strength lies in active experimentation and learning from concrete experience.
Concrete versus abstract	Some learners like to start with the concrete situation, such as the experience, while others prefer to start from the abstract, theoretical idea. This is similar to the preceding type.
Converger versus diverger	The converger is best at abstract conceptualization and active experimentation while the diverger's strengths lie in reflective observation and concrete experience (Kolb 1984: 77).
Field dependence versus field independence	Wilkin describes these as in the former mode 'perception is strongly dominated by the overall organization of the field, as "fused"' (1971: 24). In the latter mode 'parts of the field are experienced as discrete from organised background' ibid.
Focusing versus scanning	If learners have a problem to solve, focusers will examine it as a totality and generate hypotheses that will be modified in the light of new information, while scanners will select one aspect of the problem and assume it to be the solution, until subsequent information disproves it, when they have to recommence the task.
Holistic versus serialistic	This approach reflects Gestalt psychology: some learners see phenomena as a whole while others string together the parts.
Reflection versus impulsivity	This is similar to focusing and scanning and Kagan, who undertook his studies among children, wrote that 'a child who does reflect upon the probable validity of alternative solution sequences is likely to follow through the first idea that occurs to him. This strategy is more likely to end up in failure than one that involves reflection' (1971: 54–57).
Rigidity versus flexibility	Some people are rigid in their approach to learning since once they have discovered a successful method they always seek to apply it. This creates its own difficulties, since problems emerge that cannot be solved by the normal approach.

adults of almost any age can learn efficiently. Rogers records how 'training schools have found, literally to their cost, that set training periods of perhaps three weeks with formal examinations at the end produce high failure rate' (1977: 62). Hence learning and teaching methods have to be devised that allow adults to control the speed of their own learning.

SUMMARY

A theory of learning has been constructed in this chapter, based upon experientialist approaches but locating learners in their socio-cultural milieu. Adults are seen as having developing selves throughout their lifespan, although their physical bodies do undergo a gradual process of decline. Since learning begins with experience, the relationship between the adults' biographies and their understanding of their situation is important; when that relationship is harmonious there is a tendency for the experience merely to reinforce the biography, but when there is a disjuncture then there is a strong likelihood that the learning processes will commence. However, even in these situations, there are occasions when individuals do not wish to learn – sometimes this happens with the elderly who do not wish to change, but also there are other types of individual who prefer to remain true to their biography – even if they might benefit from learning and changing.

However, there are many situations when adults embark upon self-directed learning projects, many undertaking projects lasting many hours, and this has become an important focus of attention by some learning theorists. Learning, however, is far broader than enrolling in an educational institution and embarking upon a course – it involves the whole process of social living. Nevertheless, participation studies are also an important part of the study of adult education (Courtney 1992) and this has suggested that younger adults are more likely to enrol than older ones, although with the advent of the University of the Third Age, and other organizations directly concerned with older people, this might well change.

Having examined adult learners and adult learning, it is recognized that few of the learning theorists have been examined in detail and, consequently, the next chapter is devoted to elaborating upon the work of a number of the main ones.

4 Adults learning – some theoretical perspectives

Having developed an approach to adult learning in the previous chapter it is now necessary to examine the field of adult education more broadly and to investigate some of the writings about adult learning that have been produced in recent years. This chapter, which is closely linked to the previous one, highlights the work of five major writers, each of whom, in their various ways, has examined different aspects of adult learning. Four of the writers concentrate on adult education and the fifth is an educational psychologist; three assume a psychological and the remaining two a sociological perspective. They are: Paulo Freire, Robert Gagné, Malcolm Knowles, Jack Mezirow and Carl Rogers; the main works of each referred to here are listed in the bibliography. These five have been selected because, in their differing ways, they have contributed to the theoretical knowledge of adult learning and their writings are examined here, comparing and contrasting their ideas to those presented in the previous chapters.

PAULO FREIRE

The writings of Freire are now very well known among adult educators, even though some have confessed to finding him difficult to comprehend. Freire's ideas have emerged against the background of the oppression of the masses in Brazil by an elite, who reflect the dominant values of a non-Brazilian culture. His writings epitomize an intellectual movement that developed in Latin America after the Second World War, which is a synthesis of Christianity and Marxism and which finds its theological fulfilment in the so-called liberation theory and its educational philosophy is Freire's own work. From this background, it may be assumed that at the heart of his educational ideas lies a humanistic conception of people as learners, but also an expectation that once they have actually learned they may not remain passive but become active participants in the wider world. Hence, for Freire, education cannot be a neutral process; it is either designed to facilitate freedom or it is 'education for domestication' (Freire 1973c: 79), which is basically conservative.

However, in order to understand Freire's thinking it is helpful to recall Figure 1.1 in which it was suggested that objectified culture is transmitted to the individual through the lifelong process of socialization. Since the culture that is transmitted is foreign to the values of the Brazilian people, who are its recipients, Freire claims that this is the culture of the colonizers and implicit in the process in the subordination of the culture of the indigenous people. He illustrates this in the following manner:

> It is not a coincidence that the colonizers refer to their own cultural practices as an art, but refer to the cultural production of the colonized as folklore. Similarly, the colonizers speak of their language, but speak of the language of the colonized as dialect.
>
> (Freire 1973c: 50–1)

Since a construction of reality is contained within language, the masses have a construction of reality imposed upon them, which is false to their own heritage. Thus the idea of a false self-identify emerges, one that perpetually undervalues the indigenous culture and, therefore, native people come to see themselves as subordinate. Hence, the oppressed are imprisoned in a cultural construction of reality that is false to them but one from which it is difficult to escape, since even the language used by them transmits the values that imprison them.

Through the process of literacy education Freire and his colleagues were able to design experiential situations in which the learners were enabled to reflect upon their own understanding of themselves within their socio-cultural milieu. It is this combination of action and reflection that he calls praxis (Freire 1972b: 96). Herein lies the difference between human beings and the other animals: people are able to process their experiences and reflect upon them. Through the process of reflection individuals may become conscious of realities other than the one into which they have been socialized. Freire writes that conscientization 'is a permanent critical approach to reality in order to discover it and discover the myths that deceive us and help to maintain the oppressing dehumanizing structures' (1971, cited in 1976: 225). He then expresses it slightly differently: conscientization 'implies that in discovering myself oppressed I know that I will be liberated only if I try to transform the oppressing structure in which I find myself' (ibid.). More recently, he has claimed that he no longer uses this term 'conscientization' and this may be because it has become too closely related to the Marxist idea of 'false class consciousness' which is much more restrictive than his understanding of the process. Nevertheless, Freire still regards education as 'the practice of freedom' through which process learners discover themselves and achieve something more of the fullness of their humanity by acting upon the world to transform it.

In this latter proposition it is possible to detect ideas contained in Figure 1.2, where having received and processed inputs from the objectified culture that engulfs them, learners can externalize and act back upon their socio-cultural milieu. Implicit, therefore, in Freire's formulation is a social theory of learning, although he never describes it in this manner.

How do Freire's ideas differ from those suggested in earlier chapters? Fundamentally, there is one major difference and some minor ones. In the first instance, the socio-cultural background from which his theory emerged has resulted in Freire depicting the objectified culture as being false and hostile to the culture of the indigenous learner, so that his approach is often viewed as being political rather than literacy education. However, this interpretation of culture is not something that is unique to Freire: many Marxist writers would concur that the dominant cultural knowledge and values, etc. acquired by most members of a society are the cultural perspectives allowed by an elite, so that some form of cultural hegemony exists. (See Westwood 1980 for a discussion in which this approach is applied to adult education and Bowles and Gintis 1976 for their analysis of American schooling from a similar perspective.) Thus, Figure 1.2 actually allows for such an interpretation to be assumed and, indeed, teaching might even be viewed as an activity that encourages it. Nevertheless, there is a significant difference between the model presented here and Freire's thought: he incorporates two opposing cultures into his understanding of the process – that of the ruling elite and that of the oppressed. Herein lies the crux of Freire's argument that no education can be neutral since the culture of the oppressed is in opposition to that of the elite. Hence literacy education can only assume a political perspective. The model produced earlier has not sought to analyse the culture of the United Kingdom in this way, although some sociologists and community educators might consider that such an analysis is necessary, and this will be discussed below in relation to the relevance of Freire's work for Western Europe and the United States.

However, Freire places considerable emphasis on the teacher–learner and the learner–teacher dialogue and this is similar to the two-way model of human interaction depicted in the previous chapter. Freire recognizes that the teacher may facilitate the experience upon which reflection occurs, which thus becomes a learning process. Thus Freire regards the role of the teacher as a facilitator who is able to stimulate the learning process rather than as one who teaches the 'correct' knowledge and values that have to be acquired. However, this does not differ significantly from the model produced here since the teacher is regarded here as either one who transmits cultural knowledge or one who facilitates learning. This distinction is discussed further in Chapter 5.

Freire's approach is a model for teaching adults rather than necessarily one for teaching children. It concentrates upon the humanity of the learner and places great value upon the human being, but it is more structural and political in its emphasis, whereas the one discussed here is more phenomenological and individualistic. Herein lies a slight difference in emphasis although not one that is irreconcilable since both locate individuals in their socio-cultural milieu and both regard learners as recipients of cultural information and experiences transmitted through personal or impersonal means and, also, as agents who are able to act back upon that environment in order to try to change it in some instances.

Having pointed to some of the apparent differences between Freire's approach and that discussed here, it must also be recognized that there are many similarities, including: his emphasis on the humanity of the learners; his concern that learners should be free to reflect upon their own experiences and to harmonize their reflections and actions (he calls this 'praxis') and act upon their socio-cultural milieu in order to humanize and transform it; his connection between the socio-cultural environment and individual learners; his recognition that learners are able to create their own roles rather than become role players performing roles prescribed by others. As a result of all these aspects, Freire maintains that education cannot be a neutral process. The major reason for this is that it is a social institution which is controlled by the social and political processes which almost automatically ensure that social pressures are brought to bear upon learners to conform to what is socially prescribed in both cognitive and behavioural dimensions.

Out of the political condition of Latin America has emerged a Christian-Marxist approach to education that is both humanistic and radical. Yet the term 'radical' is often the 'kiss of death' to innovative approaches, as was seen with the concept of recurrent education. However, if there is not something radical about the educational process, the question needs to be posed as to how it differs from socialization. If education actually provides people with an opportunity to process and to reflect upon their experiences, it must allow them to reach different conclusions about them and to choose whether, or not, they will behave in a conformist manner.

Since his early writings, Freire has continued to produce radical analyses of education, often writing with another author, in the form of dialogues, which he calls talking a book. These books are of interest because they help introduce readers to Freire's ideas and the way in which he develops them in discussion. There have been five books like this, the last being with Myles Horton from Highlander, and while they are inspiring they tend to confuse Freire's reflections about his own previous writings and actions with the present. This is natural in discussion but it is difficult to trace the developments in his thought from his earlier writings. Perhaps these dialogues serve as a full introduction to Freire, his world and his thoughts.

Since Freire's ideas emerged in Latin America, do they have any relevance for contemporary Western society? This is a most important question to pose, since he could be dismissed as someone whose views are of significance only within the context in which they emerged. Yet this approach would be quite wrong, since many dominant ideas and values in contemporary society owe their origins to historical cultural milieux completely different from this one. London reflected upon Freire's work in the context of North America and he claimed that in that society adult education has adopted a 'bland approach ... (a) non-controversial stance, and (a) safe and respectable perspective' (London 1973: 59). But he maintained that a:

central problem for adult education is to undertake programming that will raise the level of consciousness of the American people so that they can become aware of the variety of forces – economic, political, social and psychological – that are afflicting their lives.

(London 1973: 54)

Hence, it may be seen that London was sympathetic to the adoption of Freire's approach in North America. Perhaps his argument would have been even more compelling had he focused upon the different cultures and subcultures in America and examined whether a form of cultural hegemony actually exists. A great deal of what London has written might also be applied to some adult education that exists in the United Kingdom. Hence, it may be necessary to enquire whether adult educators actually perceive their role in this way at all. Clearly, there is some evidence to suggest that community educators, such as Lovett (1975) and Newman (1973, 1979), do actually adopt similar perspectives. More recently Kirkwood and Kirkwood (1989) reported on a community education project carried out in Edinburgh utilizing Freire's methods. However, this is a significant exception since a great deal of community education and literacy work has not assumed this radical approach. Indeed, it is possible to argue that many people in the United Kingdom are no more aware of the variety of forces that afflict them than are their counterparts in the United States, so it is an important ideal for adult educators to try to raise their level of consciousness.

ROBERT M. GAGNÉ

Gagné (1977: 284–6) has developed a model for understanding a relationship between learning and instruction. He suggests that learning progresses through the following phases as the instructional process was undertaken. These stages are: expectancy; attentive: selective perspection; coding: storage entry; memory storage retrieval; transfer; responding; reinforcement. In a later publication it was suggested that there are nine phases in instruction:

- gaining attention
- informing the learner of the objectives
- stimulating recall of prerequisite learnings
- presenting the stimulus material
- providing learning guidance
- eliciting the performance
- providing feedback about performance correctness
- assessing the performance
- enhancing retention and transfer

(Gagné *et al.* 1992: 203)

Nevertheless, there is another element of his work that is also significant to adult education and this is his types of learning. He has proposed eight types, seven of which he regards as a hierarchy and the eighth may occur at any level. These are: signal learning; stimulus–response learning; motor and verbal chaining; multiple discrimination; concept learning; rule learning; problem solving.

He claims that signal learning may occur at any level of the hierarchy and it may be understood as a form of classical conditioning, which was discussed in the previous chapter. Clearly this happens with both children and adults and it is no doubt one of the ways in which everyone acquires many attitudes and prejudices throughout the whole of their life. The remaining seven types of learning are, according to Gagné, seven stages of a hierarchy and they are now elaborated upon.

Stimulus–response learning is the same as operant conditioning in which the response is shaped by the reward. The following two types of learning, motor and verbal chaining, Gagné places at the same level in the hierarchy: the former refers to skills learning while the latter is rote learning. With both, practice is necessary to achieve correctness whilst reinforcement is necessary to ensure that the acceptable sequence is maintained. In multiple discrimination learning, Gagné moves into the area of intellectual skills; this, he suggests, is the ability to distinguish between similar types of phenomena, so that the learner is able to decide which of similar types is correct for any specific situation. In contrast to discrimination is the ability to classify. Concepts are abstract notions which link together similar phenomena so that, for instance, friendship is a concept but individual friendships are actual occurrences, education is a concept but in actuality there are educational processes. Gagné suggests that the ability to learn concepts is the next order of the hierarchy and it may be recalled that developmental psychologists, such as Piaget (1929), would claim that the ability to think in the abstract commences mostly during adolescence, so that it is necessary to recognize that the education of adults may be different from the education of children, since the levels of conceptual thought in the various learning processes are different. This is a point implicit in Gagné's hierarchy of types of learning but one that is important in relation to any consideration of andragogy. One particular type of classification is that of rules and he maintains that the ability to respond to signals by a whole number of responses is successful rule learning. At this level of thought it is clear that Gagné perceives the individual to be a little more free than some of the behaviourists and this is quite fundamental to the understanding of the education of adults.

Problem solving is the highest order of learning in Gagnés hierarchy and this occurs when the learner draws upon his previously learned rules in order to discover an answer to a problematic situation. It will be recalled that among the different styles of learning discussed in the previous chapter was the dichotomy between the flexible and the rigid learner, in which the former clearly has the mastery of more sets of rules than the latter, to assist in problem solving. Problem solving is an approach to learning and teaching used frequently in the education of adults, so the problem solving sequence that Gagné proposes is quite significant for adult educators. He suggests that the following sequence occurs, in which the flexibility is apparent. Initially a learner proposes one or more hypotheses concerning the problem and these are based upon the rules that have already been learned. These hypotheses are then tested against the actual situation and once an answer has been discovered to the problem the solution will be assimilated into the learner's repertoire of rules, so that the next time a similar situation arises the learner will not experience it as a problem. There are similarities at this point between Gagné's approach and that of Schutz and Luckmann (1974) mentioned earlier. Another psychologist whose analysis is similar to Gagné's in this context is George Kelly (1955), who claimed that all behaviour may be regarded as a form of hypothesis testing to enquire whether the actual world is really like the perception of it constructed by the individual. If it is, then the experience merely reinforces the construct, but if it is not, then the construct (hypothesis) has to be modified in the light of experience. (See Candy 1981 for a direct application of some of Kelly's ideas to adult education).

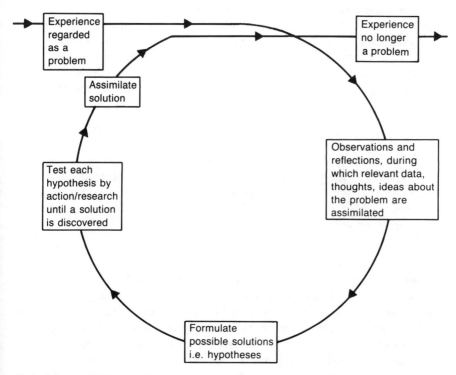

Figure 4.1 A problem solving cycle

The problem solving sequence has formed a basis of many learning exercises in adult education and in recent years a number of problem solving cycles have been devised which are similar to the learning cycles that were discussed in the previous chapter. Figure 4.1 depicts a problem solving cycle that combines the sequence proposed by Gagné with some of the ideas mentioned by Kolb and Fry (1975). Thus it may be seen from Figure 4.1 that this type of problem solving cycle actually relates back to the learning cycle but it also highlights some of the most important aspects of Gagné's hierarchy of learning. It will be recognized, however, that since Gagné starts from a psychological perspective some of the wider cultural implications of learning, discussed in the previous chapters and in the work of Freire, are not so apparent. Yet the learning process that he has highlighted is significant for adult educators, since experience is frequently a basis for learning.

MALCOLM KNOWLES

Knowles may almost be regarded as the father of andragogy because, while he did not actually invent the term, he has been mainly responsible for its popularization. Indeed, the term derives from the Greek *aner*, meaning man, and it was first used in an educational context in nineteenth-century Europe. Nevertheless, Knowles is most frequently associated with the concept which he originally defined as 'the art and science of helping adults learn' (1980: 43).

Knowles initially distinguished sharply between the way in which adults and children learn. He (1978: 53–7) claimed that there are four main assumptions that differentiate andragogy from pedagogy. These are:

- a change in self-concept, since adults need to be more self-directive;
- experience, since mature individuals accumulate an expanding reservoir of experience which becomes an exceedingly rich resource in learning;
- readiness to learn, since adults want to learn in the problem areas with which they are confronted and which they regard as relevant
- orientation towards learning, since adults have a problem centred orientation they are less likely to be subject centred.

However, in 1984 he added a fifth assumption about the motivation to learn (Knowles 1984: 12) and in his autobiographical book he added another one about the need to know (Knowles 1989: 83–5). Knowles has clearly given the idea a great deal of thought and has frequently reconceptualized it, which demonstrates his own willingness to rethink his position, a characteristic which is to be admired. However, the fact that he has reformulated the idea on a number of occasions illustrates the fact that each of the assumptions is open to considerable discussion. It might be asked, for instance, whether children are any less motivated than adults to learn about those phenomena that they regard as relevant and problematic to them and whether Knowles has actually specified all the relevant points in any discussion about the differences in adults and children learning. The fact that Knowles has, to some extent, rethought his ideas is significant since the concept of andragogy has been accepted uncritically by many adult educators in recent years. Indeed, when Knowles' work was first published in America it did stimulate considerable debate in the American journals about its validity. Initially, McKenzie (1977) sought to provide Knowles' pragmatic formulation with a more substantial philosophical foundation and he argued that adults and children are existentially different – a point with which Elias agreed although he suggested that this was not necessarily significant since men and women are existentially different but no one has yet suggested that 'the art and science of teaching women differs from the art and science of teaching men' (1979: 254). To this point, McKenzie (1979) replied that the differences between men and women, while pronounced, are not significant when related to their readiness to learn nor are they important in relation to their perspective of time. He also argued that andragogy is similar to but not precisely the same as progressivism. Yet McKenzie did not really focus upon the point that children might actually have the same readiness to learn as adults, and indeed do, when they are confronted with a problem the solution to which they wish to know.

Another set of issues arose in the debate about andragogy: Label (1978) suggested that the education of the elderly should be known as gerogogy, since education should recognize the phases of adult development; but are there only two phases in that development? Knox (1977: 342–50) would suggest otherwise, so that to include gerogogy as a separate element in the art and science of teaching would be the 'thin end of the wedge' in a multiplication of terms, which prompted Knudson to suggest that all of these should be replaced by a single concept of 'humanagogy' which is:

> a theory of learning that takes into account the differences between people of various ages as well as their similarities. It is a *human* theory of learning not a theory of 'child learning', 'adult learning' or 'elderly learning'. It is a theory of learning that combines pedagogy, andragogy and gerogogy and takes into account every aspect of presently accepted psychological theory.
>
> (Knudson 1979; 261; emphasis in original)

Perhaps Knudson's position is a logical outcome of the debate but the term 'humanagogy' has not gained any acceptance and, in any case, what makes humanagogy any different from education? It appears that Knudson has merely invented a new term for education, even though he has emphasized one aspect of the process that is regarded as significant to this study: the humanity of the participant.

In 1979, Knowles chose to re-enter the debate when he recognized that andragogy and pedagogy are not discrete processes and he claimed that 'some pedagogical assumptions are realistic for adults in some situations and some andragogical assumptioms are realistic for children in some situations' (1979: 53), and that the two are not mutually exclusive. However, since the debate was prolonged in America and as a number of questions were raised at the outside of this discussion, it is worth enquiring whether Knowles' formulation is actually correct.

Knowles placed a tremendous emphasis on the self, something with which many adult educators would agree. Knox (1977) points out that the self undergoes development throughout the lifespan and that some aspects of that development may be related to physical age. But other scholars, such as Riesman (1950), have pointed out that some adults are 'other-directed', so that when they come to the learning situation they may seek to become dependent upon a teacher. While it may be one of the functions of an adult educator to try to help dependent adults to discover some independence, it must be recognized that this may be a very difficult step for some learners. But the fact that there are other-directed people suggests that Knowles' formulation is a little sweeping in this respect.

Knowles claimed that adults have an expanded reservoir of experience that may be emphasized as a rich resource for future learning; but do not children and adolescents also have some experience that may be used as a resource in their learning? Do only adults learn from their relevant problems? What of those adults who study with the Open University or attend university extension classes? Hence, it needs to be asked whether there are any foundations for his claims.

It does appear that while Knowles has focused upon something quite significant to adult learning, his formulation is rather weak, not based upon extensive research findings, nor is it the total picture of adult learning. Indeed, it is not a psychological analysis of the learning process, it does not describe why specific aspects of experience are relevant, nor does it generate a learning sequence for an adult, so some of the claims that Knowles made for andragogy do appear to be rather suspect. It is not surprising, therefore, that in his later work he has made less all-embracing claims for this concept, nor is it surprising that even more recent works have also been rather critical of it. Day and Baskett, for instance, conclude that:

> Andragogy is not a theory of adult learning, but is an educational ideology rooted in an inquiry-based learning and teaching paradigm – and should be recognised as such . . . . It is not always the most appropriate or the most effective means of educating. This distinction between andragogy and pedagogy is based on an inaccurately conceived notion of pedagogy
>
> (Day and Baskett 1982: 150)

There have subsequently been many other criticisms of the concept of andragogy: Hartree concluded that while Knowles

> has done an important service in popularizing the idea . . . it is unfortunate that he has done so in a form which, because it is intellectually dubious, is likely to lead to rejection by the very people it is important to convince.
>
> (Hartree 1984: 209)

Tennant (1986: 113–22), writing from a psychological position, also rejects many of Knowles' arguments although he does not reject the ideas of individual autonomy which underlie much of Knowles' work.

Yet despite its apparent conceptual weaknesses and the many criticisms being levelled at the concept, it is becoming a popular term in adult education; so what are the strengths of the formulation that have resulted in its gaining support? Day and Baskett (1982) have perhaps located one of these when they suggest that it is an educational ideology, for clearly it is humanistic and this is a most frequently expressed ideology among adult educators. It also focuses upon the self-directed learner and emphasizes the place of the self in the learning process, both of which are very significant to learning theory. Additionally, it arose in a period of history in the twentieth century, which Martin (1981) has characterized as romantic, in which the value of the individual was emphasized and the boundaries of the institutions of society were weak. These boundaries resulted in an increased emphasis on integrated approaches to academic study and a wider acceptance of the ideological perspection of progressive education. Indeed, this emphasis on self-direction has resulted in Knowles' (1986) book on learning contracts assuming considerable importance in many circles.

The learning contract is one made between teacher and learner, for the learner to undertake specific work by a given date. In the tutorial that preceded it, there might also be discussion about how the work is to be undertaken, which experts should be consulted, how the work should be presented and also the standard which should be achieved. This teaching and learning method has assumed a great deal of popularity among some sectors of adult education, possibly because it does encourage individual autonomy and, maybe, because it appears less time-consuming for the teacher, but this latter assumption probably belies the reality of the situation! Another reason why learning contracts are popular at present is because of the current emphasis upon correct performance rather than correct academic knowledge, and the learning contract can be utilized in very practical ways.

Andragogy, then, was a theory that grew out of a specific period (Jarvis 1984) although Knowles emphasized certain values, such as individual autonomy, which were to transcend the 1960s when Knowles first formulated the idea. In contract learning, an adaptation of his approach is still seen as relevant to the situation. By 1986, however, the andragogical teacher had become the manager and designer of the learning process and the learning contract the agreement between the manager and the managed as to how the learning was to be undertaken. Knowles' work remains popular despite all its failings and one of the main reasons for this is probably because it reflects the ideological currents of the present time.

It may be concluded from this brief discussion that, despite the claims sometimes made on its behalf, andragogy is not a theory of adult learning, nor is it a theory of adult teaching even though its humanistic perspective might provide some guidelines for an approach to teaching adults. Is it a philosophy? Certainly, it includes within it an ideological perspective that is both idealistic and humanistic, so that it is not surprising that it has been found by many to be acceptable. However, andragogy might also be employed as a term to denote the body of knowledge that is emerging about the education of adults, in the same manner as pedagogy might be used to describe the body of knowledge about the education of children.

Knowles is, therefore, an important practitioner in the education of adults and some of the points that he has raised are based upon the humanistic ideals of education itself. It is significant that the points that he has raised are discussed within this theoretical context since, while andragogy is not a theory of adult learning, its implications are quite profound for the practice of teaching adults.

JACK MEZIROW

The work of Mezirow was cited in the opening chapter in order to illustrate how one writer's approach to learning was similar to the one being presented here. Mezirow (1977, 1981) draws upon the insights of a number of established disciplines and synthesizes them in an original manner and this section summarizes some of the ideas that he presents, although the emphasis of his work has changed in more recent years as he endeavoured to produce a more complete theory of learning. His early work will be discussed first and, thereafter, reference is made to his more recent publications.

Mezirow starts from the assumption that everyone has constructions of reality which are dependent upon reinforcement from various sources in the socio-cultural world. He calls these constructions of reality 'perspectives' and notes that they are transformed when an individual's perspective is not in harmony with his experience. In this situation of disjunction, the individual's construction of reality is then transformed as a result of reflecting upon the experience and plotting new strategies of living as a result of this assessment of the situation. Mezirow notes that life crises are times when this occurs and his conclusion is both in accord with his own observations and those of Aslanian and Brickell (1980), who discovered that people tended to return to studying as a result of life crises. Hence, the crux of Mezirow's analysis is that when a 'meaning perspective can no longer comfortably deal with anomalies in the next situation, a transformation can occur' (1977: 157). He goes on to suggest that a learning sequence is established as a result of a discordant experience, which may be depicted in the form of a learning cycle (Figure 4.2).

In a later work, Mezirow (1981: 7) extends this cycle to include the following ten stages:

1 A disorientating dilemma
2 Self-examination
3 Critical assessment and a sense of alienation
4 Relating discontent to the experiences of others

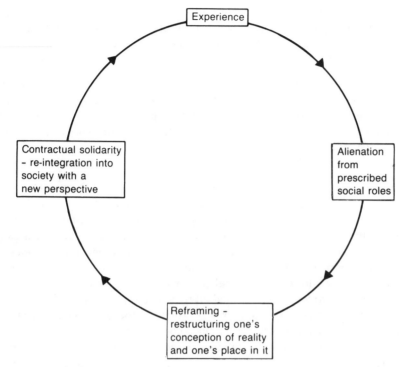

Figure 4.2 A learning cycle
Source: Mezirow (1977: 158)

5 Exploring options for new ways of acting
6 Building confidence in new ways of behaving
7 Planning a course of action
8 Acquiring knowledge in order to implement plans
9 Experimenting with new roles
10 Reintegration into society

The extent to which this is actually a sequence is not clear since Mezirow also suggests that there are two paths to perspective transformation – one sudden and the other gradual. However, he regards these transformations as 'a development process of movement through the adult years towards meaning perspectives that are progressively more inclusive, discriminating, and more integrative of experience' (1977: 159). However, there are a number of points now that perhaps require additional evidence since not all people may develop as a result of their experience, nor may they necessarily learn from it. Additionally, should an individual's universe of meaning necessarily change in the same direction to another's as he ages?

It is this movement along a maturity gradient that Mezirow regards as a form of emancipatory learning and here he draws heavily upon the work of Habermas. Emancipation is, according to Mezirow, 'from libidinal, institutional or environmental forces which limit our options and rational control over our lives but have been taken for granted as beyond human control' (1981: 5). Hence, perspective transformation is an emancipatory process

> of becoming critically aware of how and why the structure of psycho-cultural assumptions has come to constrain the way we see ourselves and our relationships, reconstituting the structure to permit a more inclusive and discriminating integration of experience and acting upon these new understandings.
>
> (Mezirow 1981: 5)

Thus it is clear that there are certain similarities and some differences between Mezirow's work and that of other theorists who consider the wider socio-cultural milieu. Both he and Freire regard education as a liberating force: Freire views it as releasing the individual from the false consciousness in which he has been imprisoned as a result of the dominance of the culture of the colonizers, but Mezirow regards the freedom from a more psychological perspective; both Freire and Mezirow focus upon the social construction of reality and regard learning as a method by which this may be changed. Like a number of theorists of adult learning, Mezirow focuses upon the idea that learning occurs as a result of reflecting upon experience, so that much of his work is relevant to understanding the learning process in socialization and in non-formal learning situations. However, he also suggests that there are different levels of reflection and he (1981: 12–13) specifies seven of these, some of which he claims are more likely to occur in adulthood:

1 reflectivity: awareness of specific perception, meaning, behaviour
2 affective reflectivity: awareness of how the individual feels about what is being perceived, thought or acted upon
3 discriminant reflectivity: assessing the efficacy of perception, etc.
4 judgemental reflectivity: making and becoming aware of the value of judgements made
5 conceptual reflectivity: assessing the extent to which the concepts employed are adequate for the judgement
6 psychic reflectivity: recognition of the habit of making percipient judgements on the basis of limited information
7 theoretical reflectivity: awareness of why one set of perspectives is more or less adequate to explain personal experience

The last three of these, Mezirow maintains, are more likely to occur in adulthood and the final one he regards as quite crucial to perspective transformation.

It was only in 1991 that Mezirow brought together thoughts that he had expressed in numerous articles and papers in *Transformative Dimensions of*

Adult Learning. Here, Mezirow sought to synthesize perspectives and research from different academic disciplines to demonstrate how adults learn. He suggests that learning is the process of making meaning from experiences as a result of the learner's previous knowledge, so that learning is a new interpretation of an experience. He goes on to show how people make meaning in a variety of different ways and he also analyses the distorted assumptions that stem from prior experiences. Making meaning is an important element in learning, although it restricts it to the cognitive domain, which is a pity since skills, emotions and even the senses are also learned from experience. This is an important study although it is not as unique as the publishers claim on the dust jacket (see, for instance, Marton *et al.* 1984).

Indeed, there is a sense in which his approach is very similar to the phenomenological approach suggested in the previous chapters: that if a person's stock of knowledge is inadequate to explain the experience, then the questioning process is reactivated. Additionally, his emphasis upon reflection is important since he has extended the analysis quite considerably. Here his approach is actually similar to that of Gagné but he concentrates upon meaning and reflection as learning. However, his idea of progress and development during the ageing process does require some further evidence since it leads logically to the idea of the 'wisdom of the elders' and to the notion that the self-knowledge of the elders is always more mature than that of younger people. Furthermore, the influence of social change plays little part in Mezirow's analysis although sociologists of late modernity (Giddens 1990, 1991) have written a great deal which would have enriched his analysis. Mezirow has, however, accepted some of the central tenets of Habermas' theory of communicative action without fully analysing the academic debate that the work has generated. Nevertheless, his approach is a significant contribution to recent literature on adult learning.

CARL ROGERS

Carl Rogers is the final theorist to be discussed in this chapter: he is a humanistic psychologist who has expounded this psychological approach in the field of education. Having this theoretical perspective it is not surprising that he emphasizes the self-actualization of the learner and he (1969: 279–97) argues that the goal of education is a fully functioning person. However, this orienation reflects the therapist in Rogers and the distinction between education and therapy is occasionally blurred in his writings. Indeed he uses therapeutic techniques for educational ends. His fusion of these two distinct activities is highlighted by Srinivasan's (1977: 72–4) discussion of the curriculum distinctions between self-actualizing and problem-centred education: emotional versus intellectual; involving the learning group in developing its own curriculum versus identification of appropriate subject matter; planning learning experiences so that learners can reassess their feelings versus building learning around a problem; support in active learning versus using prepared learning units; using a variety of audio visual approaches versus standardized printed materials and group discussion; using the group's spontaneity versus a programmed learning text; decentralized educational opportunities verus formal educational provision; participatory techniques versus teaching; assessing personal growth versus assessing learning gains. Clearly, Srinivasan has polarized the distinction since a number of the theorists mentioned in this chapter would focus upon the significance of some of the former elements in the dichotomies as significant aspects of their understanding of education. Certainly Rogers would not draw the distinction in quite the way that Srinivasan has and yet she has attempted to clarify an important conceptual issue. However, Rogers certainly comes close to Knowles in his emphasis upon the self and the need for self-development and self-direction. Knowles (1980: 29–33) specifies fifteen different dimensions of maturation and he certainly regards maturity as one of the goals of education. Like Rogers and Knowles, it will be recalled that Mezirow was concerned about the maturation process of the learner, so it must be recognized that for a number of theorists this plays a significant part in the education of adults.

Unlike some of the other writers discussed here, Rogers records the results of his approach to experiential learning within the context of graduate teaching in a university and he also records incidents of others in a formal setting who have attempted similar techniques. He suggests that experiential learning has a quality of personal involvement, but he recognizes that the teacher has a facilitating role; is pervasive in as much as it makes a difference to the learners; is evaluated by learners in terms of whether it is actually meeting their needs rather than in terms of its academic quality; has an essence of meaning. It is perhaps significant to note that while Rogers regards experiential learning as self-initiated, he does not actually dispense with the teacher, so that he is describing a different learning situation from that discussed by Tough. Nevertheless, Rogers does claim that teaching 'is a vastly over-rated function' (1969: 103).

Like Srinivasan, Rogers (1969: 157–64) regards experiential learning at one end of a spectrum but at the other he places memory learning. He claims that experiential learning is typified by the following principles:

1 human beings have a natural potentiality to learn;
2 significant learning occurs when the learner perceives the relevance of the subject matter;
3 learning involves a change in self-organization and self-perception;
4 learning that threatens self-perception is more easily perceived and assimilated when external threats are at a minimum;
5 learning occurs when the self is not threatened;
6 much significant learning is acquired by doing;
7 learning is facilitated when the learner participates responsibly in the learning process;
8 self-initiated learning involves the whole person;

9 independence, creativity and self-reliance are all facilitated when self-criticism and self-evaluation are basic;
10 much socially useful learning is learning the process of learning and retaining an openness to experience, so that the process of change may be incorporated into the self.

This approach is clearly based upon the idea that the learner is the agent and that the social structure is not too oppressive to the learner. However, omission of any discussion about the wider socio-cultural milieu appears to be a weakness in this approach, so that while the above ten principles provide considerable insight into the learning process and offer some guidelines for the teacher, they do not present a comprehensive theory of individual learning within the wider socio-cultural environment.

Overall, Rogers' approach to experiential learning has much to offer and may provide inspiration for the teacher, but it does not provide a comprehensive theory of adult learning.

SUMMARY

The work of five major theorists has been briefly examined in this chapter and the intention has been to highlight some of the similarities and some of the differences betweeen them. Both Freire and Mezirow consider the socio-cultural milieu as a significant factor in the learning process in common with the model presented earlier, although they treat culture in rather different ways: Freire has a two-cultures model of society whereas Mezirow is content to regard it as rather static and homogeneous. The process of reflection plays a significant part in the work of a number of these theorists, since they recognize that the human being is able to sift and evaluate the external stimuli received from his experiences. Experiential learning is quite central to all of their considerations, since they recognize that the adult learns most efffectively when the learning process is in response to a problem or a need. All of the writers, with the exception of Gagné, have placed considerable emphasis on the self and, although it is most exemplified in the works of Knowles and Rogers, it reflects the humanistic concerns of adult education. Even so, it is a much more debatable point as to whether the aims of education should be specified in terms of the development of the learner because the success of the educational process is then being evaluated by non-educational criteria. Perhaps, therefore, the cognitive dimension of the learning process is insufficiently emphasized in some instances, although there is a danger of polarizing or over-emphasizing formal education if Srinivasan's approach is adopted. Clearly, the academic disciplines appear to be less significant than the immediacy and relevance of problems and experiences, although there is a need for considerably more research into effective adult learning of the academic disciplines, which may occur as adults are gaining more opportunities to study for academic and professional qualifications on a part-time basis. For instance, there may be a relationship between experience and the disciplines being studied, etc. which requires more exploration. Most of the theorists focus upon the human need to learn, Rogers being the most explicit about it being basic to humanity, but none of them sought to incorporate it into a comprehensive theory of learning needs, a point to which some reference has already been made. Mezirow and Freire have both developed comprehensive theoretical perspectives but Knowles' andragogical approach appears to have achieved the status of a theory, without having been systematically worked out. In all cases there are similarities with the model produced earlier in this study but in each instance the theorist has emphasized those elements that are most central to his own consideration, so that there are also a number of points of divergence.

In a sense it has been a little artificial to separate learning and teaching and to seek to extract from these writings only that which refers to the former, since learning and teaching are interrelated and intertwined. However, it is important to try to highlight and examine some aspects of adult learning prior to discussing teaching adults; but in the following chapter it is proposed to relate the discussion of these last two chapters to the teaching of adults.

5   Teaching adults

Teaching may be an overrated activity, as Rogers (1969: 103) maintains, but it remains at the heart of the educational process, so that consideration needs now to be given to it. Hirst and Peters (1970: 78) define it as the intention to bring about learning, and if this broad definition is adopted it may be seen that any activity that is performed in order to produce learning, however it is conducted, may be considered to be teaching. Hence, it is clear that Rogers and Hirst and Peters are perhaps using the term in slightly different ways and it is, therefore, essential to clarify its use at the outset. The teacher can adopt a variety of approaches to the performance of the role: didactic, socratic or facilitative. If teachers play their role in a didactic fashion, they expound the knowledge to be learned by the students; if they are socratic, they lead students towards a conclusion to their enquiry by shrewd questioning; if they are facilitative, they create conditions under which learning can occur but they do not seek to control its outcome.

Both the didactic and the socratic approaches are teacher-centred and may lead to the teacher's perception of reality being accepted by the students, although the socratic is more likely to result in conclusions other than those held by the teacher (whereas the facilitator has little control over the outcome of the learning at all). Rogers was clearly condemning the didactic approach and, maybe, the socratic one. By contrast, the definition proposed by Hirst and Peters is sufficiently broad to include all three of the types mentioned here. Yet their definition is not broad enough to include the informal and unintended teaching that may occur in the process of human interaction, which was discussed earlier. This, therefore, raises two major questions; to what extent is unintended teaching actually teaching and to what extent is the failure to produce learning, even though it was intended, actually teaching? It was suggested earlier that the failure to bring about learning should be regarded as an unsuccessful attempt to teach rather than unsuccessful teaching. If this conclusion is to be accepted, then teaching is not the intention to produce a learning outcome but it is the provision of any situation in which learning occurs. Hence, teachers may be anyone who aids another person to learn, irrespective of whether they are part of the educational institution or whether they intended the learning to occur. But, clearly, this is too wide a definition within the context of the occupation of teacher. In this instance, a teacher may be defined as one who is employed to provide an environment in which learning may occur, so that within this framework the teacher will plan his teaching sessions with the intention to bring about learning, or with the intention of teaching.

Hirst and Peters acknowledge that teaching is not essential to education but claim that serious miseducation may occur if too much emphasis is given to this. However, it may be that this is a point at which Rogers would diverge from Hirst and Peters. They certainly do appear to place much more emphasis on the role of the teacher than many of the learning theorists discussed earlier might wish to. Learning can and does occur without a teacher but teaching is one way in which learning is facilitated, and many adult educators would claim that one of the teacher's fundamental aims should be to help the learner to become independent. Hence, it might be claimed that teaching is one of the few occupations whose aim should be to make the client independent of the practitioner, a slightly different approach to that of first school teachers who try to dissuade parents from teaching their children until they are sent to school!

Learning, then, is considered to be the most significant element in education and it will be recalled that the definition of education adopted in this study broadened it to an intended process of learning rather than restricting it to the transmission of culture. Hence the position adopted here is quite different from that proposed by Peters (1966: 25) who argued that one of the criteria for education is that knowledge of a worthwhile nature is transmitted to the learner. Rather, the humanistic basis of education adopted here places the learner at the focal point and it is, therefore, the relationship between conditions of learning and approaches to teaching that occupies the first section of this chapter. Thereafter, the processes of teaching and teaching techniques are examined in some detail.

CONDITIONS OF LEARNING AND APPROACHES TO TEACHING

In the previous two chapters a number of points have been raised about how adults learn effectively and it is now necessary to draw many of them together and to relate them to various approaches to teaching. Table 5.1 summarizes many of these conclusions.

In Table 5.1 it may be seen that the approaches to teaching that have been suggested do not actually specify a particular teaching method, only a perspective that should be adopted. Clearly, therefore, it reflects an ideological position, but then the definition of education adopted earlier in this study was normative. Knowles (1978: 77–9; 1980: 57–8) has developed a similar approach within the context of his discussion about andragogy, which again indicates the validity of the accusation levelled at it by Day and Baskett as an ideological paradigm. If they are correct, then the position adopted here

Table 5.1 The conditions of adult learning and approaches to teaching

Conditions of adult learning	Approaches to teaching
Learning is a basic human need	Teaching is not essential to learning but may facilitate it
Learning is especially motivated when there is disharmony between an individual's experience and his perception of the world	Teachers and learners need to structure the process of learning together so that it may be relevant to the experience/problem that created the felt need to learn
Adult learners like to participate in the learning process	Teaching methods should be socratic or facilitative rather than didactic in many learning situations.
Adult learners bring their own: – experiences to the learning situations – meaning systems to the learning situation – needs to the learning situation	Teachers should use these experiences as a learning resource Teachers should try to build upon the meaning system, rather than seek to be contrary to it, so that students may integrate their new knowledge with their old: methods should be used that enable students to use their previous knowledge as a resource Teachers should help students to be aware of the relevance of what they are learning; subject matter will be 'applied' rather than pure: learning will be individualized where possible.
Adult learners bring to the learning situation their own: – self-confidence – self-esteem – self-perception	Teachers need to be empathetic and sensitive to the humanity of the learner at all times and, when appropriate, always anticipate a successful learning outcome Teachers should 'reinforce' all 'correct' knowledge and understanding in order that students are enabled to maintain a high level of self-confidence and self-esteem. Teachers should provide opportunities for adult students to reflect upon 'incorrect' knowledge, so that they can 'correct' it for themselves, where this is possible. Teachers should encourage self-assessment rather than teacher-assessment
Adults learn best when the self is not under threat	Teachers need to create an ethos in which no adult feels threatened or inhibited – this is especially true at the outset of any new course of learning. Cooperation rather than competition should be encouraged
Adult learners need to feel that they are treated as adults	Teachers should not regard themselves as 'the fount of all knowledge' but they should attempt to create and facilitate a teaching and learning engagement between all the participants

Table 5.1 (contd)

Conditions of adult learning	Approaches to teaching
Adult learners have developed their own learning styles	Teachers should recognize that different learning styles exist and encourage learners to develop effective and efficient learning. Hence, teachers also need to be flexible and adopt teaching styles relevant to the teaching and learning transaction.
Adult learners have had different educational biographies so they may learn at different speeds	Teachers should encourage adults to learn at their own pace
Adults have developed a crystallized intelligence	Teachers should not be influenced by previous academic record, especially that from initial education
Adults bring different physiological conditions to the learning situation, e.g. declining visual and/or audio accuity less energy, failing health.	Teachers should ensure that the physical environment in which the teaching and learning occurs is conducive to adult learning

is ideologically similar to that of Knowles: that since education is a humanistic process then the humanity of the participants is paramount in the learning process. However, this differs from Rogers, since the purpose of education is regarded here as being to bring about learning, and the development of the individual should be viewed as an additional bonus to be gained from participation in education. What, therefore, is the relationship between learning and teaching apparent in Table 5.1? Perhaps it may best be summarized by suggesting that both the teachers' role performance and the teaching methods they employ should never undermine, but always seek to enhance, the dignity and humanity of the learner: to do less than this is a misuse of the teachers' position, immoral and falls below the high ideals of education.

Whatever links are drawn between the conditions of learning and the approach to teaching it is clear that teachers of adults do not always stand in front of the class and expound the wisdom that they consider the students need to know (see the exercise in Rogers 1973: 82–4). This is not to claim that there is no place for didactic teaching but it does suggest an approach to teaching in which exposition is less significant than it often appears to be in the education of children; the fact that it occurs with children does not necessarily mean that it is either the most efficient or human way of facilitating their learning either! However, it is clear that the teachers of adults, besides having either the relevant knowledge or experience, require certain other characteristics in order to help adults learn, including: knowledge of the educational process, appropriate philosophy and attitudes and teaching and personal skills. Hence, it is rather surprising that the preparation of educators of adults has occupied such an insignificant place in teacher education; but, since this is the topic of a subsequent chapter, no further reference will be made to it here.

Table 5.1 has not stipulated how teachers should perform their teaching role with adults but it does imply that certain styles of teaching may be more appropriate than others. In most courses preparing individuals to become teachers of adults, considerable emphasis is placed upon the variety of methods with which teachers should be familiar but much less is placed upon teaching styles. Perhaps this is a major omission from teacher training since the style that the teacher adopts may play a considerable part in the outcome of the learning. For instance, teachers may say that they are facilitative but their style might actually communicate that they expect learners to reach the outcome that they would have been taught had the session been didactic!

Perhaps the most significant piece of research that has affected thought about teaching styles is that developed by Lippett and White (1958) in a project directed by Kurt Lewin in the 1930s. They examined leadership styles of youth leaders in youth clubs with 10-year-old boys in the United States. Basically they noticed three styles of leadership: authoritarian, democratic and *laissez-faire* and discovered that group behaviour tended to be consistent with leadership style. They found that: the authoritarian leaders create a sense of group dependence on the leader, that their presence held the group together and that in their absence there was no work undertaken and the group disintegrates; the *laissez-faire* leadership results in little being done irrespective of whether the leader was present or absent; the democratic leaders achieve group cohesion and harmonious working rleationships whether or not they are actually present. However, there are a number of problems in applying these findings to adult groups, or indeed to any other teaching and learning interactions: the subjects were children; the location was a youth club; the task undertaken by the groups was a specific type of craft work. Even so, it may not be without significance that the democratic style of leadership achieved the types of results that it did.

In more recent years, and perhaps more significantly for educators of adults, McGregor's (1960) work has assumed greater importance. This stems from the field of management studies. According to McGregor, there are basically two approaches to managing people which he terms Theory X and Theory Y: the former assumes that the average human being dislikes work, needs to be controlled, directed or coerced in order to do what is required and that he prefers to be directed; the latter commences with the conception of the self-motivated adult who seeks to fulfil his own human potential. Hence, if teachers start with the perspective of Theory X they will seek to manipulate the students either by a hard approach of threats or a soft approach of rewards and permissiveness; but teachers who adopt a perspective that derives from Theory Y will be more concerned about the potentiality and growth of the students even though they may vary their approach and teaching method to suit the situation.

Hence, it is evident that the democratic approach in the research of Lippett and White and the Theory Y perspective in McGregor's work are most consistent with the philosophy of this study and with the emerging picture of the educator of adults as one who seeks to aid adult learning and to develop the full potential of the learner. However, it must be borne in mind that neither of these approaches actually prescribe the manner in which teachers should perform their role, although it does circumscribe the number of approaches that might be utilized. Perhaps Kidd summarized this perspective most clearly when he, recognizing that there are differences, pronounced his own decalogue for teachers of adults:

1. Thou shalt never try to make another human being exactly like thyself; one is enough.
2. Thou shalt never judge a person's need, or refuse your consideration, solely because of the trouble he causes.
3. Thou shalt not blame heredity nor the environment in general; people can surmount their environment (or perhaps some of their heredity) [author's addition].
4. Thou shalt never give a person up as hopeless or cast him out.
5. Thou shalt try to help everyone become, on the one hand, sensitive and compassionate and also tough minded.
6. Thou shalt not steal from any person his rightful responsibilities for determining his own conduct and the consequences thereof.
7. Thou shalt honour anyone engaged in the pursuit of learning and serve well and extend the discipline of knowledge and skill about learning which is our common heritage.
8. Thou shalt have no universal remedies nor expect miracles.
9. Thou shalt cherish a sense of humour which may save you from becoming shocked, depressed or complacent.
10. Thou shalt remember the sacredness and dignity of thy calling and, at the same time, 'thou shalt not take thyself too damned seriously'.

(Kidd 1973: 306–7)

Roby Kidd's creed summarizes much of the humanistic philosophy explicit in this discussion. Having examined some of the approaches to teaching, it is now necessary to explore the teaching process.

THE PROCESS OF TEACHING

In contrast to initial education, adult education has tended to emphasize the learner and learning more than the teacher and teaching. Traditionally, in initial education teachers and their skills have constituted a subject for discussion but rarely has that discussion sought to elaborate upon the process of teaching. Adult education has tended to regard the teacher as an adjunct to learning, often necessary and frequently important, but never as essential to it. Consequently, the process of adult learning has been explored but rarely that of adult teaching. Hence the focus of this section is upon the teaching process in adult and continuing education. Three types of teaching were mentioned earlier – didactic, socratic and facilitative – and it is necessary to recognize that they do have totally different approaches. Initially, therefore, an oversimplified model of didactic teaching is discussed. Thereafter, the socratic approach is mentioned and then the teacher-centred teaching process is combined with the learning cycle. Finally, the facilitative approach to teaching is discussed.

Didactic teaching

Teaching has traditionally been regarded as the process of making a selection of knowledge, skills, etc. from the cultural milieu, those aspects which 'it is intended that pupils should learn' (Hirst and Peters 19760: 80), and transmitting it to them by the use of some skilled technique. It has been assumed that such rewards as the teacher's approval, good grades in assignments and succession examinations (all forms of conditioning) would ensure that the pupil learned and was, therefore, able to reproduce that selection of culture thereafter.

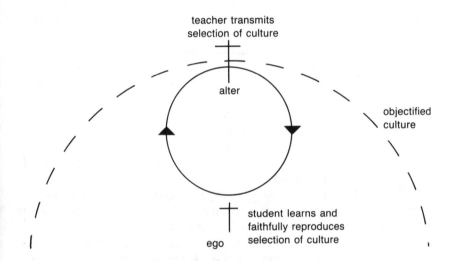

Figure 5.1 A stereotypical picture of teaching

Figure 5.1, which is very similar to Figure 3.1, locates the teaching process in the wider socio-cultural milieu and it may be seen that the teacher is the agency of transmission of a selection of culture (a curriculum). That selection may have been made by an examination board, an education committee of a profession, or an acknowledged expert in the field. The student is expected to learn that which is transmitted and to be able to reproduce it, which may equate with the lower order of Gagné's (1977) hierarchy of learning but it is certainly no higher than the middle. In terms of Bloom's (1956) taxonomy of educational objectives, the student may be expected to have understood what was transmitted and, perhaps, be able to apply it but not necessarily to be able to analyse, synthesize or evaluate it. In university education, however, it might be argued that expectations are higher than this, but Hegarty suggests that legal education may 'easily degenerate into mindless book learning . . . any student of university calibre could obtain a comfortable honours degree by doing little more than memorising the set text book in each subject and doing the occasional problem' (1976: 81). The extent to which Hegarty's assessment is applicable to all undergraduate courses is another matter, but it is doubtful if that assessment of legal education would be unique.

Not only does the level of learning not necessarily scale the heights of the learning hierarchies but the selection of what is to be learned is made by agencies other than the learner, so that the relevance to the learner of what is learned may often be reduced to the rather instrumental end of being successful in the assessment procedures, rather than being able to learn and understand something relevant to the learner. This approach frequently results in the reproduction of the status quo and while it could be argued that this is no bad thing in initial education, it is much less convincing in the education of adults.

Is there, then, no place for didactic teaching in the education of adults? Such a claim would be too sweeping, but perhaps its place is less significant than it is generally accorded to be. An exposition can actually transmit knowledge and the students may be encouraged to consider the validity of what has been presented to them; may actually provoke them to think; may facilitate learning; may motivate them to continue their learning, especially if it is superbly presented. Hence a didactic approach may prove very useful, especially if the students are encouraged to analyse what is transmitted to them, rather than merely to reproduce it.

In the past decade, as the theory of the education of adults has developed, vocational education has assumed a greater relevance and it would be fair to see that training might be regarded by some as a form of didactic teaching although many industrial trainers would claim, quite correctly, that they employ a variety of teaching and learning methods. However, didacticism is the traditional image of training and it has to be acknowledged that in many instances employers are only interested in their employees acquiring specific knowledge and skills, which has often resulted in this image. Studies, such as Marsick (1987) and Casner-Lotto and Associates (1988), demonstrate the variety of approaches used in work place learning, which would certainly deny this traditional image.

A variation on this theme is for teachers to encourage the learners to ask questions, so that they actually initiate the learning process but the teachers still provide the answers. By adopting this approach teachers overcome one of the initial problems of didactic teaching, that it may not start from a diagnostic basis. Yet it is the teachers who still transmit knowledge and expect it to be received and learned by the students who are still the receptacles of knowledge, rather than the 'creators' of it. Frequently during the education of adults, students ask questions that teachers are unable to answer, so that they discover that they can confess their ignorance without losing credibility. Indeed, it is possible to argue that a display of fallibility may help to establish the teacher's position in the group, both as a teacher and as a human being. After all, why should the teacher know everything? No other profession expects its members to be omniscient! Many conscientious teachers, having admitted that they are unable to respond to the question, ask the class if anybody in it is able to answer. Here the experience and expertise of the group can be put to good use and teachers can learn from the class as well as contribute to the class learning. However, many very conscientious teachers, when confronted with a question that they cannot answer, tell the group that they will go and find out the answer. This they do, and they inform the students on a future occasion. A certain irony emerges in this situation: the student's question has revealed a teacher's ignorance. The teacher is made aware of a learning need and goes and learns in order to provide the students with an answer. Examine closely what has occurred. The student's question facilitated the teacher's learning! But what did the teacher do for the student's learning? The teacher merely made the students more dependent, but the teacher actually became a more independent learner. Two points emerge from this: firstly, perhaps the teacher should encourage the students to seek an answer as well; secondly, it is the questioning process that facilitates independent learning and so, perhaps, a good teacher leads students from question to question rather than from answer to answer. After all, that is how the learning need becomes apparent in children, as it has been argued in earlier chapters, and it is also a way that effective learning may be facilitated with adults.

Socratic teaching

This method incorporates questioning into the teaching and learning process; it consists of the teacher directing a logical sequence of questions at the learners, so that they are enabled to respond and to express the knowledge that they have, albeit implicitly, but which they have never crystallized in their own mind. However, unless the teacher is actually skilful in the use of questions and also perceptive in responding to the students, this approach is still likely to result in an expression of knowledge reflecting the accepted body of cultural knowledge and, therefore, a type of conformity. The reason for this is that the method assumes that the learners have internalized a great deal of cultural knowledge during their socialization, which itself is a conformity producing process. Questioners ask questions in order to assist learners crystallize and express ideas and knowledge which they may have implicitly internalized but which they may never have formulated nor articulated; it is, therefore, partly a formalization of the externalizaiton process, depicted in Figure 1.2. However, conformity to and expression of the established body of knowledge is by no means wrong, and thus it is a useful method to employ, especially in teaching adults since it utilizes both their store of knowledge and their experience of life, which are quite essential learning resources in the education of adults. However, it must also be noted that if this method is used with great skill it can and does help the learners 'create' rather than reproduce knowledge. Another advantage to its use is that the learners are always actively involved in the learning process.

A learning and teaching cycle

The above discussion indicates that the teacher often plays the role of an agent in the transmission of the culture of a society in the formal educational process, even in the education of adults. However, it is clear that Figure 5.1 does not really discuss the actual process of teaching and learning, so that it is now important to draw together some of the conclusions about adult learning and these observations on teacher-centred teaching. Figure 5.2 suggests a learning and teaching cycle in which these are combined.

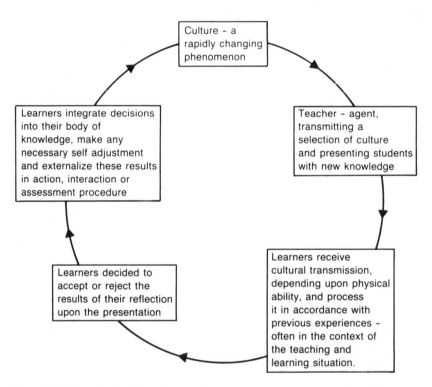

Figure 5.2 A learning and teaching cycle

It may be seen in Figure 5.2 that the teacher is an agent transmitting a selection of culture to the learner(s) and, at the same time, the teacher may have devised methods whereby the student may have opportunity to reflect upon it through discussion group, tutorial or written assignment, etc. Thus the process of reflection may be regarded as an integral part of the learning and teaching cycle. However, it must be borne in mind that unless the opportunity for reflection on the knowledge and ideas that are presented by the teacher occurs individually, the decision that a person may be influenced by the dynamics of the learning group and considerable research exists to show that group pressure results in conformity in many situations (e.g. Krech, Crutchfield and Ballachey 1962: 507–15).

However, the process of selecting that aspect of culture to be transmitted is itself an important one, but it is sometimes omitted as a phase in these considerations. Some teachers merely take for granted that they will seek to transmit all the knowledge, etc. that the examination board of syllabus specifies. Yet if teachers see themselves as agents for the transmission of cultural knowledge, it may be that they should become more active agents in deciding what they should transmit and that this should also be determined by the amount of knowledge and understanding that the student brings to the teaching and learning situation. It is, therefore, incumbent upon the teacher to diagnose the students' level of knowledge and, thereby, their learning needs, before actually endeavouring to teach anything at all. Diagnosis is, consequently, an intrinsic element in the selection of knowledge to be transmitted and this is especially significant with adults since they bring to their learning a considerable amount of previous knowledge and skill, etc. That adults do bring such resources to their learning has led some adult educators to regard themselves as facilitators of learning rather than teachers in the traditional sense discussed here.

Facilitative teaching

Teachers of adults may not always want to employ teacher-centred techniques in the performance of their role but they may wish to be more student-centred. They may seek to create an awareness of a specific learning need in the student; to confront a student, or students, with a problem requiring a solution; to provide the student(s) with an experience and encourage reflection upon it. In all of these instances the outcome of the activity should be that learning has occurred, but teachers have performed their role differently: they have facilitated learning. Hence, it is possible to reconstruct the experiential learning cycle discussed in the third chapter in order to incorporate the teacher's role in the process.

It may be seen from Figure 5.3 that teachers can create the situation in which the learning cycle is activated and, additionally, they may help in the process of observing or reflecting. But should they actually influence the process in this way? Dewey suggests that, with children, the teacher should be involved:

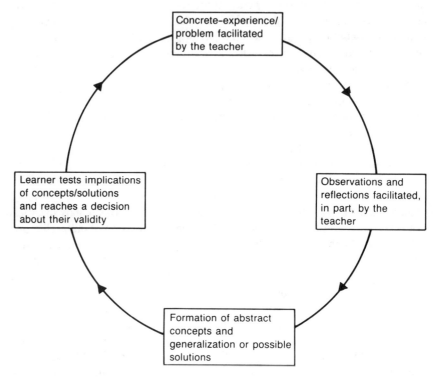

Figure 5.3 A facilitative learning and teaching cycle

Sometimes teachers seem to be afraid even to make suggestions to members of the group as to what they should do. I have heard of cases in which children are surrounded with objects and materials and then left entirely to themselves, the teacher being loath to suggest even what might be done with the materials lest freedom be impinged upon.

(Dewey 1938: 71)

Dewey goes on to warn of the opposite extreme: of teachers who abuse their office and who channel children's work along the paths that suit the teachers' purposes rather than those of the children themselves. He maintains that teachers should be intelligently aware of the capacities, needs and past experiences of those under instruction, so that they may assist them in creating a cooperative learning exercise. Obviously Dewey was writing about children learning in a progressive educational environment but the same observations are relevant to the education of adults. Indeed, it might be recalled that McKenzie (1979) recognized the similarities between progressive education and andragogy.

Thus it may be seen that the teacher's role may be that of facilitator and/or guide, but not in this instance that of the director of the learning process, since that would detract from the adult's own autonomy and independence. (See Williams 1980 for a practical outworking of some of the ideas presented here, but see Jarvis 1992 for a discussion about the concepts of self-direction and autonomy.) Thus the facilitator is one who assists in the student's learning, even to the extent of providing or creating the environment in which that learning may occur, but is never one who dictates the outcome of the experience. Consequently, it would be impossible for a facilitator to set behavioural objectives for any learning experience that may be created, although they should be expressive ones. Because the learning experience is open-ended, facilitation is often a difficult role to play since the learners may reach conclusions other than those held by facilitators but they should not seek to impose their opinions on the learners.

It should be noted in Figures 5.2 and 5.3 that the teacher has a role in the early stages of the teaching and learning cycle but that, since the teacher cannot make any individual learn and since one of the aims of adult education is the creation of the autonomous learner, the teacher plays little part in the final stages. Even in distance learning, where adults meet with a tutor for an occasional tutorial after having learned from the teaching material, the teaching and learning cycle is only recreated with the students bringing more of their own learning from the initial stages. However, it might be objected that even in these two diagrams the teacher's involvement in the learning process, even as facilitator, inhibits the student's freedom to learn. But, it may be asked, what is freedom in this context? Boud and Bridge (1974: 6), for instance, distinguish four types of freedom: pace, choice, method and content. By this they mean that students should be free to work at their own speed, choose to study particular aspects of a course, adopt whatever learning style suits them best and be free to choose what to learn. More recently, Boud, Bridge and Willoughby (1975: 18) modified this slightly and they suggest that the four types of freedom are: pace, method, content and assessment. The extent to which any of these is achievable in any institutionalized course of study is open to severe question; the expectations of the educational organization and the influence of the teacher are never completely overcome. It is doubtful whether there can be complete freedom in any type of institutionalized learning – see Candy (1991) and Jarvis (1992) for a full discussion.

Clearly the traditional teaching role does not seem to fit easily into the teaching and learning process for adults if these freedoms are considered an important element in it and class teaching seems to recede into the background. Indeed, one of the outcomes appears to be an individualized or small group approach in which the participants are engaged in the pursuit of knowledge that is relevant to their own problems or experiences. Certainly, the class as a whole is perhaps a little less significant in this approach; small group learning is frequently undertaken in adult education and individualized learning has been developed in both adult basic education and in higher education. Considerable research has been conducted into individualized learning and although it appears to have an idealistic perspective, Crane notes that:

> Unexpectedly perhaps, in view of the persuasive role played by committed Romantics in decrying the old and urging a renewed concern for the individual and individual differences, it was largely men with behaviourist training and outlook who actually produced innovations of value.
>
> (Crane 1982: 33)

Certainly the group/class versus the individual is one of the problems that emerges logically from any analysis of this type of teaching and learning. Students' learning should be regarded as their own, so the teaching and learning cycle must ultimately relate to the individual, although this does not preclude the teacher interacting with the learner(s) during the learning.

The focus of this section has been upon the teaching process and three types of teaching have been discussed: didactic, socratic and facilitative. These may be seen as being either teacher-centred or student-centred and it has been suggested that those approaches that are extremely teacher-centred may be inappropriate for some education of adults. Both of these approaches emphasize the individualistic, either the teacher or the learner, and while the following section on the specific types of method will follow this distinction, it must be remembered that the actual process is one of relationship so that it might actually be necessary to reconceptualize the teaching and learning process as one which is ultimately relationship based.

TEACHING METHODS

It is impossible in the space available in this section to elaborate adequately upon every aspect of each teaching method that can be employed in the education of adults, so it is intended only to highlight the variety of approaches that can be used. Since there is such a wide range of different methods it is initially necessary to classify them for the purposes of discussion. Chadwick (personal communication) has suggested that one approach would be to consider the three modes of search, interactive and presentational. While this is a very attractive form of classification, it might be more consistent here if the division between tutor-centred and student-centred approaches is maintained. However, it must be borne in mind that a variety of methods might be employed in any single teaching and learning process and that it might be more stimulating to the learner if such an approach were to be adopted.

Teacher-centred methods

Before individual methods are itemized, it is necessary to recognize that tutors may lead a session and still adopt two basically different approaches: be didactic and teach the subject in the traditional method of providing the information, or be socratic and seek to elicit the information from the students by careful questioning. The art of questioning is a technique that teachers should acquire, so that they are aware of how to gain the most effective response from the learners; but, frequently, it appears to be assumed that this is a skill that teachers have either naturally or as a result of their socialization process. However, this assumption may be false and it may be a skill that needs to be taught.

Seven frequently employed teacher-centred methods are discussed in this sub-section: demonstration, guided discussion, controlled discussion, lecture-discussion, lecture/talk/speech, mentoring and the tutorial.

The demonstration

This is one of the most frequent approaches to skills teaching. The teacher shows the student(s) how a specific procedure is undertaken and then they are expected to emulate the teacher. However, the demonstrator is usually very skilled so that the performance appears easy and effortless. But if the students are unable to repeat the same skill with the same fluency they may become discouraged. Perhaps this is because teachers may not have analysed their own techniques sufficiently in order to be aware of all the minutiae of correct procedures that combine to produce effortless action.

In addition, they may have acquired tacit knowledge (Polyani 1967) which they cannot articulate. Practical knowledge is extremely complex and Nyiri, for instance, suggests that it has to be 'mined out of their heads painstakingly, one jewel at a time' (1988: 21). (See also Baskett and Marsick 1992 for an edited volume which endeavours to outline a number of these significant issues.) Belbin and Belbin (1972: 44–5) suggest that if a skill is broken down into a number of discrete stages and that in both the demonstration and in the subsequent practice sessions each sequence is initially performed slowly, it is possible for learners to acquire new skills fairly rapidly. They recognize that 'it takes time for someone who hitherto has been pressed toward greater speed, to accept that a really slow performance is . . . required' (ibid.).

Additionally, it needs to be recognized that there is a possible danger in teachers being seen as role models transmitting their own imperfect skills to their students which could prevent them learning even better ways because they may not have the opportunity to be exposed to an even more accurate performance of the skill that they are endeavouring to acquire.

Guided discussion

This approach has been separated from the more general discussion techniques because it is one of the approaches that epitomizes the socratic method: it is sometimes called step-by-step discussion. In this approach the teacher has a carefully prepared sequence of questions that are directed towards the end of drawing from the learners the knowledge that they have implicitly but which they may not have articulated, crystallized or related to a wider theoretical perspective. It is a method that can be employed to elicit from students their own understanding of experiences that they have undergone. For instance, a teacher of theory may endeavour to draw from the students their understanding of some elements of a practical work experience in which they have already participated as part of their vocational education. However, the teacher should be careful not to artificialize the approach by being inflexible, since the students' responses may actually direct the discussion along paths other than those planned by the teacher. If this is so, it might be wise for the teacher to follow the students' lead and redirect the questions, although it must be borne in mind that there are times when the teacher has to ensure that the steps prepared should be followed. While this method sometimes appears simple and easy to prepare, it is one that requires confidence in the teacher as well as a great deal of knowledge and preparation.

Controlled discussion

By contrast to guided discussion, controlled discussion is quite didactic and much closer to the next method to be examined. In this approach the teacher sets the theme for the class and begins to talk about it, but the students are encouraged to contribute to the learning process or to elicit information. However, the teacher is still at the centre of the scene to whom most of the questions or comments are directed. One of the problems in this approach is that there is a tendency for only the dominant or the confident to interject so that the learning needs of the silent members of the group may not be met. If teachers want the learners to address each other they must ensure that the environment is arranged so that there is no dominant seat etc. and that the learners have eye-contact with each other. Hence, the seating must be arranged in a circular formation (with or without desks). It is difficut sometimes for teachers to change the seating arrangements of a room, especially if they arrive after many of the students, and so it is often wise to ask a caretaker to have the room arranged in the required manner in advance. If this is impossible, it is useful to explain to adult students why the room should be rearranged and, in the majority of instances, they will undertake the task themselves.

Lecture-discussion

The lecture-discussion is very similar to the previous method mentioned but it may assume a different form: a short lecture/address followed by discussion. Once again, however, it is self-evident that the teacher controls both the learning process and its content. By contrast to the previous method, the teacher has a larger initial input rather than merely focusing on the topic to be discussed, so the discussion may tend to develop or to endeavour to demonstate the weaknesses in the position taken in the lecture. It is worth remembering that unless the content of the lecture is controversial or provocative then the discussion may not be particularly valuable since it may merely rehearse the arguments previously presented.

All forms of discussion require careful preparation on the part of the teacher and a willingness to endure silence by the class especially during the early part of the discussion. It is a common failing to try to prompt the class to talk by too much early tutor intervention. Confident and talkative adults are, consequently, useful allies during early phases of a discussion session but then it may be necessary for the teacher to draw other people into the debate and help the talkative members of the group to contribute a little less. It is, however, part of the human process that the teacher should facilitate both of these aspects without injuring the self-esteem of any of the class members, so that it is often unwise even to ask individuals directly either to participate or to contribute a little less to the discussion. Hence, the social skills of the teacher are as important to the teaching and learning process as are knowledge and teaching techniques (Legge 1971a).

Lecture

Lecturing is perhaps the most frequently employed teaching technique despite all the criticisms that have been levelled against it at various times. Bergevin *et al.* define the speech, or lecture, as 'a carefully prepared oral presentation of a subject by a qualified person' (1963: 157). However, many students know to their cost that lectures are not necessarily carefully prepared on all occasions prior to delivery, nor is the presentation always given by a qualified person. Hence, this is more of a description of an ideal type rather than a definition of the lecture, so that it may be more accurately defined as 'an oral presentation of a subject', although this still leaves the definition of 'subject' open to question. Thus far the distinction between lecture, speech and talk has not been raised but it is significant to note that Beard (1976) discusses the lecture in her work on higher education but neither Bergevin *et al.* (1963) nor Legge (1971a) concentrate upon it a great deal, preferring to use the other terms, and they are more concerned with teaching adults. This reflects a little of the conceptual problems of the second chapter, but higher education has traditionally been discussed separately to the education of adults, despite the fact that students in higher education are adults. It is maintained here that this separation has been to the detriment of higher education. Bergevin *et al.* clearly regard the speech as a rather formal presentation while Legge's orientation towards non-examinable liberal adult education enables him to focus upon the less formal concept of the 'talk'.

Many criticisms have been levelled at this particular approach to teaching but, despite these, nearly all teachers continue to use the lecture method. Perhaps it is important to put the lecture in perspective and Bligh summarizes the research on this topic when he argues that:

(1) with the exception of programmed learning, the lecture is as effective as any other method of transmitting information, but not more effective;
(2) most lectures are not as effective as more active methods for the

promotion of thought; and (3) changing student attitudes should not normally be the major objective of the lecture.

(Bligh 1971: 4)

Thus it may be seen that only in the transmission of information is the lecture as effective as other methods of teaching and then it must be borne in mind that most of this research was not conducted with adult students. However, Davies (1971: 163) claims that the lecture is a useful teaching method with less able adult students. Yet adult basic education has tended not to employ the lecture approach in teaching, so that this raises questions about his claim. Hence, it is necessary to pursue this point because if the lecture is no more effective than a variety of other teaching techniques, why is it so frequently employed? This question certainly requires consideration at this point in the discussion.

It might be argued that since many educators of adults are not actually trained to perform the teaching role they do not have evidence of the effectiveness of other approaches, or that they do not know how to teach apart from the lecture, or that they do not have the confidence to attempt other approaches. This may be an argument for introducing more teacher training into the education of adults, a point that will be developed in a subesquent chapter. Additionally, it is clear that because students are familiar with this approach to teaching, or because it means that some of them may be passive learners, they prefer this approach. But these may be quite superficial and even wrong reasons: students may put pressure on a teacher to give a lecture because they may not want to reveal their level of knowledge or understanding of a topic and they may feel threatened if they think that their lack of comprehension will become apparent for others to see. Teachers, or at least some tutors, may also obtain satisfaction from having given a 'good' performance, as they may simply like it because it enables them to control the content of the session in such a way as to ensure that any gaps in their own knowledge may not become apparent, which might occur if the students directed the session. The maxim 'if you don't know a subject well lecture it' is perhaps a reflection of a teacher's sense of insecurity, especially before a class of adults. Programme planners also like the lecture method because of the ease of timetabling and room planning.

In addition, it might be argued that the lecture can be an instrument of motivation and it may be true that the superb lecture may actually produce this result; but, perhaps, few teachers actually possess such oratorial skills, and so Legge's ironic comment that 'the really hopeless teacher, i.e. the one who fails to communicate at all, drives the good student to the library to do the work for himself' (1971: 57) may be closer to the real situation! Lectures, it has been claimed (e.g. Beard 1976: 101; Legge 1971a), may be economical in teaching many students at the same time and ensuring that the whole syllabus is covered. While there may be some truth in these claims, it must be recognized that covering the syllabus without ensuring that the students learn it is far from efficient (Bligh 1971: 3) and, since there is evidence to show that the level of concentration varies at different phases of the lecture (Legge 1971a), it is difficult to ensure that learning actually occurs during the presentation. Additionally, individual learning needs may not be catered for and unless the learners have an opportunity to question the lecturer they may never actually interact with the speaker. Even if they are provided with the time to raise queries, individual students may not do so because they may not wish to reveal their ignorance or to hinder the remainder of the group. If a student does interrupt the speaker with questions, the rest of the class may become frustrated while these are answered. This is a dilemma that is intrinsic to the lecture method and it appears to have no resolution that would result in effective learning from every participant. The lecturer may seek to resolve the problems by not taking any questions but this may result in reduced learning efficiency. But even if questions occur they may interrupt the thought processes of other learners, who may then lose the flow of ideas with which they were grappling. Thus it may be seen that many unresolved problems surround this approach.

Where the lecture method is employed there are a number of errors in techniques that should be avoided: the conscientious lecturer may prepare too much material for the time available but still endeavour to complete the self-appointed task by speeding up the presentation, so that he/she actually delivers all the content but to the detriment of the learner. Hence, out of the best intentions the lecturer may hinder rather than help learning. Additionally, the lecturer may be bound to notes, even to reading them, so that little eye-contact is achieved with the class which results in the teacher being unable to detect and respond to any of the students' manifest learning needs. Hence, it may be wise for teachers to reduce the volume of notes, even to headings, sub-headings and references, in order to ensure that they have both contact and fluency of delivery. In a similar manner teachers may wish to illustrate a point by writing on the blackboard, but if they continue to speak whilst they have their back to the class some adult learners, especially those with deficient hearing, may be unable to follow every word. This is also true when a lecturer, who is not bound to notes, wanders around the room while speaking. Since the lecture has to be prepared before its presentation, it may not always be sufficiently appropriate or relevant to the learning needs of all the students and it may prove difficult for the lecturer to adjust the content of the presentation to the needs of the learners during the actual lecture.

Finally, the lecture may not provide sufficient opportunity for the adult students to remember and internalize all the ideas presented, neither may they always have the opportunity to reflect upon the knowledge transmitted after the presentation. Hence, it is useful to provide the opportunity for group discussion or question and answer during the session, or for a handout to be distributed at the end of the session, in order to help adult students memorize ideas etc. Other forms of audio-visual stimuli may also be useful in helping students to recall the information and ideas with which they have been presented.

Having raised a number of critical points about the lecture, it must still be recognized that it is a useful teaching tool, especially when it is well used, but only for the transmission of knowledge. However, it should perhaps be employed a little less frequently than it is at present and used only by those trained in its use rather than its being the basic technique used by those who are employed to transmit ideas to others.

Mentoring

There are different interpretations of mentoring although it is clearly a significant teaching method in contemporary education and training.

In his excellent book on mentoring Daloz (1986: 215–35) suggests some of the major things that good mentors do in the situations of mentoring adult students: support, challenge and provide a vision. Each of these is sub-divided into a number of different functions:

Support – listening, providing structure, expressing positive expectations, sharing ourselves, making it special.

Challenge – setting tasks, engaging in discussion, heating up dichotomies, constructing hypotheses, setting high standards.

Vision – modelling, keeping tradition, offering a map, suggesting new language, providing a mirror.

In a sense, in these instances, the role of the mentor is to help the protégés to reflect on their practice, to learn from their experiences and to improve so that they might gain more expertise. In mentoring, this is done through an in-depth relationship, a primary experience. Indeed, it is the relationship that makes mentorship so important – not just to professional practice but to life itself. It is here that the mentor gains from the relationship – but the mentee should gain as much.

Murray (1991: 5), however, points out that there are two schools of thought about mentoring: one suggests that it can be structured or facilitated, while the other maintains that it can only happen when the 'chemistry' between the two people is right. However, these are not automatically exclusive, since a facilitated relationship might actually develop into one where the chemistry appears to be right for the relationship to continue and to deepen. Clearly, in education and training, structured or facilitated mentoring is called for; but this is not something that can just be turned on and off with the passing of every two-month module etc. This has already been discovered in nursing when, as Barlow (1991) reports, short-term mentorship did not seem appropriate for clinical practice with students. Indeed, these mentors were often new staff nurses who would no doubt have benefited from being mentored themselves.

During studentship, however, some form of mentor role might be performed by the personal tutor, especially one who is acknowledged to be concerned about excellence in practice. Mentorship might also be facilitated for junior qualified staff, in the way that Murray indicates. She records a top level executive as saying:

> I'm always mentoring, both formally and informally. My role is to help my subordinates make decisions. I let them bounce ideas off me and I give my input. But ultimately, I want them to make decisions. If I were making all the decisions for them, I wouldn't need them, would I? So taking on what you call an 'additional protégé' is no great hardship for me in terms of time. It's what I do anyway.
>
> (Murray 1991: 58)

Elsewhere, she cites a mentor from AT&T Laboratories who claims that 'having a protégé from a different department helps her to bring an objectivity to the relationship that a supervisor might not have' (ibid: 61).

If the chemistry is right, however, it is the relationship which is important in mentoring – in Buber's (1959) words, it is an I–Thou relationship. But he takes it even further in his characterization of the educative relationship:

> I have characterized the relationship of the genuine educator to his pupil as being a relationship of this kind. In order to help the realisation of the best potentialities in the pupil's life, the teacher must really *mean* him as the definite person he is in his potentiality and his actuality; more precisely, he must not know him as the mere sum of qualities, strivings and inhibitions, he must be aware of him as a whole being and affirm him in his wholeness. But he can only do this if he meets him again and again as his partner in a bipolar situation.
>
> (Buber 1959: 131–2; emphasis in original)

Mentoring, then, may be seen in a variety of different ways and in all of them it is in a one-to-one situation, where the mentor seeks to assist the learners to reflect upon their practice and improve it.

The tutorial

This teaching method is more likely to occur within the formal system of education rather than in liberal adult education. However, it might be possible to classify some small classes in the latter as group tutorials. In addition, it must be remembered that in the university extension tradition a three-year course was referred to as a tutorial. But the normal use of the word refers to a teaching and learning method and, according to Davies (1971: 167–8), there are three basic types: supervision, group and practical. The first type involves a student and a tutor and the former is often expected to read a prepared piece of work to the latter and then to defend the argument in the ensuing discussion. This is quite normal practice at Oxford and Cambridge universities, but since it is labour-intensive it is not so widely practised elsewhere. Another similar use of this type of tutorial is for the student and tutor to meet after the latter has marked an assignment by the student and then the student may seek to clarify an argument or challenge the tutor's assessment grade, while the tutor may seek to explain comments, point out ways in which the work might have been improved and, even, to defend the grade that has been awarded. By contrast, group tutorials employ one tutor to a number of students. Davies (1971: 134–5), argues that the optimum number in the group depends on the ability of the tutor rather than a figure beyond which the group cannot function. Nevertheless, he suggests that six or seven is probably sufficient because of the number of possible relationships that can exist between the students. Practical tutorials may be either individual or group and are often based in a laboratory, gymnasium, work place, etc. In all of these tutorials, the tutor's role may be either didactic or socratic, although it may result in a more effective tutorial if the latter approach is adopted. Apart from teaching style, it must also be stressed that the tutorial requires a tutor who is trained and sensitive in the processes of human relations, and in the group tutorial the tutor should have some understanding of the group dynamics, or else the tutorial may fail as a teaching method.

Thus far all the teaching methods examined have been tutor-centred, but in the education of adults the tutor should play a less dominant role than that generally assumed by the teacher, so that it is now necessary to discuss these teaching methods in which the tutor also acts as facilitator.

Student-centred group methods

In this section student-centred teaching methods are considered, demonstrating throughout the discussion that since the students referred to here are adults each brings to the teaching and learning situation a vast and unique experience of life. This is a major resource, as was shown previously, since they have knowledge, reflections upon their experiences and an interpretation of meaning and purpose of life for them. Peer teaching is not, therefore, necessarily 'the blind leading the blind' as some people have claimed since it can be an approach that capitalizes on the resources of the learners themselves, although it has to be borne in mind that there may be technical knowledge etc. that none of the members of a group possesses and then the teacher may have a more didactic role. Generally, however, in student-centred teaching the teacher is a facilitator of the learning rather than a source of knowledge, and whilst responsible for creating the learning situation, teachers do not control the learning outcomes. Indeed, if they ever do this, they may actually be involved in indoctrination rather than education.

There are many different methods of teaching that might have been incorporated in this section but to discuss them all in detail would require a whole book, so fifteen different approaches have been selected here because they are frequently used, or have the potential for future use. Even so, the list does not purport to be exhaustive, but it is: brainstorming; buzz-groups; debate; fishbowl; group discussion; interview, listening and observing; panel; projects and case studies; role play, simulation and gaming; seminar; snow-balling; therapy groups; visits and study tours; workshops.

Brainstorming

Bergevin *et al.* call this an 'idea inventory' (1963: 195–6). It is an intensive discussion situation in which the quantity of ideas produced, or potential solutions offered to a problem, is more important than the quality. All the points made by the participants are recorded over the period of time mutually agreed by the group for the brainstorming to operate. No group member may criticize any idea or suggested solution during this period, irrespective of how strange or ludicrous it might appear, since this might create inhibitions in the learners contributing to the inventory. At the close of the agreed period, the group is free to analyse the points raised and to arrive at a consensus, if possible, about potential courses of action or solutions to the problem under scrutiny. Clearly this approach is an aid to creative thinking in decision making or problem solving but Davies reports one study that raises questions about the effectiveness of this method since, it is claimed, the notion of expressing 'all ideas may have a deleterious effect on the group members' (1971: 170). By contrast, he reports another in which many good quality ideas were produced, suggesting that some of the claims made for it are valid. The construction of a list of ideas, or possible solutions, may be seen as the initial stage in the facilitative learning and teaching cycle (Figure 5.3) and the next phase in the process is that of observing and reflecting upon the outcome of the first one. Since this is true of many of the methods discussed in this section no further reference is made to the theoretical perspectives outlined initially.

Buzz-groups

In many ways these are similar to the previous method, but in this approach smaller groups, usually between two and six members, are used for a short period of time during the process of a lesson in order to discuss a particular item or topic. Small groups encourage participation by all members of the class, and may help in the process of reflection. It is often a useful technique to use in conjunction with a lecture, especially to help divide the session and retain student concentration.

Debate

This is a more formal approach to teaching and learning and one that is not used so frequently in adult education although it is often regarded by students in higher education as an enjoyable leisure time pursuit. Nevertheless, Legge (1971b: 87) claims that the debate is a useful method of presenting students with sharply contrasting viewpoints and demonstrating how these different opinions can be analysed and assessed. In addition, he points out that because the debate is a staged performance it provides certain protection for the point of view expressed by the participants, even though there may be quite fierce denunciation of it. Even so, Legge suggests that opinions may be modified as a result of reflecting upon the arguments presented during the performance.

Fishbowl

The object of this method is to get as many people in the group as possible to participate and discuss their views on a given subject. It can be used in a variety of settings, although it is best used when the room is large enough to have a circle of chairs sufficiently large to get all the members of the group in one compact circle. At the same time, if there are too many in the group it is not a very useful method, and so it should be restricted to classes under about twenty students, who sit in the circle. There is then a small inner circle of chairs in which the individuals involved in the discussion sit. Those who sit in the outer circle must remain silent.

The idea of this approach is to get two or three members of a class discussing a proposition and they sit in the inner circle, with the remainder in the large outer circle. Once the discussion is underway, any member of the outer circle who wishes to participate in the discussion can do so by replacing a member of the inner circle. This is usually done by touching the shoulder of one of the inner group, when that person is not speaking (!), and then taking the inner circle seat and participating in the discussion. There can be any number of moves between the inner and outer circle with individuals coming into the inner circle as many times as they wish – but when in the inner circle participants must concede their place if they are not speaking when a member of the outer group wishes to replace them.

It is possible for the teachers to join in this discussion if necessary, although it may be that teachers do so early on to encourage others to participate, although they can do so later if they wish to redirect the discussion in specific directions. It is a useful discussion tool which allows as many people to participate as wish to while everybody is sufficiently close to the process to follow the debate.

It is often useful to put a time limit on the fishbowl – say about half of the session – so that it gives time afterwards for the class to consider and write up some of the points that they have gained from the discussion. It may be useful for the group to list the main points of the discussion in some form of feedback before they write it up.

Group discussion

Discussion reoccurs on the list because it is one of the most frequently employed teaching methods in the education of adults. Many aspects of group discussion exist, all of which could have been covered separately. Bligh mentions *free-group discussion*, which he defines as 'a learning situation in which the topic and direction are controlled by the student-group' (1971: 126) and which the teacher may, or may not, observe. He suggests that this is a useful method in which attitude change may be produced in the participants. It may also enhance human relations, self-awareness and create a willingness to consider new ideas. But if the group fails to function smoothly these positive gains may not be achieved and problems of human relations etc. may arise, which the teacher should not ignore. In contrast to this, there is *problem-centred discussion*, in which the group has a task to perform which may have been set by the tutor. The outcome of this approach may be enhanced analytical thinking, ability to make decisions and to evaluate them.

Bergevin *et al.* (1963: 95) claim that a good discussion topic should meet four criteria, it must: interest all group members; be possible for participants to acquire sufficient information to discuss it meaningfully; be clearly worded and understood; suggest alternative points of view. These criteria are a useful guide since adult students may opt out of the discussion if it is not of interest or relevance to them, or if they do not think that they have anything to contribute to or learn from the discussion. Hence, it is important for the teacher to pick discussion topics with care and to do so in conjunction with the students. Although discussion groups are frequently organized in adult teaching there are a number of weaknesses in the approach: the topic may not be suitable or relevant; the end-product may not be regarded as useful; the technique relies heavily on the ability of the participants to articulate and to listen to each other; dominant personalities tend to come to the fore and quiet people remain passive. By contrast, there are a number of strengths in this method: it encourages learners to accept responsibility for their own learning; it facilitates group sharing; it assists individuals to develop a sense of teamwork; it helps people develop a sense of self-confidence. Legge claims that many 'of the weaknesses of discussion as an aid to learning . . . result from the failure of the teacher to use the method with skill and the failure of the students to take the role of good discussion group members' (1971: 78). Hence, it is incumbent upon teachers to insure that they understand the technique and are aware of group dynamics, so that they are able to help students prepare for the role that they play and to understand the reasons why this method is used in adult teaching. Perhaps teachers are less prone to inform students about why specific teaching methods are being used than they ought to be, especially since the students are adults.

Interview

The interview, sometimes called a witness session, is not employed quite so frequently within the education of adults as it might be, but it is a technique with considerable potentiality. In this instance, the resource person is the subject to be interviewed, so both the topic and often some of the questions are prepared in advance. However, it is not a scripted exercise since this would result in an artificial situation. The aim of the technique is for the interviewer to elicit information from the resource person by means of the questions that the learners want answered. Hence, the students often prepare the questions for, and submit them to, the interviewer in advance, so that the session is relevant to their interests and learning needs. This approach may help clarify issues, provide information, explore and analyse problems and even to stimulate an interest in a topic.

Advantages of the use of this method include: it helps the resource person to communicate knowledge without having to present a lecture; it helps to articulate an idea in response to direct and relevant questions; it is relatively easy to employ; it helps the less dominant members of the group because they are enabled to submit their questions before the session. It is a technique that might be used more often when visiting specialists are not trained educators, but it must be borne in mind that the resource person need not be a visitor and it might even be one of the members of the class who has specific specialist knowledge that the remainder of the group consider relevant or interesting to them. However, the interview does not allow for detailed presentation of an argument and much of the success of the session depends upon the skill of the interviewer. If the latter talks too much, is unable to modify his approach or cannot stimulate the learners, then the interview may fail through no fault of the resource person.

Listening and observing

This is a group technique which is designed to promote active listening and observing during a lecture, speech or film, etc. Each group, or each person in a group, is given a specific task to undertake, e.g. one group may be given the job of listening for bias during a lecture while another is expected to assess the relevance of the presentation for a specific category of learners. Once the presentation is complete the group members confer amongst themselves and reach decisions that are then reported back to a *plenary session*. Plenary sessions are themselves teaching and learning periods and, in some instances, they are similar to what Bergevin *et al.* (1963: 83) call a *forum*. Listening and observing has the advantages of encouraging active listening or active observation and then of helping students crystallize their ideas about the presentation, but it may have the disadvantage of the students missing other elements of the presentation because they have concentrated upon the task that they undertook to the exclusion of all else.

Panel

Like the interview the panel can utilize both the experience and expertise of visitors to the group or it may use the class members themselves. The panel may be established with a number of slightly different approaches: each member can deliver a short address to the whole group and at the end of three or four talks there can be a period of questions and answers; the panel members can discuss aloud a specific topic for a specified length of time while the class listens to their deliberations and then the class may be invited to raise questions; the discussion between panel members might occupy the whole time; a panel might be set up merely to respond to the questions of the class, without an initial input or stimulus, but, in this instance, a considerable amount of preparation is necessary beforehand in order to ensure that the questions are forthcoming. The panel technique may be utilized in order to present opposing views on a topic and to create a wider understanding of the subject. As a method, it is useful in stimulating interest and demonstrating to a class the validity of opposing perspectives. By contrast, it has a number of difficulties: the chair needs to be proficient in the arts of chairing if the session is to be successful; the class might have to undertake considerable preparation beforehand in order to familiarize themselves with the complexities of some of the arguments; class members should have sufficient confidence to pose questions, since there is a tendency to consider that students' queries are not worthy of an expert's consideration. However, if these problems can be surmounted successfully the panel session can be both a stimulating and relevant teaching and learning method.

Projects and case studies

While these approaches are frequently employed in the education of adults, it is widely recognized that they are difficult techniques to use in courses which are assessed, since grades are generally awarded to individuals. Yet they do incorporate the highest level in Gagné's hierarchy of learning, so they are techniques that should be encouraged. There are some notable examples in liberal adult education of group projects. Coates and Silburn (1967) conducted, with their class, a sociological study of a deprived area of Nottingham and after three years of research they had gathered enough data to write a book that was subsequently published. During the course of the project the students gained considerable knowledge of the discipline, of the area of Nottingham in which the research was conducted, of the social and political processes of society and of research methods. Such approaches do not have to be restricted to the social sciences for it would be just as possible to undertake such work with the environmental, health and natural sciences. Fletcher (1980) regards community studies, such as that conducted by Coates and Silburn, as a form of practical adult education, but it must be recognized that if a class makes discoveries about a community it might want to use the results in an active manner thereafter. Tutors mounting such project type courses should be aware before they commence that this is a possible outcome of studies of this nature. Case studies are very similar to group projects but the group may seek to focus upon a specific phenomenon and in this instance it may incorporate a multi-discipline perspective. Group projects and case studies can, therefore, assume an exciting and innovative ethos, in which the class learn by doing and then use the results in a practical manner. However, the attrition rate from such classes may be greater than average, especially if the activity becomes politically orientated in the community; but more research into this is necessary.

Role play, simulation and gaming

These are other approaches to teaching in which the student group actively participates and they are included together in this section because of their similarities but discussed separately for the sake of convenience.

Role play is similar to psychodrama and socio-drama but it has educational rather than therapeutic aims. It can be employed when a tutor wishes students to experience something about which they are cognitively aware. However, it must be recognized at the outset that it is an approach that has difficulties, so it should not be used carelessly or thoughtlessly. It should be used naturally and students should feel that what they are doing fits logically into a planned learning sequence. Rogers and Lovell state that it 'often makes for a smooth, easy introduction to the techniques if at first role playing is done by the teacher' (Rogers 1973: 78), so the students see the significance of what they are undertaking. Usually role playing is a brief episode acted from someone else's life or from the role for which an individual is being prepared. Hence, in vocational education it is possible to devise many learning situations in which role play would be a most natural method to employ, and when this has been done with adult students they are often most positive about the use of the techniques. Stock (1971: 93) suggests that role play encourages active participation, enables problems of human behaviour and relationships to be presented and extends the cognitive into the emotional. Rogers and Lovell (Rogers 1973: 77–8) also indicate that students of any ability can be involved, that this approach helps to break down social barriers in the class, motivates students to learn more, telescopes time so that a longer procedure may be enacted in a brief period, and that it may be therapeutic. Hence, it is clear that the approach has much to commend it, especially in the education of people who are socially mature enough to participate seriously and then willing to reflect and to learn from their experiences.

However, it is widely recognized that some students may feel reluctant to participate and it is wise for the teacher to leave them to respond to the situation in whatever way they wish, so that they will not feel overembarrassed by it. Additionally, the technique has other disadvantages: there are difficulties relating role play to reality in some instances; role play cannot be predicted precisely, so the learning outcomes will vary with the role players; it may be time-consuming in preparation; it is hard to evaluate its effectiveness; it may create crises in individuals to which the teacher, if not trained as a counsellor, may be unable to respond competently. However, in order to help overcome this last potential problem there should always be a period of debriefing afterwards, during which students can readjust to their normal situation; and, obviously, the more the emotional involvement demanded by the role play the greater the need for a debriefing period. Indeed, if teachers do not provide it they may discover that adult students request it. Such a period also provides an opportunity to reflect upon the experience, a stage in the facilitative teaching and learning cycle. Stock (1971: 93) also claims that role playing should not be used when the educational objectives are complex, where there is any danger that they may be obscured by the involvement and he notes that bad casting may destroy the learning situation.

Role play is often a constituent element of simulation, when the teacher may involve the students in a much more complex problem and even relate it to a future occupational role in vocational education. For instance, it is possible for trainee lecturers to simulate a complete board of examiners' meeting, so that each member of the group learns something about the process before actually having to attend a meeting in a professional capacity. However, the preparation of a simulation is extremely time-consuming and unless the simulated situation relates closely to reality the point of the exercise might be lost. Since role playing is also expected in these types of learning exercises most of the problems noted above are significant here also. In addition, since simulations involve a specific number of actors it may be difficult to involve all the students in any one exercise, so the learning experiences of participant and observer will vary. Simulation should also be followed by a period of debriefing, during which time the learning experience may be reflected upon and ideas be allowed to crystallize in the minds of the participants.

Unlike the previous two techniques, gaming may not involve role play in quite the same way, and so there might be a greater cognitive element to the initial learning experience. Since there are patterns of behaviour in human interaction and regulation in social living it is possible to design games which highlight these patterns and regulations. Because the same is true of the physical universe it is possible to learn about aspects of that through gaming techniques. Rogers and Lovell (Rogers 1973: 78) note that they are aware of a Marxist economics lecturer who gets his students to play 'Monopoly' in order to demonstrate the working of the capitalist system. Other games are appearing on the market in a variety of topics but one of the problems with educational games is that their potential sale may not be large enough to attract the volume games producers and thereby keep the price low, so that, while lecturers should be aware of the games that have been commercially produced in their own area of expertise, they might also consider producing their own. Davies (1971: 169) also points out that some business games have been produced that involve role play as well. He also notes an important fact that evaluation on the use of gaming is scarce and such a conclusion is also more true in the education of adults than it is in the education of children.

Seminar

The seminar is in complete contrast to the methods discussed above since there is usually an introductory statement or paper by one, or more, students or a visiting specialist and this forms the basis for a group discussion. The thesis of the paper should be sufficient to ensure, or provoke, discussion so that it may be controversial, provocative, topical and relevant. The method has all the advantages and disadvantages of lecture-discussion but it also results in active learning by the presenter(s) of the topic as well as passive learning by the remainder of the group who are recipients of the presentation. However, the seminar may prove to be a daunting method to students if they are to teach their peers and this may prove too off-putting to ensure success. This highlights the significant fact that this method is dependent upon the ability of the presenter to provoke discussion or else the tutor may have to intervene to ensure that the session is a useful learning experience.

'Snowballing'

This is an approach that starts with each individual learner but then becomes a group process. Initially, individuals are asked to reflect upon a task, proposition, etc. and to reach some conclusions about it. Thereafter, they are asked to work in pairs and to reflect upon their original conclusions and reach a joint conclusion. Thus each individual has the opportunity to share their own thoughts and ideas with another member of the class. When this process is complete, the pairs are asked to form groups of four and to repeat the process. There is a likelihood that all will join in the discussion, knowing that they have the support of their partner from the previous stage. Each group should then elect a rapporteur to report upon the group's collective findings in a plenary session.

Gibbs (1981) advocates this approach since, initially, the individual's own experiences are utilized and all members of the class actually participate in the process. Since this method actually assists in demolishing the barriers of interaction it is a useful method to be employed early in a course, as an ice-breaking exercise. However, there is an important point to note in this method: the timing is very significant and it is very easy to overrun, so that the plenary session is cut short. Tutors have also to beware in this type of teaching and learning session, especially when the time is restricted, that they do not seek to provide a summary of the group's reports in which they super-impose their own ideas upon them. Even so, this is a useful method which can be employed with large numbers of students and which encourages full participation by all of them.

Therapy (T) groups

This is 'a method of teaching self-awareness and interpersonal relations based upon therapeutic group techniques in which individual group members discuss their relationship with each other' (Bligh 1971: 128). This approach may be employed in sensitivity training and in developing individual self-awareness, so it can be useful in certain forms of professional education where the trainees have to learn to work closely with other people in order to practise their profession effectively. However, this approach can result in situations in which the outcome is social disharmony within the learning group that may continue for long after the learning session has been completed. Indeed it is an approach that can, unless used with professional care, be damaging to an individual's self-esteem, and so it is unwise to use it unless all the participants have consented to participate and unless there is easy access to a trained counsellor.

Visits, tours and field trips

Adult education has a long history of arranging study tours both at home and abroad and also of arranging field trips. The purpose of these has always been to provide personal experience for the learner; but it should be noted that it can also provide a common learning experience for a group and that this may become a resource for further learning activities. Not only does a visit provide a learning experience, it may also help integrate a group, so that it may be a useful technique to use early in a course – although it is also recognized that it might constitute the whole of the course. It is often necessary to have some form of debriefing session, or group discussion, in order to ensure that the learning experiences are reflected upon and shared. However, there are limitations to this approach: trips take a lot of time to organize and may be relatively expensive; they may preclude some people from participating in them, especially the handicapped or those who are extremely busy with many different activities; they may have to be organized in conjunction with another party, and thus the tutor may not be totally responsible for the arrangements of the learning activity. More recently, study tours have been organized in continuing professional education but the problems of organization are exacerbated when the applicants for the course have to gain study leave, paid or unpaid, in order to participate.

Workshops

The final method to be examined in this section is the workshop, which has similarities to the project and case study method. Here a group of students are encouraged to apply theory to practice in some area of their interest or occupation. Students may actually design their own working programme or else they may participate in one devised by a tutor. In the workshop situation, students are enabled to undertake a piece of work, either individually or in groups, and the product of the exercise may be subjected to the critical scrutiny of the class for dicussion and appraisal. The end-product of such a workshop may be improved skills, a product useful to professional practice, or, merely, additional learning. This approach can be employed in liberal adult education and recently one branch of the Workers Educational Association offered a workshop on Robert Tressell. No tutor was present although the local tutor-organizer acted as convenor. The group which was convened not only studied his work *The Ragged Trousered Philanthropists* but went on to write about it and then proceeded to publish a book on the subject entitled *The Robert Tressell Papers* (WEA 1982). The group actually undertook all the production of the book, so the end-result of the workshop was a total learning experience. Hence, the workshop may be seen to provide a wide range of learning experiences and is a method that is attractive to adults, especially those who have some previous experience of a topic.

Whilst a considerable number of student-centred group methods have been examined in this section, no attempt has been made to ensure that the list is exhaustive. The main purpose has been to demonstrate that a variety of approaches exist, so that adult teaching should not always follow the same format. Additionally, a number of different methods may be employed in a single teaching session. Hence it is necessary for the teacher to be proficient in the use of a variety of methods in order to provide stimuli to the students and to enable them to learn in ways to which they are best suited. Yet, thus far, the discussion has focused only upon student-centred group methods, and so it is now necessary to examine some individual student-centred methods.

Individual student-centred methods

In contrast to the previous section, the focus in this one is the individual student and the methods that might be employed to facilitate learning. There are a variety of approaches that can be employed ranging from self-selected learning to tutor-set projects. It is proposed to discuss only eight methods in this section, chosen because of their significance to the education of adults: the assignment, computer assisted learning, contract learning, experiential, personalized systems of instruction, the practical, the personal tutorial and self-directed learning. Each is elaborated upon briefly, in the order listed above.

Assignments

Assignments are a common feature of most courses of teaching and learning and may involve, for instance, writing an essay, a case study, or a research project. In addition, assignments may have a more practical application, and students may be asked to produce a teaching aid, or some other piece of equipment relevant to their course or occupation. If more practical assignments are produced it is necessary to ensure that expert assistance is available for consultation. An advantage of encouraging students to work in media other than the written word is that adults bring to their learning their own interests and skills and these may be utilized to the benefit of the learning process. Additionally, it has to be borne in mind that the written word is only one method of communicating knowledge and it may be one which some adults have not used extensively since their initial education. At the same time, writing an assignment is perhaps the most common method by which results of research undertakings are communicated, and so adult students should seek to be proficient in the use of this medium. But the proficient use of the written word may be a skill that adults have never been taught, and so it may be necessary to diagnose adults' learning needs in the arts of writing prior to setting such assignments; and if there is a learning need tutors should help students acquire the necessary skills to undertake the task (see Sommer 1989).

Once the tutor is sure that students are able to use the written form, assignments of this nature may be set. The title of any assignment may be tutor-set, student-set, or a choice of either may be given to the group. Advantages of tutor-set assignments include: ensuring that the whole syllabus is covered and producing a standardization of grading at the end of the process. Yet grading is a subjective process, affected by many variables, including handwriting, length and style, and so it is dubious whether the latter advantage could actually be substantiated. Encouraging students to select their own topic may mean that they are more likely to choose an area relevant to either their learning needs, or interests, or both. However, there is also a tendency to choose subjects that are already known, especially if the assignment is to be graded, and this may partially defeat the object of allowing students to select their own assignment topic. Even if this disadvantage can be overcome, it is not always easy for students to select a subject which they can handle in the time or space available, so that the tutor may have to offer help to the students to get sufficient precision into their titles to enable them to do justice to their topic, within the limitations imposed upon them. Essays are perhaps the most frequently employed method, which may be because the tutors themselves were expected to write them, although projects and case studies do appear to be assuming a more important place in adult learning and teaching than they did previously. The use of these methods is significant because they enable students to follow the sequence of the learning cycle: engaging them in an analytical approach to the problem; discussing the title and its implications; collecting data to construct an argument in response to the analysis; planning a structure in which they can reveal the results of their reflections and evaluations of the data collected; showing something of the process of reflection during the sequence of the argument; reaching conclusions and testing them against the wider reality. Hence, the preparation of the written assignment is a method of learning, and setting assignments is a technique of facilitating that learning.

Usually written assignments are submitted to the tutor who marks and returns them to the student. Little training is given to tutors in marking written assignments since it is generally assumed that the tutor, as an expert in a subject, is able to assess and grade a piece of work. There are a number of problems about this assumption: that the tutor is competent to assess both the structure and content; that the completed assignment is the end-product of the learning process; that there is some objective standard against which the work is judged. Clearly some tutors do not assess the structure, only the content of the argument, even though the structure may constitute as important an element in the learning process and reveal the way in which the learners have been able to organize their thoughts and manage data. This suggests that tutors might need to be trained in the arts of marking assignments, which may be even more true when the students are adults. However, it is perhaps a totally false assumption that the completed assignment is the end-product of the learning process and it reflects the behaviourist psychology that has dominated education for so long. Many adult students do continue to reflect upon what they have written and tutors are often asked for feedback about work that they have marked. The written assignment, therefore, actually constitutes another medium through which teachers and learners engage in dialogue. Since marking may be regarded as part of that dialogue, and it is a delicate part, as the tutor may be seeking to correct misunderstandings that the adult students have acquired, it is often useful to adopt a socratic technique. Hence the tutor highlights strengths and weaknesses by means of questions, so that students are enabled to reflect upon what they have written and reach conclusions of their own, which may be more beneficial to their self-image and self-esteem than being corrected. In addition, the questions facilitate a continuing process of learning, whereas didactic comments might inhibit the learners from continuing to pursue ideas in the assignments that they have written. This is not to deny that there is a place for didactic comment, but only to claim that too much information may not be helpful, so that didacticism should play a less significant role in marking than it frequently does (Jarvis 1978). However, if grading is to be regarded as part of the teaching and learning process, perhaps the tick or the cross is the least helpful of all comments since it merely provides reinforcement, positive or negative, for what is written and, unless it is used in response to empirical fact, it suggests nothing necessarily about correctness, or otherwise – only agreement or disagreement on the part of the tutor.

Computer assisted learning

With the growth in popularity of the personalized micro-computer, it will probably not be many years before the majority of the population are familiar with its use. However, those adults who have not been familiar with the computer in their youth and who are not scientifically orientated tend to be a little overanxious about using one, so that tutors may have to introduce adult students to it gently. As the computer becomes more commonplace, so more learning packages will become available and it will be easier for educators of adults to employ this approach. Even so, the popularity of the computer might well result in more privatized learning projects, such as those discussed by Tough (1979), being undertaken; no doubt there are already a multitude of such learning activities being undertaken in Western Europe and America. Yet not all educational institutions have the facilities for adult teaching to be assisted by computer programmes, and so this approach is still in its infancy. Yet its potentiality for responding to the learning needs of students is great. Nevertheless, the lack of personalized contact with tutors may not always prove satisfying to learners, so that it does not necessarily mean that there will come a time when human teaching is redundant.

Contract learning

Knowles (1986) helped to make this approach to teaching and learning well known, as a result of his work on andragogy. Following similar principles, that adults bring a great deal of experience to learning situations, that they are highly motivated to learn and are capable of being self-directed in their learning, the idea of adult learners entering a contract with their teachers does not seem unworkable. Clearly this approach recognizes that learning is an individual process, learners have different experiences and different motivations so that classroom teaching and learning might not always be as effective and individualizing a process.

Contracts are, therefore, developed between teachers and learners spanning a variety of aspects of what is to be learned, e.g. teachers and learners may agree individually upon the aims and objectives of the learning, the resources and resource persons to be used, the date by which the learning is to be achieved and the mode by which the learners demonstrate that they have achieved the desired ends. The contract may be a written one or an informal agreement and this may depend upon whether the contract is made during a normal face-to-face course where there is frequent contact between teachers and learners, when it can be informal, or where there is less frequent contact when it may be more advisable to write the contract.

If the contract cannot be kept, it becomes the responsibility of the one who cannot keep it to renegotiate the terms with the other party so that, for instance, if students cannot achieve the desired end by the agreed date, then they take the initiative and renegotiate the contract.

It is possible to enter a contract about the grade to be awarded for a piece of work, so that the criteria for each level are agreed upon in the contract and then students demonstrate that they have met those criteria when they present their work. If the tutors do not agree then they have to demonstrate to the students why they wish either to lower or to increase the contracted grade.

In many ways this is an extremely attractive approach to teaching and learning but it is extremely time-consuming for teachers if they have big classes, more so than teaching by more traditional methods, and so they should understand the commitment that they make at the outset as well as expecting this to be understood by the students.

Experiential learning

Experiential learning is included here although it is not really a type of teaching, rather it is a whole spectrum of approaches to teaching and learning, some of which may be seen as teaching experientially. Weil and McGill (1989: 3) suggest that there are four totally different aims, values and forms of experiential learning, which they call 'villages' and these are:

- assessing and credentialling learning from life
- the basis for bringing about change in the structures, purposes and curricula of post-school education
- as a basis for raising group consciousness
- personal growth and development, increasing self-awareness and group effectiveness.

These villages demonstrate how complex is the idea of experiential learning. It should not be forgotten that many philosophers have examined this concept and a variety of major works exist on the subject, e.g. Dewey (1958), Husserl (1973), Oakeshott (1933). Oakeshott does make the point, however, that experience 'of all the words in the philosophic vocabulary, is the most difficult to manage' (1933: 9), so that it is a difficult idea to analyse, but it must be recognized that experience does point to learners' exposure to all the exigencies of life.

All learning, therefore, is experiential and so it must be asked what types of teaching might be considered to be experiential; but exponents of experiential learning would normally point to primary experience as the basis of what they regard as experiential. Consequently, when teachers provide opportunity for 'hands-on experience', even in a simulated situation, it falls within this category and, as Henry (Weil and McGill 1989: 25–37) shows, this includes a vast variety of methods, many of which have already been referred to in this chapter.

Personalized systems of instruction

The personalized system of instruction refers to the Keller Plan (Keller 1968; Boud and Bridge 1974), which is perhaps the most well known, but not the only programmed learning system to emerge. Crane (1982), for instance, refers to: Postlethwait's audio-tutorial system; individually prescribed instruction; programme for learning in accordance with needs; the personalized system of instruction. The Keller Plan consists of units of work which students study at their own pace and in their own time without a teacher. Each unit must be passed successfully before they proceed to the next one, which is referred to as mastery learning. Lectures and other learning activities are provided but attendance is not compulsory since they are regarded as an additional and occasional stimulus. Keller summarizes his plan in the following five points:

1. The go-at-your-own-pace feature, which permits the student to move through the course at a speed commensurate with his ability and other demands upon his time;

2. The unit-perfection requirement for advance, which lets the student go ahead to new material only after demonstrating mastery of that which preceded;
3. The use of lectures and demonstrations as vehicles of motivation rather than sources of critical information;
4. The related stress upon the written word in teacher–student communication; and, finally:
5. The use of proctors, which permits respected testing, immediate scoring, almost unavailable tutoring, and a marked enhancement of the personal-social aspect of the educational process.

(Keller 1968: 83)

This method has been acclaimed by Taveggia as 'proven superior to conventional teaching methods with which it has been compared' (cited by Holmberg 1981: 127). Rogers (1977) discusses British counterparts to this approach in her chapter on discovery learning but it was Leytham who elaborated a set of principles for programmed learning, when he suggested that:

- aims and objectives should be clearly specified
- materials selected for learning should relate to aims and objectives
- each new stage should only introduce sufficient new material to ensure that it is not too difficult so that students make few, or no, mistakes
- the level of difficulty of new material should be commensurate with the students' previous experience
- students should work at their own pace
- students should be active learners
- students should receive feedback
- no new stage should be inserted before the previous one is mastered

(Leytham 1971: 140)

Clearly Leytham's principles are in accord with the points stressed by Keller, with the exception of the latter's use of proctors who undertake the administration of the tests and provide the feedback. While this approach to teaching can be instituted within the educational organization, it is also clear that many of the principles of distance learning are encapsulated within these formulations. However, one of the drawbacks of this approach is that all the material that is taught and learned is selected by the teacher, and while the learner is left to learn it, it remains the teacher's choice and the learner's need is not necessarily a determining factor in the selection of content. Perhaps this is one reason why it has found a niche in adult basic education (see Crane 1982 for an example) and in higher education but, as yet, it has only established a place in liberal adult education through distance learning. Yet this approach appears to offer considerable potential as disciplines become even more specialized and interests even more diverse.

Practicals

In many professions the teaching of practical skills had, until recently, been left to the learner to copy the demonstrator, and stress been laid on learning through experience. However there has been a renewed emphasis upon the value of practice and the place of practical knowledge in recent times. Strangely this has not led to apprenticeship coming to the fore again but rather to the idea that there should be prolonged periods of practical placements so that the practical skills can be learned under the guidance of a mentor, or an expert teacher of practice. It is obvious that theory had assumed too great a significance to the detriment of practical skills, although it is possible that the pendulum might be swinging too far in the other direction, with certain government policies assuming that all relevant theoretical knowledge can be learned in the practical situation. At the same time Beard has pointed out that 'there is some evidence that this method is unnecessarily slow since students have insufficient practice and feedback' (1976: 147). Hence, there has been a gradual movement in some areas of education to teach practical skills in a simulated situation, so that students can practise the skills until they are mastered. Belbin and Belbin (1972) emphasize that most adult students, left to learn at their own pace, can master skills especially if each skill is subdivided into separate elements and each element mastered separately. It is immediately noticeable that there are considerable similarities between skill teaching and the pro-grammed learning discussed above: much of the learning is tutorless, students are left to work at their own pace and in their own time, and each phase is mastered before progression to the following one.

However, in some other forms of education for adults there is another aspect of the practical and that is the work undertaken in the laboratory. In this instance, it is necessary for the tutor to decide whether the purpose of the exercise is merely to learn the use of experimentation by repeating other people's experiments. Naturally, these are not mutually exclusive but if one of the aims is to help students understand the process of experimentation it is necessary to combine the practical with some other learning technique, such as a discussion or a tutorial, so that reflection upon the process can be stimulated and additional learning occur.

Personal tutorial

The tutorial has already been discussed from the perspective of the tutor but it can be used in order to respond entirely to the student's learning needs. In this instance, the tutor plays the role of respondent to the questions and problems raised by the adult student about the content and method of what the latter is studying. Hence the tutor is merely answering questions and the student is effectively guiding the progress of the tutorial, but when this occurs it is perhaps wise to agree beforehand upon the length of time to be allocated to the session.

Self-directed learning

In the same way as experiential learning has assumed significance in the education of adults in the United Kingdom, the idea of self-directed learning has become an important element of American thought. There is an annual conference each year on the topic.

It may well have become clear from the discussion on contract learning that self-directed learning might be regarded as a teaching technique and a development from andragogy (see Brockett and Hiemstra 1991). Certainly, Knowles regards self-directed learning as one of the manifestations of andragogy and a vital element in his understanding of contract learning. Underlying the whole idea is the idea that the individual is an autonomous learner. While there are degrees of autonomy, Jarvis (1992) endeavoured to demonstrate the paradox of this position.

However, Candy (1991) also showed that however free the learner appeared to be within the framework of an educational institution, there is still a residue of teacher influence and so he distinguished between autodidaxy and self-directed learning. He (1991: 15) regards autodidaxy as self-directed learning outside the educational institution and then he is left with the problem of clarifying what he means by learner autonomy. He (1991: 108–9) lists a number of characteristics of autonomy: conceives goals and policies independently of pressure from others; exercises freedom of choice and action; reflects rationally; is prepared to act fearlessly in accord with the foregoing; has self-mastery; individuals perceive of themselves as autonomous. He recognizes that there are threats to the idea of individual autonomy, which he then discusses. However, for the purposes of this study, the distinction between self-directed learning within an educational institution and that outside is of major significance since it is recognized here, with Candy, that the influence of the teacher is never far removed from any form of student-led learning within the institution, and it is only with distance education that learners are apparently free from the immediate presence of teachers. But, and necessarily, distance education institutions are very centralized in many ways so there is no genuine learner autonomy in this form of education either.

Thus far in this chapter there has been a division between tutor-centred and learner-centred methods and this has been done for ease of discussion. Clearly, however, in any teaching and learning session it is possible to combine a number of approaches, and it is often a useful technique in teaching adults to negotiate with them about aspects of both content and method. This is not relinquishing professional responsibility but rather exercising it in a mature manner with adult learners who may contribute greatly to the teaching and learning process. Finally, in this chapter, it is now necessary to move from methods of teaching to aids for teaching and this constitutes the next section of this chapter.

TEACHING AIDS

In the same way that teachers of adults should be aware of and able to employ a variety of teaching methods, they should also be aware of and able to use a variety of teaching aids. A multitude of different ones exist and, with the continuing growth of technology, there is an increasing sophistication of equipment. Table 5.2 lists many of the teaching aids and much of the equipment about which teachers of adults should be aware, some of which they should also be competent to use in the classroom.

Many of the aids listed in Table 5.2 are now in daily use so that they require little comment here, although there are many publications that deal with the

Table 5.2 Teaching and learning aids and equipment

		AIDS	
Audio	*Audio-visual*	*Visual*	*Learning aids*
Audio cassettes	Films	Artefacts/models	Articles/journals
Audio	Tapes	Charts	Books
recordings	Slides		
Radio	Television	Diagrams	Computer
	programmes		programmes
Records	Video-	Drawings	Handouts
	recordings	Graphs	Home experiment kits
		Illustrations	Games
		Photographs	Media programmes
		Slides	Role play
			Simulation exercises
			Study visits
			Work books/sheets

	EQUIPMENT
Basic	*Technical*
Chalkboard	Camera/cine camera
Flannelgraph/Feltboard	Cassette recorder
Flipchart	Closed circuit television
Magnetic board	Computer
Plasticgraph	Epidiascope
Whiteboard	Episcope
	Projectors – cine
	– mico
	– overhead
	– slide
	Radio
	Record player
	Television
	Video recorder

technological aspects of teaching (e.g. Stephens and Roderick 1971) which may be referred to as appropriate. Therefore, it is intended to raise only a few points here.

Initially, it is important for teachers of adults to know that such a variety of aids exist and that it is useful to have some expertise in their use. Many teaching and learning aids are produced commercially and can be purchased either by individual teachers or by the educational institution in which they are employed. At the same time, if teachers work in an educational institution with an audio-visual aids department it is always worthwhile discovering precisely what services it offers, so that lessons may be enhanced by the technical help that such a department can render. Additionally, if the library facilities in the college/institution are limited, many of the public libraries are prepared to cooperate with teachers of adults in order to ensure that they have sufficient stocks of books on a specific subject to enable class members to borrow them. Local museums also are often prepared to loan boxes of teaching materials, e.g. relevant artefacts, on specific topics if they are approached. They are, of course, also pleased to receive class visits when it is appropriate.

When teachers of adults either prepare their own aids, or use the services of the audio-visual aids department, it is wise to be aware of the laws of copyright, since infringement of these may occur out of ignorance. It is also worthwhile checking to see if their employing educational institution has signed the copyright agreement because this allows them to photocopy specific materials for use as handouts, under certain conditions to which they must adhere, without reference to the publishers themselves. Even so, many companies and organizations are prepared to grant permission for the reproduction of their materials, given acknowledgement, and so it is often advisable to seek permission from them if they themselves are not included within the agreement. Moreover, some companies and organizations will also provide teaching resources to teachers who approach them.

Such a variety of teaching aids and equipment ensures that students may be able to learn in accordance with their preferred learning style. Indeed, the greater the variety of appropriate aids employed the more likely it is that students' learning will be helped; but teachers should not employ too many aids in a single session for the sake of their performance because this artificializes the learning environment and interferes with the learning process. Considerable research has already been conducted into the relationship between learning and audio-visual communications and it is necessary for the teacher to be aware of some of this. Recently, for instance, Sless (1981) has examined the relationship between learning and visual communications and, while he admits that his own coverage is incomplete, he maintains that students are not trained in the use of visual stimuli, so that if teachers use them they must 'also show how people can learn from these forms' (1981: 77). This may be an element that educators of adults take for granted merely because adults have been recipients of visual stimuli for a long time.

Thus it may be seen that a wide variety of aids and equipment are available and the teacher is able to enrich the learning experience if some of the techniques are employed in the teaching and learning situation. It is, therefore, the responsibility of teachers of adults to be aware of what provision is made by their own educational institution and by other institutions in the locality, so that they are able to perform their role effectively.

SUMMARY

This chapter has reviewed a great deal of material about teaching adults. It began by seeking to draw relationships between learning and different approaches to teaching, in which it was recognized that the humanity of the adult students and of the teacher are paramount in the process. It was clearly seen that the adult teachers' role is rather different from that of the traditional lecturer, since while they may perform in a didactic manner, there are also socratic and facilitative styles that are often more appropriate. Different teaching styles were then discussed, and it was once more apparent that these contain within them implicit philosophies, with the humanistic one being more consistent with adult education.

In the next section of the chapter the process of learning and teaching was discussed, in which the differences between teacher-centred and learner-centred approaches were highlighted. Teacher-centred methods can be didactic or socratic whereas learner-centred methods are more facilitative. Yet it was recognized that there is a place for the former in the education of adults, but perhaps it is not quite such a dominant one as it is usually maintained. Having examined the process of learning and teaching a wide variety of teaching methods were reviewed; some were teacher-centred and others learner-centred. Since there is such a variety of methods available it should mean that teachers of adults are able to use techniques that are appropriate to the aims and content of their teaching and that they may wish to include a variety of teaching methods in any one session. In order to enrich the teaching and learning experience teachers may also wish to utilize the wide variety of aids and equipment that have been produced and the chapter concluded by briefly examining some of these.

Thus far few theorists of teaching have been examined, so in the next rather brief chapter a number of theorists are analysed.

6 Theoretical perspectives on teaching adults

In the previous chapters the processes of learning and teaching were discussed and it will have become apparent from the numerous methods mentioned that there are a diversity of approaches to teaching and many theoretical perspectives about it, so that it is now necessary to examine some of the latter in this chapter. Before undertaking this, however, it is essential to highlight the fact that since teaching and learning is a process of human interaction in which both sets of participants should be affected, it cannot be a neutral process. Indeed, it is a moral one! In this study it has been consistently maintained that education itself is humanistic and some teaching and learning processes may fall short of these ideals. Hence, in the first instance, it is necessary to consider not only the aims and content of a particular session but also the morality of the approach in relation to the participants in the process. Thereafter, it is necessary to consider the effectiveness of the methods employed, since, while there may be no single correct method, there are some techniques that should not be utilized since they fail to incorporate the morality of the educational process within them.

This chapter will, therefore, focus initially on some of the moral aspects involved in teaching and then it will examine the work of five theorists: Bruner, Dewey, Freire, Illich and Knowles.

TOWARDS A MORAL UNDERSTANDING OF TEACHING

It will be recognized from the previous discussion that teaching is both a process of personal interaction and a social process. Both of these processes have moral overtones and it is important to recognize these, although there are few studies about the morality of teaching adults, with the exception of Strike and Soltis (1985) and Goodlad *et al.* (1990) who have begun to explore the moral dimensions of school teaching. However, it is not only education that cannot be neutral, as Freire claims, for teaching itself is always a moral process.

Teaching, then, involves the possibility of a personal relationship between teacher and taught, and the ideal of this relationship might best be understood from the writings of the Jewish philosopher and adult educator, Martin Buber. In his (1959) well-known study, he focuses upon the I-Thou relationship.

But he takes it even further in his characterization of the educative relationship:

> I have characterized the relationship of the genuine educator to his pupil as being a relationship of this kind. In order to help the realisation of the best potentialities in the pupil's life, the teacher must really *mean* him as the definite person he is in his potentiality and his actuality; more precisely, he must not know him as the mere sum of qualities, strivings and inhibitions, he must be aware of him as a whole being and affirm him in his wholeness. But he can only do this if he meets him again and again as his partner in a bipolar situation.
>
> (Buber 1959: 131–2; emphasis in original)

In the beginning, for Buber, is relationship and it is here in that relationship that teaching is to be discovered. But, since Buber is describing an educative relationship between a teacher and a child, there is possibility that it could be interpreted in a non-adult educational manner. This is a fear of some writers, e.g. Burnard (1990) writing about mentorship in nursing, that this form of relationship cannot be compatible with the principles of adult education, since it is likely to create dependence and conformity. Such a claim is perfectly understandable, and it is justified if the teacher seeks to be domineering in any way. But in the spirit of the I-Thou relationship, this fear has less potency. Elsewhere, Buber illustrates his concern for humanistic principles that relate closely to those of adult education: 'The relation in education is one of pure dialogue' (1961: 125). He explains this:

> A dialogical relation will show itself also in genuine conversation, but it is not composed of this. Not only is the shared silence of two such persons in dialogue, but also their dialogical life continues, even when they are separated in space, as the continual potential presence of the one to the other, as an unexpressed intercourse.
>
> (Buber 1961: 125)

Such a relationship is at the heart of teaching, especially personal supervision and personal tutoring. It is in this primary relationship of trust that teachers can help the learners to reflect and learn, even if the learning process is difficult on occasions. Such a relationship which can be rich and rewarding may also have the potential to become personal and emotionally charged since both teachers and learners are adults. Every social interaction has this moral dimension and, therefore, the professionalism of teachers of adults is paramount if the educative relationship deepens into personal friendship.

There is at least one other dimension to the morality of teaching that needs discussing at this moment and that relates to the style of teaching adopted. Bourdieu and Passeron (1977: 5–11) assert that all pedagogic action is symbolic violence in as much as it is 'the imposition of a cultural arbitrary by a cultural power (1977: xx)'. They do raise an important issue here about the moral nature of teaching and learning of knowledge that society considers to be valuable, then how that knowledge is presented is important. For instance, if teachers assume that they have the authority to present the inalienable truth and that they are legislators of what is correct knowledge, then they are running the risk of placing themselves on too high a pedestal since they are, according to Bauman (1987) likely to be no more than interpreters. Indeed, they might be claiming both a false status for the knowledge that they present and then utilizing their position to persuade students that they should accept it – both of which actions might be regarded as having a dubious morality.

Indeed, this highlights another moral feature in the teaching and learning process, since learning is itself the process through which human beings grow and develop. Teachers exercise control over both the teaching and learning and the space that the learners occupy in the educational institution, and so a number of questions need to be posed at this juncture. Firstly, what right have teachers to influence the process of learning, and therefore of human development, so directly? Secondly, if teachers do have this right, are they suitable persons to be entrusted with this responsibility? Thirdly, are they fully aware of the significance of the teaching and learning process, so that they can exercise that control in a responsible manner? Fourthly, do they relate that process to that of human growth and development or do they merely relegate it to the process of transmitting knowledge and skills to already fully formed and developed human beings?

Clearly these are large questions, ones that are too complex for a book of this nature, although the moral dimensions of teaching are to be explored in a later study on the ethics and the education of adults. However, the significance of these questions should not be forgotten in the training of adult educators. Clearly, they have major import when considering both the teaching styles adopted and the three forms of teaching discussed in the previous chapter.

However, it must also be recognized that teacher-centred approaches do ensure that the teacher has control of the learning process, whereas learner-centred methods surrender some of that power to the students. This is a significant distinction since it has political overtones, to which reference is made in this chapter and which it is most important to realize. It will be recalled that Rogers (1969: 103) claims that for him teaching is 'a relatively unim-portant and vastly overrated activity' since he believes in the natural propensity of human beings to learn. But if the powerful in any society, profession or occupation wish to control what human beings learn, it is necessary to ensure that there are mechanisms for ensuring that learners only learn what they wish them to, so that the curriculum, a selection from culture, has to be carefully managed. Hence, for the elite, it might be claimed, it is quite necessary that teacher-centred teaching initiates the learners into acceptable cultural knowledge. Teaching is, therefore, not relatively unimportant socially nor is it neutral. It may, thus, be seen that some theories of teaching may have a political bias but, by contrast, learning is an individual activity. However, other theories of teaching focus upon the individual rather than the social process. The idealistic, political and psychological are all present in the theories of teaching explored here. Not all the writers actually concentrate upon teaching adults but yet in their different ways they are all significant in developing theoretical perspectives on teaching adults.

It will be recognized from this discussion that the moral dimension of teaching is a significant but often neglected aspect of the role. A further study of this is being undertaken at present, but many of these points will become apparent in examining the following five theorists: Bruner, Dewey, Freire, Illich and Knowles.

THEORISTS OF TEACHING

None of the following writers has actually developed a theory of teaching adults. Bruner's *Towards a Theory of Instruction* is a systematic theory of teaching but not directly orientated towards adults, while the other four are all concerned with adults but none has an explicit theory. Knowles' theory of andragogy clearly relates learning and teaching in a much more integrated approach than most, and this is to its credit, although there are other problems with it. In the remainder of this section each of these five are now discussed.

Jerome S. Bruner

Bruner, in his classic study *Towards a Theory of Instruction* (1968), recognizes that the human being is a natural learner and he claims that schools often fail to 'enlist the natural energies that sustain spontaneous learning' (1968: 127). This might appear to be an indictment upon modern schools but it is also a recognition that they perform a socializing and moulding function to equip children to take their place in society as much as an educational one. Bruner (1968: 53), therefore, recognizes that any instruction that is given in school should be regarded as having an intermediate as well as a long-term aim, the latter being that the learner should become a self-sufficient problem solver. However, it might be claimed that any didactic process, such as formalized instruction, is actually helping to create a sense of dependency in the learner rather than one of independency, especially if the school teachers are unable to detach themselves from the process and encourage independent learning in children. Consequently, by the time children grow into adults they will have learned to expect that teachers will instruct them. Indeed adult students do exert considerable pressure upon educators of adults to conform to their expectations of teachers playing a didactic and, often, an authoritative role.

It is against this discussion that Bruner's theory of instruction may be viewed. He (1968: 40–1) claims that a theory of instruction should have four main features, and these are that it:

- should specify the experiences which most effectively implant in an individual a predisposition towards learning
- must specify the ways in which the body of knowledge should be structured so that it can be readily grasped by the learner

- should specify the most effective sequences in which to present the materials to be learned
- should specify the nature and pacing of rewards and punishments in the process of learning and teaching

Clearly Bruner has posited his theory against the background of initial education, so that some of the above points appear to be diametrically opposed to some of those already mentioned in the education of adults. Yet the first of these four points is quite significant since Bruner maintains that instruction should facilitate and regulate the exploration of alternatives and a major condition for undertaking this is curiosity. It will be recalled that curiosity is aroused in adults, as well as in children, when their interpretation of their socio-cultural environment no longer provides them with relevant knowledge to cope with their present experiences. Hence, in teaching adults it is possible for the teacher to provide experiences that arouse this questioning process, so that the adult students' questioning is orientated in a specific direction. Clearly the structure and form of knowledge are significant in teaching adults and Bruner recognizes that the mode of representation, the economy of presentation and the effective power of the representation varies, 'in relation to different ages, to different "styles" among learners, and to different subject matters' (1968: 44). Hence, this second point may be seen as relevant to adult teaching. The relevance of his third point is also clear since he claims that instruction 'consists of leading the learner through a sequence of statements and are statements of a problem or body of knowledge that increase the learner's ability to grasp, transform, and transfer what he is learning' (1968: 49). Finally, all learners need some reinforcement, so the relevance of this is very evident in the education of adults. However, it must be recognized that Bruner is discussing only one type of educational method, instruction, or a didactic presentation of knowledge, and the relevance of his theory must be seen in relation to this.

There are also considerable similarities in Bruner's formulation and those in the personalized system of instruction discussed in the previous chapter, and it may be seen that Bruner has highlighted many of the points that underlay a theory of instruction. Instruction is obviously didactic and there is a sense in which, as a teaching method, it controls the amount of knowledge to be learned by the students, so that it is open to the accusations that some of the analysts discussed later in this chapter would make about it. Nevertheless, many of the more informal methods of teaching also include some teacher direction and guidance, so that they may not be quite so free of control as might appear on the surface. However, it might be true to claim that all teaching methods may be located on a continuum between student-centred and teacher-centred, and perhaps more are located towards the latter end of the continuum than adult educators might like.

While Bruner is clearly concerned about the humanity of the participants in the teaching and learning process, there is no explicit place within his principles for a humanistic perspective, although he does recognize the importance of the relationship between teacher and learner. Nevertheless, Bruner has outlined a set of principles that educators of adults should be aware of because they form part of the theoretical perspectives of teaching.

John Dewey

Perhaps Dewey is the most significant of all educationalists to the development of adult education, and so it is hardly surprising that he should be considered within this context. Many of his ideas have already been discussed in earlier chapters of this study, so it is not intended to repeat them at length here. However, Dewey was one of the major exponents of progressive education, and his earlier books were clear expositions of this position, and among his basic principles were that the concept of education had to be reconceived, so that it related to the whole of life rather than just of its early years. For Dewey, the human being is born with unlimited potential for growth and development, and education is one of the agencies that facilitates growth. Another tenet of progressivism significant to understanding Dewey's thought is the recognition that prominence is given to the scientific method; so the individual needs to start with a problem, develop hypotheses about it and test them out by examination of the empirical evidence. Hence, the problem solving method, discussed in relation to Gagné's hierarchy of learning, is significant in the work of Dewey. Dewey recognized that this resulted in a changed relationship between teacher and taught, so that teachers might facilitate and guide the learning but they should not interfere with nor control the process in the way that a didactic teacher would.

Some of the above ideas appear in *Education and Democracy* (1916) but in many ways the book that Dewey wrote on *Experience and Education* (1938) reflects some of his more developed thinking on teaching. He was concerned to contrast his approach to education to that of the more traditional schools of thought and he considered freedom and experience to be significant. Additionally, he maintained that continuity of experience and interaction between young and old are both important to learning. Hence, it is clear that Dewey was actually writing about initial education, especially after his own experiences of running a progressive, experimental school for a number of years. But it may be recognized that some significant ideas for the education of adults evolved from children's education, so it is important for the former to be aware of theoretical approaches to children's education.

Dewey considered that since experience is at the heart of human living and because continuity of experience leads to growth and maturity, then genuine education must come through experience. Hence, the teachers' role is to provide the right type of experience through which the learner may acquire knowledge and understanding and this would facilitate the process of growth and development. Learners would mature without having a structure of knowledge and the body of social rules imposed upon them. However, it might be argued that if the teachers' main task is to provide the conditions in which the students learn, and if teachers are actually directing the process when the students require help (Dewey 1938: 71), then they are involved in a much more subtle process of control than that which occurs in traditional, didactic teaching. However, Dewey does recognize that this possibility exists and he condemns those who 'abuse the office, and . . . force the activity of the young into channels which express the teachers' purpose rather than that of the pupils' (ibid.). According to Dewey, the teachers' leadership responsibilities include:

- being intelligently aware of the capacity, needs and past experiences of those under instruction
- making suggestions for learning but being prepared for the class to make further suggestions so that learning is seen to be a cooperative rather than a dictatorial enterprise
- using the environment and experiences and extracting from them all the lessons that may be learned
- selecting activities that encourage the learners to organize the knowledge that they gain from their experiences in subject matter
- looking ahead to see the direction in which the learning experiences are leading to ensure that they are conducive to continued growth

These points are collected from different pages of Dewey's work but they reflect some of his major points about teaching. It is clear from the above that Dewey's work on teaching may be related to the facilitative learning and teaching cycle (Figure 5.3) in the previous chapter and that many of his ideas are similar to those expounded in earlier chapters of this work. It was Lindeman (1926) who, influenced by Dewey, incorporated many of these ideas into adult education, so it is necessary to recognize that many elements in the theories of teaching in adult education do reflect a progressive education perspective which can be traced directly back to Dewey.

Paulo Freire

Freire's work was discussed in a previous chapter in terms of the theory of learning implicit in his writing, but the theory of teaching is much more explicit. Three elements are discussed here and these are summarized by Goulet (Freire 1973a: viii), who suggests that the basic components of Freire's literacy method are:

- participant observation of educators 'tuning in' to the vernacular universe of the people
- an arduous search for generative words
- an initial codification of these words into visual images which stimulate people 'submerged' in the culture of silence to 'emerge' as conscious makers of their own 'culture'
- the decodification by a 'culture circle' under the self-effacing stimulus

of a coordinator who is no 'teacher' in the conventional sense, but who has become an educator-educatee in dialogue with educatee-educators too often treated by formal educators as passive recipients of knowledge
- a creative new codification, this one explicitly critical and aimed at action, wherein those who were formally illiterate now begin to reject their role as mere 'objects' in nature and social history and undertake to become 'subjects' of their own destiny

Without raising issues of literacy education, the first significant point that emerges from this summary is that Freire advocates, and practises, going to those who have a learning need and listening to them, so that the educator can become the learner. While this serves a diagnostic function, it has more purposes than this because it enables the educator to learn the language of the potential learners and also to identify with them. At the outset of the teaching and learning the teacher bridges the gulf between him and the learners in order to create a genuine dialogue, without which humanistic education cannot occur.

The second significant point about this process is that the learners are encouraged to participate in dialogue and to problematize the reality in which they are immersed. This is a deliberate attempt to make the learners question what they had previously taken for granted, so that they can become aware that they have been socialized into the culture of the colonizers and that their construction of reality may be false within the context of their indigenous heritage. This occurs through the analysis and use of language, since language is a significant carrier of the universe of meaning, and through becoming aware of what has happened to them the learners are enabled to reconstruct their universe of meaning. In this process the learners are not objects of a social process but they are creative subjects within it.

Finally, Freire does not regard the educator and the learner has having mutually distinct roles but thinks that in a genuine dialogue the teacher teaches the learners who learn and teach the teacher as well. Hence, in the dialogue there is also a mutual planning of the teaching and learning, so that it is relevant to the needs of the participants. It is in this dialogue that the humanistic nature of Freire's teaching method is apparent since he (1972b: 61–5) claims that it is essential to the educational process and that it requires an intense love for and faith in man. Perhaps Freire's philosophy of teaching is summed up by a Chinese poem:

Go to people, live among them,
Learn from them, love them,
Serve them, plan with them,
Start with what they have,
   build on what they have.
      (Author unknown)

Perhaps more than in most theories of teaching, Freire emphasizes that the teacher has to reach out to the learners and learn from them in order to be able to contribute effectively to the teaching and learning process. Like other theories of teaching adults the humanity of the learners is respected and emphasized.

Two significant points need to be made at this stage in the discussion. Clearly Freire presents a radical approach to teaching and he regards it as a method by which learners can act upon their socio-political environment in order to change it. Hence, he regards the educator as the facilitator of learning and education as a process of change. The educator is not the 'fount of all wisdom' trying to fill the empty buckets: education is not a process of banking received knowledge. Rather education is an active process in which the teacher controls neither the knowledge learned nor the learning outcomes. Because of the politically radical elements in Freire, there is a danger that other aspects of his philosophy of teaching may be lost.

Freire offers a humanistic teaching method that may actually be divorced from the political radicalism, although to do so would fail to do justice to Freire's philosophy. However, he highlights the fact that teachers: have to break down the barriers between teacher and taught; should speak the same language as the learners; should be aware of how they construct their universe of meaning and what they see as their learning needs; should start where the learners are and encourage them to explore and learn from their experiences.

From Freire's unique synthesis of Christianity, Marxism and existentialism he has produced a theoretical approach to teaching that is both inspiring and challenging. That he is regarded as a political radical should not detract educators of adults from seeking to emulate elements of his method, since it epitomizes the high ideals of humanistic education.

Ivan Illich

Like Freire, Illich is a radical Christian who presents an alternative approach to education. He is included here, however, not because of his radicalism but because one of his major ideas is already finding expression in adult education in America and, to some extent, it is being incorporated into the University of the Third Age in the United Kingdom. His approach also presents a warning to those adult educators who seek to professionalize their occupation.

In order to understand Illich thoroughly it must be understood that he offers a radical critique of some of the established institutions in Western society, including medicine, the Church and teaching, and so it is necessary to summarize his concerns before they are applied to education. Illich (1977) claims that the professions dominate ordinary people, that they prescribe what the people need and institutionalize it within the professional's own territory, Hence, doctors determine when a person is ill, prescribe an acceptable remedy to the need and ensure that health cure takes place in 'hygienic appartments where one cannot be born, cannot be sick and cannot die decently' (Illich 1977a: 27). Similarly, teachers determine what children need to learn, and prescribe the educational remedy in a building which artificializes the real experiences of living. Professionals dominate people's lives, prescribing what they regard as right and proper, and the general populace are no more than the recipients of the process. This is the crux of Illich's position.

Since education has fallen into the trap of institutionalization, Illich (1973a) proposed that it was necessary to deschool society. He considered this essential because not only education but social reality itself has become schooled. Accepted knowledge and credentials for occupational advancement have become incarcerated within the institution of the school but there is no equality of access to it, so that expenditure on education is unequally distributed in favour of the wealthy. Every time some other area of social living is incorporated into a school curriculum a new class of poor is generated; so that, for instance, with the introduction of new training initiatives for young adults in the United Kingdom a new class of poor who are unable to attend the courses and gain the advantages is generated.

In precisely the same way, Illich and Verne (1976) offer a critique of lifelong education. Continuing education specialists will generate the need for more learning, prescribe how and where it should be learned and perpetuate the school system throughout the whole of the lifespan. They claim that in 'permanent education we are no doubt witnessing a further reduction of the idea of education, this time for the exclusive benefit of the capitalists of knowledge and the professionals licensed to distribute' (1976: 13). Clearly, Illich is offering a valid criticism of the process of institutionalization in Western society, and indeed in other societies as well, even though he has overstated his argument to make his point. What then does he propose as a remedy for the malady that he has diagnosed?

Illich (1973a) proposes that learning networks should be established and that resources are required to establish a web-like structure throughout a society. He (1973a: 81) proposes four different approaches which enable students to gain access to any educational resource which may help them to define and achieve their own goals: reference services to educational objects; skill exchanges; peer matching; reference services to educators at large. This clearly requires organization and some of the resources spent on the school system could be used for this purpose, and the professional teacher, liberated from the bureaucratic control of the school, would be free to provide a service to these learners who require it. Such a scheme is idealistic and revolutionary, so there is no likelihood of a society reforming its educational institution in this manner, but the free university system in America appears to be fulfilling these criteria. A free university, according to Draves is 'an organization which offers non-credit classes to the general public in which "anyone can teach and anyone can learn" (1979: 5). Some of the free universities are sponsored by traditional colleges while others are sponsored by libraries and some others are independent. They exist to coordinate learning and teaching opportunities, to introduce potential students to potential teachers. There is a national conference of free universities each year and in 1979 there were over 180 free universities established in America, with over 300,000 participants. A similar approach is appearing in the University of the Third Age in the United Kingdom at present.

Illich, then, offers a radical critique of contemporary society and of the dominant position occupied by the professionals. While his radical alternative to schooling does not appear to have gained a great deal of support in initial education, there is evidence that some adult educators are seeking to respond to the learning need in people and to create networks where teaching and learning can occur outside the institutional framework. Nevertheless, such free institutions must run the danger of ossifying and becoming established, and so it remains to be seen whether learning networks will survive and multiply in the coming decade.

Malcolm Knowles

Like Freire, Knowles was discussed in the chapter on learning theorists but, unlike Freire, he is included again because he has actually produced a text book in which he specifically discusses the two processes. It was pointed out in the previous chapter that he produced a table similar to Table 5.1, in which he specifies sixteen principles of teaching in response to conditions of learning. He demonstrates that he regards teaching as the process of designing and managing learning activities. His (1980: 57–8) principles indicate the process of teaching, and they are summarized below: the teacher

- exposes learners to new possibilities for self-fulfilment
- helps learners clarify their own aspirations
- helps learners diagnose
- helps learners identify life-problems resulting from their learning needs
- provides physical conditions conducive to adult learning
- accepts and treats learners as persons
- seeks to build relationships of trust and cooperation between learners
- becomes a co-learner in the spirit of mutual enquiry
- involves learners in a mutual process of formulating learning objectives
- shares with learners potential methods to achieve these objectives
- helps learners to organize themselves to undertake their tasks
- helps learners exploit their own experiences on learning resources
- gears presentation of his or her own resources to the levels of learners' experiences
- helps learners integrate new learning to their own experience
- involves learners in devising criteria and methods to measure progress
- helps learners develop and apply self-evaluation procedures

This list of principles clearly demonstrates the facilitative teaching style of a humanistic educator of adults. Knowles sees andragogy as embracing the process of teaching, and learning rather than merely learning or teaching, and, within this context, it is perhaps important to understand that these principles embrace progressive education for adults, so that they are rather different in perspective from the other approaches that have been examined in this chapter.

Elsewhere in the same work, Knowles (1980: 222–47) applies these principles to the process of teaching, which he regards as having seven stages: setting a climate for learning; establishing a structure for mutual planning; diagnosing learning needs; formulating directions for learning; designing a pattern of learning experiences; managing the execution of the learning experiences; and evaluating results and rediagnosing learning needs. Each of these phases is discussed briefly.

The climate of learning is perhaps more significant than many educators actually assume: Knowles includes both the physical setting of learning and the psychological ethos. He recognizes that the learning climate is also affected by the way in which teachers and the adult students interact. This is especially true in the early sessions, a point that many adult educators focus upon, so that it is significant that teachers endeavour to establish good relationships between themselves and the class and between the learners themselves, from the outset of a course. Only within this climate can diagnosis occur within which Knowles claims that there are three stages: developing a model of the desired end-state of the teaching and learning; assessing the present level of knowledge; and assessing the gap between the two. Thereafter, learning objectives can be formulated by teachers and the learners together. Having reached this stage, Knowles advocates including the adult learners in designing the pattern of learning experiences, which should contain continuity, sequence and integration between different learning episodes. It is the teachers' role to manage the learning experience and Knowles maintains that teachers should

> serve both as strong procedural technicians – suggesting the most effective ways that the students can help in executing the decisions – and as resource persons, or coaches, who provide substantive information regarding the subject matter of the unit, possible techniques, and available materials, where needed.
>
> (Knowles 1980: 239)

Finally, teachers should join with the students in both an evaluation of the process and a rediagnosis of future learning needs.

Thus it may be seen from the above sequence that Knowles clearly regards the learners as active explorers in the learning process, participating in every stage, and the teachers as resource persons for both content and process. He is obviously in accord with many of the ideas that Dewey expounded, and so unlike McKenzie (1979), it is maintained here that Knowles has applied progressive education to the education of adults. Therefore, it may be seen that the ideology of andragogy is humanistic.

SUMMARY

This chapter commenced with an introductory analysis of some of the moral issues involved in teaching, issues that need more exploration. At the same time it is possible to detect that each of the five theorists discussed in the second part point to some of these points, without raising them explicitly. It may be seen, however, that Dewey and Knowles clearly have similar humanistic, idealistic approaches to education, seeing learners as individuals who are motivated to learn, so that the tutor's role is mostly facilitative; Illich and Freire both place their analyses in a wider context, Illich as a critique of professional institutions and Freire of the power of the elite; Bruner's analysis is much more specifically in relation to instruction. No doubt Freire and Illich would not want to dispute the humanistic perspective of Dewey and Knowles although the former may consider the latter as having a restricted analysis; but, indeed, all four might well agree with Bourdieu and Passeron when they assert that all pedagogic action 'is objectively, symbolic violence insofar as it is the imposition of a cultural arbitrary by an arbitrary power' (1977: XX). Bruner may not wish to disagree too violently with this claim either, since he focuses upon man's curiosity as an activator in the process of learning.

If education is regarded as the process of learning that knowledge which society considers worthwhile, then it might be argued that skilled techniques that transmit that knowledge is 'good' education. But if education is regarded as the process of learning and understanding, then the content is less significant, and the ways in which the students are encouraged, or enabled, to learn become more significant. In this instance, it might be maintained that 'good' education is concerned with the process of learning, irrespective of what is learned, and that adult learners should become sufficiently critically aware to reject that which is incorrect or irrelevant to them. Hence, to transmit to learners accepted or received knowledge and expect them to learn it uncritically may be regarded as 'bad' education and, therefore, 'bad' teaching. If techniques are used to ensure that the students are persuaded to accept such knowledge, then it may be symbolic violence, in the way that Bourdieu and Passeron claim. However, it would not be maintained here that all pedagogic action is symbolic violence, although some of it most certainly is. Clearly there is a place for pedagogy in the education of adults, but it has been argued that it is not such a significant one as it is generally assumed to be and that the teaching method employed has to relate both to the learners and also to the nature of the topic and the knowledge being learned.

Hence, the issues raised by the more radical theorists do relate to the perspectives adopted by those educators assuming a more humanistic perspective. It is clear that there are moral and social policy issues involved in the process of teaching and while it has been one of the purposes to highlight them, it is not the intention of this chapter to resolve them. Yet the manner by which teachers resolve these issues for themselves may well affect the way in which they perform their own role, and, indeed, it is an issue with which they should be confronted during their own training.

7 Distance education

Distance education has grown in popularity in recent years, popularized by the British Open University, although its history is far older, and even university distance education occurred long before the Open University was ever dreamed about (Rumble and Harry 1982). Perhaps it actually begun with James Stuart, the founder of university extra-mural adult education, who experimented with correspondence education for women in the 1870s. There were societies for home study at about this time in both England and the United States. (See Garrison and Shale 1990 for a historical overview in the United States). Correspondence education became a relatively popular form of education for adults in the early part of the twentieth century, although it was always regarded as second best. With the development of the wireless, there were many experiments with educational radio and, naturally, now there are more high technology means of transmitting knowledge. However, it is only in more recent years that theories about distance education have begun to emerge.

Perhaps the most complete discussion of the meaning of the term is to be found in Keegan (1990: 28–47). He (1990: 44) characterizes distance education in the following manner: it has a semi-permanent separation of teacher and learner; it is influenced by the educational organization in both the preparation of the teaching materials and the support of the students; it uses technical media; it is a two-way process; it has a semi-permanent absence of a learning group. Naturally these characteristics are open to certain criticisms: for instance, it may well be true that in certain forms of distance education there is a two-way relationship between teachers and taught so that the learners may also initiate teaching and learning situations, but this is by no means universal. Consequently, this characteristic appears superfluous to any definition of the concept. Distance education is, therefore, defined here as those forms of education in which organized learning opportunities are usually provided through a technical media to learners who normally study individually, and removed from the teacher in both time and space. As each educational institution has its own procedures and provides its own facilities this definition endeavours to be narrow enough to be meaningful but not so wide as to include almost any form of learning.

Just prior to the foundation of the Open University, Otto Peters (1967 – see Stewart *et al.* 1988: 68–94 for his analysis), who was a member of an important group of adult educators at the University of Tübingen in Germany, began to develop an influential theory about distance education being a typical form of education for the age: he regarded it as: a rationalized form of industrial production; a division of labour with each individual in the course team having a different role in the production and dissemination of knowledge; mechanization, as the dissemination of knowledge was achieved through assembly line production; mass production, since there was theoretically no limit as to the number of copies of the same course that could be produced or students who could study the course once it was produced. He regarded this as a process of standardization and the beginnings of a monopoly of the educational market. (See Keegan 1990 for a clear summary of Peters' position.)

Another significant theorist of distance education is Holmberg (1989) who regarded it as a form of guided didactic conversation and who considered that there are seven postulates to distance education:

- there should be the creation of a personal relationship between the teaching and learning parties;
- there needs to be well-developed self-instructional material;
- there should be intellectual pleasure in the exercise;
- the atmosphere, language and conventions should foster friendly conversation;
- the message received by the learner should be conversational in tone, easily understood and remembered;
- a conversational approach should always be used in distance education;
- planning and guiding are necessary for organized study.

It will be clearly seen that Holmberg's approach is more humanistic than Peters' analysis, although Peters never claimed to approve all that is occurring. However, for Holmberg's approach to work it is necessary to change the whole style of academic discourse, and a considerable degree of training is necessary to ensure that course writers are empathetic to their readers.

Naturally, Holmberg's work is attractive to educators who have a humanistic approach to education, but there is a danger in making everything appear very friendly since the written word often assumes an aura of sanctity! The text appears to some readers as sacred knowledge which cannot be criticized and anything that is not included is regarded as less significant. Indeed, it is not uncommon to hear students studying distance education courses asking whether they should include material in their assignments which is not in the text! However learner-friendly the distance education, teachers and writers have to be aware that the curriculum of the distance education course is centralized and controlled, so that in this sense distance education has a tendency to be closed.

A theorist who was influential during the early years of the Open University is Charles Wedemeyer (1981); like many American writers, his concerns were self-study, independent learning and, even, individualism. He regarded distance education as an optimistic enterprise in the provision of lifelong learning – in which learners are independent of teachers. Wedemeyer's approach is optimistic but uncritical.

However, there have been dramatic changes in the world in recent years and it is now possible to extend Peters' analysis, since it is being claimed that contemporary Western Europe is entering a period of late, or post, modernity. Basically, this means that the consequences of the Enlightenment are being recognized and questioned, with some scholars actually asking whether it was actually a success. This is not the place to pursue this discussion, but distance education can clearly be seen as a sign of late modernity. Giddens (1990) suggests a number of features which typify contemporary society as being late modernity, such as: industrial-capitalistic; space-time distanciation; disembedded mechanisms and expert systems; reflexivity; individual responsibility. Distance education is the form of education that epitomizes each of these signs, and so they are now discussed in the order in which they appear here.

INDUSTRIAL-CAPITALISM

Peters has shown how thoroughly the production of distance education materials epitomizes industrial production, although he does not demonstrate its relation to the capitalist market in quite the same manner. However, inherent in capitalism are three features that can also now be discovered in distance education, namely commoditization, competition and globalization.

Once any commodity is technologically produced it becomes an object, and within a capitalist economy it is a commodity which can be sold. A distance education package, or a course, or an interactive video compact disc is a marketable commodity and one which educational institutions have been encouraged to sell. Now they have marketing managers committed to selling educational courses and, of course, the market is limited if the commodity is a course offered only at a local college or university. However, if the programme is contained within an object that can be carried away from the vendor, or even mailed or transmitted electronically to the purchaser, then it becomes a more attractive marketable commodity.

Even so, the capitalistic market is one of competition. The rhetoric of the market is that only the best quality commodities will survive, but its reality is that only the strongest and largest organizations survive irrespective of the quality of the product which they sell. Distance education now advertises its wares and buyers wish to know not only about the nature of the course being studied, but also the length of time that it will take, the qualification that will be awarded on successful completion, the number of assignments that have to be submitted and the fee that they will have to pay. Purchasers can then decide for themselves which is their 'best buy' according to their own instrumental concerns. One of the obvious outcomes of this process is that those unsuccessful institutions, irrespective of the quality of their product or of their potentiality, will lose out and may be forced to close. Hence, the large get larger at the expense of the small, unless the small discover a gap in the market etc., but the consequences of this are self-evident.

But the market cannot be limited to the local area of the producing institution. The market is bounded only by the size of the globe! Hence, globalization has entered into distance education, and many universities are running their courses internationally: for example, the British Open University is opening offices throughout the world and the University of Surrey organizes a Masters Degree programme in post-compulsory education which can be studied anywhere in the world, and so it is becoming possible to study for a British university degree in the farthest reaches of the world. Naturally, there are tremendous advantages to this – but it might also be wondered about the effect that this will have upon small indigenous universities of poor Third World countries, and once again it might lead to accusations of cultural imperialism. However, it might be much more a matter for some of trade or, as others would argue, of aid rather than anything else.

SPACE-TIME DISTANCIATION

Giddens indicates that in 'pre-modern societies, space and place largely coincide, since the spatial dimensions of social life are, for most of the population, and in most respects, dominated by ''presence'' – by localised activities' (1990: 18). In other words, students had to be in the presence of the teachers to hear their profound words. The history of the university is of students travelling to places where teachers expounded; in order to gain a degree from certain universities, residence qualifications were imposed, and so on. Now it is possible to study for, and be awarded, even higher degrees from some universities without ever being physically present, neither at the university itself nor even in the country in which the university is located. Now the teachers record their lessons and they can be studied in the students' own time and place. The learning experience is no longer immediate and face-to-face, but mediated and secondary. Distance education, by definition, symbolizes the process of space-time distanciation.

DISEMBEDDED MECHANISMS AND EXPERT SYSTEMS

Disembedding implies a process of extracting the specific localized social relations and reimplanting them within a global context of space and time. Consequently, the distance teaching institutions can be experienced, not as places to which learners travel for study with a teacher, but as the mechanisms through which the pursuit of their studies is facilitated wherever they study and at whatever time they choose to undertake their work. The distance teaching institution is disembedded and needs no campus and no geographical location.

In other words, the academy is now no longer a place, it is a disembedded process and a system – its educational offering is now a product guaranteed to provide specific learning for the purchasers; now it is not only the teachers who are important, it is the whole system – producing, packaging, marketing, processing, support services for clients, and so on. The system is removed from its localized context and now the clients and learners have to be persuaded to trust in the efficiency and expertise of the whole system. This has progressed to such an extent that there is already an electronic university!

REFLEXIVITY

The reflexivity of modernity, according to Giddens involves a constant examination and reexamination of social practices which are 'reformed in the light of incoming information about those very practices' (1990: 38). Consequently, the traditional mode of doing things is no longer sufficient justification for continuing a practice. Indeed, change in the mode of production and distribution of distance education materials will alter as new technologies initiate different ways of doing things. For instance, the interactive compact video disc, and the interactive computer program, will no doubt replace the traditional correspondence material when the market makes it a worthwhile financial investment. However, in seeking a worldwide sale such hi-tech productions will limit the size of the market able to purchase costly commodities and so many educational materials will remain in traditional, and cheaper, written form for a few more years to come.

INDIVIDUATION

As the functioning of many elements of society has become organized and distanced from everyday life, there has been a new emphasis upon the individual. Emphasis is placed upon the existential questions of humankind – upon the self and upon self-identity. People do not always feel so constrained by the demands of organizations, because they do not always have to attend them to be part of them, although they are actually controlled by their procedures in precisely the same way! Consequently, individuals feel able to follow their own pursuits, at their own time and in their own way and, to some extent, be self-determining individuals. Distance education, therefore, provides the opportunity for people to continue their education individually in their own space and at their own time and pace and have it serviced by a disembedded educational institution, an expert system.

Distance education may, therefore, be seen to fit many of the characteristics of late modernity and it may be regarded as being a symbol of this form of society. This analysis highlights some of the contemporary issues that this form of education for adults raises. It is not considered important to pursue the consequences of these any further here, although it is necessary to recognize that some practitioners of distance education attempt to overcome some of the problems implicit in the previous discussion.

For instance, while it is widely recognized that the preparation of distance education materials places a greater emphasis on the teacher and the course team in the first instance, attempts have been made to introduce elements of choice in some courses, and many others try to make the course much more personal in the style of presenting the material and even in the way that it is marked. Holmberg (1960: 14) suggested that the material had to be conversational and almost two-way, which he later came to regard as guided didactic conversation. This is true also in assessing course work that is to be returned to the distance education learners: comments might be regarded as an invitation to dialogue through the medium of the students' assignments and the tutors' comments.

The practice of distance education is now extremely common, especially with the development of desk top publishing, and this has resulted in many more people being involved in the preparation and assessment of distance education material. Naturally the quality should be high since most aspects of it can be controlled before dissemination, but the skills of becoming a distance educator are gradually being learned and taught. There are not yet many certificated courses in the techniques of distance education, although they are beginning to emerge. Few people are suggesting that practitioners should be trained before they become distance educators, in the same way as the training of educators of adults has emerged, although it will probably not be too long before initial training courses, and concurrently certificates, in distance education develop and become part of the educational scene.

SUMMARY

Distance education is growing in importance, it is being recognized by such organizations as the Commonwealth of Learning as a means by which the First World can assist the Third, but it is only recently that a theory of distance education is beginning to emerge. This chapter has examined the writings of three of the major early theorists of this mode of education and then presented a contemporary analysis.

8   Teachers of adults and their preparation

The concept of 'teacher of adults' appears on the surface to be a relatively straightforward one and, therefore, easy to discuss; but once analysed it is soon apparent that initial conceptions can be misleading and ill-conceived. Earlier in this study it was pointed out that during human interaction everybody is an agent in the transmission of culture, in fact everyone is an educator of adults. However, the topic under consideration here refers specifically to the occupation of teaching adults, so it is possible to restrict the analysis accordingly. But even then the adult education or education of adults question becomes an issue: if adult education refers specifically to a part of the education of adults, then it would be necessary to restrict the discussion to those employed part-time and full-time in that branch of the service; but, on the other hand, if the teacher of adults refers to anybody employed to teach adults in whatever capacity in education, the professions, etc., then the problem is much more complex. This problem is compounded because in the second report of the Advisory Committee on the Supply and Training of Teachers (Haycocks 1978) adult education teachers were included within the further education category, and it is stated that in the academic year 1974–75 there were: 66,500 full-time staff, 57,000 staff teaching vocational subjects part-time and another 108,000 part-time staff teaching non-vocational education. But further and adult education teachers were not specified separately. Clearly these statistics refer only to those educators employed in the educational service and not to those in the professions, and yet the confusion between further and adult education here does not help clarify the concept: indeed, it points only to the fact that administratively the adult education service is regarded as a branch of further education. Nevertheless, the Russell Report (1973: 131) indicated that there were about 1,300 full-time and 100,000 part-time staff employed in the adult education sector. Since many of the professions and other organizations employ their own teaching staff, about which it is much more difficult to obtain precise statistics, it is an extremely difficult undertaking to discover how many people are actually employed full-time and part-time in any one year to teach adults.

Mee and Wiltshire (1978: 20–1) claim that there are three main categories of adult educators employed within the local educational authority adult education service: the full-timer, the part-timer and the spare-timer. While their distinction is perfectly valid, it is a pity that they employ the term 'spare-timer', with all of its connotations, to refer to the category of adult education employment that is often referred to as part-time. Indeed, these implicit values may not actually be substantiated by their own findings, so the term 'spare-timer' is not employed here. However, it is essential to clarify what they mean by part-time adult educator: the teacher who has joint responsibility, 'part of his time being given to adult education and part to the youth service, school teaching or vocational Further Education' (Mee and Wiltshire 1978: 20). While there clearly are many people in this category it is not proposed to use the term part-time to refer to them here. Another three-fold division of adult educators was made many years earlier by Houle (1960: 35–8) who distinguished between those who teach adults on a voluntary basis, those who perform this and other educational roles on a part-time basis for remuneration, and full-time professional adult educators. Houle's category of volunteer adult educators is quite a significant one, which Elsey (1980) investigated in the United Kingdom, but one which should not be classified as a branch of the occupation of 'adult educator'.

Without exploring this any further, it may be seen that the teacher of adults, or the adult educator, may not be quite such a straightforward concept or occupation to describe and that the majority of people who appear to be classified as adult educators undertake the role on a part-time basis only. Description of the role may, therefore, be an easier undertaking than actually conceptualizing the occupation, but even this assumption may be doubtful. Houle, for instance, distinguishes between the administrative and instructional roles of the full-time professionals, suggesting that they may perform both. While this may have been true two decades ago, it is less likely to be true today. Many full-time adult educators who regard their role as tutor-organizer may be organizers of tutors more than teachers who organize as well. Additionally, principals of adult education institutes almost certainly are managers rather than teachers and Mee and Wiltshire record one principal of an adult education institute who maintained that the 'next group of principals should be accountants not educationalists' (1978: 64), reflecting accurately the trend that has occurred in the provision of local authority liberal adult education. As some adult education institutes have expanded in size it was inevitable that the managerial role would continue to develop. It is not only the full-time staff whose role is moving in this direction since many part-time staff have in recent years been employed as part-time heads of an adult education centre and their responsibility has been managerial rather than professional. In some local education authorities, however, adult education has been located within colleges of further education, community colleges, etc., and, in this instance, the role of the adult educators may be both professional and administrative, since they may be expected to teach in the college etc. and organize adult education classes in either their discipline or locality. Hence, it may not be quite so simple to describe the role of the adult educator!

Thus full-time adult educators may be employed in a variety of institutions, with or without a teaching role, while part-time and voluntary adult educators are more likely to be teachers of adults. Hence, two questions may be raised: what is the job of an educator of adults and is it even an occupation at all? Hall defines occupation as 'a social role performed by adult members of society that directly and/or indirectly yields social and financial consequences and that constitutes a major focus in the life of an adult' (1969: 5–6). Hall's definition contains four basic components: a social role, social consequences, remuneration and a major life focus. While it would be possible to dispute the validity of this definition, it does reflect considerable research findings in occupations and professions and so it is proposed to adopt it here. Once the definition is adopted it does raise some interesting conceptual issues about the teacher of adults. The social role of many full-time adult educators may be that of a manager rather than that of a teacher, but others are employed and perform the role of teacher of adults. Some may spend all their employed time in administration while others may be teachers. Yet some who are actually teachers of adults may not regard themselves as such since they see themselves as engineers, university teachers, etc. Hence, university teachers employed in a school of dentistry, for example, may teach adults all the time, without having a major administrative responsibility. But they may regard themselves as dentists or university teachers rather than as educators of adults. A similar argument may be made for adult educators in university departments of adult education. Hence, the differential status of the occupation may be reflected in the role-players' own percpetion of their occupation, which relates to the second and fourth of Hall's criteria. Thus individuals may objectly be teachers of adults but neither regard themselves as adult educators nor be employed in adult education. By contrast, many who see themselves as adult educators and employed in the education of adults may not actually teach adults. Additionally, some part-time adult educators may be employed full-time in another occupation and define their occupational role in terms of the latter occupation, while other part-time adult educators may have no other employment and regard their occupation as educators of adults. Thus the idea that adult education is an occupation is open to certain questions. That those employed in it full-time are in an occupation is not open to conjecture, but it is difficult to specify precisely what the role entails and to delineate its boundaries is even more problematic. This confusion clearly reflects some of the problems surrounding adult education itself, but it is quite fundamental to an understanding of its marginality. Whether adult education is either a separate occupation or a separate discipline raises questions that are discussed further elsewhere in this study.

Having expanded this initial problem it is now necessary to outline the other concerns of this chapter. The first continues the exploration of adult educators and their role and this is followed by an examination of the training and qualifications that adult educators have. Developments in training, especially the aftermath of the Advisory Committee's report, are examined and some possible criteria for the basis of training are then discussed. Finally, the topic of adult education as an occupation is returned to and its professionalization is discussed.

EDUCATORS OF ADULTS AND THEIR ROLE

From the above discussion it is clear that the occupation of adult education, if it actually is an occupation, is a very diverse one. This becomes even more apparent when examining the varying roles performed by different educators of adults. Teachers of adults in the professions, working in the field of higher education, are expected to research and publish in their professional field, prepare students for the appropriate qualifying examinations, and undertake whatever administrative tasks appertaining to their work that arise within their institutions. By contrast, lecturers in a university department of adult and continuing education are expected to perform all the above roles of a teacher of higher education, but also to organize university extension classes in their discipline(s), liaise with the adult education service outside the university, interview part-time staff, train them in the art and science of teaching adults and offer them support, help and advice as appropriate. A similar role is performed by Open University staff tutors. Part-time tutors in both university extension classes and in Open University tutorial work have similar class contact responsibility but the major difference in their work is that the former actually prepare their own courses whereas the latter teach a course prepared by a central course team and mark the students' work. Kirk (1976) records the sense of loneliness that some Open University part-time tutors experience because they are at the periphery of the University's tutorial activities, but similar research among university extension class tutors remains to be undertaken. A similar division of responsibility between full-time and part-time staff in the university adult and continuing education departments exists in the Workers Educational Association, so that the full-time staff have largely an administrative role although most undertake some teaching.

Similarly, part-time staff in local education authority adult education institutes tend to have a predominantly teaching role, although there are a minority who are employed in an administrative capacity. By contrast, the full-time staff perform a multifarious role which Newman (1979) characterized as:

- entrepreneurs – they have to establish courses and then ensure that there are sufficient students to make them viable;
- wheeler-dealers – they have to overcome all the problems of entrepreneurs employed in a bureaucratic education service;
- administrators – they are responsible for planning programmes and employing staff;
- managers – their job is to manage the part-time staff and the educational premises;
- animators – they have to make things happen;

- trouble-shooters – they have to deal with the multitude of problems that complex organizations like adult education institutes create;
- experts on method – they might be called upon to provide guidance and assistance to part-time adult education staff;
- campaigners – since adult education, as a marginal branch of education, is always under threat.

It is quite significant that Newman does not include teaching amongst these roles. Hence, it may be concluded that for some full-time staff in local education authority adult education teaching plays a fairly insignificant part of their work. Thus, the full-time adult educator may be regarded as a manager and an administrator as much as, if not more than, a teacher, which raises quite significant questions about the notion that adult education is an occupation undergoing professionalization, which is discussed later in this chapter.

According to Mee and Wiltshire (1978: 61–2) this diversity of role that the full-time staff play provided them with a sense of autonomy and independence that they enjoyed. Certainly autonomy and independence are significant factors in many studies of job satisfaction in work, including the extent to which this sense of independence has survived where adult education has been squeezed financially and the number of staff cut drastically as local education authorities have tried to force adult education to become a self-financing commodity. In addition, this sense of autonomy, which might also have been lost where local authorities have relocated their liberal adult education provision in community schools and colleges of further education, where there are constraints of organization, will be significant to observe in the coming decade. Another factor that contributes to educators of adults having satisfaction in their work might be because they regard it as both important to respond to people's needs and to provide another chance for the most needy (Mee and Wiltshire 1978: 95). Elsey (1980: 136) also notes that for volunteer adult literacy tutors there is an altruistic motive to their work. In contrast to this, part-time adult educators tend to acknowledge that adult education is recreational, according to Mee and Wiltshire, and this was confirmed by Graham *et al.* (1982: 57) who suggested that enjoyment was the part-timer's main reward for teaching in adult education.

Newman (1979) also depicted the part-time tutors in the same rather journalistic manner as he did the full-timers. In this instance, he categorized them by motive and type rather than by the role they perform. He described four types:

- the professionals – who spend their leisure time teaching about their full-time jobs;
- the horse's mouth – who teach about their experiences rather than any academic discipline that they have studied;
- the passionate amateurs – who teach their hobbies;
- the school teachers – who teach the discipline that they teach at school or college or that they studied when they were at college.

Like Newman, Graham *et al.* (1982: 59–63) also classify the part-time adult educators in a four-fold manner: qualified school teachers, subject specialists, professionals and apprentices. While their first three types are self-explanatory the last one does require some explanation: the apprentices are the adult educators who began by attending adult classes in the subject that they now teach and who have worked their way from student to teacher.

Despite this diversity, adult education still conforms to other occupations in a number of ways especially in the way that women tend to occupy more lower positions in the hierarchy and also to teach part-time. For instance, Verner (1964: 47) states that in America 64 per cent of paid adult educators were male but men constituted only 44 per cent of the volunteer force. Mee and Wiltshire note that 'there are probably some nine male organizers to every female' (1978: 59) in the United Kingdom. Similarly, in the higher status adult teaching, 87 per cent of responsible body (university extension work) tutors were male, but in local authority adult education provision 57 per cent were women (Hutchinson 1970). Similar findings are recorded from other research in local education authority adult education: Graham *et al.* (1982: 51) report 64 per cent of their sample were women; Handley (1981: 82) noted 73 per cent of her respondents were women; Jarvis (1982b) recorded 79 per cent of tutors in a small village adult education centre prospectus were women; Martin's (1981: 122) research revealed about two-thirds of the respondents were women. While this evidence is piecemeal and circumstantial these studies all indicate that while many women are employed in adult education they are scarcer in the higher eschelons of the work.

Unlike other occupations, however, adult education has not yet developed a direct career route from initial training into the work of an adult educator, since there has been little full-time initial training, until recently. This has had certain repercussions on the age structure of the occupational group. Verner, citing a study by Brunner *et al.* (1959), states that:

> Individuals enter the field of adult education relatively late in their careers. Brunner found the medium age to be 35.5 years. Furthermore, 23 per cent did not enter the field until they were forty-two or older, although some 34 per cent of the membership of AEA (Adult Education Association) were employed in the field by the age of thirty-one. Thus, adult education tends to recruit its leadership from other fields at the midpoint in the individual's career rather than gaining its membership directly out of college.
>
> (Verner 1964: 45)

It would be interesting to compare Brunner's findings with statistics for adult education in America in the 1990s to see if the age of entry has lowered. Since there is also little provision for inital training on the education of adults in the United Kingdom, a similar picture probably exists, although there is little published evidence to support this assumption. It is certainly true that the professions generally expect candidates entering into teaching in a particular profession or occupation to have practised for a number of years prior to entering, so that many educators of adults in these occupations tend not to commence their teaching career until they are relatively old. Mee and Wiltshire (1978: 59), however, fail to confirm this assumption for local education authority staff when they discovered that the mean age for centre organizers was 43 years, which is about the point of mid-career.

Statistics for part-time staff are also inconclusive since the National Institute of Adult Education discovered that 49 per cent of local education authority adult educators were between 35 years and 54 years, whereas 61 per cent of university extension tutors were in the same age range (Hutchinson 1970: 173). Graham *et al.* (1982: 51) recorded that their sample of part-time tutors was spread across the whole age range: 13 per cent between 20 and 29 years; 36 per cent between 30 and 39 years; 25 per cent between 40 and 49 years; 17 per cent between 50 and 59 years; 8 per cent over 60 years. By contrast, Handley (1981) recorded a much less even distribution from her sample which was, however, very small: 18.5 per cent of her male respondents, but only 2.7 per cent female respondents, were under 30 years of age, and, at the other end of the age range, 11.1 per cent of the male respondents were over 60 years. (This may suggest that, for some, teaching in adult education is regarded as a retirement occupation for a few years.) In common with Graham *et al.*, Martin (1981: 122) discovered a more even distribution of tutors by age, with a slightly greater proportion being in the 31–40 years age group.

It would not be surprising if individuals did not want to teach adults until they had achieved a degree of maturity themselves, since it requires considerable confidence if the majority of students are older than they are. Nevertheless, adult learners do not appear to mind having young teachers so long as they are seen to be competent in their subject. This acceptance by the older ones of the younger persons as teachers may itself be an indication of the speed of aspects of cultural change and the elders' realization of how difficult it is to keep abreast of developments. However, it would be most interesting to discover if more younger people would enter this field at an earlier age if there were more full-time training provision.

The main route into full-time local education authority adult teaching appears to be through school teaching or lecturing in colleges of further education (Mee and Wiltshire 1978: 60) and it will be interesting to see if more teachers enter the field at a younger age in those local education authorities which are locating their adult education provision in community schools and colleges of further education, especially as an increasing number of further education lecturers are being trained prior to entering the profession. It will also be recalled that about one-third of part-time adult educators are school teachers, e.g. Newman's (1979) typology above. The National Institute of Adult Education's survey in 1967–8 confirmed this, since 116 of the 309 respondents to a questionnaire were school teachers, of whom 79 per cent were male. A further 75 were in business, of whom 69 per cent were men and the remaining 102 were housewives. In Handley's small study, she records that 'fifteen subjects were full-time teachers, fifty four were housewives, eighteen were employed other than in teaching [and] six had part-time employment' (1981: 63). There were also four miscellaneous respondents. Thus school teaching appears to be a major full-time occupation for part-time educators of adults and this raises some quite significant questions about the extent to which teacher training equips people to teach adults, a point to which further reference will be made elsewhere in this chapter.

That so many of the part-time adult educators are housewives does call into question the assertion by Mee and Wiltshire that since 'the spare timer's career is committed elsewhere ... he is, therefore, much less affected by the feelings of insecurity which conditions the attitudes of his full-time colleagues' (1978: 93). Such a claim may be true for many of the male part-time adult educators who have full-time careers but it may be much less true of the housewives whose part-time adult education teaching is their only occupation outside the home, especially for those who fall into the category of full-time part-time adult educator. Graham *et al.* (1982) discovered, for instance, that 8 per cent of their respondents taught more than four classes per week, that is at least eight hours' classroom contact, and Jarvis (1982b) found two part-time staff in a small village adult education centre who had at least the same amount of teaching. Yet these tutors have no more job security than those who teach only one class per week. Indeed, it is the very conditions of insecurity among part-time teachers, claimed Hetherington (1980), that prevented many of them from wishing to professionalize, an assumption that itself requires further examination.

Insecurity may be one reason for the apparently rapid turnover of part-time tutors in adult education. As adult education has become increasingly more marginal and begun to vocationalize, this sense of insecurity for some of the apparently untrained adult educators has been increased. The Advisory Committee's report suggested that between 20 per cent and 25 per cent of untrained staff leave the service per annum and the average length of time spent in the form of part-time employment is about four years. Graham *et al.* (1982: 82) confirmed this statistic, having discovered 18 per cent of their sample had taught for less than one year. A quarter of the respondents in a study in Lingfield (Jarvis 1982b: 84) were new to the centre in the year of the research, but since no questions were asked about their previous teaching experience it would be false to conclude that this research also confirms the figure. Tutor mobility between centres is clearly a possibility and the extent to which it occurs is still to be investigated. The system of annual contracts certainly encourages mobility, especially if a class has not run successfully in a centre in any year, when there is no reason why the tutor should not seek employment elsewhere on another occasion. Such mobility might result in tutors becoming committed to adult education but not to the local adult education institution.

Having examined adult educators and their role it is now necessary to see the orientation towards training and to examine the assumption that Hetherington made.

THE ADULT EDUCATOR'S TRAINING
AND QUALIFICATIONS

Adult education, like most other branches of education in the United Kingdom, except initial education, has been slow to produce a national pre-service teacher training scheme. While it was hoped that this would arise from developments in the United Kingdom, which are discussed below, it does appear to be rather idealistic, although in-service training is beginning to occur nationally. Campbell (1977) and Caldwell (1981) both indicate that a similar situation prevails in North America. Indeed, many who enter adult education on a full-time basis, let alone those who are part-time teachers, have no qualification in the education of adults at all – their teaching qualifications being in the education of children. Hence, it is possible to see that the discussion about the differences between andragogy and pedagogy has practical implications, since, while there are common elements, there may be enough significant differences to raise questions about the appropriateness of a pedagogic qualification for teaching adults and, also, it is fundamental to the consideration about the extent to which adult education can professionalize.

Training for adult education teachers was raised in the 1919 Report when it was suggested that more opportunities should be provided for training (para. 261) and that such teachers 'should have adequate remuneration and a reasonable degree of financial security' (para. 271). Thereafter, tutor training occupied the minds of adult educators on a number of occasions (see Legge 1991: 59–73 for a recent summary). Peers noted that:

> The matter was raised again by the Adult Education Committee of the Board of Education in a report published in 1922 (The Recruitment, Training and Remuneration of Teachers). In a report published by the Carnegie United Kingdom Trust in 1928, the result of an enquiry undertaken jointly by the British Institute of Adult Education and the Tutor's Association, the problem of training was discussed more fully and an account was given of existing experiments. Finally, after some years of discussion by a sub-committee of the Universities Council for Adult Education, the whole ground was surveyed again with some thoroughness in a report published in 1954 (Tutors and their Training).
>
> (Peers 1972: 217)

Peers (1972: 223) claims that training for adult education should be a major activity for all extra-mural departments, but this suggestion has been slow to be adopted and, for a while after the 1954 Report, tutor training ceased to occupy a significant place in the concerns of adult education. Martin, for instance, notes his disappointment that Mee and Wiltshire, whose work was published in 1978, 'dealt so little with training' (1981: 124). Indeed, when Legge (1968) wrote about the topic in the late 1960s there were few other adult educators expressing the same interest. This is very evident from the relatively little space devoted to tutor training in the National Institute of

Adult Education's national survey which stated that the 'proportion of Local Education Authority tutors claiming some kind of training was markedly higher than among their Responsible Body colleagues (34%:8%) and [that] a higher proportion was in favour of the provision of training facilities (74%:57%) (Hutchinson 1970: 177)'. However, there were movements at this time to initiate training schemes and the East Midlands Regional Advisory Council for Further Education introduced one in 1969 which had three stages (Elsdon 1970): an introduction, a more advanced course and, finally, a certificate course which was to be validated by the University of Nottingham. This scheme was introduced, and a description of this is given by Bestwick and Chadwick (1977); it has subsequently assumed greater significance since it was the model which the Advisory Council for the Supply and Training of Teachers used for its recommendation a decade later. However, before these recommendations are discussed it is necessary to review the research that puts these developments into perspective.

As Martin noted, little empirical research was actually published during this period to demonstrate either the expressed or felt needs of part-time or full-time staff for training or the extent to which provision was being made for their training, although the Russell Report (1973) suggested that part-time staff might be prepared to be trained and argued that appropriate training should be introduced. By the time that such research was published the Russell Report's recommendation had been acted upon and the Advisory Committee Report published. Even so, Martin (1981: 122) noted that while 41 per cent of his sample of 3,313 part-time tutors in the East Anglian Regional Advisory Council area were qualified day school teachers, 37 per cent of his respondents had no qualifications or had undertaken only an induction course mounted by the local adult education institute to familiarize new recruits with the institute, its procedures and adult education generally. The remainder of his sample had a variety of teaching qualifications ranging from the City and Guilds of London Institute, course 730, and teachers certificates of the Royal Society of Arts, to specialist sports coaching qualifications. In addition, a few actually held an ACSET Stage I award. Handley discovered a similar picture in her smaller sample and she records that from:

> the total sample 49% had attended training courses for primary education, 11.8% for secondary school teaching, 11.8% for further education and 24.5% for adult teaching. Another 7.8% had attended combined further education/adult education teacher training courses, 2% had attended both primary and adult training courses and 1% secondary and adult courses. Of significance is the 23.5% who had not attended any type of training course, and the further 12.7% who were non-respondents.
>
> (Handley 1981: 72)

Graham *et al.* (1982: 54) discovered a similar picture from the sample: 30 per cent (462) had some qualification in adult education, 34 per cent had school teaching qualifications, 12 per cent had subject qualifications only but

23 per cent had received no training at all. They noted that women were more likely than men to have undertaken training in adult education, which may indicate that women who might otherwise have been restricted to the role of housewife regard this training as important to their future careers. Of the 30 per cent who had received adult education training about half had a Stage I qualification from the East Midlands and a quarter had started the second level, or City and Guilds 730, course. Only 3 per cent, however, had acquired a Stage III qualification, from either the Universities of Leicester or Nottingham, which indicates that the length of time and amount of study required to complete this course may deter some part-time staff. Bestwick and Chadwick (1977) also record that out of the twenty-eight part-timers who originally expressed interest in the East Midlands Stage III scheme, only eight actually completed it. Clearly if part-time staff are not going to spend longer than four or five years teaching in adult education, as was noted previously, then there is little incentive to study part-time for two of those years. However, possession of Stage III certificate may, in itself, be an incentive for part-time staff not to depart after a short time in the service.

The variety of courses attended by and qualifications held by part-time adult educators is considerable: Handley (1981) notes that the sixty-eight tutors in her sample who had attended courses in adult and further education held fourteen different qualifications between them. Graham *et al.* (1982: 37–46) actually list the variety of different teaching and coaching qualifications awarded by nineteen organizations whose teachers may be employed in part-time adult education and yet they did not exhaust the list by any means. In addition, it has to be recognized that professions, such as nursing, award their own variety of teaching qualifications, so that before a national scheme for the training of educators of adults can be introduced it will be necessary to work out equivalences in these qualifications. This is already occurring to some extent since nurse tutors are already being allowed to enrol as registered nurse tutors if they held specific teaching qualifications, such as the Post Graduate Certificate in the Education of Adults from the University of Surrey and the Certificate of Education (Further Education) awarded by the Council of National Academic Awards in specified colleges.

In nursing, unqualified tutor status is regarded as temporary, so all nurses appointed as unqualified tutors are expected to seek a course of study as soon as they are able. This is not the case in some other professions and neither is it in adult education. Both Handley and Martin, however, record some statistics that indicate that a number of part-time adult education staff experience the need to undertake training: Handley (1981: 76) discovered that 50 per cent of her sample would be prepared to take advantage of any training provision whereas 38.2 per cent were unsure and 11.8 per cent were unwilling to do so; Martin (1981: 12) records that 240 of his sample had actually attended the Regional Advisory Council's Stage I course during their first year of teaching adults.

It is apparent from these research findings that training educators of adults had become a significant issue by the late 1970s and that the East Midlands scheme had played an important part in the process. Yet an adult education qualification is not mandatory for practice and no qualified teacher status actually exists. Indeed, qualified teacher status, i.e. having been trained to teach children, is still regarded as valid educational qualification for adult education, and Elsdon noted that while some school teachers undertook training in adult education they 'would have been theoretically exempted' (1975: 29). Elsdon's own publication on training part-time staff may be regarded as another significant landmark in the development of training educators of adults, appearing as it did at about the time that the Advisory Committee on the Supply and Training of Teachers was giving serious consideration to this topic.

In precisely the same way as adult educators in the United Kingdom were advocating the need for training, there was a similar movement in the United States. Lindeman (1938), for instance, advocated that all students studying in school teacher training should also study 'one unit of adult education covering one whole academic year' (cited in Brookfield 1988: 96). Overstreet and Overstreet (1941) noted that most adult educators had been trained by experience and by the end of the 1940s there was concern being expressed about the extent to which adult education was a profession and the type of training necessary for this (Hallenbeck 1948). By 1964, Houle could write about the emergence of graduate study in American adult education in America, although it is still clear that the greater majority of this study was in-service rather than pre-service.

RECENT DEVELOPMENTS IN TRAINING EDUCATORS OF ADULTS

The Advisory Committee on the Supply and Training of Teachers, under the chairmanship of Prof. N Haycocks, published three reports on the training of teachers in further and adult education. The first, in late 1977, concerned itself with the training of full-time further education staff and recommended a two-year part-time Certificate of Education (Further Education) course, with a qualification to be awarded at the end of the first year for those who did not wish to progress to the second year. The first year, it was suggested, should be more practical but should be planned in conjunction with the second year centre in order to ensure continuity. This report was published at the time that school teacher education was just recovering from the reorganization forced upon it by the James Committee, during which a number of colleges of education were amalgamated with polytechnics and had either become, or expanded, their departments of education. Hence, they, and some of the colleges of education that had retained their independence, were in a position to develop certificate courses in further education and, therefore, they became centres of training for further education teachers.

These colleges, once they had been approved by their Regional Advisory Council, submitted their courses to the Council for National Academic Awards for validation. Initially, the Further Education Board received mainly submissions that led to a certificate of education but, during the first four or five years courses were developed and submitted leading to first degrees, post-graduate certificates and higher degrees. All of these courses concentrated on full-time staff, or at least upon those that had at least ten hours' teaching per week; a few demanded only five hours' class contact but this tended to be the exception. Hence, the courses were devoted almost exclusively to further education, the majority of adult educators being excluded by the teaching requirement.

In March 1978, the Haycocks Committee made its second report, the subject of which was the training of part-time staff in further and adult education and the training of full-time staff in adult education. This report commenced by reviewing the then current provision for training for adult educators and noted that the College of Perceptors and the City and Guilds of London Institute courses provided a considerable amount of training at that time. This was especially true of the City and Guilds of London Institute Further Education teachers course (CGLI 730) which attracted some 3,000 candidates in 1975 and 1976. About half of those were tutors in branches of education outside further and adult education, notably the health service professions, Her Majesty's Forces and industry. Nursing has certainly taken advantage of the existence of this course for many years although, recently, the Panel of Assessors for District Nursing withdrew recognition of it as a qualifying route for practical work teachers since it tended to be further education orientated rather than specifically orientated towards the professional clinical situation. Nevertheless, this course did attract 700 from the ranks of the part-time staff of further and adult education, but it was recognized that it is predominately a further education course, and the City and Guilds of London Institute has subsequently devised a new course (CGLI 942) which was piloted in London in 1982.

The Advisory Committee's second report focused upon the East Midlands Regional scheme and noted that this was already being regarded as a model upon which the North West Region was considering constructing its own training programme. Finally, the Committee recommended that there should be a coherent scheme of initial training for all teachers working at post-school level which should lead to the award of Certificate of Education (Further Education) and to qualified teacher status, although this was more fully developed in a subsequent report.

The Haycocks Committee then went on to outline its proposal for this scheme, which was a three-stage scheme similar to the East Midlands scheme. The first stage, it was recommended, should be widely available, as an induction, should preferably be undertaken prior to employment, although it was recognized that this was perhaps idealistic, so that it was suggested that this initial stage might be offered during the first two terms of teaching. While this proposal appears more realistic it must also be recognized that new teachers do find preparation time-consuming, so it might not be as realistic as it appears at the outset. Caldwell (1981: 8) notes that pre-service training in adult education is also something of a rarity in the United States. Table 8.1 records the suggested content of the course, which should involve thirty-six hours of attendance.

Table 8.1 The recommended content for Stage I courses

- Motives and expectations of teachers and students
- Setting aims and objectives
- Introduction to learning theory
- Planning learning situations
- Introduction to teaching aids
- Introduction to lesson
- Evaluation

In addition to learning about the above, it was suggested that new part-time teachers should have a mentor who would work closely with them. More recently, Holt (1982) has argued that there are more cost-effective ways of preparing teachers in the classroom, such as micro-teaching. While this is a useful simulated exercise there is a great deal of artificiality about it, perhaps even more than there is about a supervised lesson in a classroom. Even so, micro-teaching is a very useful tool in training teachers.

The second stage of the recommended course was to be more advanced and involved sixty hours in the classroom and thirty six hours of supervised teaching practice. This amount of supervised teaching practice certainly places the emphasis of the course on practical teaching but there is little doubt that this was both an expensive and time-consuming recommendation. Table 8.2 specifies the subjects to be studied at this level.

Table 8.2 The recommended content for Stage II courses

- Setting objectives for teaching
- Psychology of learning in post-adolescent stages of life
- Teaching methods with post-school students
- Audio-visual aids
- Teaching specialist subjects
- Context of Further and Adult Education

It was noted that each of these modules should involve between eight and twelve hours of attendance. Initially it was considered that some of this might actually be reduced by the utilization of resource based packages, which is clearly an interesting suggestion, although the final report did not make such a recommendation. Little distance learning material at this level has been produced, except the Open University's course, which is produced in conjunction with the Council of Europe. The draft scheme of this course was published in 1982 and its content includes three booklets:

- adult learners: needs, motivations and expectations
- adult learners: responding to need
- further reference booklet, containing fifteen short papers on different but relevant topics

Ventures of this nature are important for the development of adult education, since they highlight specific elements of the emerging discipline of adult education. However, it is difficult for skills based courses to be provided by distance education and while resource based packages can reduce contact time, the skills elements still involve some form of supervision.

Stage II courses are pitched at about the same level as the City and Guilds of the London Institute Further Education Teachers' Certificate, course 730. The revised course (City and Guilds 1978) includes the topic areas shown in Table 8.3.

Table 8.3 The recommended content of the City and Guilds Course 730

- Principles of learning
- Principles of teaching strategy
- Learning resources
- Course organization and curriculum development
- Assessment
- Communication
- The teacher's role in relation to students in further education

This course also has supervised teaching practice, so that it approximates even more closely to the Stage II courses. Recently, the City and Guilds have actually piloted a course (CGLI 942) which is specifically orientated to Stage II of training for adult education.

The third stage of this training, the Advisory Committee recommended, should lead to full certification and should be provided by institutions in which 'there is a substantial nucleus of experienced staff who have themselves completed courses in advanced study in education and whose major commitment is the professional education and development of teachers at the post-school stage'. No other specific location was suggested for these courses nor was the content of the curriculum specified. However, it was stipulated that the course should take one year full-time or two years part-time to complete.

In addition, the Advisory Committee recognized the diversity of adult education and made the following recommendations for the training of full-time staff:

- new, untrained teachers entering full-time teaching in adult education should embark upon the first stage off the full-time Further Education Certificate recommended in the first Haycocks Report
- for those trained as teachers, in sectors other than further education, a six-week part-time, conversion course
- for part-time adult educators who have taken Stages I and II, a Stage III course leading to a Certificate in Education (FE)
- a one-year full-time, or equivalent part-time, for those who possess the Certificate in Education (FE) for those who wish to work as organizers and administrators in adult education – leading to an advanced diploma in adult education or higher degree

Thus, it may be seen that no division between further education and adult education existed in the recommendations for initial training at all three levels and that it was only at post-certificate level that adult education was regarded as a specialism. Hence, there is a conceptual confusion in the report that is also evident in its recommendations. This was one of the criticisms made by the Advisory Council for Adult and Continuing Education (1978) in its formal response to the recommendations. In addition, it criticized them for being too narrow, for trying to combine forms of training that ought to be separated and for omitting any consideration of using the university depart- ments of adult education in initial training. These are all valid criticisms of an important but conceptually confused report, so it is not surprising that the training of education staff has developed less rapidly than that of further educa- tion staff.

By mid-1981, Graham *et al.* (1982: 1) report that there was considerable variation in provision both between and within Regional Advisory Council areas. They also noted that while areas had introduced Stage I schemes, fewer councils had approved guidelines for Stage II. Stage III schemes appeared to be assuming one of two forms: either the Certificate of Education (Further Education), as recommended by the Advisory Committee on the Supply and Training of Teachers, but in other regions consideration was being given for special arrangements with universities in which a Certificate of Education (Adult Education) would be awarded. This is a confusion that, in retrospect, the Advisory Committee might have prevented had its recommendations been a little clearer, but it must be borne in mind that in the United Kingdom adult education is usually coupled with further education for administrative purposes. However, one university (Surrey) had already introduced a post-graduate certificate in the education of adults, in which the process of teaching and learning among adults is paramount, irrespective of what professional background the trainee teacher comes from, including further education, although the specific sphere of intended teaching does constitute an option within the study and is also the area in which the teaching practical experience is gained. Thus the term 'adult education' does overcome some of the conceptual difficulties raised by the Advisory Committee's report and the scheme at Surrey allows for teachers of adults to be trained together irrespective of whether they come from adult, further or higher education or from the professions. In 1983, there was also a proposal by the new Advisory Committee for the Supply and Education of Teachers for a Certificate in Education course for all teachers, irrespective of their background.

Higher education was rarely mentioned in the above discussion since it is usually regarded as distinct from further and adult education. Even so, this division has been blurred with a number of colleges being called 'colleges of further education'. Indeed, some of the early proposals for Certificate in Education courses made to the Council for National Academic Awards specified that they were in further and higher education. The Council, however, did not recommend acceptance of many titles incorporating the term and yet most students in higher education are adults, and thus teachers in higher education are actually teachers of adults. Some initial training of teachers is occurring in some universities, but few have moved in the direction of awarding qualifications, such as Stage I etc. in higher education. Nevertheless, the London Region of the Workers Educational Association, which offers a variety of part-time courses for adults including university extension classes, introduced a training scheme for its own part-time staff, which is based on the Advisory Committee's recommendations and which is recognized as a Stage I course.

Planning schemes for the first two stages of training became the responsibility of the institutions offering the courses and validation rested with the Regional Advisory Councils until their dissolution. However, the Advisory Committee on the Supply and Training of Teachers recommended that there should be some type of national forum established in order to ensure comparability and transferability. With the emergence of credit accumulation and transfer schemes this has become a practicality.

It will be recognized that much of the preceding discussion reflects developments that occurred a number of years ago and education itself has changed since then with a greater emphasis being placed upon competence and national vocational qualifications. Even university courses are considering adopting a national vocational qualification approach and so the training of adult educators cannot remain outside these developments. Indeed, City and Guilds have undertaken pilot studies of a competence based 730 course which does not have a National Council of Vocational Qualifications approval. However, this is the direction that his course appears to be taking.

In addition, Last and Chown (1993: 234–6) report that the Further Education Unit has taken it upon itself to produce 'an entirely new competence based qualification framework for the sector' and this approach does have NCVQ approval. While they are not entirely happy with the approach, they report that they are currently preparing their own curriculum for the training of adult educators that is much more orientated to the current competence based approach. They suggest that it is in accord with some of the best practices in adult education, such as reflective learning, in a manner espoused by Schon (1983).

Having examined the education of adult educators in some detail it is now necessary to discuss the qualities of the adult educator and possible criteria for curricula of training.

THE QUALITIES OF THE ADULT EDUCATOR AND CRITERIA FOR CURRICULA OF TRAINING

While the Advisory Committee made certain recommendations for the curriculum for the first two stages of training in the education of adults, no recommendations were made about the third one. However, even the first two stages reflected the values and philosophies prevalent in the Committee at that time. Clearly, the Committee expected the initial training to be very practical, almost a survival kit for teachers. The fact that 'objectives' occur in both stages suggests that the Committee were concerning with a teacher-centred approach to teaching and one that might allow for a behavioural objectives approach, which it would be claimed here is contrary to much in the philosophy of the education of adults. Curriculum recommendations can never be free of the values of the designer, but these values do need to be assessed before accepting uncritically the curriculum content suggestions made in the report. It is also necessary to explore the relationship between curriculum recommendations for training and the role of the practitioner. Four such relationships are examined here: the role of the adult educator as the basis for the curriculum for training; the idealized, or theoretical, role of the adult educator as the basis of the training curriculum; the elements of role competency which might form a base; the demands of the emerging discipline. Each of these four possible relationships are now examined.

The role of the adult educator as a basis for the curriculum of training

Earlier to this chapter the diversity of roles of the educator of adults was discussed and the difference between the work of the full-time and part-time staff were clearly noted: the former playing an administrative and managerial role and the latter performing a predominantly teaching function. Hence, it might be argued that the full-time adult educators need a diploma in management as much as they need a certificate of education, since the current situation is one in which they may be performing roles for which they have not been trained and trained for ones they are not playing! It is perhaps significant that educational management formed a part of the final report from the Haycocks Committee (August 1983) and that over the past decade a number of management courses have emerged, and have been highly successful. At the same time, management is only one element in this complex role and it does make it difficult to prepare adult educators for every aspect of it.

Even if the role of the adult educator were to form the basis of training, a number of problems exist, such as: the extent to which it is possible to analyse such a diverse role; the fact that no analysis has been conducted scientifically and, even if it had, it would only be valid for the contemporary situation; it includes no predictions about how the role will change in the future, so that it does not constitute an adequate basis for training the next generation of adult educators. Does this mean that the training curriculum need bear no relationship to the manner in which the role is performed? No, this is certainly not the case – any role analysis should be taken into consideration when designing curricula for training adult educators but they should not form its only base.

The theoretical role of the adult educator as a basis for a curriculum of training

In contrast to the actual role of the educators of adults it might be argued that it is better to train new recruits into the role that they should play, rather than the one that current practitioners are actually performing. Yet the values in this perspective must be recognized since the varying approaches to the role – radical, political, social welfare, etc. – have been explicit in the previous discussion. Even so, many attempts have been made to construct criteria of the idealized, or theoretical, role of the adult educator and, having reviewed many of them, Campbell wrote:

> Such lists are well nigh endless, indeed tiresome – but useful to a degree. Out of this formidable, though by no means exhaustive array of analyses it is possible to identify three distinct, significant clusters of competencies marking the ideal adult educator which can be taken as generalized goals for training. The first is a conviction within the adult educator of the potentiality for growth of adults, and a strong personal commitment to adult education exemplified by the extension of his own education. The willingness to accept others' ideas, the encouragement of freedom of thought and expression is fundamental as is a dynamic rather than a static view of the field of adult education. The second is the possession of certain skills – of writing and speaking, certainly – but also the capacity to lead groups effectively, to direct complex administrative activity, and to exercise a flair in the development of programs. Finally, the adult educator must understand the conditions under which adults learn, their motivation for learning, the nature of the community and its structure. Underlying all of these, and essential, is an understanding of oneself undergirded by a sustaining personal philosophy.
>
> (Campbell 1977: 58)

Tough (1979: 181–3) echoes many of these points in his discussion of the characteristics of the ideal helper as: warm and loving; having confidence in the learner's ability; being prepared always to enter a genuine dialogue with the learner; having a strong motivation to help; being an open and growing person. Both Campbell and Tough reflect the humanistic tradition which is prevalent in the adult education, but which may be less strong in other areas of the education of adults. For instance, Gibbs and Durbridge (1976) asked Open University full-time staff tutors what they looked for in effectvie part-time tutors. The replies that they received were reported under the following headings: knowledge of the subject matter; ability to handle the subject matter; general teaching skills; classroom skills; correspondence skills; social competence; academic suitability; values and work rate; administrative competence; interesting style; systematic style; understanding style; informal, flexible style. Hence, it may be seen that more emphasis was placed upon the teacher and his teaching skills by Open University staff than upon the adult educator as a human being who facilitates adult learning. Mocker and Noble (1981: 45–6) sought to construct a fairly full list, but even they warn their readers that it is neither exhaustive nor is it a blue print for training. Their twenty-four different competencies are that an adult educator should be able to:

1 communicate effectively with learners
2 develop effective working relationships with learners
3 re-inforce positive attitudes towards learners
4 develop a climate that will encourage learners to participate
5 establish a basis for mutual respect with learners
6 adjust rate of instruction to the learners' rate of progress
7 adjust teaching to accommodate individual and group characteristics
8 differentiate between teaching children and teaching adults
9 devise instructional categories that will develop the learners' confidence
10 maintain the learners' interest in classroom activities
11 adjust a program to respond to the changing needs of learners
12 use classrooms and other settings that provide a comfortable learning environment
13 recognise learners' potentiality for growth
14 place learners at their instructional level
15 summarize and review the main points of a lesson or demonstration
16 participate in a self-evaluation of teaching effectiveness
17 provide continuous feedback to the learners on their educational progress
18 select those components of a subject area that are essential to learners
19 coordinate and supervise classroom activities
20 determine those principles of learning that apply to adults
21 demonstrate belief in innovation and experimentation by willingness to try new approaches in the classroom
22 plan independent study with learners
23 apply knowledge of material and procedures gained from other teachers
24 relate classroom activities to the experience of learners.

At first sight this list appears full and exhaustive and yet on closer scrutiny there are points with which some adult educators may wish to dispute. Indeed, this would be the case with any such list, however long it might be. The values of the person who constructs such an inventory must always be apparent in it, so that no such list could provide an undisputed basis for devising a curriculum of training. If many lists were consulted, it might be possible to distil out the common factors which might provide something of a foundation, but without an agreed theoretical perspective this approach fails to provide a problem-free approach.

It may thus be seen that attempts to devise a list of competencies for educators of adults have not been successful in the past, and there is no reason why it will be so in the future. Indeed, it is perhaps pertinent for educators to ask whether they are so happy with the developments towards competency based in education generally that they want to introduce it into the preparation of educators themselves.

A conceptual framework of professional competency

Instead of attempting to utilize every element in the professional role, Jarvis (1983: 35) has suggested that it is necessary to analyse the concept of competency and this might help provide a basis upon which a curriculum could be constructed. It was suggested that this could be built upon the triple foundations of the practitioner's knowledge, skill and attitude:

- knowledge and understanding of: relevant academic discipline(s), psycho-motor elements, inter-personal relations, moral values
- skills to: perform the psycho-motor techniques, interact with members of the role set
- attitudes that result in: a knowledge and commitment to professionalism, a willingness to play the role in a professional manner

From such a basis it should be possible to devise the content of any training curriculum but, at the same time, it allows for negotiation between all interested parties as to what is actually included. However, it might be objected that attitudes should not constitute part of the training but, since adult education is a humanistic enterprise, it is maintained here that attitude education is an important element in the preparation of educators of adults.

The demands of the discipline

The previous approach outlines only broad guidelines rather than specific content and the approaches before that have attempted to relate the training to the role performance. Yet some professions have sought to separate

theory from practice and tend to regard competence in the academic discipline underlying their practice as sufficient grounds for entry into the profession. Turner and Rushton (1976) outline the training programmes
of a number of different professions and it is significant to note the place
that the academic discipline plays and the way by which skills are under-
played. It is claimed here that new entrants to adult education should
never be trained in this manner, and even if adult education had its own
discipline, the theory should never take total precedence over the practical.

Having examined a number of different approaches to the relationship
between training and practice it is maintained that no single, simple set of
guidelines may be constructed that would enable trainers to develop a univer-
sally accepted training curriculum, so it might be appropriate at this point
to recall Legge's conclusion about training teachers of adults:

> There are many questions to which we have had no firm answers, and whole
> areas in which research has been thin. Trainers should, therefore, plan
> each course as a new venture and not allow themselves to fall into the rut
> of just repeating a previous course. It is, of course, easier and less time
> consuming to develop a standard pattern, but it is as vitally important to
> keep the experimental nature of training as it is to focus sharply on the
> objective of improving the quality of teachers in the real world of classes
> and tutorials.
>
> (Legge 1981 : 64–5)

THE PROFESSIONALIZATION OF ADULT EDUCATION?

The introduction of these new training schemes for adult education is
going to have some effect on the structure of the occupation over the
coming years and it is suggested here that this may be viewed as a stage
in the process of professionalization. Yet some writers on adult education, e.g. Elsdon (1975), Mee (1980) and Wiltshire (1981), claim that
it is already a profession. However, there has not yet been a full and
detailed analysis of adult education from the perspective of students of
occupations and professions, so these claims appear to be little more than
adult educators making claims on behalf of their own occupation (but
see Jarvis 1985). No attempt is made to analyse these claims here since
this is a separate study. However, it is maintained that the present structures of adult education conform closely to those occupations generally
regarded as semi-professions, and so the introduction of training may be
regarded as a stage in its professionalization. Jarvis (1975) suggested
that a semi-profession has the following characteristics: no firm theoretical base; no monopoly of exclusive skills nor special area of competence; the existence of rules to guide practice; less specialization than

occupations generally regarded as professions; control exercised by non-professionals; service ethic. Space forbids any full discussion of each of these points, although it is essential to note that the development of a body of knowledge about the education of adults has received a stimulus from the introduction of these training courses for adult educators – a movement towards a more firm theoretical base. However, there has been an increasing number of taught masters degree courses offered in recent years and these are becoming one of the directons that continuing professional education is taking for educators of adults. More recently, there has also been an increase in the number of doctoral students undertaking research into the processes of adult learning and the education of adults. Perhaps this is a mark of the growing maturity of the teachers of adults, irrespective of whether, or not, they constitute a professional body. It can be postulated that there will soon be a taught doctorate offered in the education of adults, taking a similar form to that in the United States of America, even though taught doctorates are still a rarity in the United Kingdom.

However, the area of competence may be teaching rather than teaching adults, so that the debate about the differences between andragogy and pedagogy may be seen in this context too. If there is no difference, then adult education has no separate discipline(s) and the adult educator is not a member of a separate occupation but a member of a branch of teaching. Yet if there is a separate area of competence in teaching adults, how does this competence differ from that of the craftsman who instructs the apprentice on the job or the salesperson who teaches the client to use the sophisticated technical equipment that the latter has just purchased? There are no rules to guide practice, at least not codified and enforceable ones, and autonomy was one aspect that gave job satisfaction, as Mee and Wiltshire (1978) highlighted. However, it has been clearly demonstrated that there is little specialization in the occupation since teachers of adults may be qualified in teaching, qualified in some other occupation or not qualified at all. With few exceptions control over adult education is now exercised by non-adult educators and there is no professional body of adult educators which can exercise the control over adult education that the British Medical Association exercises over its members. There is a strong service ethic in adult education which also conforms to the semi-professional model.

Even so, it must be recognized that this model of a semi-profession is characterized by a number of traits, which is one of its major weaknesses since there is no theoretical reason why other characteristics should not be added to or subtracted from the present list. Consequently, this type of analysis is open to some criticism, but it is also the approach that Mee (1980: 105) employs for his analysis of adult education as a profession. It is a frequent analytical approach in the study of the professions but one that is of suspect value. Another reason why it is not favoured is that it presents a rather static picture of occupations and yet they are undergoing rapid change. It is for this reason that the term 'profession' is regarded as a conceptual 'ideal type' rather than an actuality and the idea of professionalization, a process of change in the direction of the ideal type, is more frequently employed. A number of attempts to describe the process of professionalization have been published, e.g. Caplow (1954), Greenwood (1957), but that very widely accepted is the formulation by Wilensky (1964). He suggested that as occupations professionalize they undergo a sequence of structural changes which, while not invarient, form a progression.

1 The occupation becomes full-time.
2 It establishes a training school, which it later seeks to associate with universities.
3 It forms its own professional association which seeks:
   – to define the core tasks of the occupation;
   – to create a cosmopolitan perspective to the practice of the occupation;
   – to compete with neighbouring occupations in order to establish an area of exclusive competence;
   – to seek legal support for the protection of the job territory.
4 It publishes its own code of ethics to assure the public that it will service its needs.

If this approach is adapted to the analysis of adult education it may be seen immediately that it is still functioning at the first two stages of the process and the recent developments described above merely indicate that adult education has just begun the process. Yet Illich (1977) must serve as a reminder to adult education that while there may be advantages in pursuing this process, there are also many dangers.

Yet it may be asked further whether it is important that adult education should be regarded as a profession. Perhaps it is important because adult education has traditionally been regarded as marginal to education. Indeed, in this age of managerialism, perhaps the question about professionalization is redundant; it is certainly not very relevant. Changes in society have resulted in managerial and organizational effectiveness and efficiency, so that professionalism has been marginalized. All welfare services have experienced these changes and adult education has not escaped these changes. It will be argued in Chapter 10 that these changes have caused adult education to be offered as a commodity on the market and so new roles for adult educators are appearing that are much more managerial than professional, although the concept of 'professional' is being redefined in order to incorporate these new approaches.

However, a much more important question may be whether its practitioners are professional. The term 'professional' has at least three meanings: one who receives emoluments for the performance of his or her occupational tasks; one who practises an occupation generally regarded as a profession; one who is an expert since he or she is master both of a specific branch of learning and of the skill to practise the occupation based upon it. It is this last meaning to which reference is being made here, since it is much more important that adult educators be professional than it is that the occupation should be regarded as a profession. Nevertheless, if its practitioners were generally regarded as experts then it would, perhaps, be easier for the occupation to progress along the pathway of professionalization, or at least be recognized as a legitimate field of practice.

SUMMARY

Teachers of adults and their preparation has formed the basis of this chapter, which began with a consideration of the extent to which adult education is actually an occupation and ended with an analysis of the extent to which it is a profession, or even whether this is a relevant question. The first question was raised because there are comparatively few full-time adult educators and many who teach on a part-time basis. It was also recognized that many who actually teach adults full-time, e.g. those in the professions, would not regard themselves as being members of an educational occupation but would regard themselves as members of their original profession. Thereafter, the roles of the adult educator were discussed and it was recognized that the full-time adult educators may be managers, employers, entrepreneurs, trainers, supervisors but that they may not actually be educators – except when they supervise their part-time staff or train their new recruits! By contrast, the part-time educator is actually the teacher who facilitates the students' learning. The characteristics of both full-time and part-time staff were examined and it was noted that, in common with most occupational groups, it is male dominated in those areas having higher status and more power.

The qualifications of adult education staff were analysed and their lack of training in adult education noted. This led to a discussion about the introduction of a national training scheme for adult educators, having three stages rather like the East Midlands Regional scheme that was already in operation before the report by the Advisory Committee was published. The confusion between adult education and further education was noted and it was recognized that this might lead to differing schemes emerging.

The qualities of an effective educator of adults were discussed and it was recognized that any list of qualities would be a subjective assessment which hardly constituted a sufficient basis upon which to construct a programme of training. Other criteria for devising training curricula were discussed and it was concluded that every new course should be regarded as a new venture and that this would help to keep the training of adult educators experimental and prevent it from ossifying.

Finally, it was suggested that adult education may be viewed as a semi-profession in the very early stages of professionalization rather than as a fully fledged professional occupation. Having examined the concepts surrounding the education of adults, learning and teaching and the teachers of adults, it is now necessary to analyse the educational process; thus the following chapter focuses upon the relation between curriculum theory and the education of adults.

9 Curriculum theory and programme planning

'Curriculum' is a relatively common word in initial education but one used less frequently in the education of adults, while 'programme' is more common. British writers, however, do use both curriculum design and programme design reasonably interchangeably, while American writers also use the terms 'design of learning' (Verner 1964) or 'design of education' (Houle 1972). The concerns of adult education have tended to be centred around the topics that have already been discussed and yet there has always been an implicit curriculum theory and also some explicit statements of rationale for adult education. In this chapter some of these elements will be discussed and, at the same time, the curriculum theory implicit in the ideas already raised will also become apparent.

At the outset it is necessary to clarify the concept itself and, thereafter, the reasons why the term has not been employed in the education of adults will be examined. Various types of curriculum models will then be discussed including the recent movement towards modularization. This will be followed by an analysis of the elements of the curriculum, including a discussion of the concept of 'need', which has been central to considerations in adult education. There have also been many developments in assessment procedures in the education of adults and these will be examined towards the end of the chapter. Finally, there will be a brief discussion on the hidden curriculum in the education of adults.

THE CONCEPT OF CURRICULUM

The word derives from the Latin 'currere' which means 'to run' and its associated noun which has been translated as 'a course'. Hence, the word has been used to refer to following a course of study; but, like many other terms, its meaning has been subtly changed over the years and Lawton notes that 'in the past definitions . . . tended to emphasize the content of the teaching programme, now writers on the curriculum are much more likely to define it in terms of the whole learning situation' (1973: 11). Similarly Kelly suggests that it is necessary to 'distinguish the use of the word to denote the content of a particular subject or area of study from the use of it to refer to the total programme of an educational institution (1977: 3). From these two brief quotations it is possible to see that even these writers are referring to slightly different usages of the word. Perhaps Griffin's comment that curriculum refers to 'the entire range of educational practices or learning experiences' (1978: 5) summarizes the problem. The word can mean the total provision of an educational institution, it can also refer to the subject matter of a particular course of study or even to the learning that is intended. Hence, it relates to both the known and the intended, i.e. the educational organization and provision, or to the unknown and unquantifiable, i.e. the learning experiences. Perhaps the various usages of the word can be clarified slightly by Figure 9.1.

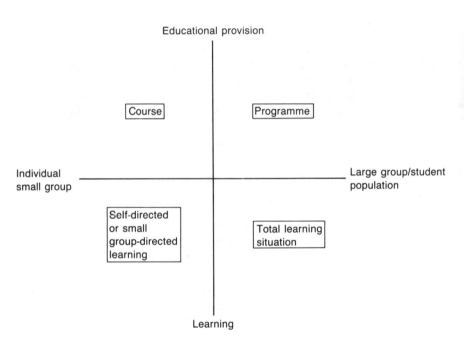

Figure 9.1 The uses of the term 'curriculum'

Figure 9.1 illustrates the different ways in which the term has been employed, especially in initial education. However, it is necessary to clarify the terms used and to explain each of the four boxes. Educational provision refers either to what is organized and offered to students by the institutions or what is organized and offered to the students by the teachers within those institutions. Learning refers to what the students actually acquired from having been the recipients of the educational provision. The large group/student population can refer to the actual or the potential student population of a whole institution, e.g. a college, or to a large part of the institution, e.g. a department within the college. The small group may refer to a single group within the department, e.g. the nursing students in a department of health studies, or to an even smaller group working together within a class.

Hence the programme may be either the prospectus provided by an educational institution, or a section of it, or it may refer to the actual number of courses that are organized after enrolment. The total learning situation refers to all the learning experiences, intended or unintended, provided by the educational institution, or by that part of it to which reference is being made.

A course may be the course of study followed by an individual within the institution or it may refer to a single course offered to a specific group of students, e.g. the nursing course. As modularization has developed, so the term 'course' has tended to refer to students' individual programmes of study. Modules, however, are individual courses. There has been a subtle, but nevertheless significant, change with the development of modularization. Previously, individual courses were usually built around the epistemological demands of an area of knowledge, e.g. a course on the sociology of the family, by the end of which students were expected to have grasped the rudiments of the subject irrespective of the number of hours that they studied beyond the hours that they were taught. This was something of an open-ended commitment on behalf of the student, but it was not really quantifiable. A module, however, is usually designated by the number of hours of learning that a student is expected to undertake, so that, for instance, a 50-hour module might involve 15 hours of teaching in the classroom, 15 hours of private study and a 20-hour assignment – although the exact constitution of the 50 hours is a matter of college policy. This 50 hours might be designated to occur over a short period of time, e.g. a few weeks (a 'short fat' module) or over a longer period. A 100-hour module, on the other hand, might involve 20 hours of classroom teaching, 40 hours of private study and a 40-hour assignment and this might occur over a period of 20 weeks (a 'long thin' module). Three important things to note about this change in curriculum design are: that more modules can be offered so that there is more student choice; that the length of the module has no relationship to the epistemological demands of the discipline; that there has been no research to examine the relative advantages of cramming a module into a short period of time, like a week, or holding it throughout a longer period, such as a semester, although it is probable that the longer period is more effective for learning but the shorter one for timetabling.

Finally, the self-directed, or the small-group directed, learning refers to the learning experiences gained by individuals working on their own projects. It must be emphasized that these terms are not all mutually exclusive since, for instance, the nursing course may be advertised in the college prospectus and the nursing students will experience learning within the total learning situation. By contrast, the self-directed learning need not occur within the context of an educational institution, e.g. the adults' learning projects discussed by Tough, so this is a slightly different understanding of the term.

It is perhaps easy to recognize how the confusion in the use of the term has arisen, since each of these terms has an affinity with the others. It is also important to note that the emphasis on learning is a comparatively recent addition and builds upon the ideas of the romantic curriculum and progressive education that were prevalent in the United Kingdom in the 1960s. At this stage it is clear that the term curriculum tends to reflect the totality of the learning as if it is a comprehensive and coherent whole, whereas programme implies that there are several parts to the whole, parts which students might choose for themselves. This is an important distinction and one that becomes more significant in any examination of the current situation in the education of adults. Certainly the scene has changed a great deal and much of the discussion about curriculum theory that occurred in the 1970s and early 1980s now appears extremely dated. This chapter will look briefly at this earlier material now before moving on to analyse the contemporary situation.

A HISTORICAL OVERVIEW OF CURRICULUM THEORY IN THE EDUCATION OF ADULTS

A great deal of curriculum theory that emerged was as a result of studies in initial education; indeed, in the United Kingdom there was an obvious reference to this with specific reference to romantic and classical curriculum models. The same was not so true in the United States where there was greater emphasis upon programme planning throughout the whole of this period. Consequently, this overview contains two sub-sections – the first stems from British writing on the subject while the second one comes mostly from the American writing, although the final aspect of this latter sub-section contains a model that Jarvis produced for the first edition of this book.

Curriculum models applied to the education of adults

Many attempts have been made to produce a satisfactory model of the teaching and learning process in curriculum terms. Frequently, reference is made back to Tyler's (1949) classic study, but Taba (1962: 425), citing Giles *et al.* (1942), has produced a model that, with slight adaptation, may be valid for the education of adults (see Figure 9.2).

This model is a reasonably familiar one within curriculum theory since it contains the elements that occur in almost every learning and teaching process. Taba wrote:

> A curriculum usually contains a statement of aims and of specific objectives; it indicates some selection and organization of content; it either implies or manifests certain patterns of learning and teaching, whether because the objectives demand them or because the content organization requires them. Finally, it includes a programme of evaluation of the outcomes
>
> (Taba 1962: 10)

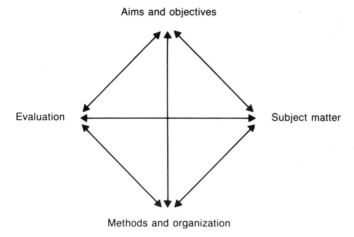

Figure 9.2 A learning and teaching process model for the education of adults

The above model may be applied to every course offered in an educational institution rather than to the overall programme and thus there may be considerable variation with the elements of the curriculum between different courses. Hence, discussion about the aforementioned elements must necessarily still remain at the level of generality.

Aims and objectives

British educators, claimed Davies, 'have been more interested in defining aims than in studying objectives, while American teachers have been more willing to think in terms of concrete objectives' (1976: 11). Certainly this claim would be true of the curriculum models of both Verner and Houle that were identified earlier in this chapter. By contrast, British theorists have focused upon the broader philosophical issues, as both Griffin (1978) and Mee and Wiltshire (1978) demonstrate, in their respective ways, the significance of aims in the education of adults. Yet the broad philosophy of educators of adults may also affect their attitude towards the concept, and use, of objectives within the design of a teaching and learning situation. Curriculum theorists have posited many types of objectives: instructional, teaching, learning, behavioural, expressive, etc. Davies (1976) discussed the whole area very thoroughly, so there is no need to expand it here. Even so, it is useful to examine the relationship between aims and objectives and to see whether the latter actually reflect the overall aims as even the general philosophy of adult education. For instance, in recent years there has been considerable emphasis given to behavioural objectives, and while these might be quite valid on a skills-based course, their usefulness in cognitive learning courses may be more questionable and contrary to the overall philosophy of adult learning. Objectives specified in behavioural terms tend to imply that the human learner will learn and behave in a manner designated by the teacher, like a pigeon or a rat! Another implication of this approach is that the teacher will adopt a didactic and authoritarian approach to teaching and this is quite contrary to the philosophy of teaching adults, a point discussed in a previous chapter. It is maintained here that any approach to teaching that designates how a learner will behave as a result of undergoing the teaching and learning process undermines the dignity of the learner and, consequently, the process of teaching and learning falls short of the high ideals of education elaborated in this study. By contrast, Eisner (1969) regards expressive objectives as evocative rather than prescriptive, which is much closer to the general philosophy of the education of adults which is advocated here. Nevertheless, behavioural objectives have a valid place in some forms of therapy, but while therapy might involve learning it is not education.

Subject matter

The content of some courses, especially those that are vocationally orientated or award bearing, is usually prescribed by the examining or the validating body. This reflects the point that the curriculum may be regarded as a selection of culture made by those who have status or power within the profession or within education. Elsewhere Jarvis (1983a: 50–53) has outlined other criteria for the selection of curriculum content in professional education including the demands of professional practice, the relevance of the topic, and its worthwhileness. However, there are courses in which the subject matter may actually be negotiated between tutor and students, but these courses tend to be exceptions rather than everyday occurrences. In liberal adult education these occurrences may be more frequent and the subject matter may depend upon the interests of the students and be negotiated between tutor and students.

Negotiated subject content may be much more common in continuing professional education since practitioners, being aware of their strengths and weaknesses in practice, will probably know what they need to learn during in-service education in order to improve the quality of their practice. Diagnosis of learning needs should have occurred prior to the course, so that it is essential for the teacher to join with the students in planning a teaching and learning programme. Often in continuing professional education it is useful to spend a planning day, a few weeks prior to the commencement of the course, mapping out the areas of the subject matter that should be covered during it. Diagnosis should always precede learning and teaching.

Organization and methods

The location of the teaching, the organization of the room in which the teaching and learning is to occur, the content of the session and the methods to be employed are all part of the educational process. They should all relate to the learners, their learning needs or wants and to their learning styles, but they are also dependent upon the expertise of the tutorial staff. The organization of the environment relates to the adulthood of the learners and to the teaching methods to be employed. Similarly, the actual methods employed by the teacher are important considerations in the educational process. Bourdieu and Passeron claim that all 'pedagogic action is, objectively, symbolic violence in so far as it is the imposition of a cultural arbitrary by an arbitrary power' (1977: 5). Hence, the methods employed are a significant factor and relate not merely to the content but also to the philosophy of the teacher. Teaching methods have already been examined in a previous chapter, so it is unnecessary to repeat any of that discussion here. But it is important to recognize the symbolic significance of the teaching method. Moreover, the symbolism becomes an immoral reality if the teaching methods employed in any teaching and learning transaction inhibit the development of, or undermine the dignity and humanity of, the learners; but it becomes moral, and good curriculum practice, when they encourage the growth and expression of humanity of the learners.

The philosophical issues involved in teaching are important considerations, especially in the education of adults, but the methods employed must also relate to the ethos of the group and the content of the session. Hence, the skill of the teacher is not only in relation to techniques but also in relation to human interaction, and it is a combination of these various factors that can lead to teaching and learning becoming an effective and stimulating process.

Evaluation

Clearly the aims and objectives that have been set for any single teaching and learning session or for a course as a whole provide one base for its evaluation. Yet these may prove to be too restrictive since the class may have deviated from the selected aims and even from the content decided upon because it followed up ideas that arose during the process itself. This may have resulted in effective learning and class satisfaction and all the participants regarded it as successful. Hence, if learning and understanding has occurred, within a humanistic context, then the education may be assessed as successful.

Yet evaluation should not be undertaken by teachers by themselves: in the education of adults the students should be full participants in the process. In non-compulsory education this occurs in any case, since as Newman forcibly reminds his readers:

> Adult education is a cruel test of a tutor's skills. It is a sink or swim business. If the tutor does not have what it takes, people stop coming. His students vote with their feet, unobtrusively transferring to other classes or simply staying away. The class dwindles week by week, leaving him all too well aware that he has been found wanting.
>
> (Newman 1979: 66)

Perhaps this is a rather dramatic portrayal of the manner by which students are actually involved in the process of evaluation. Indeed, many students are very kind to their tutors and encourage inexperienced ones. Even so, students do evaluate their tutors and the process of teaching and learning that has occurred, and so it is beneficial to all concerned to involve them in the more formal process.

The hidden curriculum

Every institution evolves its own procedures, many of which contain values that are recognized and intended but some of which may be unrecognized and unintended by those who formulate them. Some of these values have been highlighted in this chapter, such as those implicit in the teachers or students selecting the curriculum content, or in the use of various types of teaching. Yet there are others, and some of those that are unintended or recognized by the educators of adults may be apparent to the students who attend the institution, and it may be some of these that are learned and which affect their attitudes towards adult or continuing education. Hence, for instance, the differing status accorded to different types of class may be very clear to students, and those whose class is given low status may feel deprived. Examination classes may be given precedence over non-examinable leisure time study, even though the latter may actually be more academic in some instances! Courses that bring in funds to the institution may be given preference to other forms of education. There may be a profession of its being an adult education institution but the students may not be treated as adults either in the organization or in the teaching methods employed, or in the evaluation of the life and work of the institution. By contrast, other institutions may create such an ethos that the hidden curriculum purveys the humanistic ideals of education itself. The ethos of the institution is, therefore, the carrier of a message that may be received and learned by adult students who attend.

Classical and romantic models of the curriculum

The models discussed above owe their origin to theorists whose main concern was initial education, but many developments in school education curriculum theory were mirrored in the developments in adult education at this time. The classical curriculum reflected the teacher-centred approach while the 1960s emphasis on student-centred learning is reflected in the development of the romantic curriculum model.

The concepts of classical and romantic curriculum reflect contrasting educational ideologies, the latter coming to prominence in initial education in the 1960s, which has been regarded as a period of romanticism. These positions have been summarized by Lawton in two different tables and his argument is summarized here in Table 9.1.

Table 9.1 The classical and romantic curricula

Elements of the classical curriculum		Elements of the romantic curriculum	
subject-centred		child-centred	
skills		creativity	
instruction		experience	
information		discovery	
obedience		awareness	
conformity		originality	
discipline		freedom	
objectives	– acquiring knowledge	processes	– 'living' attitudes and values
content	– subjects	experiences	– real life topics and proposals
method	– didactic instruction	method	– involvement
	– competition		– cooperation
evaluation	– by tasks (teacher set)	evaluation	– self-assessment
	– by examinations (public and competitive)		(in terms of self-improvement)

Source: Lawton (1973: 22–3)

Most models must necessariy overemphasize their salient points, so Table 9.1 presents a polarization of the two curricula models. Yet the fact that the major features are highlighted means that it is possible to see immediately the significance of these formulations for a deeper understanding of the education of adults. Clearly the romantic curriculum, as formulated above, approximates to Knowles' interpretation of andragogy. It will be recalled that Knowles suggested that andragogy has four premises that are different from pedagogy: the learner is self-directed; the learner's experiences are a rich resource for learning; the learner's readiness to learn is increasingly orientated to the developmental tasks of social roles; the learner's time perspective assumes an immediacy, so that learning is problem- and performance- rather than subject-centred. Knowles (1989: 83–4) later added two other premises to this list, and his new list is: adults need to know why they are learning; adults' self-concept is of being responsible for their own lives; adults bring greater quality and quantity of experience to their new learning; adults are ready to learn what they need to know; their learning is life-centred; adults have intrinsic motivations to learn. Clearly Knowles did not formulate andragogy in curricular terminology and perhaps his failure to do so has been a major reason why the debate about it has been so wide ranging. Can andragogy be equated with the romantic curriculum? In many ways the response to this must be in the affirmative, although to label it as a formulation of the romantic curriculum and to dismiss it would do it a disservice. Embodied within it is a philosophy that is significant to adult education – the humanistic perspective – but this, it is maintained here, is a criterion of education itself.

More recently, Jarvis (1993b) has returned to the andragogy–pedagogy debate seeking to see why Knowles' work, which is so obviously wrong when applied to children and adults, has retained so much currency. It is suggested that the major variable distinguishing andragogy from pedagogy is experience, not chronological age. If this argument is accepted it is now possible to formulate the andragogy–pedagogy debate within the framework of the education for adults, which is a rather different perspective from that initially presented by Knowles. Indeed, individuals having little experience in a subject might want a more pedagogic approach whilst those having a lot of experience in an area might prefer an andagogic approach. This leads on to the possibility of conceptualizing the initial vocational education curriculum in pedagogic terms and the continuing vocational education programme in andragogic terms. From this it can be seen that it is more possible to discuss initial vocational education in traditional curriculum terms but much clearer to discuss continuing vocational education in programme terms. In both cases it must be recognized that the process occurs within the humanistic perspective of the education for adults.

Without a humanistic student-centred approach it is maintained here that learning and human development may be impaired, and this is the crux of Macfarlane's analysis of literacy education in terms of these two types of curricula, as Table 9.2 demonstrates.

Table 9.2 Macfarlane's analysis of adult literacy education in terms of two curricula models

	Curricular attitudes among advocates of the traditional curriculum	*Curricular attitudes among advocates of a student-centred curriculum*
Role of the student	Passive recipient of externally formulated process	Active participant in defining own goals and needs
The literacy process	Hierarchies, centred upon skills and stages of progress	Holistic, task centred
Tutor's view of student	One who is deprived and handicapped (and hence inferior)	An equal who is not to blame for failure
Impact on student's self-image	Relatively unimportant, a by-product of progress in skills	Purposefully enhanced
Student's view of tutor	'The expert who will cure me'	'The friend who helps me sort things out'
Dangers	Maintains dependency and lack of confidence. Transfer of skills to real world usage very doubtful	Threatens student and tutor with lack of structure and lack of perception of progress

Source: Macfarlane (1978: 156)

Once again, this type of approach over-emphasizes some of the differences but it may be seen how he suggests that the student-centred approach aids the learner's development and growth. Macfarlane notes that for either approach to be successful in any way demands quite different methods and organization. He also maintains that these different approaches have ramifications for policy, staff-recruitment, training and resource development. Yet it is clear from his own analysis that the student-centred approach is closer to the humanistic ideals mentioned earlier in this study, which are at the heart of adult education. Even so, this does not mean that all teaching need be of a facilitative style and in the following section this will be developed within the context of an analysis of some of the writings of Colin Griffin.

In the second chapter it was pointed out that continuing and recurrent education are two philosophies of lifelong education and that Griffin (1978) has examined these from the perspective of a curriculum theorist. Taking as his basis the teaching and learning process model, aims, content and method, he examines both continuing and recurrent education. His basic premise is that continuing education is related to the classical curriculum while recurrent education has a romantic curriculum basis. It will be recognized that this equation is not one that is maintained here but Griffin's analysis is important because it is a genuine attempt to apply curriculum theory to the education of adults. Griffin himself recognizes that the task he undertook was 'a tentative curriculum analysis' and herein lies its value. His study may be summarized in tabular form and Table 9.3 contains many of his major points.

Griffin's work needs to be read in detail in order to follow his arguments but it is clear from Table 9.3 that he sees a clear distinction in curricular terms between the two philosophies in the education of adults. That a practitioner may mix the two approaches is not denied but it is perhaps significant that as the 1960s were left behind, so the concept of romantic curriculum lost some of its appeal and more recently the term recurrent education has lost favour. Even so, many of the curricular aspects that Griffin discusses within this context do find their place within the wider sphere of adult education because, as it has been argued throughout this study, any form of education should have a humanistic basis if it is to achieve the high ideals of education itself.

In 1982, Griffin turned his attention to lifelong education and he noted that integration between initial education and education for the remainder of the lifespan is a significant issue that has resulted in an unbalanced policy debate, emphasizing access above all other factors. Overall, he recognized that curriculum development in the context of lifelong education is 'by no means as straight-forward as the needs/objectives/evaluation model might suggest. The coexistence of various curriculum models makes it a much more complicated affair' (1982: 119). This complexity was evident in Macfarlane's (1978) analysis and it is also clear in the distinctions drawn between initial

Table 9.3 A curriculum analysis of continuing and recurrent education

	Continuing education	Recurrent education
Aims	Professional standards of provision	Autonomous learning
	Flexible and accessible structures of provision	Personal authenticity
	Unity of response to diversity of need	Diversity of learning experiences
	Institutionalized standards of achievement and excellence	De-institutionalized criteria of performance
	Means/ends rationality model of institutional response	Assimilation of education to life-experience of individual learners
	Access to common culture	Promotion of cultural diversity in the context of meaning and goals
Content	Public criteria of learning performances	Expressive criteria of learning performances
	Subject structures reflecting forms of knowledge	Structures of knowledge contingent upon learning experience
	Mutual evaluation of subject demand	Problem solving response to conditions of alienation
	Mastery of, or initiation into, forms of knowledge and skill	Standards of learning performance relative to learning experience
	Knowledge for rational control and social mobility	Understanding for transformation through social solidarity
	Culturally appropriate institutional systems	Relevance for maintenance of sub-cultural identity
Methods	Effectiveness and evaluation	Methods stressing individual expression
	Professional criteria of relevance	Learners decide learning methods
	Professional standards based on adult learning theory	Methods reflecting diverse characteristics of learning situation
	Standards of teaching methods as a function of institutional provision	Standards as a function of a personal authenticity
	Methods reflecting the rationality of provision	Methods for transforming life-experience
	Teaching roles distinguish educational from social authority	Methods reflecting culturally significant aspects of learning

Source: Griffin (1978)

and post-initial education curricula models. Griffin, in this latter paper, highlights that policy factors of social control are fundamental to education and most apparent in the provision of lifelong education.

Implicit in the debate about continuing and recurrent education and in the distinction between classical and romantic curricula is the matter of control: who should control the learning activities; who should control the learning outcomes? etc. Since the romantic education is student-centred there is a sense in which control moved in the students' direction. This is even more evident in programme models that appeared at about this time.

In more recent writings there has been a movement away from the terminology about curriculum produced by initial educational theorists. One example of this is Bines' (1992) threefold typology of professional education training models: apprenticeship, technocratic and post-technocratic models of initial professional education. She suggests that the apprenticeship model is one which involves on-the-job instruction with some day release in order to acquire some 'cookbook knowledge' which is basically practical knowledge. Technocratic curricula consist of a threefold approach to professional preparation: transmission of some systematic knowledge; the interpretation of that knowledge as it is applied to practice; practical placements. The third model, which is a response to the weakness of the positivist approaches contained in the second model, is built upon both the experience of practice and reflection on it, so that its focus is upon professional competence, and the practical experience becomes the centre of the professional preparation. She recognizes, however, that as resources become scarce it becomes more difficult to staff practical training adequately. However, this model does not really develop a systematic epistemology, although it has a basis upon which this might be built, but it does reflect the concerns of writers like Schon (1987). Competence, however, is a most difficult phenomenon to assess, as one experiment at the University of Surrey demonstrates.

In general nurse training a few years ago it was expected that student nurses would successfully pass four practical assessments during their training. A student nurse was video-taped undertaking one of these assessment procedures and the ward sister in whose ward she was working adjudged that she had actually failed the practical assessment at the time when the video was made. It was then shown to a group of thirty experienced nurses who were on an assessment training course – about one-third of those watching would have passed the student on the performance that they witnessed, while two-thirds agreed with the ward sister and would have failed her. However, the student had already successfully passed that assessment a number of months previously! Professional competence is not necessarily an easy thing to assess. Another problem with the competence based approach to practice is that sometimes good practitioners are good because they know when not to act, as well as when to act, and it is difficult to assess the competence of active inactivity! Consequently, it does appear that the post-technocratic approach which is currently in use is one which, while it seeks to overcome some of the problems of the previous curriculum approach, still requires a great deal more refinement.

Even so, the significant thing about Bines' approach is that it seeks to reconceptualize curriculum theory in terms of professional preparation and to produce models which are appropriate for education beyond school. In addition, she has endeavoured to make a distinction between curricula for initial professional education and programmes for professional continuing education. She does not develop this latter aspect, although there are instances of this in Bines and Watson (1992). However, this approach comes much closer to the American literature on programme development, which is explored in the following section.

Programme planning models

Earlier in this chapter it was noted that some of the American theories in adult education have concentrated upon the design of education and two of these writers, Verner (1964) and Houle (1972), are examined here. In addition, a more recent model by Boone (1985) is discussed briefly. Finally, in a study of an adult education institute in the United Kingdom two models of curriculum were developed and they are modified slightly and discussed here.

A considerable proportion of Verner's (1964) study is devoted to the curriculum, and Figure 9.3 summarizes the main elements of his work.

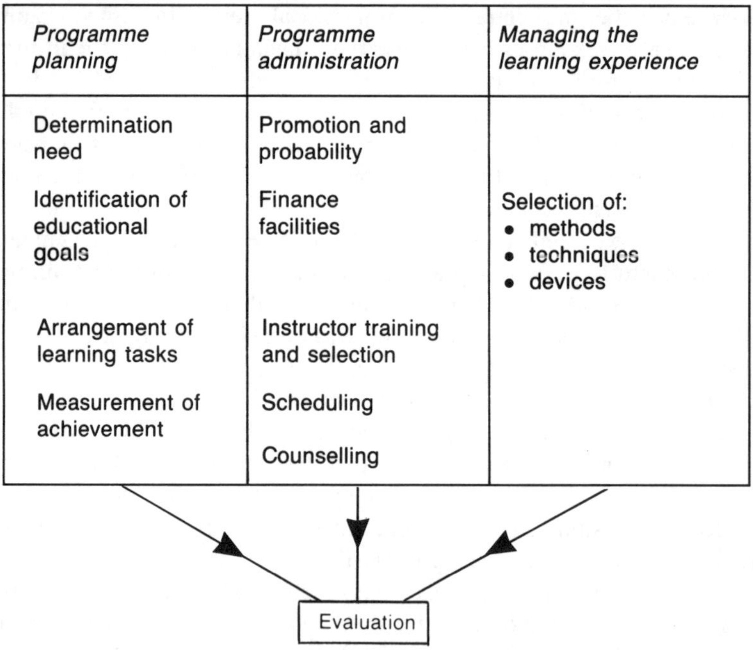

Programme planning	Programme administration	Managing the learning experience
Determination need	Promotion and probability	
Identification of educational goals	Finance facilities	Selection of: • methods • techniques • devices
Arrangement of learning tasks	Instructor training and selection	
Measurement of achievement	Scheduling	
	Counselling	

Evaluation

Figure 9.3 A diagrammatic portrayal of Verner's approach to the curriculum in the education of adults
Source: Verner (1964)

It may be seen from Figure 9.3 that Verner bases his planning on a needs meeting approach, a topic that will be considered in detail later in this chapter. He also distinguishes between planning, administration and the actual teaching, but it will be recalled from the discussion on the role of the educator of adults that the managerial and teaching roles were clearly highlighted, so that Verner's threefold distinction may be a little artificial in relation to role performance. Nevertheless, the distinction that he draws between planning and administration, on the one hand, and managing and learning experiences, on the other, does reflect the earlier discussion. Verner employs the term 'techniques' to refer to the ways in which the teacher establishes a relationship between the learner and the learning tasks, while 'devices' are the audio-visual aids that the teacher uses to assist him in his task. Verner's model is a clear taxonomy of some of the elements of the curriculum but he did not seek to build it into a comprehensive curriculum theory. It is, therefore, necessary to examine the work of Houle, one of the most well known of writers on this topic in America, who sought to illustrate the design of education.

Houle (1972), whilst recognizing the complexity of designing an educational programme, produces two different types of models. He recognizes that there are a variety of different educational situations in which a programme may be designed, and Table 9.4 illustrates the eleven different ones that he considered significant.

Table 9.4 Houle's major categories of educational design situations

Individual

c1   An individual designs an activity for himself

c2   An individual or group design an activity for another individual

Group

c3   A group (with or without a continuing leader) designs an activity for itself

c4   A teacher, or a group of teachers, designs an activity for, and often with, a group of students

c5   A committee designs an activity for a larger group

c6   Two or more groups design an activity which will enhance their combined programmes of service

Institution

c7   A new institution is designed

c8   An institution designs an activity in a new format

c9   An institution designs a new activity in an established format

c10   Two or more institutions design an activity which will enhance their combined programmes of service

Mass

c11   An individual, group or institution designs an activity for a mass audience

Source: Houle (1972: 44)

It will be seen that these various situations listed by Houle encapsulate a variety of adult learning situations, so that it is possible to fit within this framework self-directed learning, on the one hand, and planning an informative documentary television programme for a mass audience, on the other. Houle discusses each of these situations very fully in his writing, which is a most valuable exercise in the study of the design of education. Nevertheless, such a classification records nothing of the actual process that underlies the production of these educational situations, and so he goes on to produce the points that

Verner raises, but Houle does so within the context of a systems approach, which is summarized in Table 9.5.

Table 9.5 Summary of Houle's decision points in programme planning

1 Identification of possible educational programme
2 Decision taken to proceed
3 Identification of Objectives
4 Refining the Objectives
5 Designing the Format
6 Contextualising the Format
7 Putting the Plan into operation
8 Measuring the results
9 Evaluating the results

Source: Houle (1972: 47)

Houle also recognized that in the design of the format it is necessary to consider the following points: resources; leaders; methods; schedule, sequence; social reinforcement; individualization; roles and relationships; criteria for evaluation; clarity of design. In addition, he suggested that in contextualizing the format, programme planners should consider: guidance or counselling; lifestyle; finance; interpretation. This model has become quite widely cited as a clear approach to programme planning, as indeed it is, but it does omit a number of issues, some of which will be discussed later in this chapter.

Houle states that in 'applying the model to a situation, one may begin with any component and proceed to others in any order' (1972: 46–7). However, this is not really what the diagram suggests since it illustrates a sequential cycle which, while commencement may be made at any point, takes the programme designer through seven stages with the fourth and fifth stages having a number of individual facets. This model is meticulous in its production and Houle's discussion admirably thorough but it does adopt the perspective of the adult educator who is able to design an educational programme free from external constraint, which may not actually reflect the reality of what happens during the process. It is, therefore, necessary to include external factors as a variable in the process.

About the same time that Houle was producing his model, Verduin (1980) wrote a book in which he discussed curriculum building. The book claims to produce the first curriculum model for adult education, although this is rather a problematic claim in the light of the programme planning books that were already published. While he used the term 'curriculum' he did not produce a theoretical discussion of the concept, although he outlined five elements in his model: aim (which he called direction), outside political forces, goals, instruction and evaluation. In addition, he was very concerned with practical processes of planning instruction, with a behaviourist orientation. For instance, in one place he (1980: 102) produced a fivefold chart: assess entering

behaviour; specific behavioural objectives; specify learning unit and procedures; present learning unit and tasks; student performs and learns. This
was an early book in this field and one which at least recognizes the possibility
that adult education could have a curriculum.

In 1985, Boone produced a comprehensive overview of programme planning
and in this case he uses the term in rather the same way as British educators
tend to use the term workshop or specially designed course. In his approach he
examined many of the major American theories and then proceeded to produce
his own model in which he recognized two stages in programme planning: the
organization and its renewal processes and linking the organization to its publics;
two stages of design and implementation and a final stage of evaluation. This
is a very practical approach since he proceeded to list in each of these five stages
the essential elements to consider, as Table 9.6 indicates.

Clearly this is a behaviourist and empirical model, but it is quite realistic
about the way that educational activities have to offer themselves on the market

Table 9.6 Summary of Boone's model of programme planning

Stage 1 – Understanding the organization and its renewal processes, including:

- Commitment to its function
- Commitment to its structures
- Its processes
- Its commitment to using a tested framework for programme planning
- Its commitment to renewal

Stage 2 – Linking the organization to its publics, including:

- Mapping its publics
- Identifying its target publics
- Interfacing with leaders of these publics
- Collaborative assessment of needs

Stage 3 – Designing the planned programme, including:

- Translating expressed needs to macro-needs
- Translating these into objectives
- Identifying educational strategies
- Specifying intended outcomes

Stage 4 – Implementing the programme, including:

- Developing action plans
- Developing and implementing strategies for marketing the plans
- Following through on plans
- Training leaders
- Monitoring and reinforcing the teacher–learner transaction

Stage 5 – Evaluation and accountability, including:

- Determining and measuring programme outcomes
- Assessing programme inputs
- Using results for programme revision and organizational renewal
- Using results as appropriate in accounting to sponsors etc.

Source: Boone (1985)

and seek to demonstrate their usefulness. The idea of education in the market place is a theme that will be discussed further later in this chapter.

More recently, Langenbach (1988) examined a variety of curricula prevalent in adult education. He defined a curriculum model as 'a plan that creates access to education and training' (1988: 2), which illustrates that his major concern is with elements of programme planning. Nevertheless he does examine a variety of the American approaches to adult education, plus the work of Freire, from a curriculum perspective. This is one of the first text books on the topic written for adult educators.

There is, however, another approach to curriculum and programme design which stems from the work of Lawton (1973). In a recent study of one adult education centre an attempt was undertaken to include the external factors and also to include the teaching and learning process: this resulted in two different models being devised – an administrative one and an educational one (Jarvis 1982b). Here, these two models are modified slightly and their titles amended to a curriculum planning model and a teaching and learning model. The first incorporates many of the elements discussed by Verner and Houle and the second reflects the traditional curriculum model of initial education. The teaching and learning model was introduced in Figure 9.2 where the educational processes were discussed, and the curriculum planning, which is a management of the educational process, is discussed here because there are two distinct processes involved: there is the management of the educational process and the teaching and learning process and there may be many of the latter contained in one of the former processes.

The curriculum planning model contains a development of some of the elements contained in Lawton's (1973: 21) model of producing a school timetable and it is important to recognize that there is an affinity between the planning of the school timetable and the planning of the programme in the education of adults. However, Lawton's model required considerable adaptation in order to be relevant to the education of adults.

Figure 9.4 represents a much more complicated system than that depicted by Houle and Boone since it seeks to demonstrate that the educational process is exposed to the influence of the wider society and its governing bodies, as well as being affected by the philosophy of the educator. In fact, an uneasy tension may exist as a result of the interplay of the forces stemming from factors mentioned in the first three boxes. Each of these elements will be elaborated upon in a subsequent section of this chapter, but it is clear from Figure 9.4 that the system depicted here illustrates an important factor in the education of adults. This is a systems model, similar to other systems models, produced by organization theorists in order to assess the functioning of other types of organizations (e.g. Child, J. 1977: 144–78), so it may be seen how the sociological study of the education of adults may benefit from similar sociological analyses conducted in other areas of social life. Each of the elements in Figure 9.4 are discussed briefly in order to raise some of the main features of programme planning and also to enable it to be more fully contextualised.

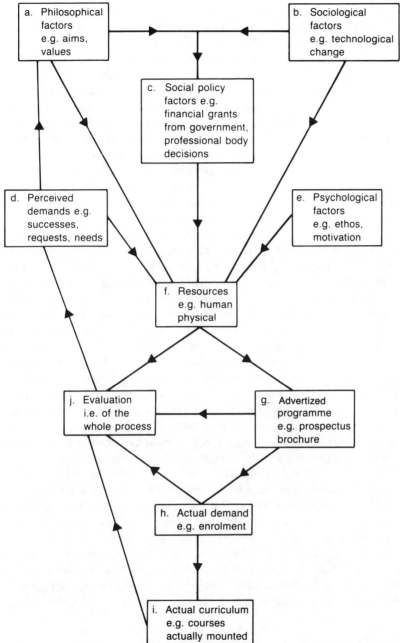

Figure 9.4 A curriculum planning model for the education of adults

Philosophical factors

Underlying every programme of education there is a philosophy, whether it is explicit or implicit, considered or rarely thought about, consistent or inconsistent; it may be a philosophy constrained by other factors, such as social policy, but it remains a philosophy. At the outset of this study a rationale for the education of adults was produced which argues that every human being has a basic need to learn and that in a rapidly changing society each individual may need to make many adjustments in order to be in harmony with the socio-cultural milieu. Most individuals will develop as a result of their experiences, although it was recognized that growth is not inevitable. This approach, however, reflects Dewey's (1916) assertion that education is a means to human growth and that growth continues throughout the whole of life. Therefore, it is maintained here that underlying every curriculum should be a concern about the development of the learners as persons. This is a humanistic, progressive perspective and one that is prevalent in adult education.

It was also recognized at the outset that society is changing rapidly and that some types of knowledge change so rapidly that they appear artificial. Hence, it is essential that some people keep abreast with contemporary developments, so that it could be argued that society has the need to produce a specific type of person who will be a lifelong learner. Education is frequently accused of being a process that moulds and controls people so that they fit into a niche in society without disrupting it very greatly. The lifelong learner may be flexible, adaptable and totally commendable, but that education should thus mould a person is a more questionable process. If educators see their role in terms of responding to the needs of the wider society primarily, they clearly have a different philosophical perspective upon education than the one being argued in this study. This does not mean that the humanistic, progressive approach to education has no concern about the needs of society, only that it sees the development of the learners as persons as they acquire a critical awareness, knowledge and understanding as more significant in educational terms.

Other philosophical perspectives may also underpin the whole of an educational programme. Elias and Merriam (1980) point out that both liberal and radical philosophies are also significant in curriculum design. Hence, it is possible to see that the literacy programme devised by Freire was considerably influenced by his own philosophy and that of his co-workers, and that this approach was totally different from literacy education in societies, such as the United Kingdom, in which this philosophical perspective is not prevalent. Even so, Freire's own programme was not free to operate without influences upon it, such as the forces operating in the wider society.

Sociological factors

It was recognized above and in the opening chapter that the curriculum itself may be regarded as a selection from culture, so that the social forces that operate upon the educational process are quite profound. Culture is changing rapidly and various aspects of knowledge are changing rapidly. Yet knowledge itself is not value-free: some has high status without being very practical whilst other knowledge has low status but is most useful (Young 1971). The relevance of knowledge is also significant in its inclusion in any curriculum (Jarvis 1978b). If curricula contain socially organized knowledge selected from culture, then it is significant to know where, why and by whom such a selection of knowledge is made. Clearly in self-directed learning and in some forms of adult education it is the learners who make the selection, but Griffin suggests that this may not occur in continuing education. However, Westwood has indicated that perhaps the selection in adult education may not be from a wide range of knowledge and she claims that since adult education is a predominantly middle-class pursuit it 'has a reinforcing role ... maintaining the status quo, engendering a state of consensus and contributing positively to the mechanisms whereby hegemony is maintained' (1980: 43). If her analysis is correct, then adult education curricula have reflected the middle-class attitudes and biases that maintain a 'bourgeois hegemony', so that it then needs to be asked whether this is a true reflection of its aims or whether it is a consequence of its existence.

No curriculum in the education of adults can escape the social pressures exerted upon it, and so it is necessary that more sociological analysis of the educational processes undertaken by adults should be conducted (see Jarvis 1985; Elsey 1986).

Social policy factors

Education is rarely free from the decisions of national and local government, and so policy factors also affect the curriculum in any educational establishment. Indeed, policy decisions in the United Kingdom have first segregated clearly continuing vocational education from liberal adult education – a separation that is more demarcated in policy than it is in practice – and then vocationalized liberal adult education. Not only have macro-curriculum decisions been affected by governmental policy, even the content of curriculum has been affected in this way. As long ago as 1859 John Stuart Mill (1962: 239) deprecated the State being involved in the content of education since he regarded it as an infringement on human liberty, but when the Manpower Services Commission was established in the United Kingdom, it forbade the inclusion of any political material in the curricula, claiming that 'inclusion in the course of political or related activities "could be regarded as a breach of ... agreement with the MSC and could result in the immediate closure of the course"' (Harper 1982). From this example it may be seen that even in a relatively democratic country, like the United Kingdom, government policy can and does exercise considerable control over the curriculum content.

Despite the government's claim that it wishes to leave a great deal to the market, it has constantly intervened in education in a way that many educationalists consider to be detrimental to education. Nevertheless, it should be recognized that even the policy decision to 'leave things to the market' has tremendous effects upon curriculum content since the market ensures the 'survival of the fittest', or in this case the more popular subjects, and enables the less popular ones to be offered at a higher fee in order to make them financially viable.

In 1987, Griffin examined adult education from this perspective, looking especially at three major models – the market model, the progressive-liberal-welfare and the social control. It will be suggested later in this chapter that the middle one of these three is being merged into the market model, as a result of government policy, but that there is still government intervention and social control in the education of adult curriculum. Indeed, it has been argued elsewhere (Finch 1984; Jarvis 1993) that a great deal of government intervention is also a matter of social engineering. (See also Jarvis 1988 for an overview of this aspect of the discussion.)

Perceived demands

Newman writes that:

> Adult education is designed in the simplest possible way to respond to demand. It is the other side of the numbers game. If classes can be closed on the basis of attendance, then they can also be set up. That is to say, if you have a group of people eager to pursue some activity, or if you have evidence of sufficient community interest you can approach your local adult education agency or centre and ask that a course be arranged, a room and basic facilities provided, and a tutor paid.
>
> (Newman 1979: 35)

This is a different approach to running courses than that often discussed by adult educators who have frequently regarded their programmes as being based upon needs. This term should be distinguished from the idea of a basic need to learn, which was discussed in the opening chapter, but since it has played such a significant part in adult education thinking it should be analysed and related to 'wants', 'interests' and 'demands'. It will have become clear from the previous discussion that education is rapidly becoming a commodity in the market, so that needs are becoming 'wants' and 'demands', and consequently the whole of this new discussion about curriculum in relation to both modularization and the market is referred to in a later section of this chapter.

Perception of demand is, therefore, one factor in the planning of a curriculum in adult and continuing education but one that is playing a larger part now than it appears to have done in the past.

Psychological factors

One of the strengths of Knowles' formulation of andragogy is that it focused upon some of the psychological factors that need to be taken into consideration in planning adults' learning. If adults are, for instance, problem-centred rather than subject-based, then more courses should be planned that have relevance to the everyday life environment. If they are going to respond to the rapidly changing socio-cultural milieu with active questioning, then the programme should include courses/sessions that provide opportunities for them to seek answers. If some adults have developed an adversion to education as a result of their experiences in initial education, everything must be done to overcome the problem from the outset including the employment of tutors able to put adults at their ease, the way the accommodation is used and the programme advertised. However, it is appreciated that some of the psychological factors may not be fully responded to in planning because there may be limited resources available.

Resources

The above discussion has already indicated the inter-relationship between the different elements of this curriculum planning model, since it would be impossible to consider resources without recognizing that these depend upon policy decisions etc. Resources may be classified as financial, accommodation and staff. Little more needs to be written about the first of these since it plays a self-evidently important part in curriculum planning. Nevertheless, it must be recognized that many education authorities make a financial grant to the educational institution and, thereafter, it is responsive to the market forces and fee income, except where funding is granted or obtained for specific activities. However, response to market forces means that the curriculum of an institution will depend upon the ability of the educational providers to perceive demands accurately or else it will result in a form of traditionalism in curriculum planning – the continuation of successful courses. Once the institution depends on the market forces, then the course fees become a significant factor in which courses are actually included in the final programme.

Accommodation for adult education has been the subject of a report by ACACE (1982c) in which it is recognized that day schools should continue to form the main accommodation resource for adult education. Clearly it makes a good deal of sense to utilize premises for this purpose when they are not being used by children, but it is necessary to recognize that such usage may inhibit some adults from participating in post-initial education because of their experiences when they attended school. Research needs to be conducted to investigate the effect of this 'poor cousin' image of adult education and it may be that if this is to remain a pattern for the future, then new schools should be built having more facilities for wider community use. The Advisory Council Report also recommends that every adult should have access to prime use accommodation, even though this may not be as close to their homes as the local school.

Increasingly it is becoming recognized that liberal adult education is a service provision and needs to be provided when students can benefit from it.

Consequently, educationalists are having to recognize that they are being required to work at 'unsocial hours', which is increasingly becoming evenings, weekends and holidays. This is also true for continuing professional education since employers, especially small ones, are loath to release staff for education and training purposes during their working hours. This does mean that teaching accommodation in colleges and universities is easier to obtain, but there is still another major resource problem, since libraries still have rather restricted opening hours, especially during normal vacation periods.

The main resource in education of most kinds is the tutor and there has been considerable discussion in this study about the tutor's role in the education of adults, so that it is unnecessary to cover this ground again. There are, however, two issues that should be mentioned here: the use of staff untrained in the art of teaching adults and the use of part-time staff to mount classes in minority subjects and interests. If there is a demand for a class in a specific topic and no tutor trained in the art of teaching adults, should the class be mounted? Since training is not mandatory then response to demand may necessitate use of untrained staff. By contrast, Hetherington (1980) suggests that part-time staff are occasionally asked by a principal of an adult education institute to mount a class in a minority interest topic. Having undertaken the commitment and a great deal of preparatory work, the part-time tutors discover that the class is closed after a few weeks because it has attracted so few enrolments and hence they lose their part-time work. This might cause hardship and it certainly would cause loss of job satisfaction. In order to organize a wide and attractive programme it might be necessary to employ tutors in this manner but the extent to which the part-time tutors should be regarded as a reserve army of labour is another matter. Unfortunately, the market mentality demands a flexible and, often, part-time work force which can be employed when there is work, and education tutors constitute part of this work force. Indeed, loyalty by an institution to its part-time staff from year to year might well result in the tutors seeking additional training and providing a better service to the students.

Advertised programmes

Two major issues here that need some discussion are the actual programme and the way that it is advertised, and both will be discussed in turn.

In the preparation of the programme at least three educational issues must be taken into consideration: scheduling, balance and level. The actual time when courses are programmed is a major curriculum issue since potential students may not be free to attend a class, even an in-service one, if it clashes with their work. Hence, it may be necessary for professional in-service education courses to be mounted on days when the pressure on that specific occupational group is least. In adult education classes it might be necessary to vary the time when they commence, since some topics may be attractive to those who commute to work and who might prefer a Saturday morning class to an evening one. Clearly it is impossible to satisfy every demand since a mutually convenient time for all potential students may be impossible to discover and, even if it were, it may not be convenient for the caretaker! Hence, it may be necessary for different approaches to teaching and learning to be created if scheduling cannot be satisfactorily achieved, such as learning networks, individualized learning, etc.

Mee and Wiltshire (1978: 41) rightly point out that much adult education seeks to respond to several publics, so that when adult educators refer to the idea of a balanced curriculum they may be suggesting that the balance should suit the demand. This is a different conception of balance to that in compulsory education when it might refer to the balance between different forms of knowledge or to that between the cognitive disciplines and physical skills, etc. Clearly, then, within the education of adults these considerations should play a significant part since the balance between supply and demand is hardly sufficient educational rationale for producing a programme of courses. It may be appropriate, therefore, to regard the concept of balance as an ideal to be aimed at, so that a balance may be created between the market forces and the minority interests. Hence, a variety of learning needs should be catered for, but, however broad the programme offered, it is certain that not everybody's interest can be included within it, so it may be necessary to organize an educational advisory service or learning networks in order to respond to these demands. Since these latter topics are discussed later in this chapter no further reference is made to them here.

However, it is necessary to recognize that if there is a learning need that should be responded to in terms of human justice then there is sufficient reason for organizing an unbalanced programme. Hence balance in a programme will ultimately depend upon the philosophy of the curriculum designer and balance in itself is not a phenomenon to be achieved at all costs.

Mee and Wiltshire (1978: 33) discovered that the subject matter for courses in the programmes of adult education institutes that they analysed consisted of: 51 per cent craft courses (personal care, household and leisure); 24 per cent physical skills (maintenance of health, physical fitness and leisure); 12 per cent languages; 6 per cent other intellectual courses; 5 per cent courses for disadvantaged groups. However, when the university extension classes were included, the academic component was 25 per cent of the actual programme offered. It is clear that craft and physical skill courses comprise the greater proportion of the advertised programme, so that it does tend to reflect a recreational, demands orientated approach to education rather than a compensatory programme. But, it may be asked, to what extent does the advertised programme actually reflect the philosophy of the providers or the actual demand of likely students? Clearly, Mee and Wiltshire's findings provide a valuable basis from which to discuss the balance of the curriculum and they, themselves, raise vital questions about this. Perhaps, wisely, they refrained from suggesting answers and yet it is important that answers are sought since only by undertaking research at this level will the advertised programme ever relate to other elements in the curriculum planning model.

The concept of 'level' may be considered within a very similar theoretical framework, and this is becoming more important as credit is being awarded for modules of study at different levels; for instance, the National Council for Vocational Qualifications is trying to establish a national credit-based system at different levels, four of which are considered as being lower than higher education, and the university credit accumulation and transfer system also has three levels of first degree and also both honours level and masters level credits. (These developments will be discussed more fully in the next chapter.) The curriculum, because it seeks to respond to people with different educational interests and backgrounds, has to achieve a balance in levels suitable for a wide potential student body. Nevertheless, those who wish to pursue their studies in considerable depth may be disadvantaged if no, or few, advanced courses are offered. However, as higher education is gradually becoming more flexible and, therefore, more accessible to adults, it has become necessary to build progression routes, at different levels, to help adults gain access to advanced study. Further education colleges and adult education institutes are now offering a variety of lower level courses that provide access to universities and institutes of higher education. However, this requires considerable planning and liaison between the various providers, which may not actually occur. Consequently, there are emerging systems of liaison in which an agreement is reached between the providers of different levels of education to ensure that progression routes are open to adults.

Courses and programmes must be advertised and two issues need to be considered here: to advertise successfully is a professional undertaking but to advertise too successfully may be contrary to the high ideals of education itself. Rogers and Groombridge claimed that adult education is

> a service needing constant promotion and visibility [but] it remains largely unpromoted and directly invisible; where sympathetic understanding of all modern media is needed, it continues hopelessly to rely on methods which would have looked out of place in the late nineteenth century.

They (Rogers and Groombridge 1976: 76) suggested a variety of approaches that might be employed, including: focused distribution; a supplement in a local newspaper; direct mailing; skilful cultivation of the local press in order to ensure good coverage of newsworthy items; militant publicity. Obviously post-compulsory education must reach out to the wider populace and many of these suggestions are now included in the advertising programmes of many educational institutions. However, with the new market orientation of the education for adults, advertising has become a more prominent feature, with higher educational institutions competing against one another for students through mass advertising campaigns. The education of adults has become a market orientated commodity with advertising becoming more professional and commercial. Indeed, it is perhaps now necessary for education to take stock of what is occurring and for educators to ask if this is the route down which they wish to travel in the coming years!

Advertising, as an occupation, is often accused of employing immoral, or at least questionable, methods. While the accusation is rarely substantiated it is important that education should not be seen to use methods to promote its courses that create a sense of need in, or manipulate, potential students. These techniques may be regarded as immoral and certainly fall short of the high ideals of education. Hence, it is important to prepare good publicity and to disseminate it widely, but the means used to persuade people to enrol on courses must always be in accord with the ideals of education; other means do not justify the ends.

Actual demand

At the commencement of the academic year, semester or term, the enrolment period brings the preparatory work into focus. The extent to which the advertised programme prepared by the educators actually responds to the demands of the potential students may now be revealed. In a recent study, Sargant (1991) discovered that 36 per cent of the adult population had been involved in some form of academic study over the previous three years. She also discovered that there was a considerable variation in the places where they studied: at a college (34 per cent); at home (39 per cent); at work (15 per cent); at a training centre (7 per cent) being the most popular. The subjects that they studied varied considerably: business, vocational and office, comprising 26 per cent; 12 per cent studied languages; 11 per cent mathematics, computing and science; 11 per cent the social sciences and the caring professions; 11 per cent handicrafts and DIY; 7 per cent engineering; 6 per cent arts and culture.

Clearly the programme may not respond to everybody's learning needs, and so there has arisen in recent years educational advisory services that can help potential students to find another course in the prospectus that responds to their interests or to discover another educational institution offering the course that the student requires. Adult education institutions are not the sole providers of this service; public libraries, citizens advice bureaux and careers service offices have all contributed greatly to this, so liaison between providers and advisers is very necessary to ensure that an efficient advisory service exists. In the Advisory Council for Adult and Continuing Education's report on this topic, it notes that, for instance, the Guildford Adult Education Week held in the public library was a 'collective effort involving many agencies, including the University and the Women's Institute' (ACACE 1979c: 15). In fact, over twenty agencies, either advisers or providers, cooperate every year during the enrolment period to inform the general public of the courses that they can follow, offer advice about where they can find the courses that they wish to study and even to counsel enquirers about the educational requirements that they might need in order to pursue certain careers or seek specific qualifications. This service has been made even more effective since the County Library Service has a computerized record of the majority of adult courses offered throughout Surrey. This is but one example of how response to demand can be met and adult education offer a genuine service while it still seeks to inform people about the proposed content of the educational programmes of a number of providers.

Education and Guidance services actually exist in a variety of local education authority areas throughout the country, which also has its own national association – the National Association for Educational Guidance for Adults – although these associations are not evenly spread throughout the country. A useful source for addresses for these organizations is the National Institute for Adult Continuing Education Yearbook.

However, it must be realized that the provision of special weeks to promote education for adults may be motivated by the providers' need to attract students, so while it may be viewed as an altruistic service, it may also be continued as part of an advertising campaign mounted by adult education. Mixed motivation is obviously present in the providers but the offer of such a service is in keeping with the humanistic ideals of adult education.

Courses that fail to enrol sufficient students during that period may be closed immediately, or allowed to run for a few weeks to see if student enrolments increase. However, each year a number of courses may be closed, so that the educational institution might offer no course in specific topics. This may be the place at which curriculum innovation may commence; the creation of learning networks, self-help groups, etc. may find some support and if cooperation between providers could be increased it might be possible to employ peripatetic teachers with self-help groups.

Actual curriculum

The actual content of the teaching programme of any educational institution, depending totally or partially upon voluntary participation, must, therefore, to some extent, rely on the response to the prospectus. Yet it will be recalled that demand itself is hardly sufficient reason for inclusion in the curriculum of any particular topic, so that there must be a place for some minority interests. Even so, the extent to which economically unviable courses may be continued does depend upon the philosophy underpinning the educational institution's curriculum and upon the social policy factors that affect the funding arrangements for specific courses.

The actual curriculum of an educational institution is more than its programme of courses, as will be recognized from the discussion about the way in which the term is employed. Because it can refer to the total learning situation, the whole ethos of the institution, its hidden curriculum and the teaching and learning curriculum are all united at this point.

Evaluation

In Figure 9.4 it will be noted that the curriculum planning model demands that educators of adults should evaluate many of the elements of the process. The basis of this evaluation must be educational philosophy but even that may be called into question by other demands in the programme. In addition, there are certain factors that may be evaluated by other criteria, e.g. the use of physical resources by financial criteria, the whole of the operation by criteria of organizational efficiency, since the educator of adults clearly plays an administrative and managerial role. Hence, it is necessary to utilize the criteria of management in evaluating the planning and implementation of the curriculum, but because the end-product is an educational curriculum the major criterion by which the whole is evaluated must remain the educational philosophy of the educators of adults.

The above discussion has sought to highlight some of the major elements in the curriculum planning model and it is clear that the curriculum, when employed in the context of the toal learning situation provided by the educational institution, has connotations for organization and management that demand that those full-time staff employed in this role should have additional training if they require it.

Having undertaken a historical overview of work in this area, it is now necessary to look briefly at one or two recent developments in this field.

NEW PERSPECTIVES ON PLANNING EDUCATION PROGRAMMES FOR ADULTS

The idea of 'need' has traditionally been the base upon which curricula in the education of adults have been constructed, although it will have become apparent from the above discussion that this now appears to be changing, and ideas about market demand have come to the fore. Indeed, in the 1980s there has been a tremendous change in the way that education has been viewed and by the end of this period it has been completely commoditized and education has been viewed as a marketable good. This section examines this change, starting with the concept of need and demonstrating how it has changed. Thereafter the idea of the market will be examined with reference to modularization, certification, advertising and quality. It will be seen that the traditional approach to curriculum theory is being replaced by one which has great similarities to the programme planning literature.

Needs

The concept of 'need' has been regarded as one of the bases of the adult eduation curriculum and the moral overtones of the term have provided adult education with an apparently deep and unquestionable rationale for its existence. That the adult educator could provide an educational programme that responded to the needs of individuals and communities has been an ideologically important factor to those whose occupation is at the margins of the educational service. The Russell Report (1971: 5) was unable to provide a consistent analysis of the term but used it to provide legitimation to the activities undertaken by adult education. Mee and Wiltshire (1978) showed clearly how full-time adult education staff regarded their work as compensatory, while part-time staff viewed it as recreational. Hence, for the full-time staff 'needs' was a more significant term. The Advisory Council for Adult and Continuing Education has also adopted the term (ACACE 1982b) but the term is clearly confused and, on occasions, 'wants' or 'interests' could be substituted for 'needs' without any change in meaning, although the moral overtones would be lost in the process.

That such a substitution is possible suggests that the term requires considerably more analysis before it could be regarded as a basis for a curriculum theory. Indeed, once such an analysis is undertaken, it is not difficult to concur with Hirst and Peters when they suggested that 'a major book could be written solely round the problems raised by the emphasis or needs and interests' (1970: 33). They actually specify a number of different ways in which the term may be used to illustrate their contention: diagnostic, e.g. a poor person needs more wealth; basic, e.g. the need for a bed; biological, e.g. the need for oxygen; psychological, e.g. the need for love and security; functional, e.g. the teacher needs his books. Clearly they have not exhausted the possibilities, and Bradshaw (1977) specified four more types of need of which social workers should be aware: normative, felt, expressed and comparative needs. Halmos (1978) drew attention to the distinction between primary and secondary needs: the former referring to bodily requirements while the latter are learned or acquired. Needs can also be classified as individual, community or societal. From the above discussion it can be appreciated that the concept of need is ill-defined and, therefore, an inadequate basis for curriculum development.

Educational analysis of the concept has revealed a number of other reasons why it may be a dubious concept to employ in this context. Dearden (1972), illustrated its weaknesses in a number of ways: those needs diagnosed as such against a norm may be rebutted by rejecting the validity of the norm, since it is not absolute (perhaps the exception to this is the basic learning need referred to in the opening chapter); those expressions of need that imply motivation may be rejected since learners may not want what they actually need, and needs and wants are not synonymous concepts; needs are not free from value judgements despite their apparent objectivity; needs are not empirically based. Dearden concedes that it 'might be said in connexion with needs and the curriculum. . . . that there are certain general injunctions about needs which do have a point in that they lay down something called "basic policy"' (1972: 54–5). Dearden's criticisms may be less familiar to adult educators, however, than that made by Wiltshire (1973) who rightly claimed that the use of the term begged a number of significant questions and he specifically noted that, by giving adult education an ethic of service to the needy, it drove a wedge between thinking and practice, which prevented practice from being fully analysed. Lawson (1975) has also highlighted some of the weaknessees of the concept, concentrating upon the value judgement and the prescriptive issues. While he (1975: 37) maintains that needs statements should not be abandoned he does appeal that they should be recognized for what they are. Paterson (1979: 242) has also criticized the use of the word because he claims that the idea implies that people have the right to achieve a specific level of educational attainment, whatever that might be, and this is patently not the case. Even more recently, Armstrong (1982) has suggested that needs meeting is both an element in liberal ideology and also a justification of compensatory education. Yet do such needs exist? Coates and Silburn (1967) claimed that no such needs exist. Illich noted the implicit ideological bias in the term and claimed that 'Need, used as a noun, becomes the fodder on which professions were fattened into dominance' (1977: 22–3). This suggests that the term is used in order to achieve power and that need is the creation of the power seeker. Illich's strictures are perhaps appropriate for continuing education since it will no doubt develop considerably in the next few years and continuing educators may seek to justify their existence. Perhaps, therefore, the need to learn, as recognized by the potential learner, is a better basis for the education of adults and perhaps learning needs rather than eduational needs are more significant.

Once a learning need is recognized by a potential student, then it creates a want, an interest or a desire. The learner may, therefore, exert pressure upon an educational provider to respond to his or her demands. But 'wants', 'interests' and 'demands' are not words that occur so frequently in the vocabulary of adult educators, nor do they carry the same moral overtones as does the term 'need'. However, they are terms that are analytically more convincing and it has been argued that demand may be one of the foundations of adult education curricula which does not detract from the value of the education (Jarvis 1982a). It was also suggested that if adult education actually became demand orientated, it might conceivably break away from the ethos of middle-class respectability that it carries at present.

However, it might be asked whether this analysis is only theoretical or whether adult education has managed to reach out and respond to people's demands. Mee and Wiltshire claimed that there

> seems to be some sort of national concensus that these are the things (their core curriculum) that institutions of adult education ought to be offering to the public and that there is something wrong if these subjects are not given something like their due place in the programme.
>
> (Mee and Wiltshire 1978: 41)

Commenting upon their work, Keddie (1980: 54) suggests that their findings merely indicate that adult education has been operating a provider's model rather than a needs model of curriculum. If she is correct it is even less likely that there has been a response to demand, or even tremendous attempts to discover it, and the needs meeting ideology has merely provided legitimation for the retention of the status quo. Even if there had been outreach to discover expressed learning needs, or demands, they are not in themselves sufficient reason for the inclusion of the appropriate learning activity in the curriculum. The demands have to be considered within the overall scheme and it is essential that curriculum planners ensure that their response is not mindless.

Needs, then, provided an unsatisfactory basis for a welfare model of educational provision, one with which theorists were most unhappy but which appeared to provide an important rationale for the provision of education for adults. The theorists were already suggesting that 'want' or 'demand' might be better bases for a great deal of the provision – although it might be appropriate to recognize that the provision of adult basic education might be justified in terms of citizens rights or even justice (Jarvis 1993a). Radicals, however, were undermining 'needs' in a variety of ways during this period, and in the same way as Illich was arguing that needs might be created, Marcuse (1964: 4–6) discussed the idea of true and false needs: the former being vital to human life and the latter superimposed upon individuals by societal interests and which may become repressive. Implicit in this analysis is the idea that the needs created in people are 'product of a society whose dominant interest demands repression' (Marcuse 1964: 5). Indeed, these needs might be created through advertising etc., so that people feel that they need a certain commodity and feel the need to purchase it, and the dominant interests are those of the providers, or suppliers of the commodity, which in this instance is education.

As governments have provided less financial support for educational institutions throughout the 1980s, educational institutions have been forced to find additional funding from student fees. This has been especially true with the education of adults, where there has traditionally been even less government support and local government has found it easier to cut back funding. Consequently, education has become a marketable commodity seeking to respond to the demands of potential students. Such language does not seem that strange for many adult educators because there is one sense in which it has always marketed education, albeit under the banner of a 'needs meeting' approach! However, selling a whole course might be a different undertaking, but selling a course a piece at a time is much easier – and this has been facilitated by modularization. Hence, most new courses have modular designs which allow for flexible study. This is even more appropriate where there are learning packages, which enable packages of learning material to be marketed like any other commodity.

Education in the market place

The language of the market place is something which has been familiar to liberal adult education for many years, but it is only now becoming a part of the vocabulary of other educators. Even so, it is necessary to recognize that education has become a marketable commodity like other commodities, and that educational institutions are more like other commercial organizations. Indeed, educational organizations have increasingly been forced to seek new markets, and this has caused them to become more competitive and flexible.

Continuing vocational education has become a rapidly expanding field, and with universities and colleges all seeking to offer additional education to those who are in work, functional degrees and diplomas, e.g. the MBA degree, have become commonplace. Colleges and universities are striving to attract more students to their taught higher degrees (both masters degrees and doctorates), and even engaging in competition to recruit more students by seeking to undercut their rivals in terms of the fees that they charge or even the amount of remission that they are prepared to award for prior educational experience. In addition, it is being recognized that potential students might not be able to gain educational release in working time, and so educational courses are not being offered during evenings and at weekends and distance education is becoming much more widely accepted. Courses are becoming modularized, irrespective of epistemological considerations, so that they can be more flexible and be marketed as independent units or as parts of a wider qualification. Flexibility and costs have become major concerns and academic qualifications have become symbols of the education which has been purchased. Indeed, it is now common to find educational institutions advertising the symbol of the education, that is the qualification to be gained, rather than the knowledge to be learned or the advantages of studying that specific field of knowledge. Indeed, recently the National Vocational Qualification advertisement for training read: 'If you're buying training, make sure you get a receipt', and the receipt was the qualification! (*Guardian* 19 October 1993)

Other forms of general adult education for adults, through adult education classes, have traditionally not been certificated. Liberal adult education, for instance, has been a part of the educational provision for many years. Indeed, the folk high schools in Denmark, university extra-mural classes in the United Kingdom and the 150-hour programme in Italy have all eschewed certification. However, the market ethos has now overtaken many of these systems and there is discussion about certificated courses in Danish folk high schools and liberal adult education is rapidly moving towards a fully certificated form in the United Kingdom. Now the educational qualification is a sign of the cultural capital possessed by individuals and through the purchase of additional educational commodities the sign can be changed to demonstrate the amount of knowledge consumed through the institutionalized learning process and so these courses are becoming certificated. With the introduction of accreditation of prior experiential learning (APEL), the commodity can be bought at discount prices in the educational market place and wise buyers seek the best purchases for their own purposes. It is significant that often the courses that are certificated are the same, or similar, to those which were previously not certificated – change but no change – or as Baudrillard suggests:

> Everything is in motion, everything is changing, everything is being transformed and yet nothing changes. Such a society, thrown into technological progress, accomplishes all possible revolutions but these are revolutions upon itself. Its growing productivity does not lead to structural change.

(cited in Kellner 1989: 11)

Educational institutions advertise their courses, just like other market providers. Indeed, the Further Education Unit, among others, has recognized this trend and produced pamphlets on marketing strategy for adult and continuing education (FEU 1990). Indeed, the educational market is now international, with many institutions of higher education advertising their courses throughout the world, and many of them adopting a variety of modes of delivery, including distance education.

However, it is more often than not the sign that is advertised – Study for a University Degree – rather than the education itself. In order to attract the consumer the commodity must become a sign, according to Baudrillard, who defines consumption as 'a systematic act of the manipulation of signs' (cited in Poster 1988: 21). Individuals are, therefore, free to purchase their own education, if they can afford it, and develop in the direction that they wish, or at least in one of the directions that they are offered through the market. They can reinforce their own understanding of themselves through the educational signs, among other signs, that they display. Indeed, the more prestigious the commodities, the greater the sign value.

Certificates and credits

All forms of education for adults are now being certificated, and new approaches to qualifying certificates have emerged, two of which are discussed here, and they are National Vocational Qualifications and credit accumulation and transfer.

National Vocational Qualifications (SVQ – Scottish Vocational Qualification in Scotland)

Not only has education become a commodity, it is one which has to be assessed in terms of its outputs. Considerable emphasis is now being placed upon the competencies that are gained as a result of the learning. Competence is 'the possession and development of sufficient life skills, knowledge, appropriate attitudes and experience for successful performance in life roles' (Hermann and Kenyon 1987: 1). Whilst knowledge, skills and attitudes might also be included within the general framework of competence, it is extremely difficult to assess all of these from the perspective of performance because individuals do not always perform consistently in accord with their own theoretical position, as Argyris and Schon (1974) have demonstrated. They argued that people had 'espoused theories' and 'theories in use': the former are the perspectives which individuals will say guide their behaviour whilst the latter are those which may be detected from a close observation and analysis of behaviour. They are not necessarily consistent and while the performance may be regarded as more important than the espoused theory, the coupling of knowledge and skills in any definition of competence is over simple.

In vocational terms, a competency may be defined as 'a performance capability needed by workers in a specified occupational area' (Hermann and Kenyon 1987: 1). Different levels of competence have been designated in National Vocational Qualifications:

- Level 1 – performance of routine and predictable work activities
- Level 2 – performance of work activities involving greater individual responsibility and autonomy than Level 1
- Level 3 – skilled performance of activities, involving complex and non-routine work. Some supervisory activity may also be involved at this level
- Level 4 – complex, technical, specialized and professional activities, including planning and problem solving. There is personal accountability at this level
- Higher Level – competence in pursuit of a senior occupation, including the ability to apply fundamental principles and techniques. Extensive knowledge and understanding is necessary to underpin competence.

(Summarized from Oakeshott 1991: 52)

Performance must be tested using valid assessment methods and endorsed by the best current practice. The standards are set by the Lead Industrial Bodies – that is the organization, or occupational grouping, which has been given this responsibility. Since it is the performance being assessed, it is not necessary for individuals having their competencies assessed to have attended a training course beforehand – it is the ability to perform the job that is important. This is regarded as the most efficient, since it allows for the shortest routes to be taken to the point of assessment, although the value of experience is not ruled out by this approach.

While it is clearly necessary to assess performance in the work situation, trying to categorize all performances into a few levels is a problematic undertaking, especially those which are demanded infrequently by the demands of the job. However, this approach has moved assessment away from the theoretical and artificial to the actual place of performance; but the assumptions underlying this approach are probably as problematic as those underlying more traditional modes of assessment, since successful performance on one day is no guarantee of it on another. Much more problematic, however, is the process of trying to subdivide an occupation into its competencies and arriving at a complete list upon which there is general agreement – indeed, the whole is always more than the sum of its parts!

However, a complex process of designating competencies and testing them is being evolved at the present time, although the surrounding bureaucracy is clearly too great and some providers of courses seeking NVQ accreditation have expressed dissatisfaction with it.

Even so, it is becoming possible to gain NVQs for participation in voluntary activities as well as vocational ones. Tiernan (1992) records how the Royal Society of Arts has recognized the skills involved in voluntary work and has introduced an Advanced Diploma in the Organization of Voluntary Groups, based on the NVQ model.

In addition, there is a movement towards introducing a more general set of qualifications that will relate to, but not replace, the current General Certificate qualifications; these are General National Vocational Qualifications (GNVQ). These qualifications are more work related than subject related, although it is anticipated that they will achieve compatibility with the normal General Certificate – it is claimed that level 3 GNVQ will be equivalent to an Advanced Level General Certificate of Education (Smith 1993).

Credit accumulation and transfer

Once courses are modularized, it becomes possible to award some form of accreditation for each module. Standardized credits for educational achievement in continuing education were first discussed in America in the late 1960s. A National Task Force of the National University Continuing Education Conference in 1968 provided a definition of a continuing education credit as: 'Ten contact hours of participation in an organized continuing education experience under responsible sponsorship, capable direction and qualified instruction' (Long 1978: 2). Long records how this idea developed and how the idea of accrediting experience developed from this, so that accreditation of Prior Experiential Learning (APEL) emerged from within the same framework. However, the movement towards standardized Accreditation of modules developed much more slowly in the United Kingdom, although it was heavily influenced by the American experience. Eventually, it was accepted by the Council for National Academic Awards in 1986. Since the Council only accredited higher education courses, its credit scheme related to the different levels of the undergraduate degree and the taught Masters courses. It assumed that an undergraduate degree has three levels, relating to each of the three years and that each year was equivalent to 1,200 hours of study. Consequently, the first year of an undergraduate degree was seen as a Certificate and worth 120 credits at level 1; completion of two years was equivalent to the Diploma of Higher Education and was the equivalent of the Certificate plus a further 120 credits at level 2; a bachelor's degree was worth 360 credits, at least 60 of which had to be obtained at level 3 and not more than 120 at level 1. An honours degree had to include 120 credits at level 3 and no more than 120 at level 1. A taught Master's degree consisted of 120 credits at M level and herein lay one of the major mistakes that the Council made, since a taught Master's degree has always been the equivalent of one full year's study (i.e. 120 M level credits) followed by a dissertation. This mistake by the Council effectively devalued the taught Master's degree by at least one-third.

Having produced a system that gradually achieved widespread acceptance it became possible for students to study some modules in one educational institution and gain accreditation for that work and then to transfer to another institution to gain further credits. Many universities and colleges, while subscribing to the scheme, will only award their own degrees if at least a substantial proportion of the credits have been gained in their institution, and this proportion is often as high as two-thirds of the whole. This is understandable, since there is not yet a national undergraduate or taught Master's degree, although there might have been if the Conservative government had not abolished the Council for National Academic Awards. The Open University now administers the remnants of the Council's scheme, and many of the Council's former 'clients' (the polytechnics) now have university status and award their own qualifications.

This principle has been utilized at lower level courses and even in liberal adult education where there has not been any assessment of achievement. For instance, in one or two places 'passport' type schemes have been introduced whereby a record of attendance at courses has been retained by students who could then produce their own record as part of their own learning portfolio in seeking credit for their previous learning experiences. Assessment of prior learning has become widely accepted in post-compulsory education in the United Kingdom, with two types appearing: a general and a specific credit. The former is often given as a general remission of part of a course for the overall learning experiences in which students have engaged, while the specific credit refers to remission of part of a course of study because of previous successful study in that specific area of knowledge. While assessment of prior learning in the general sense is a recognition of the broad learning of adults, there is a danger that it will be given to induce students to specific courses because it will enable them to complete it sooner and more cheaply, etc. This danger becomes greater as education is being underfunded and colleges and universities are having to attract as many students as possible in order to make their courses viable. Specific credits are content based and, consequently, there is a greater certainty that academic standards and subject coherence will be retained.

Accreditation is becoming a normal part of the education of adults, even of liberal adult education, as it becomes part of mainstream general education. The process of integration into mainstream education is something that adult educators would generally welcome, but the price for this is high. In many ways accreditation is contrary to the ethos of liberal adult education – an ethos which is being destroyed by the policies of the Conservative government of the early 1990s. At the same time, if education is to be regarded as a passport to occupation or further study it is necessary to have some form of recognition for the standards achieved in those courses, and accreditation is, therefore, a necessary part of this process.

As liberal adult education is moving towards accreditation in order to continue to get some funding from the government, it is also being recognized that many people do not want to study for additional qualifications. Consequently, some courses are being offered which seek to combine both those students seeking the award and others who are learning for learning's sake. Research will have to be undertaken to discover the extent to which this is successful. The alternative will have to be self-financing liberal adult education courses which will result in decreasing provision as fewer potential students will be able to afford the fees, and it will probably become even more open to the accusations that it is a middle-class leisure time pursuit.

Naturally, there are a number of other reactions to this and one of these is the emphasis being placed on self-directed learning, the study of which is becoming very prevalent throughout the United States and elsewhere (Candy 1991, *inter alia*). In addition, new forms of educational opportunities are emerging, such as free universities (Draves 1980) and the University of the Third Age, where no credit is given since the learning is about human being and becoming rather than human having and consuming (Jarvis 1992). Here people can learn, grow and develop, even within a market framework, but without reference to qualifications.

It is becoming difficult to imagine that academic standards are being maintained with all the changes that are occurring, despite the valiant efforts of nearly all major educational institutions to introduce systems of quality control.

Quality

Curriculum evaluation was the normal manner through which educators assessed their work, although much of this was conducted in initial education. It was often assumed in adult education, for instance, that if tutors retained their students throughout the allocated duration of their course then they must be acceptable. Another approach was that of elaborating upon the principles of good practice (see Council on the Continuing Education Unit 1984). Periodic reviews by both local and governmental inspectors were another sufficient check of the overall standard. However, this is now beginning to change under the influence of the market, and now the language of quality is appearing in adult and continuing education.

The definition of the concept, however, is much more problematic. Quality has been defined as effectiveness, efficiency and even student or client satisfaction. However, equating quality with any of these is to be guilty of the naturalistic fallacy, because quality simply cannot be equated to another value. Quality is quality and this differs considerably from efficiency, since it is possible to be adjudged efficient even though the outcome is poor, and so on. Additionally, quality has been used in relation to quality teaching, quality learning, etc., but in these instances there is a tendency towards tautology. Quality is also used in relation to the outcomes of the teaching–learning transaction (see Müller and Funnell 1991). Thus it may be seen that this is by no means an obvious concept, although it does appear to be treated as rather self-evident at times. (See, for instance, FEU 1989, where the concept is assumed throughout rather than clarified.)

More recently, the ideas of good practice and quality assurance have been brought together in two research projects conducted by de Wit (1992, 1993) who writes that:

> Although there is no agreed definition of quality, there are several key themes in the current debate, which focus attention on the whole network of resources and procedures in CE. These themes are
>
> fitness for purpose
> need for a strategic approach
> meeting customers' expectations
> a cycle of continuous improvement
> a cohesive system of interconnected processes
>
> (de Wit 1993: 7)

While any attempt to distil the main characteristics from such an abstract concept is fraught with danger, this approach is more correct than that of equating the concept of quality with any specific characteristic, in the manner that some of the previous descriptions have done. De Wit's study seeks to draw together in a practical manner some of the main issues that are generally agreed to constitute quality in continuing education, and she produces a clear and practical checklist, under each of the following headings;

- Policy
- Staff
- Courses
- Marketing
- Teaching and Learning
- Outcomes

Under each of these headings there are a number of questions that course teams and evaluators might ask about continuing education provision to ensure that good practice is being carried out in all instances. Clearly it does not overcome the conceptual problem, but this it acknowledges. It does, however, seek to provide practical guidelines within the limits it sets itself.

CONCLUDING DISCUSSION

Of all the chapters in this book that have had to be revised, this has included amongst the most new material, reflecting the changes that have occurred within the educational system since the book was first published a decade ago. At that time there was more concern about curriculum theory in the education of adults, almost as if it could have utilized some of the theory that had emerged from initial education. However, society was already undergoing considerable changes as monetarism gained ground and educational provision for adults was being underfunded. It is, however, only since the mid-1980s that the changes have been so rapid. Programme planning has assumed a much more significant place as education has been regarded as a marketable commodity and the ethos of business and commerce is that of the educational institution. It might be asked whether this process is one with which educationalists agree. The response might be negative but the reality is that these are the policies by which the United Kingdom government has responded to the current global situation. Other governments might have responded slightly differently, but the fact remains that providers of education for adults are now much more concerned with the educational market place and all that that entails than they are with the more traditional curriculum theory.

SUMMARY

This chapter has sought to draw together from a variety of sources theoretical perspectives on the curriculum that are relevant to the education of adults. It commenced by pointing out that this material is relatively sparse and this is, perhaps, because adult education in the United Kingdom has used the term programme rather than curriculum. Having examined the terms course, programme and total learning situation, a number of curriculum models were then analysed. It was recognized that the situation has changed considerably since theorists in the education of adults examined curriculum models. Thereafter the manner by which the education of adults has been forced to change as a result of social circumstances was briefly referred to and it was shown that education has become a marketable commodity, resulting in a totally different language and approach to education.

The traditional language of 'needs' has changed to 'demands' and education is a commodity supplied by educational providers. As a commodity, education has to undergo examination for quality and, consequently, the language of quality assurance has become part of the vocabulary of those who prepare and provide modules or courses. Since the clients of the educational institution may wish to purchase only a single module, a new procedure of certification has emerged and some of the efforts to standardize the forms of certification were discussed.

This is clearly a new language and a new approach to education. It makes education more flexible, more open and enables students to choose only those elements of a course that are relevant to the student. In this manner, these new developments have merit, but questions must remain as to the overall wisdom in proceeding down the present path.

10 The provision of education for adults in the United Kingdom

Since the 1944 Education Act it has been the duty of the Secretary of State for education

> to promote the education of the people of England and Wales and the progressive development of institutions devoted to that purpose, and to secure effective execution by local authorities, under his control and direction, of the national policy of providing a varied and comprehensive educational service in every area.
>
> (cited from the Russell Report 1973: 25)

Later in the same Act of Parliament, the requirements are specified:

> Section 4.1: Subject as hereinafter provided, it shall be the duty of every local education authority to secure the provision for their area of adequate facilities for further education, that is to say:
> a. full-time and part-time education for persons over compulsory school age; and
> b. leisure time occupation, in such organised cultural training and recreative activities as are suited to their requirements, for any persons over compulsory school age who are able and willing to profit by the facilities provided for that purpose.
>
> (cited from Stock 1982: 12)

It is clear, from the above quotations, that since the 1944 Education Act it has been the duty of every local education authority in the United Kingdom to make provision for lifelong education, but it will be recognized immediately that the educational model implicit in this Act is a front-end model, and that no consideration was given to the idea of an integrated curriculum. Even so, the vision of the 1944 Act was long term and idealistic and this is as significant as other parts, e.g. the structure of initial education, of this most influential statute. During the propsperous period of the 1950s and 1960s there was a considerable expansion in the provision of education for adults. Yet this branch of education has remained marginal, and recent economic and policy decisions have merely reinforced this position. Indeed, as each new financial restriction was imposed upon the education budget, adult education suffered disproportionately. This has resulted in the demise of the ideals of those who framed the 1944 Education Act. It will have been noted in the previous chapter that the education of adults now functions in the market place with little financial support from government or local education authority; it almost seems as if the government would wish to have liberal adult education privatized. There are many problems in creating an educational market, not the least being that the poorer people can ill-afford the opportunities that education beyond school-ing offers. Indeed, the market has no place for welfare or moral concern and so the ethos of many educational institutions is undergoing rapid change, dashing the ideals of those who framed this Act and who anticipated that it would 'contribute towards the spiritual, moral, mental and physical develop-ment of the community by securing that efficient education . . . to meet the needs of the population of their area' (1944 Education Act: Section 7).

In contrast to the forces to restrict the provision of low-cost liberal adult education there have been changes in the world of work that have caused continuing vocational education to assume a central place within many pro-viders' programmes. Indeed, it could be argued that education has become the 'handmaiden of industry' (Kerr *et al.* 1972) and that educational providers are having to restructure their provision to meet this new demand. At the same time, adult educational providers are striving to retain a liberal adult education programme. Nevertheless it would be contrary to the ideals of the 1944 Education Act and to the nature of education itself if the whole person were not taken into consideration in the provision of continuing education in the future.

Since the education authorities have had only limited budgets with which to provide an education service for adults, and this budget has been continually slashed as a result of government policies, their provision has been restricted and it has rarely been possible to offer the comprehensive service that was envisaged. Hence, the purpose of this chapter is to examine the provision made for the education of adults and some of the organizations that support the service. Consequently, it will be recognized that less emphasis will be given to industrial and commercial provision than to that of the local authorities. The chapter contains four main sections: the providers; recent developments in provision; organizations that support the service; recent research in the education of adults. This fourth section is included here since much of the research has been initiated by the organizations that support the education of adults. The chapter concludes with a brief discussion and summary.

THE PROVIDERS OF EDUCATION FOR ADULTS

From the terms of the 1944 Education Act it is clear that the local education authority provision is part of the Welfare State, and this has been shown to be too expensive for a society with a contracting economy. Consequently, the past fifteen years have seen the dismantling of much of the welfare provi-sion. Liberal adult education has become much more expensive, the local service restructured and curtailed and those who work in it have tended to doubt whether it will survive as a state provided service. Indeed, there is some doubt as to whether the Local Education Authorities themselves will survive much longer in their present form. In addition, the 1988 Education Reform Act laid upon local authorities only the duty to provide further education in their areas, and this could be much more vocational than the traditional liberal adult education service. As a result of these changes, a variety of other providers have emerged, many of which are private enterprises, and others voluntary associations.

The Guildford Adult Education Week, for instance, has over twenty different participant organizations each year, including: the University of Surrey, the Guildford College of Further and Higher Education, the Workers Educational Association, the Adult Education Institute, the County Library Service, the Careers Service, the Women's Institute, the Friends of Guildford House, the French Circle, etc. Yet this list, which is incomplete, does not make explicit the concept of a provider of education for adults, and Legge (1982) makes it clear that this is a difficult undertaking. It will be recalled that the definition of education adopted here is 'any planned service of incidents having a humanistic basis directed towards the participant's learning and understanding'. Hence any provider, or facilitator, of a series of incidents directed towards learning, provided that they have a humanistic basis, may be considered within this discussion. But to isolate all of these providers would be another task, and one that Legge (1982) has already done most admirably, so that this discussion is limited to the main providers: the local education authorities, the universities, the colleges of further and higher education and, finally, some of the other providers are mentioned briefly including the Workers Educational Association.

The local education authorities

It will be recognized that the place of these authorities is becoming less influential in modern Britain. Indeed, their role in education beyond school was further curtailed when the government took the control of Further Education from them and created a Further Education Funding Council to administer the total funding of this sector of education. Even some of the activities of the traditional liberal adult education institutes, which still remain within the jurisdiction of the local authorities, are funded by this central Council and are bid for by the institutes in precisely the same way as do the colleges of further and higher education.

The liberal adult education service has remained largely under the control of the local authorities; whether it is administered as a separate service or as part of a broader one depends upon the specific authority. For instance, some authorities have endeavoured to retain a free standing adult education service; others have combined it with the school service and created community colleges; while others have combined it with other services, such as the Youth Service, and called it continuing education.

However, other changes can be expected in the near future since it is widely believed that the Conservative government of the early 1990s will reorganize local government itself in the next few years and this will inevitably affect the way that the liberal adult education service is provided at local levels.

Separate institutions of adult education tend to have a centre, with a small full-time staff, and perhaps a little amount of prime use accommodation. The institutes utilize classrooms from local schools and colleges on an evening, and occasionally on a day-time basis. Mee (1980) discusses how adult education functions on this model. However, when adult education and further education are separated, the curriculum of the former tends to be mainly based upon leisure time and hobby activities – not that there is anything wrong in this since these activities may contribute to the growth and development of the students in a variety of ways. Perhaps the content of the curriculum is, however, one of the reasons why adult education has remained a low status marginal activity. Even so, there is some overlap between the educational programmes offered by institutes of adult education and colleges of further education, where both are in the same local education area, and this occurs especially in ACCESS, Youth Opportunities and other forms of certificated courses. Such duplication is one reason why liaison between providers is necessary. However, there are some local education authority areas in which there is an adult education institute but not a college of further education and in these instances the former may seek to fulfil many of the functions of the latter, including offering courses sponsored by the Training and Enterprise Councils.

While many adult education institutes were formed after the 1944 Education Act, Kelly states that:

> The tradition of the non-residential centre can be traced back to the mechanics' institutes and working men's colleges of the nineteenth century, but few of these survived as educational institutions into the twentieth century. It was the Educational Settlements Associations (from 1946 the Educational Centres Association) which took the lead in developing the modern movement and at the same time provided a link with the historic past.

> (Kelly 1970: 383–4)

Perhaps Kelly underplays the degree of continuity between the mechanics' institutes and the contemporary adult education institutes and Devereux (1982) would appear to suggest that in London, at least, this was more apparent than Kelly claims. However, discussion upon this point will be pursued no further here, since historical analysis is beyond the scope of this study. Nevertheless, it may be seen that the history of adult education has been one in which institutes, rather than schools or colleges, have been the location of the education offered.

Perhaps the most well known of all the adult education provision made by local education authorities are the community colleges, associated with the name of Henry Morris. Morris, who was chief education officer for

Cambridgeshire, had a passionate belief in lifelong education and an interest in architecture. He had a vision of the educational institution becoming the centre of the village community in almost the same manner as the ecclesiastical institution had been in a bygone age. Morris (1956, cited in Fletcher 1980: 16) claimed 'that the centre of gravity in education and the culture it transmits should be in that part which provides for youth and maturity . . . Our main means to this end is to group our local communities round their colleges and secondary schools.' Under his direction, in the 1930s, the first four village colleges were opened and, after the Second World War, other colleges were opened in Cambridgeshire and elsewhere (Jennings). The village college incorporated the village hall, adult classrooms, rooms for other public meetings and organizations and the secondary school. Fairbairn (1971) actually provides a plan of the Countesthorpe school which had a community education department within a comprehensive school. However, the idea of utilizing a large comprehensive school as the basis for a community school has subsequently been adopted in a number of places, such as the Sutton Centre in Nottinghamshire (Wilson 1980), the Abraham Moss Centre in Manchester, and the model has been copied in Grenoble in France. There appears to be tremendous advantages in providing all the community facilities on one campus (see Fletcher's [n.d.] study of the Sutton Centre).

Less adventurous and expensive experiments in community colleges have been started by other local education authorities, and in these instances they have merely designated one portion of a local secondary school for work with adults, employed one or more members of staff with some form of adult education specialism, and called it a community college. These colleges have clearly been useful in rural areas where it would not be financially viable to run a free-standing adult education institute.

The universities

In 1867, James Stuart, who was a fellow of Trinity College, Cambridge, delivered a course of lectures in various cities organized by the North of England Council for Providing Higher Education for Women, and this is generally regarded as the start of the university extension movement (Kelly 1970: 219). The movement was actually sanctioned by the Universty of Cambridge in 1873 with the first course commencing in Derby on 8th October of that year. Thereafter, the universities of Oxford and London offered classes and by 1983 there were twenty-five universities in England and Wales which had a department with extra-mural responsibility and provided a university extension service in their regions. These universities had the designation of Responsible Body, which entitled them to receive a grant from the Department of Education and Science towards the cost of organizing adult education classes of a university standard in their designated area. This was the only aspect of the normal work of a university which was open to the scrutiny of Her Majesty's Inspectorate.

However, the Responsible Body status was abolished by the government and all universities are now being encouraged to provide continuing education for adults, including those which were formerly polytechnics and which only received their university status in the early 1990s. It is currently expected that the grant given by the government for liberal adult education will be curtailed in real terms and that only certificated courses will receive a grant, as of right, although it is anticipated that the government will not withdraw all funding from non-certificated courses. In one sense this is advantageous to adult education since it is mainstreaming the provision for education for adults, but it has a number of major disadvantages including the fact that the liberal adult education as learning for learning's sake is subsumed and those who cannot afford to pay for such courses will be disadvantaged. It is currently believed that universities will be invited to bid for some monies in order to enable them to provide some uncertificated programmes, although it is believed that it will be a severely restricted amount.

However, another major change has occurred in the past ten years and that is the growth in continuing professional education offered by the universities. In this sense the traditional universities have moved in the direction of the former polytechnics and are providing courses of a similar nature. Indeed, many subject departments now have part-time taught masters degrees, some of which have been constructed and mounted in conjunction with large employing organizations.

It must be recognized from the outset that the polytechnics and colleges of higher education frequently provided both vocational and advanced courses in general education for adults. There was considerable debate about the extent to which polytechnics should play similar roles to universities or whether they should retain the function for which they were originally established – to provide opportunities for adults to follow work related eduction at an advanced level on either a full-time or a part-time basis. If the polytechnics and colleges of higher education were actually able to provide this service then non-university higher education would have had the means of creating a lifelong system of education, and Wood (1982: 9–11) indicated that continuing education, at least, was being seriously considered by many of these institutions. Despite these considerations the pressure to respond to the demands of the young adults and to concentrate resources on initial education has resulted in much of the work of such institutions being similar to university-type undergraduate education.

By the early 1990s it was clear that the government intended to change the status of the polytechnics and some of the colleges of further and higher education and it eventually created a national system of higher education with most of the institutions having the title of 'university'. The former polytechnics and the older universities now appear to be similar in their provisions of adult and continuing education. However, the former polytechnics are more advanced in the manner by which they market modular courses and the older universities are having to adapt their provision in order to prepare for the new method by which adult and continuing education is to be funded.

There is a danger in all universities that extra-mural staff may be seen as tutor organizers who have expertise in a subject, other than the provision of adult education. Their competence may no longer be seen in academic terms but only in terms of marketing and provision and adult and continuing education be regarded only as systems rather than as fields of research in their own right. One of the reasons for this is that there have been few universities that actually offer courses that lead to an academic qualification in the education of adults. Like American universities, however, there has been a gradual movement in this direction and there are now an increasing number of universities offering courses of study that lead to a university post-graduate qualification in adult education. Once these are established, the academic status of the discipline may be raised.

It is important at this point to raise a conceptual problem, one which will be elaborated upon in the final chapter. Adult education has always been viewed as liberal adult education and this has recently been subsumed within the concept of continuing education. All departments in universities are being encouraged to offer continuing education courses in their areas of expertise and, in some cases, they are employing their own marketing officers – often personnel who have some expertise in the specific discipline but who are not necessarily regarded as experts in the field. Consequently, the provision of continuing education is being seen by the universities as a marketing exercise rather than a specialist academic area. This raises quite major questions about what should constitute the field of study of continuing education and whether it should be regarded as a separate academic discipline in universities.

The universities have also been involved with other aspects of adult education including tutor training, research and writing books and papers for publication (Thornton and Stephens 1977). Research and publication are normal functions of a university academic but tutor training is one that occurs less frequently (see Jarvis and Chadwick 1991). However, members of university extra-mural departments do often train the part-time staff that are employed to teach in their part-time external provision. Even so, this initial preparation was not generally institutionalized.

Many of the classes provided by the universities are offered in their own centres but others are organized and mounted in conjunction with local authority, or Workers Educational Association, provision. A small staff of academics, often having the title 'staff tutor' and sometimes not being regarded as part of the university's academic staff, organize the extension service, but it may be seen from this statement that once again adult education tends to have low status compared to other branches of education. Few universities have yet actually offered part-time degree programmes for adults, despite the fact that the Open University demonstrated the extent of the demand (Tight 1982), but the new funding arrangements in 1995 will almost certainly create a part-time degree system in the universities in the long run.

There has been one notable exception to this failure to respond to the demand for education at an advanced level by adults: Birkbeck College, a constituent college of the University of London, is concerned exclusively with adult students. This college is named after Dr George Birkbeck who was professor of natural philosophy at Anderson's Institute in Glasgow when he offered courses of lectures to adults in that city at the start of the nineteenth century. Birkbeck College has offered a wide range of courses, including part-time masters degree programmes, for mature students for many years. The University of London has also offered part-time undergraduate level study at Goldsmiths' College and it has also provided the opportunity for part-time mature students to take external degrees and diplomas.

More recently, a major advance in the provision of part-time higher education for adults has been the establishment of the Open University. This is funded direclty by the Department of Education and Science and offers a range of courses at undergraduate level, a smaller amount of post-graduate work and a programme of short courses. The undergraduate programme is modular in structure, with each module being equivalent to a year's part-time study. In addition, there are some half credit courses but these also span a year's study. Students were expected to accumulate six credits for the award of a degree and eight for an honours. However, this has recently changed to bring the Open University into line with the Credit Accumulation and Transfer scheme adopted by the other universities which requires students to complete only six modules for an honours, although their level has to be specified. Not all modules are regarded as being of the same degree of difficulty, so the courses are offered at three levels. The Open University has now introduced a taught higher degree (B.Phil) and a small research degree programme; this latter innovation demonstrates that there is a demand from a number of people who would like to pursue academic research as a leisure time interest. Some of the Open University's undergraduate courses may be studied by associate students who are not registered for a degree and who may have no intention of registering for one. In addition, the Open University offers a programme of short courses in both continuing and community education. After a decade of existence the Open University began to offer courses in adult education itself, with both tutor training courses and a third level half credit course in education for adults which commenced in 1984. After a quarter of a century the Open University is expanding its activities throughout the world, indicating the tremendous need adults experience for more education and also demonstrating one of the strengths of having an entrepreneurial approach to adult and continuing education.

Distance teaching in its present form, especially that employed by the Open University using the media as an integral part of the course design, is a new development, although some of the larger established correspondence colleges might dispute this and regard it as merely a development in their own work. Nevertheless, since the establishment of the Open University it has acquired considerable significance and a number of established universities, e.g. Surrey, are also experimenting with courses of study through distance learning. Hence, at the time of writing there seems a distinct possibility that more opportunities for adults to pursue their own academic interests, and even vocational continuing education, by this method will arise in the foreseeable future. While the Open University pioneered the idea of distance learning undergraduate programmes, other countries in the world have rapidly developed similar versions, as Rumble and Harry (1982) have clearly demonstrated. With the advent of advanced technology new forms of distance education are beginning to appear, so that cable networks are being used, computer link-ups are common, teleconferencing is occurring and, more recently, inter-active compact video disks are being seen as developments that will affect the provision of education for adults at university level.

The Further Education section of the educational system of the United Kingdom has also been removed from local government control and the Further Education Funding Council has been given the financial responsibility for this sector. This not only includes the colleges of further and higher education, it also includes some adult education, especially that which is award bearing. This means that even free-standing adult education institutes have to apply to the Funding Council for financial support for some of their work, resulting in a clear distinction between those aspects of adult education that can be funded, vocational and award-bearing, and those which will increasingly have to become self-financing. Leisure time adult education is apparently becoming a privatized commodity for those who can afford it.

Less advanced work related to the education of adults is undertaken by the colleges of further education. The distinction between higher and further education often appears to be blurred but advanced further education is usually regarded as being that education which is above the General Certificate in Education (Advanced Level). Since many colleges of further education offer courses that are generally recognized as being advanced further education it is difficult to differentiate between institutions offering higher and those offering further education.

Indeed, many colleges of further and higher education are entering liaisons with their local universities so that they can offer, under franchise, parts of their degree courses; one common arrangement is for the college to offer the first year of an undergraduate degree course and then the students attend university for the final two years. This movement illustrates the fact that the first degree is systematically being downgraded and the taught masters degree is replacing it as the necessary stage to have been achieved by people in the professions, etc.

Many colleges, however, offer education for adults in courses leading to: a vocational award; General Certificate of Education; awards of other validating agencies. In addition, many provide short courses for vocational or general interest that carry no academic qualifications upon completion. Nevertheless, many of these courses do attract many adult students, and thus the general image of these colleges as catering exclusively for young adults (16–19 years old) who are reaching the end of their education is now misleading. However, the change in the image may only be completed when the front-end model of education has finally lost its currency and a form of lifelong education is seen to be the basis of education. Then these colleges may be regarded as colleges of continuing or recurrent education, although Illich and Verne (1976) do warn of the dangers of too much institutionalization of lifelong education.

More recently, some local education authorities have established departments of adult education within colleges of further education, so that general adult education is being located in the institutions that also provide vocational education. This is, clearly, a movement in the direction mentioned above – that of creating colleges of continuing education. There are a number of advantages to this, despite the warnings of Illich and Verne, as the colleges of further and higher education can become the focal point for the local provision of education for adults; the distinction between vocational and non-vocational education, which is already blurred, becomes even less apparent; the duplication of provision between the colleges and the adult education institutes may be avoided and the resources of the colleges may be even more fully utilized. By contrast, there are a number of potential problems in this policy including the exacerbation of the status differential between those staff whose main work is in teaching advanced vocational courses and those whose work is in general, non-vocational education, a point highlighted by Mee and Wiltshire (1978). However, a general, non-vocational education class may actually achieve a higher academic level than that of the vocational one but since there may be no examination to demonstrate it, the general, non-vocational education course may be accorded lower status. Other potential disadvantages include: a greater likelihood to fail to respond to demand from small groups of individuals since they may be less likely to make their requests to employees of large bureaucratic organizations than they are to staff from local adult education institutes and the likelihood that examination courses will always be given precedence over liberal adult education. As this movement has occurred in some areas, as was mentioned earlier, it will be interesting to see if there are differences in the variety of provision between authorities that have implemented it and those that are retaining a distinction between the two branches.

Further and higher education colleges are increasingly playing a major role in all forms of training, retraining and continuing vocational education. This reflects the vocational nature of their work since their inception. Increasingly these colleges are becoming colleges of adult and continuing education and they are beginning to assume the function of a community college, similar to that to be found in the United States.

The Workers' Education Association

Founded in 1903 by Albert Mansbridge as Association to Promote the Higher Education of Working Men, but soon renamed, the Workers' Educational

Association also had Responsible Body status from the Department of Education and Science and after the Russell Report (1973) the Association stressed its work with industry and the socially disadvantaged, in accordance with the recommendations made in the Report. The Association is a national voluntary body, divided into seventeen districts in England and Wales, plus a further three in Scotland and one in Northern Ireland. Each has its own full-time secretary and a few full-time tutor organizers who both teach on the programme and are involved in its development.

However, each local branch is autonomous, so that the members' interests constitute one of the basic criteria for the content of the programme for any one year. Often this programme is arranged in conjunction with a local education authority provider, so that in such instances duplication in the programme should not occur. While it is the members of the local branches who contribute to the programme planning, each branch offers its courses to the general public so that it depends on the extent to which members are aware of local interests as to whether the classes actually attract many non-members of the association. Since most branches do not have their own premises, each programme is usually offered in premises hired by the association and it is often the same set of premises as the other providers use, e.g. a local school.

During the funding crises of the late 1980s the existence of the WEA was threatened but it managed to survive. Even so, its existence as a large voluntary organization depending on government support is fairly precarious as the government continues to withdraw financial support from liberal adult education. Additionally, the extent to which its work with the Trades Unions will continue to have government support after 1995 remains an open question.

Some other providers of education for adults

It will be recalled from the discussion at the outset of this section that the concept of provider is difficult to define, so it would be possible to take the broadest interpretation and examine the work of a multitude of different educationally orientated institutions, including museums and art galleries, etc. However, only three main types of provision are mentioned here – the residential colleges, independent educational organizations and some other voluntary associations – and it must be appreciated that even this is an arbitrary division because some of the voluntary associations run their own residential colleges, e.g. the Women's Institute has its own college, Denman College, near Oxford.

Residential colleges

There are basically two types of residential college: those that run long courses lasting about an academic year or more and those that organize mostly short courses. There are currently eight of the long-term college, Ruskin College being the oldest while Northern College was founded more recently in 1977. The other six colleges are: Coleg Harlech, Co-operative College, Fircroft, Hillcroft, Plater and Woodbrooke. There was a ninth college, Newbattle Abbey, in Scotland but this was closed when the Scottish Office withdrew its financial support. All the aforementioned colleges offer courses for mature students of both sexes, with the exception of Hillcroft which is for female students only. Two of these colleges have a religious foundation: Plater being a college of the Church of Rome and Woodbrooke being organized by the Society of Friends. Many of the students who attend these colleges receive grant aid, although some attend on scholarships awarded by the Trades Union Movement, this being especially true for some attending Ruskin and Northern colleges. Frequently the courses studied by students at these colleges lead to an award of a diploma, validated by a university, and while these courses are entities in their own right, they also provide sufficient qualification to enable their holders to proceed to a university in order to read for a degree.

Apart from these nine long-term residential colleges there are, according to Legge (1982), about fifty short-term residential colleges which organize short, work-related courses. Often these courses are organized by the college in conjunction with specific companies for the latter's employees and run during the weekdays, while at the weekend they run liberal adult education courses for the general public. Some of these colleges are owned by universities, others by local education authorities, whilst some are private enterprises. Many employ a full-time principal, or warden, but use specialist part-time staff on the specific courses that are organized.

Independent education organizations

Apart from the independent short-term residential colleges there are a number of other independent organizations offering a variety of educational services to adults, e.g. correspondence colleges, conference centres, language schools, commercial schools and industry's own schools and centres. Correspondence colleges offer courses in a variety of areas, especially in the sphere of the General Certificate of Secondary Education, but it is difficult to ascertain the number of adult students enrolling with these colleges each year. The private language schools are flourishing at the time of writing since English as a foreign language is becoming increasingly important for foreign nationals who wish to reside in the United Kingdom and because it is used so widely in international trade and commerce. It would be difficult to describe all the different types of education offered by these various independent organizations, indeed it is a study in itself, but their existence is evidence of the demand for education that exists and which is often met in an open market situation.

By contrast to these organizations, it is probably true to claim that the largest providers of information in the United Kingdom are the media and it might be claimed that they constitute a major element in the education of adults in the country. Obviously the tabloid newspapers offer little in the way of systematic education for their readers but they do constitute a source of information regularly provided for many people. Unlike these, the so-called 'quality press' and many of the local newspapers offer regular financial and legal columns, systematic analyses of the current political and economic situations, and even columns about architecture and antiques. Indeed, Rogers and Groombridge (1976: 171) record how some educational courses have been offered through the newspapers. Radio and television, likewise, provide a similar service to their listeners and viewers and these have certainly become a major instrument in the transmission of culture. The Open University has utilized both in a much more systematic manner than any other educational institution in the United Kingdom, but in other parts of the world they are also used for this purpose and with the growth of local radio in the United Kingdom these media, apart from when they are employed in a more systematic manner, raises a conceptual issue – do they actually provide education as opposed to being media through which learning occurs? Obviously they are the latter, but are they also the former? For somebody following a series of documentary programmes or who reads regularly the analysis of the contemporary political scene, for instance, they provide the material for a planned series of learning episodes on a self-directed basis. Whether it is the editor or the viewer/listener/reader who is the planner is irrelevant; the fact remains that they are planned and systematic, so that they constitute the basis of a curriculum.

Professional journals and magazines also constitute a medium through which education occurs. Indeed, there are a number of plans for universities to run their continuing professional education degree courses using these professional journals as a distance teaching medium. Naturally, the universities and colleges will not publish their whole course in the journals, but this is indicative of the way that both continuing professional education and distance education are developing.

Voluntary organizations

The Workers' Educational Association has already been mentioned but apart from it there are many voluntary organizations which provide education. The Women's Institute was mentioned previously and it is one of the three major providers of education for women, the others being the Townswomens Guilds and the womens clubs. The Women's Institute receives a grant from the Department for Education towards its educational activities and it has also cooperated with the Open University in mounting one of the latter's courses. These associations may, in some ways, be compared to the Workers' Educational Association and should be regarded as major providers of education for adult women.

Among the voluntary organizations that provide education are the churches, both at national and local level, which have always sought this role, and while they are often regarded as only promulgators of a spiritual message, they have always sought to enable their members to learn about a wider variety of matters. Indeed, the Methodist Church has its own distance education department which runs courses in adult religious education, and other denominations have introduced innovative approaches for training both lay preachers and candidates for the pastoral ministry.

Education, then, occurs at work, at home and during leisure, in an educational or an informal setting; the amount provided is impossible to quantify but it does mean that facilities for a life of learning exist in the United Kingdom. Perhaps the fact that it is neither institutionalized nor formal, that it is not all provided by the state and that it is often on an unplanned and uncoordinated basis means that the ideal of state provision of lifelong education for all, on a voluntary basis for adults, has not yet been achieved in the United Kingdom. Whether it is even possible or desirable to have a total state system of education for adults is open to debate, but it must be recognized that in a society where privatization is the norm it is most unlikely that such a system would ever be considered. Indeed, Knowles (1980a) made the point that flexibility could happen only if there is the freedom for this to occur. Nevertheless, the vast amount of provision for the education of adults that has been documented above does not exhaust the provision, as will be seen in the following section of this chapter.

RECENT DEVELOPMENTS IN THE PROVISION OF EDUCATION FOR ADULTS

The past decade has been one of perceptual change for the education of adults and to document them here would require another book. Indeed, a retrospective study of this period would render a tremendous service to historical research and so the purpose of this section is only to paint an overview. This brief section, consequently, does no more than highlight some of the main changes, including: the commoditization of education for adults; the blurring of the boundaries between higher and further education; adult basic education and training; education for the elderly; educational guidance services for adults.

The commoditization of education for adults

The magnitude of the change that has occurred is captured by Thompson's open letter to whoever is left, in which she asks if there is anybody who cares much for the radical tradition in adult education any more since so much of the current debate is about market forces which is being conducted by

> grey men in suits, with executive briefcases and brightly coloured ties, skilled in business speak, [who] manage the decisions that deliver fresh batches of new consumers in search of education commodities in lecture halls staffed at the chalk face by contract labour whose terms and conditions of employment have been so deregulated as to ensure maximum exploitation at minimum cost
>
> (Thompson 1993: 244)

Not only has education become a commodity that is sold in the market place, often in intense but polite competition between the educational suppliers, but the type of education being offered has become more vocational and training no longer appears to be anathema to liberal adult educators. The outcome of this process is that the providers of education have had to become more like commercial organizations, often to the chagrin of the educators themselves.

Once there is a commodity concept, then the goods can be marketed widely and, consequently, there has been an internationalization of education for adults over this past decade. Distance education has enabled universities and other providers to offer courses throughout the world. In addition, with the improvement in communications, there has been a considerable expansion of interest in the education for adults worldwide, with book series examining international issues and the *International Journal of Lifelong Education* focusing entirely on this sphere of activity. In addition, the International Council of Adult Education has continued to play a major role, especially in seeking to link the less developed countries with those which are more wealthy.

The education of adults has also necessarily become more flexible, so that a variety of new approaches have been introduced during this period. One example of this has been the increasingly frequent provision of modular courses which has allowed adults to study a relevant part of a course but not the whole, to gain credit for what has been studied and to transfer that credit to another institution if it provides other relevant courses. This flexibility is a reflection of the way in which education is being redesigned to meet the changing conditions of contemporary society. Indeed, this approach is becoming commonplace in continuing professional education, where it is increasingly possible to gain taught masters degrees through the acquisition of credit for individual modules.

The fact that credit transfer is occurring means that there have to be brokers in the transaction. Initially the Council for National Academic Awards introduced the scheme, but when the government dissolved the Council some of its activities were assumed by the Open University. But as other universities are moving towards modular schemes, so they are issuing transcripts for their modules and there is growing up something of a mutual recognition of credit. At the same time, this has led to some problematic situtations, where individuals are getting two qualifications for one set of studies. For instance, advanced standing, or remission of part of a course because of a previous qualification, can result in individuals being able to gain the second qualification while undertaking much less work than other students who have no remission even though the subject of the previous qualification bears no relationship to the qualification for which remission is granted. This form of credit remission is a form of penalizing those who do not have qualifications already.

Credit transfer is one form of accreditation of prior learning experiences. However, the introduction of this has been beset with difficulties since some providers will grant remission for prior learning experiences that bear little or no relationship to the courses being studied while others are much more rigorous. This means that those institutions whose qualifications are easier to obtain will be advantaged in marketing their courses that cost them less financially and require less time to complete. Indeed, market forces may well create a form of qualification inflation, so that as more people gain qualifications the value of each falls.

Even so, the recognition of the learning undertaken in the process of daily living as an entry qualification for courses is something to be encouraged since adults do acquire a considerable amount of knowledge and skill as a result of daily living. It is becoming increasingly possible to gain entry into courses at all levels as a result of the growing acceptance of accreditation of prior learning, even though some institutions do not have formal procedures for testing it. However, there are some subjects where this is more difficult, such as mathematics and the pure sciences, so that this will almost certainly lead to different periods of time for studies leading to specific qualifications, such as bachelors degrees, etc.

Accreditation, or credentialing, has been a major development in education, especially in vocational education. Emphasis on vocationalism has, itself, been increasing during this period 'as learning for learning's sake' is being relegated to leisure and pastimes. Indeed, in some local authorities liberal adult education has been administered by the leisure rather than the education department. Liberal adult education will almost certainly not be destroyed by these present trends, but it will be changed and become a more expensive activity for those who wish to pursue it.

The blurring of the boundaries between further and higher education

At the time when the former polytechnics achieved university status, many of the colleges of further education changed their names to colleges of further and higher education. These colleges also wished to teach at first, and even second, degree level although they had no degree-awarding rights. Consequently, they continued to develop liaisons with universities, both new and established, in order to offer some of their degree courses. The result has been that there has developed a franchise arrangement, whereby these colleges teach the first year of some of the university courses. Significantly, these courses tend to be ones which are followed by adults, rather than by those younger people studying first degrees by the normal route.

Not only have these colleges been teaching the first year of university degree courses, they have also been preparing adults to enter higher education through ACCESS courses. At the same time a number of universities have mounted their own access courses, even though these have traditionally been part of the further education sector (Ryle 1993). These courses originally began with Fresh Horizons-type courses, pioneered by the City Literary Institute in London from as early as 1966 (Hutchinson and Hutchinson 1978), initially on a part-time basis but later as full-time courses. The idea was to provide a one-year full-time, or its equivalent, course in new subjects that would prepare people for a change in their career. Once students on these courses gained full-time maintenance grants, they tended to grow in number.

There were two other developments that led to ACCESS courses as they have currently developed; the first was the special provision made for members of deprived groups, including ethnic minorities, to study for entry into the professions. But the major influence was the development of the Open College networks – firstly, from Nelson and Colne College in conjunction with institutions of higher education in the north-west of England, especially what was then called Preston Polytechnic. The idea behind the courses run by Nelson and Colne College was to prepare adults to enter higher education and for them to bypass the General School Certificate in Education (Advanced Level) by being guaranteed entry to an institution of higher education if they were successful in the courses being studied. These types of arrangements proliferated and a number of Open College networks appeared throughout the United Kingdom. Davies and Robertson elaborate the basic principles of Open Colleges; they should:

- be genuinely open
- set no limit for individuals' personal or intellectual growth
- receive and validate courses meeting community needs
- offer credit for courses
- offer courses at different levels
- be democratic and federal
- initiate educational developments and promote and market courses throughout the area of its operation
- link post-16 education with higher education.

(Davies and Robertson 1986: 109–10)

By the early 1990s the Open College Network had become widespread and the Unit for the Development of Adult Continuing Education (UDACE) published a handbook of good practice which contains some seventy examples drawn from across the country (Mager 1991).

Adult basic education

Despite all of these developments in the education of adults it must be recognized that it is not that many years ago that the prevalence of adult illiteracy in the United Kingdom, thought to have been eradicated by the introduction of compulsory education, was first recognized. Indeed, Cardy and Wells (1981: 5) point out that provision to cope with adult illiteracy only began this century in 1975 and that this was initially organized by the Adult Literacy Resource Agency, established as a specialist division under the auspices of the National Institute of Adult Education. This agency disbursed grants from central government to the local education authorities in order to stimulate an awareness of the problem. As a result of the British Broadcasting Corporation's involvement in the field with the television programme

On the Move, the demand for basic education grew enormously, so that from 1 April 1980 the government established the Adult Literacy and Basic Skills Unit (ALBSU), as an agency of the National Institute of Adult Education, with an initial grant for a period of three years and with a remit to develop:

> provision designed to improve the standards of proficiency for adults, whose first or second language is English, in the area of literacy, numeracy, and those related basic communication and coping skills without which people are impeded from applying or being considered for employment
>
> (ALBSU, n.d.: para 1.1).

It will be noticed that both numeracy and life skills were included in this remit, which made it far broader than the original area of concern. The remit was in accordance with the recommendations of the Advisory Council for Adult and Continuing Education (1979b) which also specified that adult basic education should include language, number and life skills. Among the other recommendations of this report were that the Department of Education and Science and the Welsh Office should establish a strategic plan for adult basic education over the next decade and than an Adult Basic Education Unit should be established. Even so, it did appeal that the increased provision of adult basic education should not be made at the expense of other adult and further education provision. It was also quite significant that the New Training Initiative, which was initiated by central government and funded by the then Manpower Services Commission, included some of the main aspects of adult basic education within its recommended curriculum. In addition, the Advisory Council for Adult and Continuing Education recommended that it should be included in courses for the unemployed (ACACE 1982d). Little *et al.* (1982) noted that, while adult education provision for the black communities in the United Kingdom tends not to consider their needs very adequately, adult basic education was still needed by many of them.

In the past decade adult basic education has mushroomed and now there are a multitude of different approaches, all of which are tremendously important and many very innovative. Amongst them, English as a Second Language has become important in a multicultural society. Gurnah points out, for instance, that illiterate migrants coming from some Third World societies live perfectly adequate lives in their own countries, but on coming to England they discover that literacy 'especially English, assumes an importance entirely out of proportion to what they would consider to be the key issues of their lives (1992: 196). In an edition of *Adults Learning* devoted to adult basic education in the city of Sheffield, the significance of, and innovations in, adult literacy are fully discussed, involving the use of literacy assistants, the cooperation of higher education, involvement of the local community and the local education authority.

Literacy, however, is only one element in these new developments. Rodd (1992) records how another scheme sought to involve employers in 'workplace basic skills training'. He tells how that gained little support from some employers and that when they were trying to introduce the idea to employers they were forced to concentrate on the likelihood of increased productivity and harmonious labour relations rather than the individual development of the learners. This is significant since the local Training and Enterprise Councils (TECs) are influenced to a considerable extent by employers. Rodd goes on the point out that there is a danger that 'the narrow and short-term interests of training providers, increasingly dependent on outcome-related funding, will define the nature of literacy provision (1992: 56). Other schemes, however, do demonstrate that some employers are examining ways of maximizing their work forces' potential through educational projects; Hughes and Mayo (1991), for instance, describe how the city of Oxford initiated a project with Ruskin College, whereby the course centred on individual staffs' perceived needs rather than on the training that the employers considered necessary.

While work-place learning is an important part of adult basic education, it is clear that many individuals who receive training do not find it stimulating or even worth their time. Payne (1993: 275), writing about the University of Leeds project, records how 38 per cent of non-manual and 44 per cent of manual workers considered their training to be poor or unsatisfactory, as opposed to 17 per cent of manual and 23 per cent of non-manual workers who described their training as good or excellent. He goes on the show how many people had educational aspirations that went far beyond the work place. Once adults cultivate a desire to learn they know no bounds, and many strive for a rich liberal adult education!

Finally, in this section, it is important to note that the continued high level of unemployment means that a new area of educational work amongst adults has emerged – that of education for the adult unemployed. Many schemes are being run throughout the country, and Senior and Naylor (1987: 48) suggest that they organize four different types of courses: life and study skills; employment skills; job getting skills; interest classes. Naturally, not all of these forms of adult education are basic education, although adult basic education was mentioned twice as frequently by providers of life and study skills as any other. Senior and Naylor (1987: 49) go on to point out that there is little provision for welfare rights, or social or local issues among the first three types of course provided. Indeed, they conclude that there is 'a singular lack of education which aims to help individuals and groups to influence events that shape their lives and to search for alternatives to a social organisation one of whose basic values is full employment' (1987: 90).

Pre- and post-retirement education

It will be noted in the remit given to the Adult Literacy and Basic Skills Unit which finally achieved regular government support and became independent of the National Institute of Adult Continuing Education, that the reason why adults should receive basic education was because without these skills they would be unable to apply for, or unlikely to be considered for, employment, rather than because it might actually help the individuals develop and grow. It is this interface between work and non-work that constitutes the theme for some of the discussion about the education of older adults that is being examined here. Pre-retirement education has been among the most rapidly expanding areas of education for adults in the United Kingdom in the latter half of the twentieth century, and Coleman claimed that:

> The foundations of the pre-retirement education movement in the United Kingdom were laid during the years 1955–1959, in Scotland by the efforts of the late Dr Andrew Hood when he was Lord Provost of Glasgow; and in England and Wales through the work of the late Mr W.A. Sanderson, secretary of the Gulbenkian Foundation.
>
> (Coleman 1982: 7)

Much pre-retirement education is organized by local authority adult education, provision although industry and commerce also mounts its own courses. However, many of the courses appear to be rather instrumental in terms of these aims and it has been argued elsewhere that they should include a much greater emphasis upon individuals and their own perspectives upon their approaching retirement (Jarvis 1980). Curriculum development is clearly a very important issue in this form of education, and Coleman (1982: 60–72) recorded a course which he conducted during his own research. This was a useful inclusion since it both demonstrated an educator of adults at work and showed the type of content that the participants themselves considered they needed.

One of Coleman's recommendations was that: the Department of Education and Science along with the industrial and voluntary sector supports the establishment of a national organization which shall be recognised as the focus for pre-retirement education in England and Wales (1982: 95–6). In an important post-script to the research the chairman of the Pre-Retirement Association wrote, 'that the Department of Education and Science was recognising the Pre-Retirement Association as the appropriate national body. Funds were being made available on an initial three year basis, to enable the PRA to create an educational development group' (cited in Coleman 1982: 99). Hence, it may be seen that this was another area in the education of adults which central government had viewed as significant enough in recent years to invest monies. However, this support was not continued through the following decade and, as the recession of the late 1980s developed, many industrial companies which had previously organized their own courses, often through their Welfare Departments, ceased to run courses.

However, not all pre-retirement courses were successful, as Phillipson and Strang (1983) showed very clearly in their in-depth study. They (1983: 184) demonstrated that not all courses created a more carefully planned retirement and that many courses addressed issues relevant to only one group of employees, usually management. However, they also pointed out that these courses often came too late for many of the participants and that there was a case for mid-life planning courses, so they (1983: 215–21) arranged an experimental one in which they demonstrated that individuals had already begun to plan for retirement in mid-life and that there is a case for offering planning support at a much earlier age. This is still an issue with which the Pre-Retirement Association of Great Britain is concerned.

By contrast to education before retirement, the education of the elderly after retirement is also gaining an important place in the education of adults, which is not surprising since there are now so many more adults who have retired. Indeed, Glendenning (1985: 7) points out that in the United Kingdom there were approximately 2.4 million elderly by 1901 and in 1991 that figure had increased to 9.9 million. Similarly, there were 3.1 million who lived beyond 65 years in 1900 in USA but by the year 2000 there will be 32 million. There is, therefore, a large potential market into which the education for adults might expand. Even so, it has to be recognized that older people have less educational capital to bring to future education, and there is a strong relationship between the amount of previous learning and the enrolling on future courses. Consequently, the fact that the next generation has more learning might be a strong indicator that education for elders will continue to expand in the coming generations. In America the elderly have been attending university summer schools and Zimmerman (1979) records the enthusiasm with which they tackle their studies. The 'université du troisième age' has been widely acknowledged as an exciting venture in France and now the University of the Third Age is developing rapidly in the United Kingdom. But the education of the elderly does not have to carry a university label to be popular; some holiday camps are now filled in out of season times with elderly adults seeking to learn, and thus another element in the education of adults is emerging.

Indeed, it will be recalled that Label (1978) actually suggested that this area was becoming a separate branch of education and that it should be called gerogogy. However, this suggestion has not been widely accepted but although Battersby (1990) has sought to reintroduce the term the term remains as little more than a remainder of the place of the elderly in the education of adults.

Educational guidance services for adults

As the amount of provision of education for adults has increased, so there has been an increasing need to provide a guidance and counselling service to assist those who need both to find their way around all that is offered and also to discover the best route for those seeking more education to achieve their goals. These local services began in the 1970s in an uncoordinated manner, with one of the first being started in Northern Ireland in 1967. This initiative grew rapidly and in the 1980s a Standing Conference of Associations for Guidance in Educational Settings (SCAGES) was established. By the time that the NIACE Yearbook for 1993–4 was published, the term 'learning guidance' was being used, and as the Yearbook points out this service is still locally organized:

> In some areas provision is made primarily through the local careers service, in others through free-standing educational guidance services for adults. Training and Enterprise Councils are developing an increasingly visible co-ordinating role through such initiatives as the 'Gateways to Learning' scheme.
>
> (NIACE Yearbook 1993–4: 75)

The Careers Service in the United Kingdom has, as a result of the 1993 Trades Union Reform and Employment Act, now come under the responsibility of the Secretary of State for Employment and there are currently on-going discussions about which agencies are going to organize these services in the future. In addition, the Royal Society of Arts organized a national conference in 1993 in order to launch its own report on guidance, and as a result the RSA and the Council for British Industry have launched a National Advisory Council for Careers Education and Guidance.

Some recent trends in the education of adults have been examined in this section, although it is acknowledged that the choice was somewhat arbitrary. It would have been possible to have included many others but the reason for choosing these developments has been in order to illustrate that while adult education remains marginal, elements in the education of adult are assuming a greater significance and that central government is beginning to play a greater role in this provision. If this trend continues then, as Cantor (1974) suggested, the rudiments of a policy of recurrent education are appearing in a piecemeal fashion, but the term being employed is continuing education.

Having examined some of the recent trends in the education of adults, the main organizations and associations in the field will now be considered.

ORGANIZATIONS INVOLVED IN THE EDUCATION OF ADULTS

Over the past ten years central government has apparently removed itself, and certainly removed local government, further from the direct administration of those forms of education which relate to adults. At the time of writing, liberal adult education is among the only forms of adult education controlled by local government and, with future local government reforms in the pipeline, this arrangement may not last for long. Even some of the work of local authority adult education is funded by the Further Education Funding Council. Further education has expanded into the fields of education for adults significantly during the past ten years and, consequently, this sector of education is now one of its main providers. Higher education is also a major provider, especially since the creation of the new universities, but also with the growth and development of the Open University. The latter institution is one of the largest educational institutions providing liberal adult education courses at degree level, but clearly all the other universities organizing their extra-mural programmes are doing the same. In addition there is the Workers' Educational Association, which is the largest voluntary organization providing exclusively education to adults in the United Kingdom with much of its funding coming from the Further Education Funding Council. Both further and higher education are providing continuing professional education for adults at all levels, although much of it is classified as mainstream since it is award bearing. Neither of these sectors of education will be discussed here in any further detail since the purpose of this section is to examine briefly some of the organizations that affect, or have affected, adult education policy and practice. Seven major ones are discussed: the now defunct Advisory Council for Adult and Continuing Education (ACACE), the National Institute of Adult Continuing Education (NIACE), the Universities Association of Continuing Education (UACE), Standing Conference on University Teaching and Research in the Education of Adults (SCUTREA), the Educational Centres Association (ECA), Association for Lifelong Learning (ALL), University of the Third Age. However, it would also have been possible to have discussed many others, some of which are mentioned briefly in the final paragraph of this section.

The Advisory Council for Adult and Continuing Education

The Russell Report (1973: 54) recommended that the Secretary of State should establish a Development Council for Adult Education for England and Wales. However, in 1977 an Advisory Council was established, and the actual change in the wording of the title is significant. The Council was initially established for three years and it was subsequently granted a three year extension before it was discontinued. During the final year of this latter period the Advisory Council concluded that it had fulfilled its remit and it proposed that its successor should be a completely new body which might be called the Continuing Education and Training Services Commission (ACACE 1982e: 3). Before this recommendation is examined, it is necessary to recall the original terms of reference of the Advisory Council, which were:

> To advise generally on matters relevant to the provision of education for adults in England and Wales, and in particular:
> a) to promote co-operation between the various bodies in adult education and review current practice, organization and priorities, with a view to the most effective deployment of the available resources; and
> b) to promote the development of future policies and priorities, with full regard to the concept of education as a process continuing throughout life
> (cited from Taylor 1978: 209–10)

The membership of the Council was the perogative of the Secretary of State who nominated individuals to serve as members in a personal rather than in a representative capacity and, as Taylor pointed out, its brief was extremely wide and it had few limitations placed upon it. In the Council's own review of its work, it pointed out that it had: published reports on enquiries into policy and organizations, curriculum and programme development and fact finding; provided written statements and oral evidence in response to policy and consultative papers published by other bodies; made public statements on educational matters. At the time this report was published the Council had published five discussion papers, twenty-three reports (with up to thirteen more to appear in its final year) and had prepared and submitted thirty-two written responses to policy and consultative papers published by other bodies (ACACE 1982e: 7). These publications provided the most extensive and comprehensive analysis of adult and continuing education ever produced in the United Kingdom and focused the minds of many upon this aspect of education. However, the Council considered that it had fulfilled its remit and recommended to the Secretary of State that a Continuing Education and Training Services Commission be established. However, this was an ambitious proposal, as the Council recognized, so it proposed that an interim body should be established, having three main purposes:

1　To review regularly the facilities available in England and Wales for the continuing education and training of adults
2　To initiate, and respond to requests for, advice and help in the development of all aspects of continuing education and training
3　to identify areas of provision in need of specific development and to undertake or sponsor innovative and experimental work so as to encourage and enable the most effective country-wide provision appropriate to particular local circumstances

(ACACE) 1982e: 3)

The Council recommended that this new body should have five years in which to demonstrate its worth but considered that the establishment of some such body is necessary in England and Wales. However, the Secretary of State did not accept these proposals and the National Institute of Adult Continuing Education was given additional grant aid in order to fulfil some of these functions. Having completed six years, the Council was discontinued and the National Institute of Adult Continuing Education assumed some of its activities, albeit in a different form.

The National Institute of Adult Continuing Education

This association was formerly the National Foundation of Adult Education and it was founded in 1946. In 1949 this new body merged with a much older one, the British Institute of Adult Education (established in 1921), to become the National Institute of Adult Education. However, the term 'national' is a little misleading because it refers only to England and Wales, since Scotland had its own Institute and Northern Ireland its own National Association. The National Institute of Adult Education (NIAE) was originally located in London but is currently based in Leicester. The Institute has a small professional staff and its main function is to promote the study and general advancement of adult education. Legge (1982: 183–4) suggests that it seeks to achieve this by: facilitating the exchange of experiences by conferences and meetings, especially its annual study conference; acting as a clearing house or the collection and dissemination of information about adult education through the publication of books, journals and research reports, perhaps the most well-known journal being *Adults Learning and Studies in the Education of Adults*; seeking to encourage and conduct research into adult education; developing cooperative relations with other bodies concerned with adult education throughout the world. By 1993, however, two further functions had been provisionally added: representing the interests of adult learners and bodies that serve them, and renting, leasing, buying or selling property to facilitate its work (NIACE 1993a: 1).

Not only did the institute add new functions, it adopted the title 'NIACE – The National Organisation for Adult Learning' in which it endeavoured to demonstrate that its national concerns were for adult learners, irrespective of the branch of education in which they studied. It clearly sees itself having a major advocacy role for adult education in the immediate future, and as the only national organization of its type, it has a significant role to play in this rapidly changing world.

Universities Association for Continuing Education

Prior to 1947 the universities liaised with each other through the Universities Extra-Mural Consultative Committee, but, in that year, the Universities Council for Adult Education was formed. More recently, it inserted the element of continuing education. Universities having an extra-mural responsibility had a seat on this council and its functions consisted of disseminating information about the universities' involvement in extra-mural adult education, which was done both through an annual conference and through the establishment of occasional working parties.

During the 1980s this association changed from a group concerned with extra-mural liberal adult education to the wider remit of university education for adults, and universities not having a major extra-mural function were able to join. With the creation of the new universities, UCACE expanded once again. The polytechnics actually had their own association (Polytechnic Association for Continuing Education PACE) and so when the two associations merged, the new title adopted was the Universities Association for Continuing Education. This association serves as an advocate for university continuing education, conducts its own research and provides a focal point for policy discussions about research and teaching in university continuing education.

Standing conference on university teaching and research in the education of adults

If UACE is more concerned with policy and advocacy, SCUTREA assumes more of the role of a professional association. Universities which have either a teaching or a research function, or both, in the education of adults may have membership. In addition, individuals who are actively involved in university teaching or research in this field might apply for individual membership. Like the other bodies mentioned, this organization has established an annual conference and it has also established a number of working groups in various disciplines in order to bring together academics who have interests in specific areas of the education of adults, such as the sociology of the education of adults, psychology of adult learning, etc. There was discussion about a possible merger of SCUTREA and UCACE but since the functions of the two organizations are different, although overlapping, they have continued to retain their respective identities.

The Educational Centres Association

This association was established in 1947 as a result of a decision of the Educational Settlements Association to change its name and to broaden its membership (Allaway 1977: 41–2); it is a national, voluntary body which seeks to represent all those centres which cater specifically for the education of adults. Allaway (1977: 106) estimated that one-third of all adult education centres were in membership with the association in the mid-1970s and, in addition, there is also a category of individual membership. Since the association grew out of the Educational Settlements Association, it is hardly surprising that it has a democratic philosophy and seeks to support the educational centres in a national context. Like other associations, it organizes conferences for its members and also seeks to disseminate information about adult education as widely as possible.

Association for Lifelong Learning

This association was formerly called the Association for Recurrent Education but, as was pointed out earlier in this book, the concept of recurrent education fell into disfavour when it was recognized that few societies could afford such a system. Consequently, this association eventually changed its name in order to reflect the current situation. The association is of more recent origin than the older associations mentioned above and seeks to provide a focus for all who are concerned about: achieving a radical but principled reform of compulsory schooling; establishing a comprehensive post-16 system; extending information and guidance; ensuring more learning opportunities for adults; creating financial support systems to help those in need return to education; advocating lifelong learning as a citizen's right. It seeks to disseminate information to all its members through a regular newsletter. In addition, it publishes discussion and occasional papers on significant issues within lifelong education and, like most of the bodies thus far mentioned, it organizes conferences and workshops.

University of the Third Age

The University of the Third Age was founded in Toulouse, in France, in 1974 and really commenced in the United Kingdom in the early 1980s. It is not a university in the technical sense and it has no campus. It is a rapidly growing voluntary association, or rather an association of associations since local associations are independent. The University of the Third Age provides a non-formal system of adult education to its members. It adopts the principle that anybody can teach and anybody can learn, and its courses are organized locally and are not certificated. Members pay an annual fee in order to join and they can then attend classes organized by the association. The concept of the University of the Third Age has now extended throughout the world, with there being an international movement and international visits.

A variety of other associations could also have been examined here, including the Townswomen's Guild, the Women's Institute and the Adult Literacy and Basic Skills Unit. This last organization was established in 1980 and became independent of NIACE about ten years later. It is responsible for improving the standards of proficiency for adults in literacy, numeracy and adult basic education generally. In addition, there are tutors' associations, principals' associations and various other interest groups that meet to provide a forum for their own members. There are also some regional associations that meet on a regular basis. Nevertheless, there is no one single national body that draws together all who are involved in adult and continuing education in either an individual or corporate capacity, or which speaks for all whose occupation is in the field of the education for adults. The National Institute is obviously the association that comes closest to performing this function and its draft strategic plan for the period 1993–6 suggests that it is seeking to play this role.

Apart from the associations already discussed there are a number of other associations whose role in the world of adult education impinges upon the work of adult educators in the United Kingdom; five of those are mentioned here. The International Council of Adult Education is located in Ontario, Canada. This council publishes a quarterly journal, *Convergence*, which provides a basis for comparative adult education. In the United States, the American Association of Adult and Continuing Education was created in 1982, as a result of a merger between the National Association of Public Continuing and Adult Education and the Adult Association of the United States of America. The association is based in Washington and publishes two journals, *Adult Education Quarterly* and *Adult Learning* which appears ten times per annum. Naturally, there are other associations in America concerned with the topic but this one is noted here not only because of its journals, but because it has initiated many other studies that are useful to adult educators in the United Kingdom. In Europe, the European Bureau of Adult Education is based in the Netherlands and Spain and has membership from the United Kingdom, and UNESCO has a lifelong education unit based in Paris and another centre in Hamburg, both of which initiate publications on adult education. Finally, the newly formed European Society for Research in the Education of Adults has been based in the University of Leiden in the Netherlands. Naturally, this is only a selection of the organizations that either provide or seek to support education for adults, but these are mentioned to indicate some of the more influential ones in respect to adult education in the United Kingdom.

One of the most significant elements in the work of many of the associations mentioned above has been their support for research into adult education, and so the final section of this chapter focuses upon this important topic.

RESEARCH IN ADULT AND CONTINUING EDUCATION

Some of the organizations mentioned above have sponsored considerable research in this field but clearly the research reports from the Advisory Council for Adult and Continuing Education will remain some of its most outstanding contributions to the development of this branch of education. Certainly there has never been a period in the history of the education of adults in the United Kingdom when as many research publications of such significance have appeared in such a brief span of time. Additionally, the National Institute of Adult Continuing Education has either cooperated in or initiated a number of major research projects. The Further Education Unit has also sponsored a number of projects in adult education.

In addition to these organizations' research, the universities and UCACE have also been granted some funding from the Universities Grants Committee and some Trusts in order to conduct research. The UGC grants were made at a time when university departments were seeking to establish themselves as academic departments, rather than extra-mural providers of adult education, in the light of the research selectivity exercises being conducted across the university system. The change from extra-mural department to academic department demonstrates that the education of adults is being taken seriously as an area to be studied, but since there is little research funding available these departments have not yet been able to establish as firm an academic base as many of them would like. In addition, university academics have conducted a considerable amount of non-funded private research which has resulted in some excellent publications.

As previously mentioned, universities have also awarded higher degrees and diplomas for research in the education of adults, and especially in various branches of nurse education, and while many of the studies remain in university shelves it is possible to obtain them through the inter-library loan service. In addition to these, a number of universities have published their own series of research monographs. The University of Manchester has an influential series of Manchester Monographs; the University of Nottingham has published a number of influential books and booklets; Leeds, Surrey and other universities have also produced their own literature; the Open University has also produced two different courses in the education of adults. Many other universities are now running taught Master's courses in adult and continuing education, which results in both a higher level of scholarship through teaching, and more dissertations of either a research or development nature from students which add to the volume of research being conducted at the present time. Hence, it may be seen that adult and continuing education is becoming the focus of much more research attention than ever before. The theme of research will be elaborated more fully in the final chapter.

SUMMARY

Adult education has been the 'poor cousin' (Newman 1979) of the education service since its inception, but as Cantor (1974) suggested there are policy changes occurring and continuing education is beginning to assume a place of importance within the education service. It is significant that as continuing education becomes an acceptable form of education, the term adult education appears to be declining in significance. Naturally, in an industrial society where the speed of change is so rapid, vocational continuing education is of paramount importance, but to lose the liberal adult education tradition would be tragic for education as a whole. Thus the human needs of the learners must be taken into consideration in the provision of education for adults as are the demands of the wider society. It might be argued that ultimately there is no difference between the two and that professional development should also result in personal development. While this may occur, it need not always be the case, nor need personal growth result in professional development. Ultimately, the quality of education provided for adults must relate to the learners and their needs as well as to society and its demands.

One further point that needs to be noted here is that the growth and development of research in the education of adults is of significance in as much as it is adding to the body of knowledge about this branch of education, and this continues to construct the foundations of an academic subject in adult and continuing education which, in its turn, provides a theoretical basis upon which the occupation of educators of adults might be established.

This chapter has indicated that adult and continuing education, at least in the form of continuing education, has emerged as a significant branch of the education service as a whole. Continuing education, especially in its vocational form, may emerge as a branch of education that is far from the 'poor cousin' of education but a question mark must hang over the future of traditional liberal adult education. Apart from noting this change in the education of adults, this chapter has recognized the foresight of those who framed the 1944 Education Act and the provisions that were made for the establishment of an adult education service.

11 Towards an understanding of practice, theory and research

The relationship between theory and practice and research is one that was touched upon in the last chapter; it has consistently recurred in adult and continuing education in recent years and it is upon this theme that this chapter focuses. In 1974, for instance, Argyris and Schon raised the problem of the relationship between theory and practice when they made the distinction between espoused theory and theory in use; the former being the theory to which practitioners give allegiance whilst the latter is that theory which can be constructed as a result of observing their performance. They recognized that there was not always congruency between the two; indeed, they (1974: 7) actually claimed that there may, but need not, be compatibility between them at all. However, what the practitioners espouse may relate to what they learn during their professional preparation in the classroom whilst what they practise may relate to what they learn in practice, and further reference will be made to this later. At the same time Argyris' and Schon's concern was not really with the body of knowledge as theory, but only the manner by which practitioners made sense of the world and increased their effectiveness within it.

More recently, the relationship between the body of knowledge, as theory, and practice has re-emerged in the United Kingdom (Bright 1989) and in the United States (Cervero 1991), although it was a topic of concern in America in adult education as early as 1964 (Jensen *et al.* 1964), when Jensen thought that adult education borrowed from the foundation disciplines. This approach is one which is perfectly understandable, but it will not be accepted here. In Bright's more recent edited book a number of issues were raised that are of significance, but perhaps the most important for this chapter was Usher's (1989) discussion, especially where he called for more analysis of practical knowledge. The conclusion of his paper was, effectively, that it is necessary to return to the writings of Ryle (1963) who, as early as 1949, differentiated between *knowledge how* and *knowledge that*. Discussion of practical knowledge has not constituted a significant aspect in adult education literature in the English language and so the purpose of this chapter is to extend that discussion by considering it in relation to theoretical knowledge and to research in the field (see also Jarvis 1994).

However, it is suggested here that in order to understand fully the field of study, which is the focus of research, it is first necessary to understand the idea of a field of practice and then the theory about it, so that the first section examines the idea of a field of practice, the second looks at the idea of practical knowledge, the third at theoretical knowledge, and finally this analysis is related to the idea of researching the field.

ADULT AND CONTINUING EDUCATION AS FIELDS OF PRACTICE

Adult education is a field of practice. This appears to be a fairly unproblematic claim on the surface, but as all the discussion in the earlier chapters of this book illustrate, it becomes a problem since reference has been made to adult education, professional education, continuing professional education, and many other terms. The education of adults is not one field of practice, but many! They can occur within educational institutions or outside of them; in professional or community settings; they can be vocational or leisure time occupations, etc. The only common phenomenon is the educational process which occurs in a variety of fields of practice. Conceptually, the thing that they all have in common is that they involve an educational process, and the major conceptional problem that now arises is not 'what is education?' but 'what is educational?'

No attempt will be made here to resolve this problem, but it is clear that the common feature of all of these fields of practice is the practical activity. In order to practise it, some practical knowledge is necessary. Hence it becomes necessary to understand the concept of practical knowledge; and this constitutes the subject for the next section.

THE CONCEPT OF PRACTICAL KNOWLEDGE

Teachers of adults, then, are practitioners and education is a practice. In order to be an expert teacher of adults it is necessary to know how to teach them. As an educational practice, there are considerable similarities with school teaching, although this relationship is not explored here since it goes beyond the remit of this chapter.

However, Ryle (1963: 40–1) made the point that knowing how to play chess means that the player does not have to be able to articulate the rules, only observe them during the performance. He suggested, in rather the same way as did Argyris and Schon (1974) about theory in use, that so long as the player observes the rules and so long as the chess player is seen to obey the rules, onlookers know that the chess player knows how to play the game. In a similar manner Nyiri (1988: 19) discussed the knowledge necessary to know how to ride a bicycle. He pointed out that this ability is learned, not through knowing the theories of dynamics underlying riding the bicycle, but rather by trial and error.

Consequently, it is necessary at this point to ask what relationship exists between the actual performance of the action and the knowledge in the mind: that is, what makes practical knowledge knowledge? This is a much more difficult question to answer because the chess player might not always be able to articulate the rules of chess and the bicycle rider might not know the scientific rules that explain how balance might be maintained and the bicycle be ridden. Is it just the ability and the confidence to perform the correct actions, because they have been habitualized and memorized! Is *knowledge how* no different from *being able to*? Clearly it is not – knowing how to perform the action is not the same as having the skill to do it, and so learners can be taught the procedures about how to perform a skill but they still have to learn how to do it for themselves. In addition, learners can be taught that if they perform a skill in a certain manner, there are most likely to be certain outcomes; in other words, they can learn *knowledge that* in the classroom but then test it in practice.

However, the chess player knows when the rules are being broken and the cyclist is aware when someone else has not got the confidence to ride the bicycle. Naturally, this gives rise to the idea that some elements of practical knowledge are tacit (Polyani 1967), or even that it is merely a matter of confidence that the skill performance is correct, and so no actual thought need go into why it is correct until such time as an action does not quite fit the situation. At this point of disjuncture the actor has to think about it and perhaps devise some new ideas that need to be tried out in practice. If they work, then they can be internalized but their precise formulation may be forgotten, for practical knowledge is fundamentally pragmatic and presumptive upon the world, and the relationship between this form of theory and practice is pragmatic. In fact, practical knowledge is not only *knowing how*, in Ryle's terms, but it is also *knowing that* something will most likely occur given certain conditions and having the *tacit knowledge* that develops through experience. Practical knowledge consists of a combination of forms of knowledge.

How then is practical knowledge learned? Nyiri suggested that:

> One becomes an expert not simply by absorbing explicit knowledge of the type found in textbooks, but through experience, that is, through repeated trials, 'failing, succeeding, wasting time and effort . . . getting a feel for a problem, learning when to go by the book and when to break the rules'. Human experts thereby gradually absorb 'a repertory of working rules of thumb, or "heuristics", that, combined with book knowledge, make them expert practitioners'. This practical heuristic knowledge, as attempts to simulate it on the machine (computer) have shown, is 'hardest to get at because experts – or anyone else – rarely have the self-awareness to recognize what it is. So it has to be mined out of their heads painstakingly one jewel at a time'.
> (Nyiri 1988: 20–1; all quotations from Feigenbaum and McCorduck 1984)

Whether education is one, or many, fields of practice is irrelevant since this discussion is applicable to the practice of the education of adults, whether it be adult or continuing education. Practical knowledge of education can be learned partly in the classroom and then in practice from experts, and it is grounded in the field of practice. This is confirmed from students' reports on teaching practice – they say that they try things out to see if they work, they observe other teachers performing and they learn from experience. They learn the process by direct participation in it. Clearly practice is an important area for learning, and Schon (1983) highlighted the fact that many practitioners are not mindless in the performance of their occupation, but that they are responsive to new situations and reflective in practice in order to improve their overall performance.

Such an analysis as this has led to calls to reintroduce the apprenticeship model of training school teachers in the United Kingdom, and this could also be extended to the preparation of adult educators as well. However, there are some fundamental weaknesses with this claim, namely:

- that if there is no research into, or agreement about what constitutes, good practice then what every practitioner learns from any experienced practitioner must be acceptable, even though not all experienced practitioners are experts;
- that not all aspects of practice can be learned through observing the expert because unusual situations are likely to occur in most forms of professional practice, and so all practitioners are likely to experience something in the course of their practice that they have not been able to observe in their apprenticeship with the expert;
- if there is only apprenticeship then every new practitioner needs to reinvent every aspect of the wheel, which is an even greater waste of time than learning some aspects of practice in the classroom first!

Hence it is advantageous to have a body of knowledge about how the education of adults is undertaken, whether this be about teaching, curriculum design, management, etc. in the field, and this should be gathered from observation of practice rather than from theoretical explication of how a procedure should be performed, a teaching method practised or a lesson prepared.

Preparation for teaching adults should, therefore, include both the classroom instruction and book knowledge about how to undertake certain aspects of practice, about how to cope with the normal and the abnormal situation and, generally, to discuss the field of practice. At the same time, preparation for practice that does not include a great deal of experience in the practical situation is artificial and unrealistic. Exposure to experts in practice is an essential part of learning practical knowledge. Nyiri (1988) claimed that a great deal of practical knowledge is learned through exposure to custom, convention and ritual. But it also has to be recognized that exposure to bad practice is also a way of learning because learners not only learn from experts, they learn from the mistakes of others. Naturally, this approach is traditional but the transmission of the ethos of practice is necessarily conventional and conservative. But social change is gradual and a great deal of practice adapts to, rather than initiates, change.

Hence, it is possible to construct a body of practical knowledge through research that is about the practice of the education of adults and applicable to both adult and continuing education. Once this body of practical knowledge about education has been constructed, it might be called a body of educational knowledge or even a body of adult educational knowledge, etc. Does this mean, howver, that education is a discipline, like other social sciences? Response to such a question must be negative. The body of educational knowledge is a body of applied knowledge which is hypothetically drawn from the other social sciences. The point about this is that in everyday life actions are performed that, if they are ever analysed, might be seen to fall into the ambit of distinct but applied disciplines – such as psychology or sociology or philosophy. However, in everyday life people do not, when they think about how they are going to behave, always consciously decide that they are going to use a little bit of psychological, a lot more philosophical, some sociological knowledge, etc. and mix it together to constitute the practical knowledge underlying a specific behaviour. However, there may be times when actors are aware that they have applied some philosophical ideals etc. to their behaviour, so that it would be untrue to claim that the foundations of practical everyday knowledge are never recognized. (See Heller 1984: 185–215 for a discussion on everyday knowledge.) The same is true of educational knowledge – it is a unique constellation of applied knowledge that falls within the ambit of the other social science disciplines. It is only independent in as much as it relates to the fields of practice and this can be demonstrated in the following manner: it is possible to have a philosophy of adult education or a sociology of continuing medical education, but it is not possible to have an adult education of sociology or a continuing education of psychology, and so on.

The body of practical knowledge of the education of adults, therefore, is a unique mixture of applied knowledge from the various social science foundation disciplines, but it is not a pure discipline in itself. It is, however, an integrated subject – rather than a discipline – that can be learned in university or college and practised in the field; and the field can and should be researched, in as far as this is possible, in order to discover 'good' practice, so that the body of knowledge of practice might grow and become even more sophisticated.

There is necessarily a close link between the body of practical knowledge and practice. However, it is necessary to explore this relationship a little more specifically here. Traditionally, it has been argued that the body of knowledge (or theory) of practice should be taught before the new recruits enter the field, so that they can implement what they have learned in the classroom when they get into practice. This rather positivist approach, however, is flawed, as Schon (1983) showed when he pointed out that practitioners do learn in and from practice and when he argued for an end to technical rationality.

Indeed, it could well be claimed here that this body of practical knowledge does not determine practice. If it did, it would imply that practitioners mindlessly perform their professional duties in a totally unchanging world. Consequently, it is suggested here that this form of theory does not determine practice but neither does practice totally determine theory, but rather, as Lukes (1981: 396ff) suggested, it is a relationship of underdetermination. If it were not such a relationship, then actions would be predetermined and the social world would be regarded as unchanging and unchangeable. Such a view of both society and humankind is unacceptable, and so it is suggested here that there must be some incongruence between even the body of practical knowledge and practice itself, but that it would constitute a much bigger problem if there were congruency rather than incongruence.

This body of knowledge is the theory of practice, but there are also other bodies of knowledge and these are *about* practice, and this constitutes the topic for the next section of this chapter.

FURTHER THEORETICAL ANALYSIS INTO ADULT AND CONTINUING EDUCATION

It has been argued earlier that there are many fields of practice in the education of adults and that the educational process is common to each. Hence it is possible to argue that in whatever field of practice individuals are teaching, they can have a common body of practical knowledge, which is one form of theory about education. But there is another, one which can best be epitomized by the term *knowledge why*. The disciplines provide a comprehensive analytical framework within which questions about the education of adults might be posed.

Each of these fields of practice constitutes a potential field of study by scholars from the individual disciplines, so that a sociologist might study adult and continuing education, or a philosopher develop a philosophy of continuing professional nurse education, or an economist study the economics for adult basic education, etc. There is, therefore, a second form of theory which consists of the bodies of knowledge drawn from the individual disciplines about separate fields of practice, and these are bodies of knowledge driven by the demands of the discipline concerned and not by the demands of practice.

There are, therefore, two distinct types of theory and the differences might be demonstrated in the following manner. Practical theory is: applied; utilizable across all the fields of practice; driven by the educational practice itself; its knowledge base is integrated. Discipline based theory is not formulated in order to be applied in a direct manner; refers to specific fields of practice; is driven by the demands of the discipline; its knowledge base is predominantly from a single discipline.

RESEARCH INTO ADULT AND CONTINUING EDUCATION

Having analysed the concepts of theory and practice and begun to explore their inter-relationship, it is now necessary to explore the relationship of these to research, and Usher's and Bryant's (1989) study has perhaps undertaken this most consistently thus far in the literature of adult education. Their contention that this is a triangular relationship in which each affects the other is full accepted here. But having argued that there are two forms of theory, or bodies on knowledge, it has to be recognized that any research project must initially be firmly located in one or the other – it must either be seeking to analyse the practical or it must come from a perspective of one or other of the disciplines

Research into practical knowledge

Since adult and continuing education is practice based, it is important for research into practice to discover both what actually occurs in the field and what is considered to be 'good practice'. In a sense the expert in practice appears to be the best person to research it and it was Stenhouse (1975) who argued that the teacher should be a researcher. That the practitioner should be the researcher is something that might be encouraged although it might be argued that this approach to research is subjective and, therefore, invalid. However, it can also be argued that precisely because it is subjective it is valid, since only those engaged in practice can understand fully what it means to work in practice. Practical knowledge is necessarily subjective, although when it is written down it tends to assume the appearance of objectivity. However, there are considerable dangers in research of this nature becoming no more than descriptive responses to practice and research reports being little more than developmental diaries.

There is, however, a much greater problem with the practitioner-researcher and this has been implicit throughout the discussion of practical knowledge. Argyris and Schon point out that there is a difference between espoused theory and theory in use and that practitioners are not necessarily aware of this discrepancy; and both Ryle and Nyiri claim that expert practitioners find it difficult to articulate their practical knowledge. Consequently, expert practitioners might not always be the best persons to research their own practice. But this does not mean that they should not be encouraged to do so, neither does it mean that they might not be able to research contingent aspects of their practice.

Something of a paradox has now emerged because it is possible to argue that non-practising researchers might well be objective and observe practice very precisely and accurately but their accounts of practice might lose a great deal of the subjective. By contrast, practitioner-researchers might not always be able to articulate all the aspects of their practice because of the implicit nature of their practical knowledge. Certain aspects of practical knowledge and their relationship to practice might, therefore, be unresearchable! However, practitioner-researchers might get closer to the reality of the situation than non-practising ones. The naturalistic paradigm to research, therefore, might be the best for understanding the practical and individuals involved in practice might understand more fully aspects of practice than those who stand outside and observe. Naturalistic research, whilst subjective, has still to be carefully designed to ensure its validity, and Reason and Rowan (1981: 239–50) suggest eight criteria for this: all researchers require a high quality of awareness; they must engage in personal development; the research must be conducted in cooperation with others; the research cycle needs to be repeated; different form of knowing should be inter-related; contradiction should be employed systematically; a variety of different perspectives should be employed; the research should be replicable. Criteria such as these help overcome the dangers of subjective research alluded to earlier in this section.

Research into knowledge why

Perhaps little needs to be written about this because each of the disciplines are driven by their internal logic. Hence, a sociology of adult education or a policy analysis of adult basic education, for instance, must be conducted by experts in their respective fields of sociology and policy analysis. Since some of these fields are poorly developed – there are no really thorough ethical analyses of adult education, nor are there any comprehensive philosophical studies of continuing professional education in any field, for example – there is a temptation for practitioners in adult and continuing education to analyse their fields from the practitioners' perspectives without having an adequate grounding in these academic disciplines. Whilst this is quite understandable, and maybe it is necessary while research in adult and continuing education from these perspectives is still in its infancy, such research does not enhance greatly the academic credibility of such research undertakings. Consequently, it is necessary for adult and continuing education to be the subject of research by expert researchers from the social sciences and the humanities.

It might be asked, therefore, if there is any relationship between these two approaches. Clearly, they have different baselines: the body of knowledge emanating from practice is based upon the demands of practice whereas the second approach is driven by the internal logic of the individual disciplines. Both forms of research overlap since they both examine the same fields of practice, but there is a distinctiveness about each that makes them separate from each other.

SUMMARY

Traditionally, adult and continuing education have been provider orientated and their concerns have been in curriculum design, marketing the courses, teaching and evaluating them – as this book has endeavoured to demonstrate.

Systematic research in practical knowledge in these fields has been undertaken much more in America than in the United Kingdom, although the current changes in education in the United Kingdom have resulted in many more pragmatic studies in recent times. There is a need now for practitioners and scholars in the United Kingdom to replicate more of the American research in order to discover the extent to which the apparent similarities are real. Research of this nature can then be embodied into the curriculum training of new recruits to the field of practice.

However, there is a dearth of research from the disciplines and this is urgently required. But, it might be argued, that since this is not driven by practice it is a luxury that cannot be afforded in times of economic stringency. However, research of this nature provides a great deal more understanding of the field of practice within the wider social context and the purpose of 'pure' research is to discover and understand rather than to use the results in an instrumental manner. This is not to suggest that they may not be useful, only that their usefulness is perhaps subsidiary to the quest to understand.

As emerging fields of practice, some of which are going to grow in significance in years to come (such as continuing professional education, educational gerontology, vocational training), it is becoming increasingly important that more research should be undertaken in these fields, and understanding some of the issues has been one of the other main purposes of revising this book.

Selected further reading

(These books are listed in order of publication date and not in order of rank)

1 TOWARDS A RATIONALE FOR THE PROVISION OF EDUCATION FOR ADULTS

Education and Democracy, J. Dewey (1916)
This is a classical study in the field of education which should be read by all who are involved in the education of adults because Dewey grapples with many of the problems that concern them. In a sense, this book contains the foundations of a philosophy of lifelong education.

Adequacy of Provision, ed. E.M. Hutchinson (1970)
This report is now mainly of historical interest since it has been surpassed by the more recent ACACE (1982b) report. Nevertheless, it does contain valuable material about participation in adult education in England and Wales.

An Introduction to Lifelong Education, P. Lengrand (1975)
The author of this book has been at the forefront of the movement to promote lifelong education in Europe. It is an easy book to read but it raises quite succinctly many important issues.

The Lifelong Learner, R. Gross (1977)
This is a small book that introduces readers to the concept of lifelong learning and to the idea that life is an invisible university. Stimulating and enjoyable reading.

The Adult's Learning Projects, A. Tough (1979) (2nd edn)
This is a most important study containing the report of Tough and some of his research colleagues into self-directed learning. Not only is the book a research report but it also raises significant issues relating to theory and practice in the education of adults.

ACACE Report: Adults: Their Educational Experience and Needs (1982)
This research report was published after this chapter had been written otherwise some of the data from it would have been included. The report contains data form a national survey of 2,460 interviews in England and Wales and is based upon the idea of participation in continuing education rather than adult education. It is a very important research report about adult and continuing education, and more recent information may be found in Sargant (1990).

Handbook of Adult and Continuing Education, ed. S. Merriam and P. Cunningham (1989)
The American Association of Adult and Continuing Education has published a handbook, or series of books, at various intervals since 1934. This is the latest. It contains 48 chapters which provide an overview of the situation in the United States. It is a valuable introduction to understanding the current developments in adult education in the USA at the present time.

Lifelong Education for Adults: An International Handbook, ed. Colin J. Titmus (1989)
This is a significant book of readings, comprising 128 articles about various aspects of lifelong education. Each chapter is by a reputable scholar in the field and provides an introduction to the area. It is not a book for buying, but it is one which provides a most valuable overall picture of the complex field.

An International Dictionary of Adult and Continuing Education, P. Jarvis (1990)
This is a thorough introduction to many of the major concepts in the field. It contains over 5,000 references and provides a background against which adult and continuing education may be studied.

Learning and Leisure, N. Sargant (1990)
This is a research report about 4,608 adults' learning and leisure habits. This report updates the research cited in the previous two exmaples, showing how many people are, or have been, involved in education. In addition, it also reveals some findings about adult leisure time preoccupations. It was a timely report and one which is worthy of study.

Adult Education: Evolution and Achievements in a Developing Field of Study, J. Peters, P. Jarvis and Associates (1991)
This book was commissioned by the Commission of Professors of Adult Education to the American Association for Adult and Continuing Education. It contains chapters by some of the leading authors in America, and four from non-North American scholars. It is a 'state of the art' book covering many of the major areas of the field.

Paradoxes of Learning, P. Jarvis (1992)
Paradoxes of Learning reflects many of the ideas that are contained in this opening chapter and extended in an existentialist direction. Learning is treated here as the force that drives and assists the human essence to develop and become a recognizable element with the body in the human being. Since this process does not occur in isolation, it does lead to some paradoxical situations and some of these are explored in this book.

2 A CONCEPTUAL FRAMEWORK FOR ADULT AND CONTINUING EDUCATION

Learning to Be, E. Faure (1972)
UNESCO's important report on lifelong education. This is a very important document and one with which all who are involved in the education of adults, especially in the vocational sphere, should be familiar.

Pedagogy of the Oppressed, P. Freire (1972a)
This is Freire's classic book which all who are interested in the theory of the education for adults should read. It summarizes his radical humanistic position, in which he sees education as a way of humanizing the world. In addition, it contains clear statements of his analysis of education into two types – banking and problem posing.

Cultural Action for Freedom, P. Freire (1972b)
This short book encapsulates many of Freire's most significant ideas. The book is difficult to read, unless the reader has a sociological background, but the ideas that Freire discusses are very important and they repay the hard work of careful study.

Recurrent Education: A Strategy for Lifelong Education, OECD (1973)
This is a clear statement of OECD's policy on recurrent education in the 1970s. The report discusses the concept, sees the scene of recurrent education and highlights important points.

Foundations of Lifelong Education, ed. R.H. Dave (1976)
This book consists of eight papers, by seven authors, on lifelong education. Each is written from the perspective of a different academic discipline and provides a wealth of ideas about lifelong education.

Continuing Learning in the Professions, C.O. Houle (1980)
This book has rapidly assumed importance in the sphere of continuing education as a major work. It is not only a book about the concept, it is a practical book about the application of continuing education in the differeent professions. Houle is one of America's foremost theorists of adult education and, if for no other reason, it is well worth educators in the professions being aware of the ideas it contains.

Adult Education and Community Action, T. Lovett, C. Clarke and A. Kilmurray (1983)
This book records Lovett's work in Northern Ireland and provides a theoretical perspective on community education. It raises significant issues about the relationship between community education and community action.

Effective Continuing Education for Professionals, R. Cervero (1988)
The main aim of this book is to identify the chief elements of effective practice for continuing professional education practitioners. It is a practical book raising issues which are relevant to all areas of continuing professional education.

Britain: Policy and Practice in Continuing Education, ed. P. Jarvis (1988)
This is a small book in the Jossey Bass 'New Directions in Continuing Education' series. It contains ten chapters, written by different authors, examining continuing education in a variety of different settings in Britain. While it was written for an American audience it does capture the situation in the United Kingdom at this period.

The Long Haul, M. Horton (1990)
This is Horton's autobiography, the writing of which was assisted by Judith and Herbert Kohl. It is an exciting story of radical adult education, written in a direct and non-theoretical manner. An excellent introduction both to Highlander and to radical adult education.

3 THE ADULT LEARNER AND ADULT LEARNING

Participation

Access to Education for Non-participant Adults, V. McGivney (1990)
This is an excellent introduction to the study of participation and one of the few studies which endeavours to examine why specific groups of adults do not enrol in education after school.

Learning and Leisure, N. Sargant (1990)
This is a survey of 4,608 adults conducted in February 1990, analysing their involvement in adult learning and leisure. Clearly written, atheoretical, but an important survey which provides significant information about adult participation.

Why Adults Learn, S. Courtney (1992)
This is an attempt to provide the basis of a theory of participation; it adopts a sociological perspective and provides an introduction to the North American literature on this subject.

Adult Learning

How Adults Learn, J.R. Kidd (1973) (revised edn)
Written by one of the most well-known of all adult educators, this is a thorough, interesting and readable book. It displays a humanistic approach to adult learning and reflects both the scholarship and the commitment of its author.

Adult Development and Learning, A.B. Knox (1977)
This is a massive study, much of it given over to the adult, his development and place in the wider world. Despite its size and the breadth of its referencing it is a relatively easy book to read.

Adults Learning, J. Rogers (1977) (2nd edn)
Perhaps the most well-known book on this topic in the United Kingdom, published as a paperback and easily obtainable, this book is well written, easy to read and full of good material. However, the topics covered are wider than adults learning and much of the book is in fact about teaching adults.

Adult Learning, R.B. Lovell (1980)
This is a concise text book, reviewing the research and raising questions about the findings and conclusions. It is precise, quite thorough and a good introduction to the subject.

The Reflective Practitioner D. Schon (1983)
This book has become a classic, catching the mood of contemporary theory. It is perhaps the most frequently cited book on learning in professional practice and it contains the basis of a theory of reflective learning.

Experiential Learning, D.A. Kolb (1984)
This book draws together many of Kolbs thoughts and contains a full account of both his learning cycle and also of the work that he has undertaken on learning styles.

The Experience of Learning, ed. F. Marton *et al.* (1984)
This book provides a clear analysis of learning and learning style, written by a variety of authors from the UK and Scandinavia. It is a good academic study and should be read by anybody seeking to develop a theoretic understanding of learning. Most of the research reported, however, has been conducted within a higher education setting.

Adults Learning in the Social Context, P. Jarvis (1987)
This book contains the full discussion of the theory of learning presented in this chapter, including the research methodology. The book offers a social science theory of learning rather than a psychological one.

Psychology and Adult Learning, M. Tennant (1988)
This is a careful and good introduction to the psychological literature and its relationship to adult learning. It offers a clear and critical analysis of some of the major schools of psychology.

Learning in Adulthood, S. Merriam and R. Caffarella (1991)
This book offers a comprehensive guide to adult learning literature, from an American perspective. It is clear and thorough, and for anybody wishing to get to know developments in America, this book provides a helpful introduction.

Paradoxes of Learning, P. Jarvis (1992)
This book is a development upon *Adult Learning in the Social Context*. Written from both a social and an existentialist perspective, the book explores learning within a variety of social situations.

4 ADULTS LEARNING – SOME THEORETICAL PERSPECTIVES

Pedagogy of the Oppressed, P. Freire (1972)
In this short book Freire works out his understanding of the influence of the dominant culture upon the oppressed. He discusses fully his 'banking' concept of education which is his criticism of the formal educational process and he claims that the outcome of the educational process is a freedom that enables individuals to enter into a creative relationship with their world.

The Conditions of Learning, R.M. Gagné (1977) (3rd edn)
This is an important study in which Gagné explores aspects of learning, including those discussed in the previous chapters. While it is not about adult education, or specifically about adult learning, much of what he has written is relevant to adult and continuing education.

The Modern Practice of Adult Education, M. Knowles (1980) – revised and updated
This is a large book in which Knowles offers a guide to the theory and practice of adult education. Knowles has been a prolific author and this book contains many of his mature ideas. This edition is important since it includes his response to the andragogy–pedagogy debate that the publication of the first edition of this book stimulated.

Freedom to Learn for the 80's, C. Rogers (1983)
This is a thorough revision of his *Freedom to Learn* in which Rogers presents his ideas about experiential learning. The original has become a classic and this is an important updating of his ideas about the excitement of learning and, even more significantly, his existentialist philosophy of education – one which many traditionalists find extremely difficult to accept.

Using Learning Contracts, M.S. Knowles (1986)
In this text Knowles shows how he has extended his theory of andragogy to incorporate the use of learning contracts. It is a useful book about how Knowles has used self-directed learning and learning contracts and there are practical examples. It is a useful book for anybody who uses, or wants to use, contracts in teaching and learning. Knowles advocates written contracts, although some might feel that this is too formal.

Learning to Question, P. Freire and A. Faundez (1989)
This book is one of the lesser known talking books which Freire has prepared in which the two authors engage in discussion about learning through problem posing. It shows very clearly that Freire's understanding of this approach to learning is a socratic approach to teaching.

The Making of an Adult Educator, M.S. Knowles (1989)
Knowles has had a considerable effect on the development of adult education and while the level of theory has developed so that his work is no longer at the centre, this is an interesting autobiographical sketch of the man and his work.

Transformative Dimensions of Adult Learning, J. Mezirow (1991)
After many papers published in a variety of journals, Mezirow finally published a full-length book about his theory of transformative learning. This is a full book, tersely written in places, in which he attempted to incorporate a great deal of information. It is an important book for theorists of adult education but there is a sense in which he still needs to publish a book in which he brings together all of the papers he has written about this subject.

Principles of Instructional Design, R.M. Gagné, L.J. Briggs, W.W. Wager (1992) (4th edn)
This is an update of a book produced first in 1974 – it shows how Gagné and his colleagues related learning to instruction and it is relevant to many approaches to the education of adults in the 1990s.

The Texts of Paulo Freire, P.V. Taylor (1993)
There are a number of books about Freire, mostly symposia, but this text is a thorough analysis of Freire's writing by an author who is critically aware of what Freire has written. It is not an introduction to his work but it is an excellent critical analysis.

5 TEACHING ADULTS

The Management of Learning, I.K. Davies (1971)
A very thorough book, useful to anyone who teaches in post-compulsory education, whether their area is cognitive or skill based. It is both a guide through the literature and handbook on how to teach, even though it is now a little dated. The book has a behavioural bias, but is useful to teachers working within an institutional setting.

Helping Others Learn, P.A. McLagan (1978) (revised edn)
A handbook, not mentioned in the chapter, in which the author guides readers through the techniques of teaching adults – a simple but useful little book.

Teaching Adults, A. Rogers (1986)
This book is directed specifically to adult education, containing chapters on both teaching and learning. It is clearly written and a useful introduction; it contains some useful exercises which can help an inexperienced teacher.

The Craft of Teaching, K.E. Elbe (1988) (2nd edn)
This is a book aimed at teaching in higher education rather than adults, but there are relevant aspects which adult educators might find useful.

Adults Learning, J. Rogers (1989) (3rd edn)
Despite its title, this book is a well-written basic introduction to teaching adults. It is descriptive and realistic, covering most of the essential elements in teaching adults. The book has become one of the most well-known texts in this area and, as a relatively cheap paperback, it is good value for any teacher of adults.

The Skillful Teacher, S. Brookfield (1990)
This is a rather personalized approach to teaching, in which the author decribes how he plays the role of teacher of adults. In common with many of Brookfield's books, there is a relatively good bibliography.

Adult Learning Methods, ed. M. Galbraith (1990)
This edited book starts with reference to learning theory and the second part contains chapters on many of the different teaching methods, each written by a different adult educator. While the book is American in its orientation, there is much in it to commend itself to educators of adults worldwide.

Workshops that Work, eds. T. Bourner, V. Martin and P. Race (1993)
This is a simple 'how-to' book which outlines 100 different ideas for designing practical teaching sessions and workshops. It is not meant to be critical or theoretical in any way and so it includes theoretical ideas that are in need of debate, but many of the suggestions are very practical and workable.

6 THEORETICAL PERSPECTIVES ON TEACHING ADULTS

Experience and Education, J. Dewey (1938)
This is a short book, written after Dewey's experiences with progressive education. It is orientated towards initial education, but both the philosophy and many of the ideas are most appropriate to the education of adults.

Towards a Theory of Instruction, J.S. Bruner (1968)
This is a well-known study of teaching which, while it is especially appropriate for teaching school children, has a number of points that adult educators might wish to consider. This is especially true in the way that Bruner sees instruction within his wider philosophical perspective.

Deschooling Society, J. Illich (1973a)
This is one of Illich's many books on a variety of subjects which focus upon his concerns about professionalization and institutionalization. He has clearly a part to play in making educators critically aware of the process in which they are engaged and some of the solutions that he poses are significant for branches of adult education such as community education. It is wise to see Illich's work as a whole rather than merely regarding him as an idealistic critic of schooling.

Ethical Issues in Adult Education, ed. R. Brockett (1988)
This is the only book in adult education which raises the ethical issues. The chapters are written by practising adult educators rather than moral philosophers, so the book is practical in orientation. Only one chapter, by Rosemary Caffarella, examines teaching.

Please note that two of Freire's and two of Knowles' books have already been included in selected reading for earlier chapters.

7 DISTANCE EDUCATION

Learning at the Back Door, C. Wedemeyer (1981)
This book starts from the premise that all people are learners and that the educational institutions have not always catered for all of these needs – hence, learning at the back door. It suggests that with the development of new technologies, learning opportunities are now open throughout the lifespan. An optimistic book.

Distance Education: International Perspectives, ed. D. Stewart, D. Keegan and B. Holmberg (1984)
This is a poorly produced book but provides an excellent overview of the field, with extracts from the writings of many of the major early writers on the subject.

Theory and Practice of Distance Education B. Holmberg (1989)
This is an excellent introduction to many of the issues about distance education. It is practical and introduces the reader to Holmberg's own attempts to make distance education a two-way inter-personal communication.

Foundations of Distance Education, D. Keegan (1990) (2nd edn)
This is a comprehensive introduction into theoretical perspectives on distance education; it introduces readers to the main thinkers and provides clear insights into their work. Additionally, the book provides some practical points about planning distance education systems, although it does not enter into the minutiae of the issues involved in preparing distance education texts.

Theoretical Principles of Distance Education, ed. D. Keegan (1993)
This is a comprehensive introduction to the theory of distance education, written by scholars from an international perspective.

8 TEACHERS OF ADULTS AND THEIR PREPARATION

Training for Adult Education, K.T. Elsdon (1975)
This book, now a little dated because of the recent rapid developments in training, remains the only one published in the United Kingdom that seeks to explore the rationale for, and provides a number of models of, training. Therefore, it is an important book to read for anyone concerned to place training in a broad, theoretical, framework.

Training of Adult Educators in East Europe, ed. J. Kulich (1977)
One of a series of monographs published by the University of British Columbia, providing a description of the training programmes for adult education being organized in Eastern European societies. It is an interesting study, especially for those interested in comparative education.

Preparing Educators of Adults, S.M. Grabowski *et al.* (1981)
One of the series of studies produced by the Adult Education Association of the United States of America, containing chapters on different aspects of training in America. This book is thorough and most interesting to read.

The Training of Part-Time Teachers of Adults, T.B. Graham *et al.* (1982)
This is a research report conducted by members of the Department of Adult Education at the University of Nottingham. The empirical study is thorough and enlightening but there are few theoretical references and a very limited bibliography. Nevertheless, this is an important piece of work because it documents the present situation in respect to training very thoroughly.

Training the Educators of Adults, A. Charnley, M. Osborn and A. Withnall (1982)
The National Institute of Adult Education has published a number of reviews of existing research in specific fields of adult education. This is a thorough review of a great deal of literature. It provides a comprehensive introduction and some comparative material.

Training Adult Educators, ed. S. Brookfield (1988)
This is a book containing some of the most important essays written in American adult education about the way in which the training of adult educators has developed in America. For anyone interested in the development of training, this is an important book.

Training Adult Educators in Western Europe, ed. P. Jarvis and A. Chadwick (1991)
This book contains chapters by sixteen adult educators about the development of training in their own country. The project was conceived before the fall of the Berlin Wall, so the focus is upon Western Europe – but this is the only full account of the preparation of adult educators in these countries and constitutes data for any study of developments in this area.

9 CURRICULUM THEORY AND PROGRAMME PLANNING

Developing Programs in Adult Education, E.J. Boone (1985)
This is a comprehensive coverage of the American literature, providing both a basic theory and a practical understanding of programme design.

Curriculum Models in Adult Education, M. Langenbach (1988)
This is a text book covering a wide variety of curriculum models, mostly from American sources although there is a discussion of Paulo Freire's approach to adult literacy. In a sense, this book is more than just curriculum theory since it introduces the reader to a selection of North American thinkers and their approaches to the education of adults.

Developing Professional Education, ed. H. Bines and D. Watson (1992)
This book emanates from one university department in the United Kingdom and so it contains both the strengths and weaknesses of that department. Nevertheless there are some useful chapters explaining how academic staff in that department have conceptualized their approach to the design of education.

Approaches to Good Practice in Quality Assurance in Continuing Education, P. de Wit (1993)
This is an interim report of a research project examining good practice in quality assurance in non-vocational continuing education. The report covers a great deal of ground, examining the practices in a number of universities and produces a most helpful checklist of questions that any course team might need to ask. It is excellently written and obtainable from The School of Continuing Studies, University of Birmingham.

10 THE PROVISION OF EDUCATION FOR ADULTS IN THE UNITED KINGDOM

The Education of Adults in Britain, D. Legge (1982)
This book is written by an adult educator whose involvement in the education of adults has spanned many years and the depth and breadth of his experience is apparent throughout. The author has unravelled much of the complexity of adult education provision in Britain and this book provides a fine source of reference for anyone interested in this aspect of adult education.

Ageing, Education and Society, ed. F. Glendenning and K. Percy (1990)
A book of readings prepared by the Association for Educational Gerontology raising many of the most important issues about education in later life.

The Learning University, C. Duke (1992)
This book suggests ways in which universities are developing in the latter part of the twentieth century: much of which impinge upon the manner in which the education of adults will develop. A good introduction to current thinking.

11 TOWARDS AN UNDERSTANDING OF PRACTICE THEORY AND RESEARCH

Adult Education as Theory, Practice and Research, R. Usher and I. Bryant (1989)
As university adult educators began to undertake more research, it became important to consider the relationship of theory and practice to each other and to research. This book is an excellent study of this inter-relationship.

Bibliography

Adult Literacy and Basic Skills Unit (n.d.) *Guidelines for Special Development Projects*, London: Adult Literacy and Basic Skills Unit.

Advisory Council for Adult and Continuing Education (1978) *The Training of Adult Education and Part Time Further Education Teachers – a Formal Response from the Advisory Council for Adult and Continuing Education*, Leicester: ACACE.

—— (1979a) *Towards Continuing Education*, Leicester: ACACE.

—— (1979b) *A Strategy for the Basic Education of Adults*, Leicester: ACACE.

—— (1979c) *Links to Learning*, Leicester: ACACE.

—— (1980) *Regional Provision for the Training of Part Time Adult Education Staff*, Leicester: ACACE.

—— (1981) *Protecting the Future for Adult Education*, Leicester: ACACE.

—— (1982a) *Continuing Education From Policies to Practice*, Leicester: ACACE.

—— (1982b) *Adults: Their Educational Experience and Needs*, Leicester: ACACE.

—— (1982c) *Prime Use Accommodation for Adult Education*, Leicester: ACACE.

—— (1982d) *Education for Unemployed Adults*, Leicester: ACACE.

—— (1982e) *The Case for a National Development Body for Continuing Education in England and Wales*, Leicester: ACACE.

Alford, H.J. (ed.) (1980) *Power and Conflict in Continuing Education*, Belmont, California: Wadsworth Publishing Co.

Allaway, A.J. (1977) *The Educational Centres Movement, 1909–1977*. NIAE in association with the Educational Centres Association.

Allman, P. (1982) 'New perspectives on the adult: An argument for lifelong education', *International Journal of Lifelong Education* I (1).

Allman, P. (1984) 'Self-help learning and its relevance for learning and development in later life', in Midwinter, E. (ed.) *Mutual Aid Universities*, London: Croom Helm.

Apps, J.W. (1979) *Problems in Continuing Education*, New York: McGraw Hill Book Co.

Argyle, M. (1974) *The Social Psychology of Work*, Harmondsworth: Penguin.

Argyris, C. (1982) *Reasoning, Learning and Action*, San Francisco: Jossey Bass.

Argyris, C. and Schon, D. (1974) *Theory in Practice: Increasing Professional Effectiveness*, San Francisco: Jossey Bass.

Armstrong, P.F. (1982) 'The "needs meeting" ideology in liberal adult education', *International Journal of Lifelong Education* I (4).

Aslanian, C.B. and Brickell, H.H. (1980) 'Americans in transition: life changes and reasons for adult learning', in *Future Directions for a Learning Society*, New York: College Board.

Ausbubel, D.E., Novak, J.S. and Hanesian, E. (1978) *Educational Psychology: A Cognitive View*, New York: Holt, Rinehart and Winston.

Barlow, S. (1991) 'Impossible dream: why doesn't mentorship work in UK nurse education', *Nursing Times* 87.

Baskett, M. and Marsick, V. (eds) (1992) *Professionals' Ways of Knowing: New Findings on How to Improve Professional Education*, San Francisco: Jossey Bass.

Battersby, D. (1990) 'From andragogy to gerogogy', in Glendenning, F. and Percy, K. (eds) *Ageing, Education and Society*, Association for Educational Gerontology, University of Keele.

Bauman, Z. (1987) *Legislators and Interpreters*, Cambridge: Polity Press.

—— (1992) *Intimations of Modernity*, London: Routledge.

Beard, R. (1976) (3rd edn) *Teaching and Learning in Higher Education*, Harmondsworth: Penguin.

Belbin, C. and Belbin, R.M. (1972) *Problems in Adult Retraining*, London: Heinemann.

Berger, P.L. and Luckmann, T. (1991) *The Social Construction of Reality*, London: Penguin.

Bergevin, P., Morris, D. and Smith, R.M. (1963) *Adult Education Procedures*, New York: Seabury Press.

Bestwick, D. and Chadwick, A. (1977) 'A co-operative training scheme for part-time teachers of adults' in *Adult Education* 50 (4). Leicester: NIAE.

Bines, H. (1992) 'Issues in course design', in Bines, H. and Watson, D. (eds) *Developing Professional Education*, Buckingham: SRHE and Open University Press.

Bligh, D.A. (1971) *What's the Use of Lectures?* Exeter: D.A. and B. Bligh, Briar House.

Bloom, B. (ed.) (1956) *Taxonomy of Educational Objectives – Book I. The Cognitive Domain*, London: Longman.

Boone, E. (1985) *Developing Programs in Adult Education*, Englewood Cliffs, New Jersey: Prentice Hall.,

Boone, E.J., Shearon, R.W., White, E.E. *et al.* (1980) *Serving Personal and Community Needs through Adult Education*, San Francisco: Jossey Bass.

Borger, R. and Seeborne, A.E.M. (1966) *The Psychology of Learning*, Harmondsworth: Penguin.

Boshier, R. (1980) *Towards a Learning Society*, Vancouver: Learning Press.

Botkin, J., Elmandjra, M. and Malitza, M. (1979) *No Limits to Learning*, Oxford: Pergamon Press.

Boud, D. and Bridge, W. (1974) *Keller Plan: A Case Study in Individualized Learning*, Institute of Educational Technology, University of Surrey.

Boud, D.J., Bridge, W.A. and Willoughby, L. (1975) 'P.S.I. now – a review of progress and problems', *Journal of Educational Technology* 6 (2).

Bourdieu, P. (1973) 'Cultural reproduction and social reproduction' in Brown, M. *Knowledge, Education and Social Change*, London: Tavistock.

Bourdieu, P. and Passeron, J.-C. (1977) *Reproduction in Education, Society and Culture*, London: Sage.

Bourner, T., Martin, V. and Race, P. (eds) (1993) *Workshops that Work*, Maidenhead: McGraw Hill.

Bowles, S. and Gintis, H. (1976) *Schooling in Capitalist America*, London: Routledge and Kegan Paul.

Boyle, C. (1982) 'Reflections on recurrent education', *International Journal of Lifelong Education* 1 (1).

Bradshaw, J. (1977) 'The concept of social need in Fitzgerald, M., Malmos, P., Muncie, J. and Zeldin, D. (eds) *Welfare in Action*, London: Routledge and Kegan Paul/OUP.

Bright, B. (ed.) (1989) *Theory and Practice in the Study of Adult Education*, London: Routledge.

Brockett, R. (ed.) (1988) *Ethical Issues in Adult Education*, New York: Teachers College, Columbia University.

Brockett, R. and Hiemstra, R. (1991) *Self-Direction in Adult Learning*, London: Routledge.

Brookfield, S. (1979) 'Supporting autonomous adult learning groups', *Adult Education* 51 (6). Leicester: NIAE.
—— (ed.) (1988) *Training Educators of Adults*, London: Routledge.
—— (1990) *The Skillful Teacher*, San Francisco: Jossey Bass.
Brown, H. (ed.) (1973) *Knowledge, Education and Social Change*, London: Tavistock.
Brundage, D.H. and Mackeracher, D. (1980) *Adult Learning Principles and their Application to Program Planning*, Toronto: The Ontario Institute for Studies in Education.
Bruner, J.S. (1968) *Towards a Theory of Instruction*, New York: W.W. Norton and Co.
—— (1979) *On Knowing*, Cambridge, Mass.: Belknap Press of Harvard University Press.
Brunner, E., da S., Nicholls, W.L. and Sieber, S.D. (1959) *The Role of a National Organization in Adult Education*, New York: Bureau of Applied Social Research, Columbia University.
Bryant, I. (1983) 'Paid educational leave in Scotland', in *International Journal of Lifelong Education* 2 (1).
Buber, M. (1959) *I and Thou*, Edinburgh: T&T Clark.
—— (1961) *Between Man and Man*, London: Fontana.
Burgess, P.D. (1974) *The Educational Orientations of Adult Participants in Group Educational Activities*, Unpublished doctoral thesis, University of Chicago.
Burnard, P. (1990) 'The student experience: adult learning and mentorship revisited', *Nurse Education Today* 6 (5).
Caldwell, P.A. (1981) 'Preservice training for instructors of adults', in Grabowski, S. *et al. Preparing Educators of Adults*, San Francisco: Jossey Bass.
Campbell, D.D. (1977) *Adult Education as a Field of Study and Practice*, Vancouver: Centre for Continuing Education, University of British Columbia.
Candy,P.C. (1981) *Mirrors of the Mind*, Manchester Monographs 16, Department of Adult and Higher Education, University of Manchester.
—— (1991) *Self Direction for Lifelong Learning*, San Francisco: Jossey Bass.
Cantor, L.M. (1974) *Recurrent Education – Policy and Developments in OECD Member Countries; United Kingdom*, Paris: OECD.
Cantor, L.M. and Roberts, I.F. (1972) (2nd edn) *Further Education in England and Wales*, London: Routledge and Kegan Paul.
Caplow, T. (1954) *The Sociology of Work*, Minneapolis: University of Minnesota Press.
Cardy, E. and Wells, A. (1981) *Adult Literacy Unit: Development Projects 1978–80* London: Adult Literacy and Basic Skills Unit.
Carp, A., Peterson, R. and Roelfs, P. (1974) 'Adult learning interests and experiences', cited in Cross, K. (ed.) (1981) *Adults as Learners*, San Francisco: Jossey Bass.
Cashdown, A. and Whitehead, J. (eds) (1971) *Personality, Growth and Learning*, London: Longman.
Casner-Lotto, J. and Associates (1989) *Successful Training Strategies*, San Francisco: Jossey Bass.
Cervero, R. (1988) *Effective Continuing Education for Professionals*, San Francisco: Jossey Bass.
—— (1991) 'Relationships between theory and practice', in Peters, J., Jarvis, P. and Associates, *Adult Education: Evolution and Achievements in a Developing Field of Study*, San Francisco: Jossey Bass.
Chadwick, A.F. (1980) *The Role of the Museum and Art Gallery in Community Education*, Department of Adult Education, University of Nottingham.
Charnley, A., Osborn, M. and Withnall, A. (1980) *Review of Existing Research in Adult and Continuing Education: Vol. I – Mature Students*, Leicester: NIAE.

—— (1982) *Review of Existing Research in Adult and Continuing Education: Vol VIII – Training the Educators of Adults.* Leicester: NIAE.

Charters, A.N. *et al.* (1981) *Comparing Adult Education Worldwide*, San Francisco: Jossey Bass.

Child, D. (1977) (2nd edn) *Psychology and the Teacher*, London and New York: Holt, Rinehart and Winston.

—— (1981) (3rd edn) *Psychology and the Teacher*, New York: Holt, Rinehart and Winston.

Child, J. (1977) *Organization – A Guide to Problems and Practice*, London: Harper and Row.

City and Guilds of London Institute (1978) *730 Further Education Teachers' Certificate*, London: CGLI.

Coates, K. and Silburn, R. (1967) *St Ann's: Poverty, Deprivation and Morale in a Nottingham Community*, Department of Adult Education, University of Nottingham.

Coleman, A. (1982) *Preparation for Retirement in England and Wales*, Leicester: NIAE.

Collins *Dictionary of the English Language* (1979) London and Glasgow: Collins.

Coombs, P. and Ahmed, M. (1974) *Attacking Rural Poverty*, Baltimore: Johns Hopkins University Press.

Cooper, C.L. (ed.) (1975) *Theories of Group Processes*, London: John Wiley and Sons.

Council for National Academic Awards (1991) *Handbook 1991–1992*, London: CNAA.

Council on the Continuing Education Unit (1984) *Principles of Good Practice in Continuing Education*, Maryland: CCEU.

Courtney, S. (1981) 'The factors affecting participation in adult education: an analysis of some literature', *Studies in Adult Education* 13 (2).

Courtney, S. (1992) *Why Adults Learn*, London: Routledge.

Crane, J.M. (1982) 'Individualized learning: an analysis of the theoretical principles with illuminative references from the experientially-evolved practices of an individualized learning system developed in an adult basic academic upgrading programme', unpublished MSc dissertation, University of Surrey.

Cross, K.P. (1981) *Adults as Learners*, San Francisco: Jossey Bass.

Dadswell, G. (1978) 'The adult independent learner and public libraries', in *Adult Education* 51 (1) Leicester: NIAE.

Dale, S.M. (1980) 'Another way forward for adult learners: the public library and independent study', in *Studies in Adult Education* 12 (1).

Daloz, L. (1986) *Effective Teaching and Mentoring*, San Francisco: Jossey Bass.

Dave, R. H. (ed.) (1976) *Foundations of Lifelong Education*, Oxford: Pergamon Press (for UNESCO Institute for Education).

Davies, D. and Robertson, D. (1986) 'Open college – towards a new view of adult education', *Adult Education* 59 (2): 106–14.

Davies, I.K. (1971) *The Management of Learning*, London: McGraw Hill Book Co.

—— (1976) *Objectives in Curriculum Design*, London: McGraw Hill Book Co.

Day, C. and Baskett, H.K. (1982) 'Discrepancies between intentions and practice: Re-examining some basic assumptions about adult and continuing professional education', *International Journal of Lifelong Education* 1 (2).

Dearden, R.F. (1972) '"Needs" in education', in Dearden, R.F., Hirst, P.H. and Peters, R.S. (eds) *A Critique of Current Educational Aims (Part I of Education and the Development of Reason)*, London: Routledge and Kegan Paul.

Dearden, R.F., Hirst, P.H. and Peters, R.S. (eds) (1972) *A Critique of Current Educational Aims (Part I of Education and the Development of Reason)*, London: Routledge and Kegan Paul.

Devereux, W. (1982) *Adult Education in Inner London 1870–1980*, London: Shepheard-Welwyn/ILEA.

Dewey, J. (1916) *Education and Democracy*, New York: The Free Press.

—— (1938) *Experience and Education*, London: Collier Macmillan.

—— (ed.) (1958) *Experience and Nature*, New York: Dover Publications.

de Wit, P. (1992) *Quality Assurance in University Continuing Vocational Education*, London: HMSO.

—— (1993) *Approaches to Good Practice in Quality Assurance in University Continuing Education*, Universities Association for Continuing Education Working Paper 3, University of Birmingham.

Draves, W. (1979) 'The free university network', *Lifelong Learning – The Adult Years* 3 (4).

—— (1980) *The Free University – a Model for Lifelong Learning*, Chicago: Association Press.

Duke, C. (1992) *The Learning University*, Buckingham: Open University Press in association with Society for Research in Higher Education.

Durkheim, E. (1956) *Education and Sociology* (trans. S.D. Fox), New York: The Free Press.

Eisner, E.W. (1969) 'Instructional and expressive educational objectives', in Popham, W.J., Eisner, E.W., Sullivan, H.J. and Tyler, L.L. (eds) *Instructional Objectives*, Chicago: Rand McNally.

Elbe, K. (1988) (2nd edn) *The Craft of Teaching*, San Francisco: Jossey Bass.

Elias, J.L. (1979) 'Andragogy revisited', *Adult Education* 29: 252–6.

Elias, J.L. and Merriam, S. (1980) *Philosophical Foundation of Adult Education*, Malabar, Florida: Robert E. Krieger Publishing Co.

Ellwood, C. (1976) *Adult Learning Today*, London: Sage Publications.

Elsdon, K.T. (1970) 'The East Midlands Scheme', *Adult Education* 46 (4). Leicester: NIAE.

—— (1975) *Training for Adult Education*, Department of Adult Education, University of Nottingham in conjunction with NIAE.

—— (1981) *New Directions: Adult Education in the Context of Continuing Education*, London: Department of Education and Science.

Elsey, B. (1980) 'Volunteer tutors in adult education', *Studies in Adult Education* 12 (2).

—— (1986) *Social Theory Perspectives on Adult Education*, Department of Adult Education, University of Nottingham.

Eurich, N. (1985) *Corporate Classrooms*, Princeton, New Jersey: Carnegie Foundation for the Advancement of Teaching.

Fairbairn, A.N. (1971) *The Leicestershire Community Colleges*, London: NIAE.

—— (1978) *The Leicestershire Community Colleges and Centres*, Department of Adult Education, University of Nottingham.

Faure, E. (1972) *Learning to Be*, Paris: UNESCO.

Feigenbaum, E. and McCorduck, P. (1984) *The Fifth Generation*, New York: Signet.

Finch, J. (1984) *Education as Social Policy*, London: Longman.

Fitzgerald, M., Halmos, P., Muncie, J. and Zeldin, D. (1977) *Welfare in Action*, London: Routledge and Kegan Paul/Open University Press.

Fletcher, C. (1980a) 'The theory of community education and its relation to adult education', in Thompson, J.L. (ed.) *Adult Education for a Change*, London: Heinemann.

—— (1980b) 'Community studies as practical adult education', *Adult Education* 53 (2). Leicester: NIAE.

—— (1982) 'Adults in a community education centre', *International Journal of Lifelong Education* 1 (3).

—— (n.d.) *The Challenges of Community Education*, Department of Adult Education, University of Nottingham.

Fletcher, C. and Thompson, N. (1980) *Issues in Community Education*, Lewes: Falmer Press.

Flude, R.A. (1978) 'A course in rural community action', *Adult Education* 51 (3). Leicester: NIAE.

Flude, R. and Parrott, A. (1979) *Education and the Challenge of Change – a Recurrent Education Strategy for Britain*, Milton Keynes: Open University Press.

Fordham, P., Poulton, G. and Randle, L. (1979) *Learning Networks in Adult Education*, London: Routledge and Kegan Paul.

Fowler, J. (1981) *Stages of Faith*, New York: Harper & Row.

Freire, P. (1971) 'A few notions about the word "concientization"', *Hard Cheese* No. 1. Reprinted in Dale, R., Esland, G. and MacDonald, M. (eds) *Schooling and Capitalism* (1976), London: Routledge and Kegan Paul/Open University Press.

—— (1972a) *Cultural Action for Freedom*, Harmondsworth: Penguin.

—— (1972b) *Pedagogy of the Oppressed* (trans. M.B. Ramer), Harmondsworth: Penguin.

—— (1973a) *Education for Critical Consciousness*, London: Sheed and Ward. Reprinted under the title *Education: the Practice of Freedom*, London: Writers and Readers Publishing Cooperative.

—— (1973b) 'Education, liberation and the Church', *Study Encounter* 9 (1).

—— (1973c) 'By learning they can teach', *Convergence* 6 (1).

—— (1978) *Pedagogy in Process. The Letters to Guinea-Bissau*, London: Writers and Readers Publishing Cooperative.

—— (1985) *The Politics of Education*, London: Macmillan.

Freire, P. and Macedo, D. (1987) *Literacy: Reading the Word and the World*, London: Routledge.

Freire, P. and Shor, I. (1987) *A Pedagogy for Liberation*, London: Macmillan.

Freire, P. and Faundez, A. (1989) *Learning to Question: a Pedagogy of Liberation*, Geneva: World Council of Churches.

Further Education Unit (1989) *Supporting Quality in YTS*, London: FEU.

—— (1990) *Developing a Marketing Strategy for Adult and Continuing Education*, London: FEU.

Gagné, R.M. (1977) (3rd edn) *The Conditions of Learning*, New York: Holt, Rinehart and Winston.

Gagné, R.M., Briggs, L. and Wager, W. (1992) (4th edn) *Principles of Instructional Design*, Fort Worth: Harcourt Brace Jovanovich.

Galbraith, M. (ed.) (1990) *Adult Learning Methods*, Malabar, Florida: Krieger.

Garrison, R. and Shale, D. (eds) (1990) *Education at a Distance*, Malabar, Florida: Krieger.

Gelpi, E. (1979) *A Future for Lifelong Education* (2 Vols) (trans. R. Ruddock), Manchester Monographs 13, University of Manchester.

Gibbs, G. (1981) *Teaching Students to Learn*, Milton Keynes: Open University Press.

Gibbs, G. and Durbridge, N. (1976) 'Characteristics of Open University tutors (Part 2): Tutors in action' *Teaching at a Distance* (7), Milton Keynes: Open University.

Giddens, A. (1990) *The Consequences of Modernity*, Cambridge: Polity Press.

Giles, H.H., McCutcheon, S.P. and Zechriel, A.N. (1942) *Exploring the Curriculum*, New York: Harper.

Glendenning, F. (ed.) (1985) *Educational Gerontology: International Perspectives*, London: Croom Helm.

Glendenning, F. and Percy, K. (eds) (1990) *Ageing, Education and Society*, Association for Educational Gerontology, University of Keele, Staffs.

Goodlad, J., Soder, R. and Sirotnik, K. (eds) (1990) *The Moral Dimensions of*

Teaching, San Francisco: Jossey Bass.

Gould, A. (1979) *Towards Equality of Occupational Opportunity*, Association of Recurrent Education. Discussion Paper 5, Centre for Research into Education for Adults, University of Nottingham.

Grabowski, S.H. *et al.*(1981) *Preparing Educators of Adults*, San Francisco: Jossey Bass.

Graham, T.B., Daines, J.H., Sullivan, T., Harris, P. and Baum, F.E. (1982) *The Training of Part-Time Teachers of Adults*, Department of Adult Education, University of Nottingham.

Greenwood, E. (1957) 'Attributes of a profession', *Social Work* 2: 44–55.

Griffin, C. (1978) *Recurrent and Continuing Education – a Curriculum Model Approach*, Association of Recurrent Education, School of Education, University of Nottingham.

—— (1979) 'Continuing education and the adult curriculum', *Adult Education* 52 (2). Leicester: NIAE.

—— (1982) 'Curriculum analysis of adult and lifelong education', *International Journal of Lifelong Education* 1 (2).

—— (1987) *Adult Education as Social Policy*, London: Croom Helm.

Groombridge, B. (1972) *Television and the People*, Harmondsworth: Penguin.

Gross, R. (1977) *The Lifelong Learner*, New York: Touchstone Books, Simon and Schuster.

Gurnah, A. (1992) 'Editorial', *Adults Learning* 3 (8).

Hall, R.H. (1969) *Occupations and the Social Structure*, Englewood Cliffs, New Jersey: Prentice Hall.

Hallenbeck, W.C. (1948) 'Training adult educators', in Ely, M. (ed.) *Handbook of Adult Education in the United States*, Center for Adult Education. Republished in Brookfield, S. (ed.) (1988) *Training Educators of Adults*, London: Routledge.

Halmos, P. (1978) 'The concept of social problem', *Social Work and Community Course DE206*, Block 1, Milton Keynes: Open University Press.

Handley, J. (1981) 'An investigation into the training needs of part-time tutors, with particular reference to the development of courses at ACSTT Stage II level', unpublished MSc dissertation, University of Surrey.

Harper, K. (1982) 'Colleges warned against "politics" in YOP courses', *Guardian* 29 November, p. 22.

Harries-Jenkins, G. (1982) 'The role of the adult student', *International Journal of Lifelong Education* 1 (1).

Harris, W.J.A. (1980) *Comparative Adult Education – Practice, Purpose and Theory*, London and New York: Longman.

Hartree, A. (1984) 'Malcolm Knowles' theory of andragogy: a critique', *International Journal of Lifelong Education* 3 (3): 203–10.

Harvey, B., Daines, J., Jones, D. and Wallis, J. (1981) *Policy and Research Adult Education*, Department of Adult Education, University of Nottingham.

Haycocks, J.N. (1978) *The Training of Adult Education and Part-Time Further Education Teachers*, Advisory Committee on the Supply and Training of Teachers, London.

Head, D. (1977) 'Education at the bottom', *Studies in Adult Education* 9 (2).

Hegarty, T.B. (1976) 'Education for the legal profession', in Turner, J.R. and Rushton, J. (eds) *Education for the Professions*, Manchester: Manchester University Press.

Heller, A. (1984) *Everyday Life*, London: Routledge and Kegan Paul.

Henry, J. (1989) 'Meaning and practice in experiential learning', in Weil, S. and McGill, I. (eds) *Making Sense of Experiential Learning*, Buckingham: Open University Press in association with SRHE.

Hermann, G. and Keynon, R. (1987) *Competency Based Vocational Education*, London: Further Education Unit.

Hetherington, J. (1980) 'Professionalism and part-time staff in adult education', *Adult Education* 52 (5). Leicester: NIAE.

Hilgard, E.R. and Atkinson, R.C. (1967) (4th edn) *Introduction to Psychology*, New York: Harcourt, Brace and World, Inc.

Hilgard, E.R., Atkinson, R.L. and Atkinson, R.C. (1979) (7th edn) *Introduction to Psychology*, New York: Harcourt Brace Jovanovich.

Hirst, P.H. and Peters, R.S. (1970) *The Logic of Education*, London: Routledge and Kegan Paul.

Holmberg, B. (1981) *Status and Trends of Distance Education*, London: Kogan Page.

Holmberg, B. (1960) *On Methods of Teaching by Correspondence*, Lund: Gleerup.

—— (1989) *Theory and Practice of Distance Education*, London: Routledge.

Holt, R. (1982) 'An alternative to mentorship', *Adult Education* 55 (2). Leicester: NIAE.

Hopper, E. and Osborn, M. (1975) *Adult Students: Education, Selection and Social Control*, London: Frances Pinter.

Horton, M. with J. and H. Kohl (1990) *The Long Haul*, New York: Anchor Books.

Hostler, J. (1977) 'The education of adults', *Studies in Adult Education* 9 (1). Leicester: NIAE.

—— (1978) 'Liberal adult education', *Studies in Adult Education* 10 (2).

Houghton, V. (1974) 'Recurrent education: a plea for lifelong learning' in Houghton, V. and Richardson, K. (eds) *Recurrent Education: A Plea for Lifelong Learning*, London: Ward Lock Educational/Association of Recurrent Education.

Houghton, V. and Richardson, K. (eds) (1974) *Recurrent Education: A Plea for Lifelong Learning*. London: Ward Lock Educational Association of Recurrent Education.

Houle, C.O. (1960) 'The education of adult educational leaders', in Knowles, M. (ed.) *Handbook of Adult Education in the United States*, Washington, DC: Adult Education Convention of the USA.

—— (1961) *The Inquiring Mind*, Madison: University of Wisconsin Press. Republished as a second edition in 1988 by The Oklahoma Research Center for Continuing and Professional Higher Education, University of Oklahoma.

—— (1964) 'The emergence of graduate study in adult education', in Jensen, G., Liveright, A.A. and Hallenbeck, W. (eds) *Adult Education: Outlines of an Emerging Field of University Study*, Washington, DC, Adult Education Association of the USA.

—— (1972) *The Design of Education*, San Francisco: Jossey Bass.

—— (1979) 'Motivation and participation with special reference to non-traditional forms of study', in OECD 1977, Vol 3.

—— (1980) *Continuing Learning in the Professions*, San Francisco: Jossey Bass.

Houston, R.P., Bee, H., Hatfield, E. and Rimm, D.C. (1979) *Invitation to Psychology*, New York: Academic Press.

Howe, M.J.A. (1977) *Adult Learning*, Chichester: John Wiley and Sons.

Hoy, J.D. (1933) 'An enquiry as to interests and motives for study among adult evening students', *British Journal of Educational Psychology* 3 (1).

Hughes, K. and Mayo, M. (1991) 'Opening up personal development, *Adults Learning* 3 (4).

Hughes, M. (1977) 'Adult education on the cheap: an extension of adult education provision into the school classroom', *Adult Education* 50 (4). Leicester: NIAE.

Husen, T. (1974) *The Learning Society*, London: Methuen.

Husserl, E. (ed.) (1973) *Experience and Judgment*, London: Routledge and Kegan Paul.

Hutchins, R.M. (1970) *The Learning Society*, Harmondsworth: Penguin.

Hutchinson, E. and Hutchinson, E.M. (1978) *Learning Later*, London: Routledge and Kegan Paul.

Hutchinson, E.M. (ed.) (1970) 'Adult education – adequacy of provision', *Adult Education* 42 (6). Leicester: NIAE.

Illich, I. (1973a) *Deschooling Society*, Harmondsworth: Penguin.

—— (1973b) *After Deschooling, What?* London: Writers and Readers Publishing Cooperative.

—— (1977) 'Disabling professions', in Illich, I., Zola, I.K., McKnight, J., Caplan, J. and Shanken, R. (eds) *Disabling Professions*, London: Marion Boyars.

Illich, I. and Verne, E. (1976) *Imprisoned in a Global Classroom*, London: Writers and Readers Publishing Cooperative.

Illich, I., Zola, I.K., McKnight, J., Caplan, J. and Shanken, R. (eds) (1977) *Disabling Professions*, London: Marion Boyars.

Jarvis, P. (1975) 'The parish ministry as a semi-profession', *Sociological Review* 23: 911–22, University of Keele.

—— (1978a) 'Students' learning and tutors' marking', *Teaching at a Distance No. 13*, Milton Keynes: Open University Press.

—— (1978b) 'Knowledge and the curriculum in adult education: a sociological approach', *Adult Education* 51 (4). Leicester: NIAE.

—— (1980) 'Pre-retirement education: design and analysis', *Adult Education* 53 (1). Leicester: NIAE.

—— (1981) 'The Open University unit: andragogy or pedagogy?', *Teaching at a Distance No. 20*, Milton Keynes: Open University Press.

—— (1982a) 'What's the value of adult education?' *Adult Education* 54 (4). Leicester: NIAE.

—— (1982b) *Adult Education in a Small Centre: a Case Study in the Village of Lingfield*, Department of Adult Education, University of Surrey.

—— (1983a) *Professional Education*, London: Croom Helm.

—— (1983b) 'Education and the elderly', *Adult Education* 55 (4). Leicester: NIAE.

—— (1983c) 'The lifelong religious development of the individual and the place of adult education', *Lifelong Learning: The Adult Years* 6 (9).

—— (1984) 'Andragogy: a sign of the times', *Studies in the Education of Adults* 16: 32–8.

—— (1985) *The Sociology of Adult and Continuing Education*, London: Croom Helm.

—— (1987) *Adult Learning in the Social Context*, London: Croom Helm.

—— (1990) *International Dictionary of Adult and Continuing Education*, London: Routledge.

—— (1992) *Paradoxes of Learning*, San Francisco: Jossey Bass.

—— (1993a) *Adult Education and the State*, London: Routledge.

—— (1993b) 'Pedagogy, andragogy and professional education', paper presented at the International Conference on the Training of Adult Educators, Wadham College, Oxford.

—— (1984) 'Learning practical knowledge', *Journal of Further and Higher Education*.

—— (ed.) (1988) *Britain: Policy and Practice in Continuing Education*, San Francisco: Jossey Bass.

Jarvis, P. and Chadwick, A. (eds) (1991) *Training Adult Educators in Western Europe*, London: Routledge.

Jarvis, P. and Walters, N. (eds) (1993) *Adult Education and Theological Interpretations*, Malabar, Florida: Krieger.

Jennings, B. (ed.) (n.d.) *Community Colleges in England and Wales*, Leicester: NIAE.

Jensen, G., Liveright, A.A. and Hallenbeck, W. (eds) *Adult Education: Outlines of an Emerging Field of University Study*, Washington DC: Adult Education Association of the USA.

Jessup, F.W. (ed.) (1969) *Lifelong Learning – A Symposium on Continuing Education*, Oxford: Pergamon Press.

Johnstone, J.W.C. and Rivera, R.J. (1965) *Volunteers for Learning*, Chicago: Aldine Publishing.

Kagan, J. (1971) 'Developmental studies in reflection and analysis', in Kidd, A.H. and Rivoire, J.E. (eds) *Perceptual Development in Children*, New York: International Universities Press. Reprinted in Cashdow, A. and Whitehead, J. (eds) (1971) *Personality, Growth and Learning*, London: Longman.

Kallen, D. (1979) 'Recurrent education and lifelong learning: definitions and distinctions', in Schuller, T. and Megarry, J. *World Yearbook on Education 1979: Recurrent Education and Lifelong Learning*, London: Kogan Page.

Katz, D. (1960) 'The functional approach to the study of attitudes', *Public Opinion Quarterly* 24: 163–77.

Keddie, N. (1980) 'Adult education: an ideology individualism', in Thompson, J.C. (ed.) *Adult Education for a Change*, London: Heinemann.

Keegan, D. (1990) *Foundations of Distance Education*, London: Routledge.

—— (ed.) (1993)*Theoretical Principles of Distance Education*, London: Routledge.

Keller, F.S. (1968) 'Good-bye, Teacher . . . ', *Journal of Applied Behaviour Analysis* 1.

Kellner, D. (1989) *Jean Baudrillard: From Marxism to Postmodernism and Beyond*, Cambridge: Polity Press.

Kelly, A.V. (1977) *The Curriculum: Theory and Practice*, London: Harper and Row.

Kelly, G.A. (1955) *The Psychology of Personal Constructs*, New York: Norton.

Kelly, T. (1970) (3rd edn 1990) *A History of Adult Education in Great Britain*, Liverpool: Liverpool University Press.

Kidd, J.R. (1973) *How Adults Learn*, Chicago: Association Press.

Killeen, J. and Bird, M. (1981) *Education and Work*, Leicester: National Institute of Adult Education.

Kirk, P. (1976) 'The loneliness of the long distance tutor', *Teaching at a Distance No. 7*, Milton Keynes: Open University.

Kirkwood, C. (1978) 'Adult education and the concept of community', *Adult Education* 51 (3). Leicester: NIAE.

Kirkwood, G. and Kirkwood, C. (1989) *Living Adult Education*, Milton Keynes: Open University Press.

Knapper, C.K. and Cropley, A.J. (1985) *Lifelong Learning and Higher Education*, London: Croom Helm.

Knowles, M.S. (1978) (2nd edn) *The Adult Learner: A Neglected Species*, Houston: Gulf Publishing Co.

—— (1979) 'Andragogy revisited II', *Adult Education* 3: 52–3, Washington DC.

—— (1980a) *The Modern Practice of Adult Education*, Chicago: Association Press.

—— (1980b) 'The growth and development of adult education', in Peters, J. and Associates, *Building an Effective Adult Education*, San Francisco: Jossey Bass.

—— (1986) *Using Learning Contracts*, San Francisco: Jossey Bass.

—— (1989) *The Making of an Adult Educator*, San Francisco: Jossey Bass.

Knowles, M. and Associates (1984) *Andragogy in Action*, San Francisco: Jossey Bass.

Knox, A.B. (1977) *Adult Development and Learning*, San Francisco: Jossey Bass.

Knudson, R.S. (1979) 'Andragogy revisted: Humanagogy anyone?', *Adult Education* 29: 261–4, Washington DC.

Kohlberg, L. (1981) *The Philosophy of Moral Development Vol. 1 – Essays in Moral Development*, San Francisco: Harper.

Köhler, W. (1947) *Gestalt Psychology*, New York: Liveright Publishing Corporation.

Kolb, D. (1984) *Experiential Learning*, Englewood Cliffs, New Jersey: Prentice Hall.

Kolb, D.A. and Fry, R. (1975) 'Towards an applied theory of experiential learning', in Cooper, C.L. (eds) *Theories of Group Processes*, London: John Wiley and Sons.

Krech, D., Crutchfield, R.S. and Ballachery, E.L. (1962) *Individual in Society*, New York: McGraw Hill.

Kulich, J. (ed.) (1977) *Training of Adult Educators in East Europe*, Vancouver: Centre for Continuing Education, University of British Columbia.

—— (1982a) *Adult Education in Continental Europe: An Annotated Bibliography of English Language Materials 1975–9*, Vancouver Centre for Continuing Education, University of British Columbia.

—— (1982b) 'Lifelong education and the universities: a Canadian perspective', *International Journal of Lifelong Education* 1 (2).

Kumar, K. (1978) *Prophecy and Progress*, Harmondsworth: Penguin.

Label, J. (1978) 'Beyond andragogy to gerogogy', *Lifelong Learning: The Adult Years* 1.

Labouvie-Vief, G. (1978) 'Models of cognitive functioning in the old adult: Research needs in educational gerontology', in Sherron, R.H. and Lumsdon, D.B. (eds) *Introduction to Educational Gerontology*, Washington DC: Hemisphere Publishing Co.

Lacey, A.R. (1989) *Bergson*, London: Routledge.

Langenbach, M. (1988) *Curriculum Models in Adult Education*, Malabar, Florida: Krieger.

Last, J. and Chown, A. (1993) 'Teacher training in adult education', *Adults Learning* 4 (9) 2344–6.

Lawson, K.H. (1975) *Philosophical Concepts and Values in Adult Education*, Department of Adult Education, University of Nottingham. Reprinted in a 2nd edition and published by the Open University Press.

—— (1977) 'Community education: a critical assessment', *Adult Education* 50 (1). Leicester: NIAE.

—— (1982) 'Lifelong education: concept or policy?', *International Journal of Lifelong Education* (1) (2).

Lawton, D. (1973) *Social Change, Educational Theory and Curriculum Planning*, London: Hodder and Stoughton.

Legge, D. (1968) 'Training adult educators in the United Kingdom', *Convergence* 1 (1).

—— (1971a) 'The use of the talk in adult classes', in Stephens, M.D. and Roderick, G.W. (eds) *Teaching Techniques in Adult Education*, Newton Abbot: David and Charles.

—— (1971b) 'Discussion methods', in Stephens, M.D. and Roderick, G.W. (eds) *Teaching Techniques in Adult Education*, Newton Abbot: David and Charles.

—— (1981) 'The training of teachers of adults', in Harvey, B., Daines, J., Jones, D. and Wallis, J. (eds) *Policy and Research Adult Education*, Department of Adult Education, University of Nottingham.

—— (1982) *The Education of Adults in Britain*, Milton Keynes: The Open University Press.

—— (1991) 'Educators of adults in England and Wales', in Jarvis, P. and Chadwick, A. (eds) *Training Adult Educators in Western Europe*, London: Routledge.

Lengrand, P. (1975) *An Introduction to Lifelong Education*, London: Croom Helm.

Lester-Smith, W.O. (1966) *Education – An Introductory Survey*, Harmondsworth: Penguin.

Leytham, G. (1971) 'The principles of programmed learning', in Stephens, M.D. and Roderick, G.W. (eds) *Teaching Techniques in Adult Education*, Newton Abbot: David and Charles.

Lindeman, E. (1988) 'Preparing leaders in adult education' (speech given to Pennsylvania Association for Adult Education, 18th November). Published in Brookfield, S. (ed.) *Training Educators of Adults*, London: Routledge.

—— (1961; first published 1926) *The Meaning of Adult Education*, Montreal: Harvester House.

Lippitt, R. and White, R.K. (1958) 'An experimental study of leadership and group life', in Maccoby, E.E., Newcomb T.M. and Hartley, E.L. (eds) *Readings in Social Psychology*, New York: Holt.

Little, A., Willey, R. and Gundara, J. (1982) *Adult Education and the Black Communities*, Leicester: ACACE.

London, J. (1973) 'Reflections upon the relevance of Paulo Freire for American Adult Education', *Convergence* 6 (1).

Long, H. and Lord, C. (eds) (1978) *The Continuing Education Credit Unit: Concept, Issues and Use*, Georgia, USA: University of Georgia Center for Continuing Education.

Lovell, B.R. (1980) *Adults Learning*, London: Croom Helm.

Lovett, T. (1975) *Adult Education, Community Development and the Working Class*, London: Ward Lock Educational.

—— (1980) 'Adult education and community action', in Thompson, J.L. (ed.) *Adult Education for a Change*, London: Heinemann.

Lovett, T. and Mackay, L. (1978) 'Community based study groups', *Adult Education* 51 (1). Leicester: NIAE.

Lovett, T., Clarke, C. and Kilmurray, A. (1983) *Adult Education and Community Action*, London: Croom Helm.

Luckmann, T. (1967) *The Invisible Religion*, London: Collier-Macmillan.

Lukes, S. (1981) 'Fact and theory in the social sciences', in Potter *et al.* (eds) *Society and the Social Sciences*, London: Open University Press in association with Routledge and Kegan Paul.

Maccoby, E.E., Newcomb, T.M. and Hartley, E.L. (eds) (1958) (3rd edn) *Readings in Social Psychology*, New York: Holt.

McCullough, O. (1980) 'Analyzing the evolving structure of adult education', in Peters, J. and Associates *Building on Effective Adult Education on Enterprise*, San Francisco: Jossey Bass.

McGivney, V. (1990) *Access to Education for Non-Participant Adults*, Leicester: NIACE.

Macfarlane, T. (1978) 'Curriculum innovation in adult literacy: the cost of insularity', *Studies in Adult Education* 10 (2).

Mace, J. and Yarnit, M. (eds) (1987) *Time Off to Learn*, London: Methuen.

McGregor, D. (1960) *The Human Side of Enterprise*, New York: McGraw Hill.

McIntosh, N. (1974) 'The Open University student', in Tunstall, J. (ed.) *The Open University Opens*, London: Routledge and Kegan Paul.

McIntosh, N.E. (1979) 'To make continuing education a reality', *Oxford Review of Education* 5 (2) and republished by ACACE, Leicester.

McKenzie, L. (1977) 'The issue of andragogy', *Adult Education* 27: 225–9, Washington DC.

—— (1979) 'Andragogy revisited: Response to Elias', *Adult Education* 29: 256–61, Washington DC.

McLagan, P.A. (1978) *Helping Others Learn*, Massachusetts: Addison-Wesley.

Mager, C. (1991) 'Open college networks', *Adults Learning* 3 (4): 97–8.

Mannings, R. (1986) *The Incidental Learning Research Project*, Bristol Folk House: Adult Education Centre.

Mannion-Watson, C. (1982) 'An evaluation of a pilot course on the teaching of study skills to Sixth Form students', unpublished MSc dissertation, University of Surrey.

Marcuse, H. (1964) *One Dimensional Man*, reprinted in 1986 by ARK paperbacks, London.

Marsick, V. (ed.) (1987) *Learning in the Workplace*, London: Croom Helm.

Martin, B. (1981) *A Sociology of Contemporary Cultural Change*, Oxford: Basil Blackwell.

Martin, L.C. (1981) 'A survey of the training needs of part-time tutors in a region', *Studies in Adult Education* 13 (2).

Marton, F., Hounsell, D. and Entwistle, N. (1984) *The Experience of Learning*, Edinburgh: Scottish Academic Press.

Maslow, A.H. (1968) (2nd edn) *Towards a Psychology of Being*, New York: D. Van Nostrand Company.

Mee, G. (1980) *Organisation for Adult Education*, London: Longman.

Mee, G. and Wiltshire, H. (1978) *Structure and Performance in Adult Education*, London: Longman.

Merriam, S. and Caffarella, R. (1991) *Learning in Adulthood*, San Francisco: Jossey Bass.

Merriam, S.B. and Cunningham, P. (1989) *Handbook of Adult and Continuing Education*, San Francisco: Jossey Bass.

Merton, R.K. (1968) *Social Theory and Social Structure*, New York: The Free Press.

Mezirow, J. (1977) 'Perspective transformation', *Studies in Adult Education* 9 (2).

—— (1981) 'A critical theory of adult learning and education', *Adult Education* 32 (1), Washington DC.

—— (1991) *Transformative Dimensions of Adult Learning*, San Francisco: Jossey Bass.

Mezirow, J. and Associates (1990) *Fostering Critical Reflection in Adulthood*, San Francisco: Jossey Bass.

Midwinter, E. (1975) *Education and the Community*, London: Allen and Unwin.

—— (ed.) (1984) *Mutual Aid Universities*, London: Croom Helm.

Mill, J.S. (1962) 'On liberty' (First edn 1859). Reprinted in *Utilitarianism*, London: Fontana Library Collins.

Mocker, D.W. and Noble, E. (1981) 'Training part-time instructional staff', in Grabowski, S. *et al. Preparing Educators of Adults*, San Francisco: Jossey Bass.

Moemeka, A.A. (1981) *Local Radio – Community Education for Development*, Zaria, Nigeria: Ahmodu Bello University Press.

Molyneux, F., Low, G. and Fowler, G. (ed.) (1988) *Learning for Life*, London: Croom Helm.

Molyneux, F. (1992) 'The learning society: Rhetoric and reality', in Small, N. (ed.) *The Learning Society: Political Rhetoric and Electoral Reality*, Association for Lifelong Learning, University of Nottingham.

Morris, H. (1956) 'Architecture, humanism and the local community', paper read at RIBA on 15 May, and published in Fletcher, C. and Thompson, N. (eds) (1980) *Issues in Community Education*, Lewes: Falmer Press.

Morstain, B.R. and Smart, J.C. (1974) 'Reasons for participation in adult education courses: a multivariate analysis of group difference', *Adult Education* 24 (2), Washington DC.

Müller, D. and Funnell, P. (eds) (1991) *Delivering Quality in Vocational Education*, London: Kogan Page.

Murray, M. with Owen, M. (1991) *Beyond the Myths and Magic of Mentoring*, San Francisco: Jossey Bass.

Newman, M. (1973) *Adult Education and Community Action*, London: Writers and Readers Publishing Co-operative.

—— (1979) *The Poor Cousin*, London: Allen and Unwin.

NIACE (1993a) *Yearbook of Adult Continuing Educaiton 1993–4*, Leicester: NIACE.

NIACE (1993b) *Draft Strategic Plan 1993/6*, Leicester: NIACE.

Nyiri, J. (1988) 'Tradition and practical knowledge', in Nyiri, J. and Smith, B. (eds) *Practical Knowledge: Outlines of a Theory of Traditions and Skills*, London: Croom Helm.

Nyiri, J. and Smith, B. (eds) (1988) *Practical Knowledge: Outlines of a Theory of Traditions and Skills*, London: Croom Helm.

Oakeshott, Michael (1933) *Experience and its Modes*, Cambridge: Cambridge University Press.

Oakeshott, M. (1991) *Educational Guidance for Adults: Identifying Competences*, London: Further Education Unit.

Overstreet, H. and Overstreet, B. (1941) 'The making of the makers', in Overstreet, H. and Overstreet, B. (eds) *Leaders for Adult Education*, New York: American Association of Adult Education.

Parker, S. (1976) *The Sociology of Leisure*, London: Allen and Unwin.

Paterson, R.W.K. (1979) *Values, Education and the Adult*, London: Routledge and Kegan Paul.

Pavlov, I.P. (1927) *Conditioned Reflexes*, New York: Oxford University Press.

Payne, J. (1993) 'Too little of a good thing', *Adults Learning* 4 (10).

Peers, R. (1958) *Adult Education – A Comparative Perspective*, London: Routledge and Kegan Paul.

Peters, J.M. and Gordon, S. (1974) *Adult Learning Projects: A Study of Adult Learning in Urban and Rural Tennessee*, Knoxville: University of Tennessee.

Peters, J. and Associates (1980) *Building an Effective Adult Education Enterprise*, San Francisco: Jossey Bass.

Peters, J., Jarvis, P. and Associates (1991) *Adult Education: Evolution and Achievements in a Developing Field of Study*, San Francisco: Jossey Bass.

Peters, R.S. (1966) *Ethics and Education*, London: Allen and Unwin.

—— (1972) 'Education and the educated Man', in Dearden, D.F., Hirst, P.H. and Peters, R.S. (eds) *A Critique of Current Educational Aims (Part I of Education and the Development of Reason)*, London: Routledge and Kegan Paul.

Peterson, R.E. *et al.* (1979) *Lifelong Learning in America*, San Francisco: Jossey Bass.

Phillipson, C. and Strang, P. (1983) *The Impact of Pre-Retirement Education*, University of Keele, Department of Adult Education.

Piaget, J. (1929) *The Child's Conception of the World*, London: Routledge and Kegan Paul.

Polyani, M. (1967) *The Tacit Dimension*, London: Routledge and Kegan Paul.

Popham, W.J., Eisner, E.W., Sullivan, H.J. and Tyler, L.L. (1969) *Instructional Objectives*, Chicago: Rand McNally.

Poster, C. and Krüger, A. (eds) (1990) *Community Education in the Western World*, London: Routledge.

Poster, M. (ed.) (1988) *Jean Baudrillard: Selected Writings*, Cambridge: Polity Press.

Potter, D. *et al.* (eds) (1981) *Society and the Social Sciences*, London: Open University Press in association with Routledge and Kegan Paul.

Pursaill, J. (1989) *National Vocational Qualifications and Further Education*, London: Further Education Unit.

Reason, P. and Rowan, J. (eds) (1981) *Human Inquiry*, Chichester: John Wiley and Sons.

Reischmann, J. (1986) 'Learning en passant', paper presented at AAACE, Hollywood, California.

Richardson, M. (ed.) (1979) *Preparing to Study*, Milton Keynes: Open University Press.

Riegel, K. (1973) 'Dialectic operations: The final period of cognitive development', *Human Development* 16 (3).

Riesman, D. (1950) *The Lonely Crowd: A Study of Changing American Character*, New Haven: Yale University Press.

Rodd, M. (1992) 'Change for the better? Recent developments in adult literacy', *Adults Learning* 4 (2).

Roderick, G.W., Bell, J., Dickenson, R., Turner, R. and Wellings, A. (1981) *Mature Students in Further and Higher Education*, Division of Continuing Education, University of Sheffield.

Rogers, A. (ed.) (1976) *The Spirit and the Form*, University of Nottingham, Department of Adult Education.
—— (1986) *Teaching Adults*, Milton Keynes: Open University Press.
Rogers, C.R. (1969) *Freedom to Learn*, Columbus, Ohio: Charles E. Merrill Publishing Co.
—— (1983) *Freedom to Learn for the 80's*, New York: Merrill-Macmillan
Rogers, E.M. (1962) *Diffusion of Innovations*, Glencoe, Ill.: The Free Press.
Rogers, J. (ed.) (1973) *Adults in Education*, London: British Broadcasting Corporation.
—— (1977) (2nd edn) *Adults Learning*, Milton Keynes: Open University Press.
—— (1989) (3rd edn) *Adults Learning*, Milton Keynes: Open University Press.
Rogers, J. and Groombridge, B. (1976) *Right to Learn*, London: Arrow Books.
Rumble, G. (1982) *The Open University of the United Kingdom*, Milton Keynes: Distance Education Research Group, The Open University.
Rumble, G. and Harry, K. (1982) *The Distance Teaching Universities*, London and Canberra: Croom Helm.
Russell, L. (1973) *Adult Education: A Plan for Development*, London: Her Majesty's Stationery Office.
Ryle, G. (1963) *The Concept of Mind*, London: Peregrine Books.
Ryle, M. (1993) 'A case for collaboration', *Adults Learning* 4 (9): 240–1.
Sargant, N. (1990) *Learning and Leisure*, Leicester: NIACE.
Scheler, M. (1926) *Die Wissens former and die Gessellschaft*, Leipzig: Der Neue-Guist Verlag.
—— (1980) *Problems of Sociology of Knowledge* (trans: M.S. Frings), London: Routledge and Kegan Paul.
Schon, D.A. (1983) *The Reflective Practitioner*, New York: Basic Books.
Schuler, T. and Megarry, J. (eds) (1979) *World Yearbook on Education 1979: Recurrent Education and Lifelong Learning*, London: Kogan Page.
Schutz, A. and Luckmann, T. (1974) *The Structures of the Life World*, London: Heinemann.
Senior, B. and Naylor, J. (1987) *Educational Responses to Adult Unemployment*, London: Croom Helm.
Sherron, R.H. and Lumsden, D.B. (eds) (1978) *Introduction to Educational Gerontology*, Washington DC: Hemisphere Publishing Company.
Sidwell, D. (1980) 'A survey of modern language classes', *Adult Education* 52 (5). Leicester: NIAE.
Skinner, B.F. (1951) 'How to teach animals', *Scientific American* 185 (6).
—— (1971) *Beyond Freedom and Dignity*, Harmondsworth: Penguin.
Sless, D. (1981) *Learning and Visual Communication*, London: Croom Helm.
Small, N. (ed.) (1992) *The Learning Society: Political Rhetoric and Electoral Reality*, Association for Lifelong Learning, University of Nottingham.
Smith, A.L. (1919) 'Adult Education Committee Final Report', reprinted in 'The 1919 Report', Department of Adult Education, University of Nottingham.
Smith, G. (1993) 'BTEC GNVQs and developments in vocational education', *Adults Learning* 4 (5). Leicester: NIACE.
Sockett, H. (1981) 'Editorial introduction', *Educational Analysis* 3 (1).
Sommer, R. (1989) *Teaching Writing to Adults*, San Francisco: Jossey Bass.
Srinivasan, L. (1977) *Perspectives on Non-formal Adult Learning*, New York: World Education.
Stenhouse, L. (1975) *An Introduction to Curriculum Research and Development*, London: Heinemann.
Stephens, M.D. (1981) 'The future of continuing education', *Adult Education* 54 (2). Leicester: NIAE.

Stephens, M.D. and Roderick, G.W. (eds) (1971) *Teaching Techniques in Adult Education*, Newton Abbot: David and Charles.

Stewart, D., Keegan, D. and Holmberg, B. (eds) (1984) *Distance Education: International Perspectives*, London: Routledge.

Stock, A. (1971) 'Role playing and simulation techniques', in Stephens, M.D. and Roderick, G.W. (eds) *Teaching Techniques in Adult Education*, Newton Abbot: David and Charles.

—— (1982) *Adult Education in the United Kingdom*, Leicester: NIAE.

Straw, J. (1992) 'Broadcasting and a learning society', *Adults Learning* 4 (2): 4–1.

Strike, K. and Soltis, J. (1985) *The Ethics of Teaching*, New York: Teachers College, Columbia University.

Surridge, R. and Bowen, J. (1977) *The Independent Learning Project: A Study of Changing Attitudes in American Public Libraries*, Public Libraries Research Group.

Taba, H. (1962) *Curriculum Development: Theory and Practice*, New York: Harcourt, Brace and World.

Tabberer, R. and Allman, J. (1981) *Study Skills at 16 Plus*, Slough: National Foundation for Educational Research.

Taylor, J. (1978) 'The Advisory Council for Adult and Continuing Education', *Adult Education* 51 (4). Leicester: NIAE.

Taylor, P.V. (1993) *The Texts of Paulo Freire*, London: Routledge.

Tennant, M. (1986) 'An evaluation of Knowles' theory of learning', *International Journal of Lifelong Education* 5 (2): 113–22.

—— (1988) *Psychology and Adult Learning*, London: Croom Helm.

Thompson, J.L. (ed.) (1980) *Adult Education for a Change*, London: Heinemann.

Thompson, J. (1993) 'Learning liberation and maturity', *Adults Learning* 4 (9): 244. Leicester: NIACE.

Thorndike, E.L. (1928) *Adult Learning*, London: Macmillan.

Thornton, A.H. and Stephens, M.D. (eds) (1977) *The University in its Region*, Department of Adult Education, University of Nottingham.

Tiernan, K. (1992) 'Taking credit for voluntary work', *Adults Learning* 4 (2). Leicester: NIACE.

Tight, M. (1982) *Part-time Degree Level Study in the United Kingdom*, Leicester: ACACE.

—— (1991) *Higher Education: A Part-time Perspective*, Buckingham: Society for Research into Higher Education in association with Open University Press.

Titmus, C. (1981) *Strategies for Adult Education – Practices in Western Europe*, Milton Keynes: Open University Press.

—— (1989) *Lifelong Education for Adults: An International Handbook*, Oxford: Pergamon Press.

Toennies, F. (1957) *Community and Society* (trans. C.P. Loomis), Michigan: Michigan State University Press. Published in the United Kingdom as *Community and Association* by Routledge and Kegan Paul, London.

Tough, A. (1979) (2nd edn) *The Adult's Learning Projects*, Toronto: Ontario Institute for Studies in Education.

Tough, A. (1981) (3rd edn) *Learning Without a Teacher*, Toronto: Ontario Institute for Studies in Education, Educational Research Series No. 3.

Tuijnman, A. (1989) *Recurrent Education, Earnings and Well-being*, Stockholm: Almqvist and Wiksell International.

Tunstall, J. (ed.) (1974) *The Open University Opens*, London: Routledge and Kegan Paul.

Turner, J.R. and Rushton, J. (eds) (1976) *Education for the Professions*, Manchester: Manchester University Press.

Tyler, R.W. (1949) *Basic Principles of Curriculum and Instruction*, Chicago: University of Chicago Press.

Usher, R. (1989) 'Locating adult education in the practical', in Bright, B. (ed.) *Theory and Practice in the Study of Adult Education*, London: Routledge.

Usher, R. and Bryant, I. (1989) *Adult Eduction as Theory, Practice and Research*, London: Routledge.

Venables, P. (1976) *Report of the Committee on Continuing Education*, Milton Keynes: Open University Press.

Verduin, J. (1980) *Curriculum Building for Adult Learning*, Carbondale: Southern Illinois University Press.

Vermilye, D.W. (ed.) (1977) *Relating Work and Education*, San Francisco: Jossey Bass.

Verner, C. (with assistance from C. Booth) (1964) *Adult Education*, Washington DC: Center for Applied Research in Education, Inc.

Wedemeyer, C. (1981) *Learning at the Back Door*, Madison: The University of Wisconsin Press.

Weil, S. and Mcgill, I. (eds) (1989) *Making Sense of Experiential Learning*, Buckingham: Open University Press in association with SRHE.

Westwood, S. (1980) 'Adult education and the sociology of education: an exploration', in Thompson, J.L. (ed.) *Adult Education for a Change*, London: Heinemann.

Wilensky, H.A.L. (1964) 'The professionalization of everyone?', *American Journal of Sociology* LXX: 137–58.

Williams, E. and Heath, A.E. (1936) *Learn and Live*, London: Methuen.

Williams, G. (1977) *Towards Lifelong Education: A New Role for Higher Education Institutes*, Paris: UNESCO.

Williams, G.L. (1980) 'Adults learning about adult learning', *Adult Education* 52 (6). Leicester: NIAE.

Wilson, S. (1980) 'The school and the community', in Fletcher, C. and Thompson, N. (eds) *Issues in Community Education*, Lewes: Falmer Press.

Wiltshire, H. (1973) 'The concepts of learning and need in adult education', *Studies in Adult Education* 5 (1). Reprinted in Rogers, A. (1976) *The Spirit and the Form*, University of Nottingham, Department of Adult Education.

—— (1976) 'The nature and uses of adult education', in Rogers, A. (ed.) *The Spirit and the Form*, University of Nottingham, Department of Adult Education.

—— (1981) 'Changing concepts of adult education', in Elsdon, K. (ed.) *New Directions: Adult Education in the Context of Continuing Education*, London: Department of Education and Science.

Witkin, H.A. (1965) 'Psychological differentiations', *Journal of Abnormal Psychology* 70: reprinted in Cashdown, A. and Whitehead, J. (1971) *Personality, Growth and Learning*, London: Longman.

Wlodkowski, R. (1985) *Enhancing Adult Motivation to Learn*, San Francisco: Jossey Bass.

Wood, D. (1982) *Continuing Education in Polytechnics and Colleges*, Department of Adult Education, University of Nottingham.

Woodhall, M. (1980) *The Scope and Costs of the Education and Training of Adults in Britain*, Leicester: ACACE.

—— (1988) 'Economic and financial implications of recurrent and continuing education', in Molyneux, F., Low, G. and Fowler, G. (eds) *Learning for Life*, London: Croom Helm.

Woodley, A., Wagner, L., Slowey, M., Hamilton, M. and Foulton, O. (1987) *Choosing to Learn: Adults in Education*, Buckingham: Society for Research into Higher Education in association with Open University Press.

Workers' Education Association (1982) *The Robert Tressell Papers: Exploring 'The Ragged Trousered Philanthropists'*, obtainable from Robert Tressell Workshop, c/o Robert Tressell House, 25 Wellington Square, Hastings, East Sussex.

Yarrington, R. (1979) 'Lifelong education trends in community colleges', *Convergence* XII (1–2).

Yeaxlee, B.A. (1929) *Lifelong Education*, London: Cassell.

Young, M.F.D. (1971) 'Curricula as socially organized knowledge', in Young, M.F.D. *Knowledge and Control*, London: Collier–Macmillan.

—— (ed.) (1971) *Knowledge and Control*, London: Collier–Macmillan.

Zimmerman, F.E. (1979) 'Elder hostel '78 at Adelphi University', *Lifelong Learning: The Adult Years* III (3).

Index

- 5 AUG 2003

LEEDS COLLEGE OF BUILDING LIBRARY
NORTH STREET
LEEDS LS2 7QT
Tel. (0113) 222 6097 and 6098

1 5 AUG 2003